International Management

ANANT R. NEGANDHI
University of Illinois

CALIFORNIA SCHOOL OF PROFESSIONAL PSYCHOLOGY
LOS ANGELES

ALLYN AND BACON, INC.
BOSTON · LONDON · SYDNEY · TORONTO

Library of Congress Cataloging-in-Publication Data

Negandhi, Anant R.
  International management.

  Bibliography; p.
  Includes index.
  1. International business enterprises—Management.
2. Comparative management. I. Title.
HD62.4.N438 1987   658'.049   86-14189
ISBN 0-205-08809-0
ISBN 0-205-10550-5 (International Edition)

Series editor: Jack Peters
Production coordinator: Helyn Pultz
Editorial-production service: CRACOM Corporation
Cover coordinator: Linda K. Dickinson

Printed in the United States of America

10 9 8 7 6 5 4 3 2   90 89 88 87

TO

Erna, whose tomorrow is today
and
Chhotubhai, whose yesterday is tomorrow,
which makes
my today and tomorrow more enjoyable

Contents

List of Cases

Preface

This book is designed for classroom use in International Business and International Management for advanced and undergraduate-level courses.

The focus of the book is managerial. Although attempts were made in the introductory chapter to provide a broad overview of the changing character of the international business environment, trade and international theories and related topics, the rest of the book is devoted to analyses of various managerial functions undertaken in international corporations.

Strategic policy-level issues, such as business-government relations, ownership, control of overseas subsidiaries, centralization of decision making, and strategic long-range planning are covered in the first half of the book. The second half deals with important functional areas, such as human-resource management, production and logistics, marketing, and financial management.

To reinforce understanding of important theories and concepts, relevant cases have been provided at the end of each chapter.

Unique characteristics of this book are the comparative analyses of strategies and practices of American, European, and Japanese international corporations, as well as extensive use of empirical and theoretical studies.

The author's five large-scale studies of more than one thousand companies in twenty industrialized and developing countries form the core of this book.

Various drafts have been used in undergraduate, graduate, and executive M.B.A. classes at the University of Illinois from 1983 to 1986. The student's responses and suggestions were very helpful in improving the final draft. I am most thankful to all of them.

Mr. William Emmons and Mr. Mannsoo Shin, doctoral students at the University of Illinois, carried the major load of collecting and organizing the research material, preparing useful notes, and reading the various chapters. To these young men and emerging international business scholars, I owe a deep sense of gratitude.

The critical comments of the reviewers greatly improved the book, and I thank them for their insight: J. J. Boddewyn, Baruch College; Goli Eshghi, Illinois State University; Stephen J. Kobrin, New York University; Duane Kujawa, University of Miami; Ernest W. Ogram, Jr., Georgia State University; S. Benjamin Prasad, Ohio University; Ilkka A. Ronkainen, Georgetown University; John K. Ryans, Jr., Kent State University; J. Francis Truitt, University of Washington.

Much of the typing and retyping of the drafts was done through the Word Processing Center of the College of Commerce and Business Administration. I am thankful to Ms. Carol Halliday and her colleagues, Mrs. Debbie Loos and Mrs. Freda Poe for their help.

As senior editor at Allyn and Bacon, Inc., Mr. Jack Peters's encouragement to develop this volume went far beyond commercial interest and acted as a real stimulus to undertake this venture. Copy editing was done by the CRACOM Corporation. My sincere thanks to them.

Finally, my wife and our two teenagers, Pia and Amin, made my task easy in every way. Thank you, Family.

A.R.N.

Part I

International Business Environment

- *The World of International Business*

- *International Corporations and Governments: Control Issues and Social Responsibilities*

Chapter 1

The World of International Business

About This Book

This book concerns the management of international business operations with an emphasis on international managerial practices. It provides a comparative profile of the managerial practices of United States, European, and Japanese companies. These management practices are analyzed to pinpoint their strengths and weaknesses in contributing to firms' survival, growth, and profitability in the international marketplace.

The coverage of managerial aspects includes:

- Formulating and implementing strategies
- Designing organizational structures
- Policy making and control
- Decision making and headquarters and subsidiary relations
- Long-range planning and environmental scanning
- Manpower management

- International production: choice of technology and other important logistical issues
- Export marketing
- Marketing management
- Financial management
- Ethics and social responsibilities

The environmental constraints in managing global operations are integrated within the discussion of actual practices. Furthermore, to sensitize students to a fast-changing, international business environment, this book discusses in this and the next chapter the changing characters of international business and its environment.

In this introductory chapter, the discussion covers the following:

- International business in the world economy
- United States' role and stake in international business
- Growing importance of multinational companies
- Changing character of international business
- Challenge to United States dominance in world business
- Newcomers in international business
- New forms of conducting international business

At the end of this chapter is a brief review of the theoretical and analytical paradigms used to explain intercountry trade and investments and the various organizational and managerial practices of international corporations. The chapter ends with an outline of the book's organization.

International Business in the World Economy

Although the world economy has been beset with structural problems, especially since the 1973 oil crisis, international trade and investment have been increasing. Trade among nations grew from $136 billion in 1960 to $2 trillion in 1980.[1] A 15% growth rate in international trade is predicted for the 1980s. By 1988, the trade volume will be five trillion United States dollars. This is more than the increase in either the gross domestic product (GDP) or the industrial production in major industrialized countries (Figure 1-1). Foreign private investments have also increased more rapidly than the GDP or the industrial production.[2] The growth in international trade is equally distributed among the developed and developing countries. Japan, West Germany, and other European Common Market Countries, as well as many of the developing countries, such as Brazil, Mexico, Singapore, India, and South Korea, all have experienced sizeable increases during the 1968–1980 period.

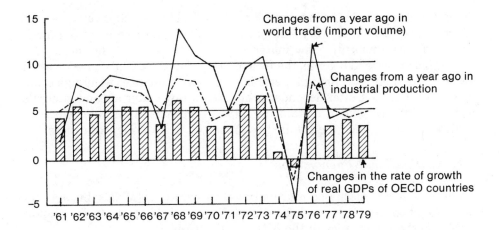

Notes: 1. *The above figures exclude Communist-bloc countries.*
        2. *The rates of growth of real GDPs of the 24-member countries of OECD are based on 1975 prices translated at the exchange rates which prevailed in 1975.*

UN–MBS, OECD–Main Economic Indicators, OECD–National Accounts of OECD Countries.

Figure 1-1 Changes in the rate of growth of world trade, production, and real GDP (*Source: White Paper on International Trade: Japan 1981,* Tokyo: Japan External Trade Organization (JETRO), 1981, p. 69. Statistics were derived from UN-MBS, OECD-Main Economic Indicators, OECD-National Accounts of OECD countries.)

United States Stake in International Business

The United States plays a significant role in world trade and investment, accounting for 12% of the world's total trade and for a hefty 46% of the world's stock of direct foreign investment.[3] Today, many large United States companies derive one third to one half of their total earnings from foreign countries. The United States giants, such as Exxon, Ford Motor Company, Texaco, IBM, and ITT, depend heavily on foreign earnings.[4]

The United States operates over 11,000 subsidiaries in 74 countries on 6 continents.[5] There has been a fivefold increase in the number of foreign subsidiaries owned by United States companies since World War II. One third of the total work force of United States multinationals is employed abroad. In recent years, one out of nine jobs in the United States manufacturing sector is attributed to foreign sales, while some 30% of United States farm products are being exported. In his 1983 State of the Union message, President

Reagan reconfirmed his commitment to free world trade and investment, declaring that "Each and every American has a stake in international trade."[6]

To secure important raw materials, minerals, and metals for United States industries and defense, the United States multinationals have invested over 30% of their total foreign assets in extractive industries in foreign countries.[7] Yet United States dependence on foreign raw materials and minerals is increasing every year. Metals and minerals such as aluminum, asbestos, potassium, gold, and zinc are largely imported from foreign countries.

The Multinational Phenomenon

This chapter has discussed multinational corporations (MNCs) but has not elaborated on their roles and significance in the world economy. It will now examine the importance of the MNCs specifically.

These firms are variously referred to in the literature as "international corporations," "transnational corporations," and "multinational corporations." The terms "multinational corporation" and "international corporation" will be used interchangeably in this book. Accordingly, the precise definition of MNCs is not of central importance.

However, as a point of reference, I here provide the United Nations' Center for Transnational Enterprises definition of multinational corporations:

> Multinational Corporations are enterprises which own or control production or service facilities outside the country in which they are based. Such enterprises are not always incorporated or private; they can also be cooperatives or state-owned entities.[8]

Another useful definition identifying the important attributes of such firms is provided by Phatak. He writes:

> A multinational company is an enterprise that has an interlocking network of subsidiaries in several countries, whose executives view the whole world as its theater of operations, and who therefore obtain and allocate financial, material, technical, and managerial resources in a manner conducive to the achievement of total enterprise objectives.[9]

Fayerweather refers to them as "multicultural, multinational global-spanning systems."[10]

According to one count, about 500 such large firms exist in the world.[11] They represent approximately one half of the industrial output of noncommunist countries.[12] And their dominance in world trade is increasing. For example, in 1950, United States MNCs (some 250 firms) accounted for 17% of the total sales of United States manufacturers; by 1967, the percentage increased to 42%, and by 1974 to 62%.[13]

The Changing Character of International Business

Major changes occurring in international business have a significant impact on the economies of both industrialized and developing countries. These developments represent a challenge to the United States firms' dominance in international business. The changes include:

1. Newcomers in international business and their newfound competitive advantages
2. The increasing role of state-owned enterprises in international trade and investments
3. New forms of conducting international business

I shall briefly outline these changes and their implications for United States businesses.

Challenge to United States Dominance

Although the United States still holds the lion's share of the world's total foreign private investment (46%), her position has slipped in the last decade. The share of West Germany, Switzerland, Japan, and Canada, however, is increasing. As shown in Table 1-1, the United States' share in foreign private

Table 1-1 Foreign direct investment abroad for developed countries, 1970–1972 and 1978–1980

Country		Outflow of FDI		
	1970–1972	*%*	*1978–1980*	*%*
United States	7,649	57.8	19,547	46.3
United Kingdom	1,597	12.0	5,756	13.6
Germany, Fed. Rep. of	1,161	8.8	4,262	10.1
Canada	316	2.4	2,617	6.2
Japan	481	3.6	2,552	6.0
France	455	3.4	2,359	5.6
Netherlands	564	4.3	2,210	5.2
Total above	12,223	92.3	39,303	93.0
All other	1,022	7.7	2,942	7.0
Grand total	13,245	100.0	42,245	100.0

Source: Transnational Corporations in World Development, Third Survey. (New York: United Nations Center on Transnational Corporations, United Nations), p. 19.

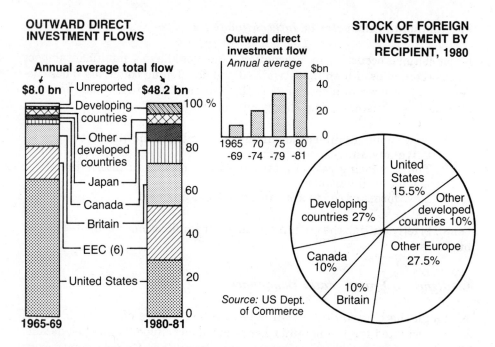

Figure 1-2 Outward direct investment flows (*Source: The Economist,* November 7, 1984.)

investment had decreased from 57.8% in 1970–1972 to 46.3% by 1978–1980. During the same period, West Germany and Japan recorded about a threefold to fivefold increase of their shares. The impact of Japanese and European investments, both here in the United States and elsewhere, is a formidable challenge to the United States' position. Multinational companies, once a United States phenomenon, now not only come from Europe and Japan but also from developing countries such as Brazil, India, South Korea, and Mexico. The United States accounted for 65% of all direct foreign investment between 1965 and 1969; her share declined to 28% during 1980–1981, while Japan increased her share from less than 2% to 7.5% during the same period. Furthermore, as we will see later, the United States is becoming a prime host to foreign companies.[14] This changing scene is portrayed in Figure 1-2.

A similar trend is also noticeable in the new overseas subsidiaries established by United States, European, and Japanese companies.[15]

In spite of the considerable lead the United States firms enjoyed before and immediately after World War II, the differences between large United States and European enterprises are narrowing quickly. For example, Franko cites a major shift in international business:

1. In 1959, an American company was the largest in the world, in 11 out of 13 major industries—namely, aerospace, automotive, chemicals, electrical equipment, food products, paper, petroleum, pharmaceuticals, textiles, and commercial banking. By 1976, the United States was leading in only 7 out of 13. Three of the non-American leaders in 1976 were German, one was British-Dutch, and one was Japanese.
2. The number of U.S. companies among the world's top 12 declined in all industry groups except aerospace, between 1959 and 1976. Continental European companies increased their representatives among the top 12 in 9 out of 13 industries; the Japanese scored gains in 8.
3. Continental European companies scored particular gains in six industries: chemicals, automotive vehicles, primary metals, metal products, commercial banking and pharmaceuticals. The number of the Continental European companies on the list of the world's top 12 in each industry equaled or exceeded the number of the U.S. companies in 1976.[16]

As shown in Figure 1-3, the United States' position of leadership in such major industries as chemical, plastic, steel, semiconductor, integrated circuits, and even in aircraft is deteriorating quickly. Only the computer industry seems to be steadfast, but here too the Japanese are narrowing the gap.[17] Some international experts, such as Vogel[18] and Thurow,[19] predict that unless United States companies and the government do something, the United States' dominance as an industrial power may be replaced by Japan.

As Thurow writes:

America faces a problem that is simply put. The huge technological edge enjoyed by Americans in the 1950s and 1960s has disappeared. . . . We are now faced with competitors who have matched our achievements and may be in the process of moving ahead of us. . . . When our effortless superiority has vanished, the American economy has been absorbed into a world economy. For most goods there is now a world market—not just an American market. Competition is world-wide—not just American.[20]

Newcomers to International Business

Japanese and West European companies, particularly the German, Swiss, and Dutch, have been among the most aggressive in increasing their shares of the world's trade and investment. The United States' share of world trade has declined from 18% in 1960 to 12.1% by 1980, whereas West Germany and Japan increased their shares from 3.5% and 1.4% in 1960, to 11.4% and 6.8% in 1980, respectively.[21] Japanese foreign direct investment increased from $591 million in 1975 to $4.1 billion in 1980.[22]

Moreover, the United States market has become a major battleground for international trade and investment. The United States is now the second

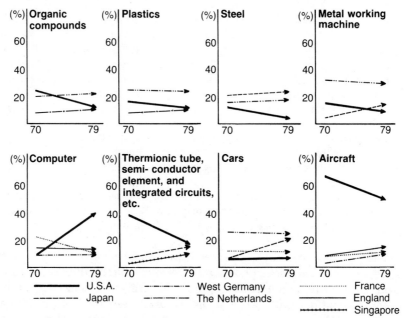

Notes: SITC (Rev. 1) codes of different items are as follows: organic compounds 512, plastics 581, steel 67, metal working machine tools 715, computers 7143, television sets 7241, radio 7242, thermionic tubes, semiconductor elements, and integrated circuits, etc. 7293, cars 7321, air craft 734.
Source: UN–YITS

Figure 1-3 Position of major industries of the United States in world markets (Changes in the shares of major industrial nations in world markets) (*Source: White Paper on International Trade: Japan 1981*, Tokyo: Japan External Trade Organization, 1981, p. 16).

largest host country in the world for foreign companies. The growth of foreign investment in the United States is staggering. For example, between 1975 and 1979, the number of foreign manufacturing firms in the United States almost tripled; it increased from 1,246 to 3,433.[23]

Among the ten leading foreign countries investing in the United States, West Germany and Japan recorded the highest growth. The number of West German firms operating in the United States increased from 203 in 1974 to 710 in 1978, while during the same period Japanese firms increased from a mere 48 in 1976 to 203 in 1978.[24] Table 1-2 presents the foreign investment positions established in the United States by Canadian, British, Western European, and Japanese companies. The Japanese, although dotting the world with their exports and capital investments, now seem to be concentrating on United States and European markets. The industrial countries attracted nearly 49% of Japan's $2.59 billion direct investment in manufacturing during 1983.[25]

Table 1-2 Foreign direct investment position in the United States, year end 1981 (in millions of dollars)*

Source of investment	Total	Petroleum	Manufacturing	Trade	Insurance	Other
Canada	12,212	1,547	5,787	1,285	402	3,191
United Kingdom	15,527	−212	5,910	4,362	2,360	3,107
Europe, excluding						
United Kingdom	42,178	14,834	13,106	6,281	2,389	5,568
Japan	6,887	7	1,111	4,128	217	1,424
Other	12,955	1,637	3,619	1,678	528	5,493
Total	89,759	17,813	29,533	17,734	5,896	18,783
As percent of total						
Canada	13.6	8.7	19.6	7.2	6.8	17.0
United Kingdom	17.3	−1.2	20.0	24.6	40.0	16.5
Europe, excluding						
United Kingdom	47.0	83.3	44.4	35.4	40.5	29.6
Japan	7.7	0.0	3.8	23.3	3.7	7.6
Other	14.4	9.2	12.3	9.5	9.0	29.2
Total	100.0	100.0	100.0	100.0	100.0	100.0

Note: Dollar totals may not be exact because of rounding.
Source: U.S. Department of Commerce, *Survey of Current Business*, August 1982, p. 37.

Foreign investors in the United States are not only active in the so-called high-tech and chemical industries, but lately they have entered retailing and agriculture. Today, as Robert Ball writes in *Fortune*, "Whether they know it or not, shoppers from California to the Carolinas are buying from Europeans."[26] Over 10% of the United States' grocery business is now owned by Europeans, including two of the top ten supermarket chains, A&P and Grand Union.[27]

The Newcomers' Competitive Edge

The high growth rate of the European and Japanese multinationals has been attributed to higher expenditure for research and development, resulting in improved capabilities for product and process innovations. Other MNCs have also been characterized as being more adaptable than their United States counterparts.

Twenty years ago, the French journalist and author Jean-Jacques Servan-Schreiber warned Western Europe about the United States' invasion of European industries. He attributed her success to management style, technological knowledge, and practices. It seems that the Europeans and Japanese took this warning seriously and responded with counterchallenges. In more specific terms, as Franko writes:

> By the 1970s, large non-American companies had learned how to systematically manage modern, multidivisional organizations—and had perhaps improved on U.S. practices by adopting more collegial, less adversarial management styles.[28]

Besides improved capacities in product innovations and production processes, growth in productivity of manufacturing in Germany, France, and Japan outstripped those gains in the United States. Labor productivity doubled during the 1967–1977 decade in Japan; and it increased by 70% in Germany, compared with a 27% increase in the United States (Figure 1-4).

During the 1970s, the United States had the lowest rate of productivity growth of any major industrial nation. In the private sector, the growth rate dropped from 3% during the 1950s and 1960s to approximately 2% during the 1970–1977 period (Figure 1-5).

This decrease in labor productivity has been attributed both to a lack of adequate capital investment and to a decrease in research and development expenditures. It is estimated that today the average United States plant is twenty years old; the average age of a plant in West Germany is twelve, and in Japan ten.[29]

Research and Development Activities

Commenting on United States management attitudes and concerns for product and process developments and capital investments, Thurow writes:

> American management has also let the time over which investments must pay for themselves grow so short that they will not undertake the basic research and development, make the necessary investments, or build the service networks necessary for long-run survival.[30]

Recently, United States research and development expenditures, as a proportion of the gross national product (GNP), are declining, while those of Germany, Switzerland, and Japan are increasing. West German, Swiss, Dutch, and Japanese privately funded research and development expenditures, as a percentage of the GNP, have come to surpass those of the United States (Figure 1-5).[31] The close ties between government and business in Western Europe and Japan have also been cited as instrumental in achieving higher growth rates for their industrial enterprises.

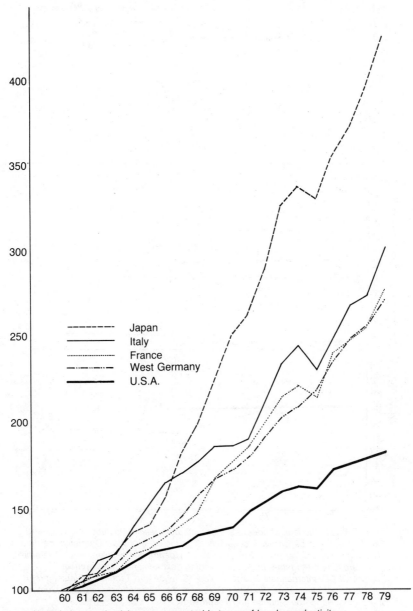

Figure 1-4 Trends in physical labor productivity of manufacturing workers (1960 = 100) (*Source: White Paper on International Trade: Japan 1981,* Tokyo: Japan External Trade Organization, 1981, p. 51.)

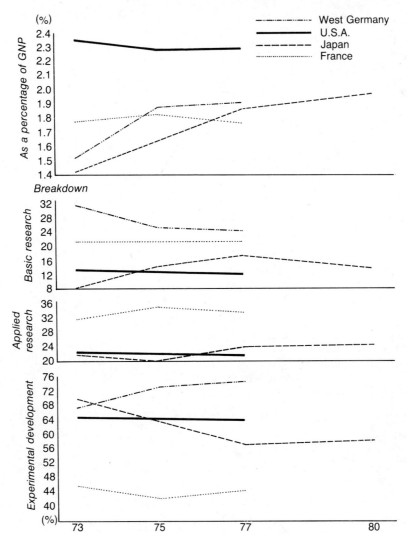

Note: 1. Due to the lack of adequate statistics, data relating to Japan for 1973 and data for 1975 and beyond lack continuity. 2. In the case of West Germany, the data are not divided into "applied research" and "experimental development." Therefore, they were lumped together under the heading "experimental development."
Source: OECD, International Statistical Year, Science and Technology Indicators, Main Economic Indicators; Statistics Bureau of the Prime Minister's Office, Summary of a Survey Report on Science and Technology.

Figure 1-5 Trends in the R & D expenditure of major industrial nations (*Source: White Paper on International Trade: Japan 1982*, Tokyo: Japan External Trade Organization, 1982, p. 67.)

Before further discussing the orientation of this book, I will briefly outline three additional challenges in international business. These are:

1. Emergence of multinational companies from developing countries
2. State-owned enterprises
3. New methods of conducting international business

Multinationals from the Third World

A common image of the multinational company is that of a large firm from an industrialized country investing in both industrialized and developing countries. This perception of the multinational phenomenon is essentially correct. Today about 95% of the world's multinational companies originate in industrialized countries and about three quarters of total foreign investment is in developed countries. However, in the last few years, a new breed of multinationals has been emerging from the developing countries. The stock of capital and technology is now sufficient in some developing countries to enable them to invest overseas.

Partial available statistics concerning multinational firms from developing countries suggest a high rate of growth among them. For example, Louis Wells identified some 1,100 projects undertaken by those firms. Important in this group are Brazil, Argentina, Mexico, India, Hong Kong, Taiwan, and South Korea.[32] The U.N. Center on Transnational Corporations reports more than 180 intercountry investments in Latin America.[33] Developing countries have invested over $1.5 billion in Thailand, Indonesia, the Philippines, and Hong Kong.[34] By 1980, some 200 Indian companies had invested over $100 million overseas[35] and additionally generated construction contracts for $2.5 billion in 22 countries.[36] According to a recent survey, 15 leading developing countries have invested over $120 billion abroad; they had established some 1,964 subsidiaries of which 938 were engaged in manufacturing. In terms of overseas subsidiaries, Hong Kong led the group with 527 subsidiaries, followed by India with 383.[37]

What are the main advantages these firms enjoy in the international marketplace? Studies on the attributes and functions of MNCs from developing countries suggest the following:

1. More adaptable and "appropriate" scaled-down technology
2. Willingness to enter into joint venture partnership with the local firms and state-owned enterprises
3. Lower cost of producing goods and services, and lower demands on profit and profit remittance[38]

Multinationals from the Third World have begun to offer serious competition to the MNCs of the industrialized countries. For example, in the construction contract race in the Middle East, the United States has fallen behind such developing countries as South Korea, Brazil, India, and Taiwan. South Koreans have surpassed even the aggressive Japanese and West German companies.[39]

State-owned Enterprises in International Markets

State-owned enterprises are growing in relative importance both in national and international economic relations. The role of the state and of state-owned enterprises is by no means new. Beginning in some countries in the 1930s—during the Great Depression—and increasingly during the period after World War II, nation-states around the world have considerably expanded their role and their influence in the socioeconomic and cultural lives of their citizens. Indeed, in many instances, the "visible hand" of the state has replaced Adam Smith's "invisible hand" of the marketplace. For example, government expenditures, as a percentage of the GNP, have risen as high as 53% in Sweden. In such highly industrialized countries as the United Kingdom, Austria, Japan, France, and West Germany, governments are spending over 40% of their GNPs. Among the industrialized nations, only the United States government spends less than 30% of her total GNP.[40]

In most nations, governments own and control postal and telecommunications services, electricity, airlines, and steel industries. As a provider of jobs, the public sector employs some 33% of the gainfully employed in Austria, 29% in Britain, 21% in West Germany and the Netherlands, and 19% in France and the United States.[41] The prime motivations for the increasing influence by these states are: (1) to safeguard the health and economic well-being of the people; (2) to narrow the widening gap between the rich and the poor; (3) to maintain ecological and environmental balance; (4) to safeguard consumer interests; (5) to eliminate or reduce the monopolistic and oligopolistic powers of big businesses; (6) to generate industrial and economic growth; and (7) to provide needed jobs, especially in the less developed areas of the country.[42]

The public sector has entered into manufacturing, distributing, and providing goods and services traditionally reserved for private hands. The public sector's industrial enterprises employ 10% of the total manpower in many industrialized and developing countries. Moreover, state-controlled companies produce 85% of the noncommunist world's oil, 40% of its copper, 33% of its iron ore and bauxite, 54% of its steel, 35% of its polyethylene, and 20% of its automobiles.[43]

As Hugh D. Menzies points out in his provocative article: ". . . while U.S. companies in basic industries have borne the brunt of the new state challenge, their brethren in high-technology businesses are not entirely immune."[44] Privately owned companies in high-technology industries, such as semiconductors, aerospace, chemicals, and petrochemicals now see their counterparts, the state-owned enterprises, commanding some share of the world's market. For example, the United States' stronghold in the semiconductor business is now being challenged by an international consortium initiated by the French government. The United Kingdom has recently set up a state-owned company in the United States to purchase technology and to lure highly qualified personnel. Although United States aircraft companies dominated the sky until now, a dogfight has already begun. Some of the challengers are indeed the state-owned companies, such as the four partners in the West European consortium Airbus Industrie and Brazil's Embraer. The former, backed by an interest-free loan of $1 billion by the French, West German, and British governments, has already sold over 350 planes at very competitive prices and terms. Brazilian companies, besides selling in the domestic market, have already made inroads into the United States and other foreign markets.[45]

New Forms of Conducting International Business: Countertrade

Since the industrial revolution of the nineteenth century, national and international economic relations have been facilitated by monetary exchange. As more countries become actively involved in international trade, goods are increasingly being acquired through direct trade of some other goods, or by parallel, but linked, cash purchases. Commonly known as countertrade, these forms of trade account for over 25% of total world business. Some of the recent examples of such countertrade deals in international business include:

1. The Brazilian government required foreign automakers to export automobiles and trucks, worth $21 billion, in return for the duty-free import of spare parts from overseas locations.
2. Sweden got a commitment from General Electric to sell Swedish products in overseas markets in return for a Swedish contract to build engines for Sweden's JAS fighters.
3. The New Zealand Meat Board agreed to sell $200 million worth of frozen lamb to the Iranian government in exchange for crude oil.
4. Russia is buying construction machinery from Japan's Komatsu and Mitsubishi companies. The Japanese are taking Siberian timber.[46]

In the past, countertrade used to be practiced by the controlled economies of the Soviet Union, East European countries, and Third World countries. Recently, however, these practices began to spread widely, and countries such as Canada, Switzerland, Sweden, even the United States have joined the trend. As Robert D. Schmidt, Vice-Chairman of Control Data puts it: "Everybody is at it; more countries are demanding reciprocity."[47] State-owned trading companies in communist and developing countries are playing an important role in countertrade agreements. In industrialized countries, plans are underway to establish Japanese style general trading companies to cope with this new reality in international business. Recent estimates indicate that one hundred United States companies, such as General Motors, General Electric, Sears, Roebuck and Company, Westinghouse Electric, Occidental Petroleum, and Exxon have set up trading companies to handle countertrade. In 1979 there were twenty-seven countries requiring countertrade; by 1983 this list swelled to eighty-eight countries.[48] Throughout this book I have attempted to incorporate the impact of these environmental changes on the management strategies, policies, and practices of international corporations.

To integrate my analysis of management practices, I will need some sort of theory or paradigm. In the next section, I will briefly review the major theories of international business.

To sum up, it is clear that the international business environment and the nature of international economic relations are changing rapidly. International executives of the 1980s will be obligated to develop a keen sense for these environmental changes to take advantage of the opportunities in the world's marketplace.

Theories of International Business

There are basically two sets of theories of international business: the international trade theories, explaining how intercountry trade takes place, and theories of direct foreign investment, explaining intercountry investment in manufacturing and service activities and the management of these activities.

International Trade Theories

Mercantilism (1500–1700). Being linked to the development of the nation-states of England and Europe, mercantilism was a loose-knit body of ideas and practices established by many mercantilists such as Thomas Mun and Jean Bodin. They were primarily concerned with national wealth, believing that national power is based on an economic foundation. They also believed that a country's wealth and self-sufficiency depended on the exports exceeding the imports. Thus one characteristic of mercantilism was a policy of encouraging exports and discouraging imports.

The mercantilists were, however, unable to provide an explanation on what trade benefits are realized between two nations.

Adam Smith (1800s). Being influenced by the individualism around the beginning of the nineteenth century and by the Industrial Revolution, Adam

Smith emphasized the importance of individual freedom. He believed that if the individual is permitted to pursue his or her own interest without interference from the state, he or she will promote the well-being of all by the "invisible hand."

Classical Economic Theory (mid-1800s). A new economic theory, proposed by Adam Smith and David Ricardo, provided the principles that underlie the working of the capitalist system. The major principles of classical theory were:

1. Preference of the individual's interests over the state's
2. Division of labor for trade specialization
3. Perfect competition and a free market
4. Labor as a key production factor

The classical economists were able to show that the real basis for trade, either domestic or foreign, is the mutual advantage that can be secured. According to the classical theory, countries will maximize their real incomes if they specialize in the production of commodities they are best fitted to produce and to exchange them against the products of another country.

Comparative Advantage Theory. David Ricardo showed that a nation might properly import goods it could make itself with a lower expenditure of labor as long as its relative efficiency in making other exportable goods was greater. He suggested that specialization, based on absolute cost advantage, would not be possible because of the immobility of both capital and labor. Thus the important principle here is that a country should not produce all of the goods it can make cheaper but only those it can make cheapest.

John Stuart Mill and Terms of Trade. John Stuart Mill addressed the question of how international values are determined. He not only recognized that the value of a foreign commodity depended on the quantity of the home product exchanged but he identified the brackets (ratios) within which trade could take place.

Weaknesses of the Classical Theory. Both Mill and Ricardo stated the doctrine of comparative advantage only in terms of labor costs. It would be valid if there were no other scarce resources. The classical economists also believed that labor and all productive factors are mobile within a country and immobile among nations. Pure competition and the most efficient allocation of resources also meant that full employment of workers was considered to be the norm.

In spite of those flaws, one strong theoretical contribution of the classical theory is its ability to show how countries have become better off as a result of specialization and trade based on comparative advantage.

Beril Ohlin's Theory.[49] Beril Ohlin, a Swedish economist, argued that trade between countries was merely a special case of trade between regions. He introduced the factor-advantage concept. Each region is best equipped to produce the goods that require large proportions of the factors relatively abundant there; it is, on the other hand, least fit to produce goods requiring large proportions of factors scarcely endowed. Thus, once specialization and trade begin, each country will tend to produce goods requiring large quantities of the plentiful factors and tend to produce few goods requiring large quantities of the scarce factors.

As in the classical economic theory, Beril Ohlin's theory of international trade has been criticized for several restrictive assumptions, which are:

1. The absence of transfer costs in the international movement
2. Perfect competition
3. Full employment of all factors of production
4. Fixed supplies of homogeneous factors of production
5. The absence of technological innovation
6. Perfect immobility of the factors of production among nations

Theories of Direct Foreign Investment

Classical economists were mainly concerned with international trade (export and import) and the overall political economy of a nation. However, the industrial revolution in England and Europe and consequent technological developments in the new world (the United States) shifted attention from trade to direct investment and to the transfer of technological and management knowledge. The classical theories were limited in scope to explain these newer phenomena in international economic relations. Three prominent theories explaining foreign direct investment and the multinational's behavior and strategies are briefly reviewed next.

Product Life Cycle Theory. Whereas traditional theory is based on the free availability of information and stable production functions, the product life cycle (PLC) models are based on assumptions that the flow of information across national borders is restricted and products undergo predictable changes in their production and marketing characteristics over time.

According to this theory, a product goes through several stages of development. The first stage is to introduce a new product into the large domestic market with heavy research and development expenditures. The second stage is to export the product. As the product matures, it becomes more standardized with more competitors. Then the firm has to decide whether to invest in a foreign subsidiary. If foreign manufacturers begin to produce the product, the firm is likely to set up a foreign subsidiary to maintain its market share abroad and to recapture the remaining rent from the product's development. At the next stage the subsidiary may serve third country markets to exploit economies of scale. In the final stage of this model, new competitors arise to challenge the position of the original firms.[50]

Louis Wells identified five distinct stages in the product life cycle:

1. Developing a product for the domestic market through research and development activities
2. Exporting domestic products to overseas markets
3. Setting up manufacturing facilities in other industrialized countries, exporting goods from these subsidiaries to developing countries
4. Setting up manufacturing facilities in developing countries (e.g., manufacturing radios and televisions in Taiwan, South Korea, Singapore)
5. Exporting goods to the United States market from developing countries (e.g., televisions from South Eastern countries to the United States)[51]

The results of many empirical tests of this model indicate that it was useful for understanding the flow of manufactured goods across international borders. Also, when additional factors such as the size of the firm and the oligopolistic elements of the industry structure are introduced, the model becomes a fairly powerful tool to explain the flow of foreign direct investment. However, in recent years, with the reduction of trade barriers and technological diffusion around the world, the PLC theory has lost much of its explanatory power. The multinational firm itself, as Giddy has pointed out, "has succeeded in developing a number of other strategies for surviving in overseas production and marketing."[52]

Fayerweather's Paradigm: Unification versus Fragmentation. Fayerweather attempted to explain the conflicting demands on the multinationals in terms of *unification* versus *fragmentation*. The unification strategy corresponds to the firm's desire to integrate its global units into one entity, whereas the fragmentation strategy indicates the necessity of adjusting policies and practices according to the environmental demands of the various nation-states.

These conflicting demands differentiate the international business operations of an MNC from a large domestic company. The latter is generally operating in a single homogeneous environment of a given nation; consequently, the integration of strategies and policies is easier to accomplish. The MNCs, on the other hand, not only face heterogeneous, but also very complex socioeconomic, political, and cultural environments in different nations.

Chandler's Thesis.[53] The historian Alfred Chandler, in his study of one hundred of the largest United States industrial firms, found that as firms attempted to grow through product and geographical diversification, they changed from centralized structures to multidivisional structures. The multidivisional structures were largely autonomous, and each major division typically retained considerable autonomy in its decision making. However, major strategic and policy decisions were still undertaken by the corporate headquarters.

The reliability of Chandler's prediction, that *structure follows strategy,* has been investigated at the national and international levels with some positive results. The Harvard Group suggested that the multinational firm's structure will evolve from using export, or foreign departments to handle its overseas business, to formulating an international division. Then the company becomes by orientation an international corporation, which is indicated by the emergence of a multinational concept with geographical area and product concentrations. Finally, the MNC moves into a matrix organizational form and perhaps eventually becomes a transnational enterprise, owned and operated by the citizens of several different nations.

Using a similar set of expectations, Lawrence Franko and Michael Yoshino found similar trends among European and Japanese MNCs, respectively.[54] That is, the organizational structures of these MNCs have evolved from an export division, to an international division, to a separate international corporation, and finally to a divisionalized structure with product and area concentrations. Table 1-3 shows the various stages of the internationalization of firms and the corresponding changes in their organizational structure, control, and other management practices.

As the firm's overseas business activities increase, it will go through the stages of the standardization of production, product innovation and diversification, and the global rationalization of production and marketing processes. This, in turn, will necessitate corresponding changes in ownership, control policies, and practices (e.g., from a minority equity holding in overseas subsidiaries to a majority or a 100% equity holding; and from informal, loosely controlled mechanisms to more formalized control systems).

Limitations of Unification versus *Fragmentation, the Product Life Cycle, and Structure Follows Strategy Paradigms.* The research studies based on Chandler's theoretical rationale emphasize the internal aspects of organizational policy making and do not pay enough attention to the external environmental forces impinging on the structure follows strategy construct.

Second, the "rightness" of congruence between the firm's strategy and its structure is inferred through the economic performance criteria, although the connection between strategy, structure, and performance has not yet been empirically verified.[55] It is conceivable that a firm's economic and financial

Table 1-3 Evolution and growth of international business and corresponding changes in organizational structures, formalizations, ownership policies, control strategies, and staffing policies

Evolution and growth of international business	A. Evolution of organizational structure	B. Other structural characteristics	C. Ownership policies	D. Control strategies	E. Staffing policies
I. Initial stage	Export dept.	Loose, formal relationships	Minority HQ* equity	Indirect, loose coupling	Host country national in charge
II. Early production stage	Export dept./ international division	More formalized relationships between HQ* and sub†	Minority or 50–50 equity	Indirect control through technical personnel	Home country nationals in charge
III. Standardization of production process— mature stage few products	International division	Increased formalized relationships	Majority or 100% equity in subsidiary operation	Direct control, tight coupling	Host country nationals in charge
IV. Product innovations and growth through diversification	Product/area bases for structuring of organization	Increased formalization	Minority or 50–50 equity	Indirect control through personnel	Home country or third country nationals in charge
V. Quest for global rationalization	Product/area bases for structuring matrix type organization	Increased formalization	Majority or 100% equity in subsidiary	Direct control	Host country nationals in charge

*Hq: Headquarters
†Sub: Subsidiaries

performance may be primarily a result of market, economic, and political conditions rather than of the firm's strategy and structure.[56]

Most of the field research was done during the late 1960s and early 1970s, and was undertaken in the industrialized countries, where free and competitive market conditions were prevalent and government interference was minimal. It was easy then to overemphasize the internal aspects of organizations and underemphasize the "macro" or external environmental conditions.

Since the 1973 oil crisis, economic and market conditions have changed drastically in both developed and developing countries. Government intervention and regulations that used to be the hallmark of centralized and developing economies have now also become pervasive in industrialized countries.

Fayerweather, in his construct of unification versus fragmentation, specifically recognized the influence of environmental factors. However, he too has overemphasized the leverage and power of the multinationals vis-à-vis the nation-states by assigning to MNCs the role of the *central actor.*[57]

Given the rapid changes in international business environments, I have adhered to the following assumptions in writing this book.

Environmental Demands and Adaptive Strategy

The MNCs' strategies are influenced by the demands made by constituents in both the host and the home countries. On the basis of this premise, I hypothesized that the MNCs' strategies should be in congruence with the home and host countries' policies and demands.

To be effective in the varied environments of home and host countries (varied demands and policies of home and host countries), the MNCs may have to devise different strategies for their home offices and each of their subsidiary operations. In other words, a *master plan* (such as those of IBM or Coca Cola, which require 100% equity ownership in all foreign operations) might not be workable. Structures and processes of the headquarters and subsidiaries must be consistent to cope with the home and host countries' demands (environments).

The lack of congruence between the demands of the home and host countries and the headquarters' and the subsidiaries' strategies, will be reflected in tensions and conflicts between headquarters and subsidiaries, between headquarters and host, as well as home countries, and between subsidiaries and host countries. Figure 1-6 indicates the multiactor's game I visualize in the international business arena.

Organization of This Book

This book is divided into three parts:

   I. International Business Environment
  II. Strategic Aspects of International Business Corporations
 III. Functional Aspects of International Business Operations

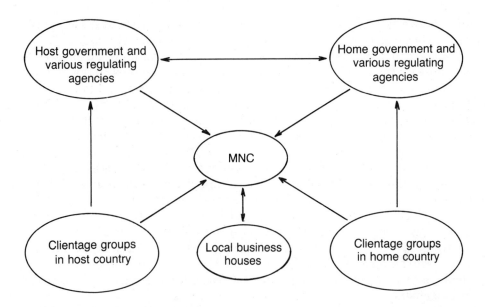

Figure 1-6 MNCs and their challenges

Part I contains two chapters. In *Chapter 1* I have endeavored to highlight the role of international business in the world economy, the United States' stake in international business, the emergence of multinational companies, the changing character of international business, and the challenge to United State dominance in international business.

Chapter 2 provides an overview of the interactions between multinationals and nation-states. It discusses the issues concerning the controlling and ethical and social responsibilities of international corporations.

Part II contains four chapters. *Chapter 3* discusses the structure follows strategy paradigm advanced by Alfred Chandler, and its use by the Harvard Multinational Enterprise Project Group for examining the organizational structure of United States, European, and Japanese multinational companies. This chapter then reviews the current studies on the MNCs' organizational designs and structures.

Chapter 4 discusses the various strategic and policy issues of multinational corporations, which include the focus of policy decisions, policies as control devices, ownership of subsidiaries, modes of control, and means and sources of control.

Chapter 5 outlines the relative influence of headquarters and foreign subsidiaries in decision making. It also analyzes the nature and intensity of conflicts between the headquarters and the subsidiary. Lastly, it discusses the impact of these conflicts on the firm's growth and profitability.

Chapter 6 analyzes the nature of environmental scanning and long-range planning undertaken by multinational corporations. It discusses the concepts of environmental scanning and long-range planning first, and follows with the actual practices. Lastly, it analyzes the impact of environmental scanning and long-range planning on the firm's growth and profitability.

Part III covers the major functional aspects of international business corporations.

Chapters 7 and 8 discuss manpower management practices. Various aspects of managing the labor work force are discussed in *Chapter 7*. These include the impact of sociocultural factors on employee morale, motivation and productivity, manpower planning, job analysis, and selection and promotion practices. *Chapter 8* discusses various issues on managing managers in overseas subsidiaries. These include: sources of recruitment, advantages and disadvantages of the home, host, and third country's nationals; needed qualities of an overseas manager; and the feasibility of transferring advanced management practices into developing countries.

Chapter 9 covers international production and logistics. Issues to be covered are the choice of technology, decisions concerning plant location and size, and the sources of materials and parts.

Chapters 10 and 11 discuss marketing management in international corporations. Topics include the assessment of the world markets, export marketing, and the impact of sociocultural and environmental factors on decisions concerning product design and developments, promotion and advertising practices, pricing policies, and channel distribution.

Chapter 12 covers the managerial financial issues involved in managing international business operations. Its topics are the management of capital resources, the sources of capital, and the management of foreign exchange fluctuation.

As stated in the beginning of this chapter, the focus is on the managerial and comparative issues of international management. The managerial aspects concern the actual strategies, policies, and practices of international corporations and will cover major strategic and operational aspects of international business. The comparative approach contrasts United States, European, and Japanese companies. The main aim is to examine the strength and weakness of the various practices, and to assess their impact on the survival, growth, and profitability of international corporations.

To highlight the strategies, policies, and practices of United States, European, and Japanese corporations, several cases with differing contexts are at the ends of the chapters. I hope the discussions and analyses of these cases will reinforce the learning process.

Discussion Questions

1. Although the relative position of United States involvement in world business is decreasing, her stakes in international business are expected to continue to grow in the future. Why is that so?
2. How do the United States' foreign operations benefit their domestic economy?
3. During the last two decades, the United States' MNCs have become larger in size; however, they are facing more competition from MNCs of other nations than before. How would you account for such a situation?
4. Many big Asian multinational firms are competing with many United States businesses in the domestic market, as well as in the international market, today. In which industries are they mostly involved, and what kind of competitive edge do they enjoy?
5. In what areas and under which situations will state-owned enterprises be able to provide formidable challenges to private MNCs?
6. Discuss the differences in the arguments of the various contending theories of international business as proposed by Fayerweather, Vernon, and Negandhi.
7. What would future implications of each theory be on:
   a) Growth potentials of United States firms in the international marketplace
   b) Economic relations between Europe and the United States
   c) Economic relations between Japan and the United States
   d) Economic relations between developing countries and the United States

Endnotes

1. Jay I. Olnek, *The Invisible Hand* (Greenwich, Conn.: North Stonington Press, 1982), p. 100.
2. *White Paper on International Trade, Japan 1981* (Tokyo: Japan External Trade Organization (JETRO), 1981).
3. United Nations, *Transnational Corporations in World Development: Third Survey* (New York: United Nations, 1983), p. 19.
4. *Forbes*, July 4, 1983, p. 114.
5. Joan P. Curhan, William H. Davidson, and Rajan Suri, *Tracing the Multinationals* (Cambridge, Mass.: Ballinger Publishing Co., 1977), pp. 19, 22–23.
6. President Reagan's State of the Union Message, January 21, 1983.
7. U.S. Department of Commerce, *Survey of Current Business*, August 1982.
8. United Nations, *Multinational Corporations in World Development* (New York: United Nations, 1973), p. 23.
9. Arvind V. Phatak, *Managing Multinational Corporations*, (New York: Praeger Publishers, 1974), pp. 21–22.
10. John Fayerweather, *International Business Strategy and Administration* (Cambridge, Mass.: Ballinger Publishing Co., 1978), pp. 1–2.
11. Raymond Vernon, *Storm over the Multinationals* (Cambridge, Mass.: Harvard University Press, 1977), p. 12.
12. Ibid., p. 13.
13. Ibid.

14. *The Economist*, November 7, 1984.
15. Curhan, Davidson, and Suri, *Tracing the Multinationals* (Cambridge, Mass.: Ballinger Publishing Co., 1977), pp. 17–55.
16. Lawrence G. Franko, "Multinationals: The End of U.S. Dominance," *Harvard Business Review* 56, 2 (November-December 1978): 95–96.
17. Yoshi Tsurumi, *The Japanese are Coming* (Cambridge, Mass.: Ballinger Publishing Co., 1976), p. 24.
18. Ezra F. Vogel, *Japan As Number One* (Cambridge: Harvard University Press, 1978).
19. Lester Thurow, "A Strategy for Revitalizing American Industry," *California Management Review* XXVII, 1 (Fall 1984): 9–41.
20. Ibid., p. 9.
21. *U.S. News and World Report*, June 9, 1980, p. 23.
22. *White Paper on International Trade: Japan 1982* (Tokyo: Japan External Trade Organization (JETRO), 1982), pp. 60–62.
23. J. Arpan and S. D. Ricks, "Foreign Direct Investment in the United States," *Journal of International Business*, 10, 3 (Winter 1979): 85.
24. Ibid.
25. *Wall Street Journal*, November 29, 1984, p. 1.
26. Robert Ball, "Europe's U.S. Shopping Spree," *Fortune*, December 1, 1980, p. 84.
27. Ibid.
28. Lawrence G. Franko, *The European Multinationals* (Stamford, Conn.: Greylock, 1976), p. 98.
29. F. L. Hartley, "World Trade in the '80s: Will We Be Competitive?," paper presented at 1980 World Trade Conference, Chicago, April 7, 1980.
30. Thurow, "Strategy," p. 20.
31. Franko, *Multinationals*, p. 98.
32. Louis T. Wells, Jr., "Foreign Investors from the Third World," in *Multinationals from Developing Countries*, ed. Krishna Kumar and Maxwell G. McLeod (Lexington, Mass.: Lexington Books, 1981), p. 23.
33. U.N. Commission on Transnational Corporations, *Transnational Corporations in World Development: A Re-examination* (New York: United Nations, 1978), pp. 246–247.
34. Ibid.
35. Ram Gopal Agrawal, "Third World Joint Ventures: Indian Experience," in *Multinationals from Developing Countries*, p. 128.
36. Aggarwal, Raj, and Inder P. Khera, "Foreign Operations of Third World Multinationals: A Literature Review and Analysis of Indian Companies," *The Journal of Developing Areas* (In Press).
37. Louis T. Wells, Jr., *Third World Multinationals: The Rise of Foreign Investment From Developing Countries* (Cambridge, Mass.: MIT Press, 1983), pp. 2–10.
38. David A. Heenan and Warren J. Keegan, "The Rise of Third World Multinationals," *Harvard Business Review*, 57, 1 (January-February, 1979): 101–109.
39. "U.S. 'Arrogance' Costs Firms Billions," *Engineering News* 203, 22 (November 29, 1979): 22.
40. "The State in the Market," *The Economist*, December 30, 1978, pp. 37–58.
41. Ibid.
42. Ibid.
43. Hugh Menzies, "U.S. Companies in Unequal Combat," *Fortune*, April 9, 1979, p. 103.
44. Ibid., p. 104.
45. Ibid.

46. *Business Week*, July 19, 1982, p. 139.
47. Robert D. Schmidt, quoted in *Business Week*, July 19, 1982, p. 118.
48. *Business Week*, March 12, 1984.
49. Bertil Ohlin, *Interregional and International Trade* (Cambridge, Mass.: Harvard University Press, 1933).
50. Louis T. Wells, Jr., ed., *The Product Life Cycle and International Trade* (Boston: Harvard University Press, 1972), p. 15.
51. Ibid.
52. Jan H. Giddy, "The Demise of the Product Cycle Model in International Business Theory," *Columbia Journal of World Business* XIII, 1 (Spring 1978): 97. Also see Raymond Vernon, "The Product Cycle Hypothesis in a New International Environment," *Oxford Bulletin of Economics and Statistics* (November 1979): 255–267.
53. Alfred D. Chandler, *Strategy and Structure* (Cambridge, Mass.: MIT Press, 1962).
54. Lawrence G. Franko, *The European Multinationals*, and Michael Yoshino, *Japan's Multinational Enterprises* (Cambridge: Harvard University Press, 1976).
55. J. R. Galbraith and D. A. Nathanson, *Strategy Implementation: The Role of Structure and Process* (St. Paul, Minn.: West Publishing Company, 1978), p. 37.
56. Joe Bain, *Industrial Organization* (New York: John Wiley and Sons, 1958).
57. Fayerweather, *International Business Strategy*, Chap. 2, pp. 1–9.

Additional Readings _____

Articles

Aharoni, Yair. "The State-Owned Enterprise as Competitor in International Markets." *Columbia Journal of World Business* (Spring 1980): 14–22.

Root, Franklin R. "Some Trends in the World Economy and Their Implications for International Business Strategy." *Journal of International Business Studies* (Winter 1984): 19–23.

Speth, James Gustave. "Questions for a Critical Decade." *Columbia Journal of World Business* (Spring 1984): 5–9.

Young, John A. "Global Competition: The New Reality." *California Management Review* (Spring 1985): 11–25.

Books

Bergsten, C. Fred. *The United States in the World Economy.* Lexington, Mass.: Lexington Books, 1983.

Dunning, John. *International Production and the Multinational Enterprise.* London, Eng.: George Allen & Unwin, 1981.

Kindleberger, Charles P., and Audretsch, David B. *The Multinational Corporation in the 1980s.* Cambridge, Mass.: MIT Press, 1983.

Negandhi, Anant R., and Baliga, B.R. *Tables are Turning: German and Japanese Multinational Companies in the United States.* Cambridge, Mass.: Oelgeschlager, Gunn & Hain, Publishers, Inc., 1981.

Chapter 2

International Corporations and Governments: Control Issues and Social Responsibilities

The last chapter discussed some major changes in the international business environment. These included: the increasing importance of international trade and investment in the world economy; the increasing challenge to United States dominance in international business; the rise of European and Japanese multinational companies; and the emergence of state-owned enterprises and multinational firms from Third World countries. It also briefly discussed the increasing importance of barter or countertrade in international transactions.

Cumulatively, these changes have accelerated the competitive pressures in the international marketplace. Coupled with the highly competitive environment, international companies are also facing diverse demands from various governments.

Basically, three significant issues are involved concerning the interaction between international corporations and governments. First, the issue of the divergence in the objectives and goals of the firms and their governments are giving rise to tension and conflict between them.

Second is the issue of controlling the activities and actions of international corporations by the governments. Third is the larger issue pertaining to the overall ethical and social responsibility of the corporation to the community and the nation.

Both the home and the host countries have raised questions concerning all three issues.

Tensions and conflicts between the multinationals and nation-states, and the controls over their activities by governments directly impinge on their organizational strategies, policies, and practices. These two aspects are discussed first.

The issue of ethical and social responsibility affects the very basic survival and growth of the international corporation. This will be discussed at the end of this chapter.

Our discussion of tension and conflict between multinationals and nation-states will begin by briefly reviewing the ongoing public debates, followed by identifying the conflict and the conflicting issues between them. Lastly, the controlling aspect will be discussed at some length.

The Setting

Increased attention has been focused on the impact of multinational corporations (MNCs) on the national economy, employment, balance of payments, security, national defense, foreign policies, national sovereignty, and the social and economic development plans of the host countries.

This upsurge of concern on the impact of the MNCs can easily be seen from the numerous inquiries and investigations. Such august bodies as the U.S. Senate Finance Committee, the United Nations, and many learned societies have formally dealt with this subject.[1] Likewise, many professional associations, such as the British–North American Research Association,[2] the National Association of Manufacturers,[3] the National Foreign Trade Council,[4] and a number of prestigious universities both here and abroad, have embarked on issues relative to the impact of multinational corporations.

The issues raised and the intensive dialogue on the subject have augmented the sensitivity of those involved. This has resulted in an optimistic outlook on the one hand and pessimistic overtones on the other hand.

Optimism and Pessimism and Off Balance

The so-called optimists see the MNC as the most powerful engine of progress ever invented by humans. Referring to the positive role played by the multinationals, Mr. Maisonrouge, Chairman of the IBM World Trade Corporation, said, "They have become agents of change and progress, for they are building what, to all intents and purposes, must be considered a new world economic system—one in which the constraints of geography have yielded to the logic of efficiency."[5]

In supporting this view, Mr. Kendall, Chairman of the Pepsi Cola Co., has echoed, ". . . from this new conception of the world as a single system will come a richer, and far more rewarding life for us all—not simply as Americans, but as human beings."[6]

Businesspeople are not alone in advocating the positive aspect of the multinationals. Some academicians have also become ardent believers. For example, Professor Benoit has argued:

> The MNC may be viewed as a powerful engine for diffusing the benefits of superior management and technology across national boundaries, thereby improving the world's allocation of resources and taking fuller advantage of the economies of scale. . . . Contrary to what many suppose, there is no fundamental clash between the MNC and the host government. Indeed, the MNC can contribute notably to host country national objectives, given adequate encouragement and sensible control. . . .[7]

Arguing against the benefits derived from the operations of multinational corporations, many nation-states believe that the presence of multinationals is a deterrent to their socioeconomic development, as well as to their sovereignty. Shaker, for example, seems to have reflected the sentiments of many leaders of developing nations:

> However zealously the advocates of the multinational corporation may promote its virtues, there is basically no such thing as a truly international corporation. The subsidiary owes its allegiance to corporate headquarters in the United States from whom it takes its orders and by which it is guided accordingly. While the corporation itself wields powerful political influence, it is at the same time an instrument of U.S. foreign policy. Nation-states will not long tolerate foreign control and domination of their industries and other economic institutions. Developing nations are seeking their own patterns of

development for their society and are reassessing their positions *vis-à-vis* the international corporations.[8]

Reflecting the same concern in a somewhat milder tone, the United Nations group on MNCs reports:

> The divergence in objectives between nation-states and multinational corporations, compounded by social and cultural factors, often creates tensions. Multinational corporations, through a variety of options available to them, can encroach at times upon national sovereignty by undermining the ability of nation-states to pursue their national and international objectives. Moreover, there are conflicts of interest regarding participation in decision-making and the equitable division of benefits between multinational corporations and host as well as home countries. In recent years the situation has been sharpened, on the one hand by changes in the internal sociopolitical conditions of many countries, and on the other, by shifts in bargaining positions. As a result, existing arrangements are frequently questioned and new ones are sought.[9]

Such an intense dialogue is further compounded by "offensive" strategies taken by the multinationals and other concerned groups (e.g., consumers, labor unions, and host developing countries).

Analysis of Conflicts and Conflicting Issues: Developing Countries

Sources, Patterns, and Trends of Conflicts

As one can see from Table 2-1, approximately one half of the 260 serious disputes during 1975–1979, which resulted in nationalization, expropriation, or other types of takeover by the host countries, concentrated on petroleum and mining industries. The table also shows that the highest proportions of investment disputes occurred in Latin America (45% of the total disputes) and were followed by Africa (29%). The manufacturing sector recorded the least amount of disputes (14%), whereas, relatively speaking, the Asian region has had the least number of conflicts (12%). A larger stock of investment in a given country may have given rise to a larger number of conflicts and takeovers. For example, Latin America represented 17.2% of the total United States' investment, and over 80% of the United States' total investment in the developing countries recorded 45% of the total disputes between MNCs and developing nations.

Table 2-1 Disputes between United States firms and developing countries: by region and sector*

Industry	Latin America	Africa	Geographic Area Middle East	Asia	Total	Percent
Petroleum-related	26	23	28	7	84	32
Mining and processing	35	9	0	0	44	17
Banking and insurance	6	17	5	10	38	15
Public utilities	13	0	1	0	14	5
Manufacturing	20	5	0	10	35	14
Other	18	21	3	3	45	17
Total	118	75	37	30	260	
Percent	45	29	14	12		100
Percent of U.S. total foreign investment*	17.2	2.0	†	4.3	23.5	

*Survey of Current Business, August 1977.
†Less than 1%.
Source: Nationalization and Expropriation of U.S. Direct Private Foreign Investment: Problems and Issues, Report to the Congress by the Comptroller General of the United States, Washington, D.C.: May 20, 1977, p. 2.

Hawkins's study indicates a changing picture of the disputes between MNCs and developing countries. The wave of nationalization and expropriation in the extractive sector was declining (from 50% of the total disputes from 1946 to 1966, to 39% from 1967 to 1971, and to 37% from 1972 to 1973), whereas for the manufacturing sector it increased from 27% from 1961 to 1966, to 40% from 1972 to 1973. Regionally, Latin America still dominates the scene, except during the period 1967 to 1971, when large numbers of disputes started occurring in Africa.[10]

Changes from Political Ideology to Economic Rationality

The detailed analysis of the cases of serious disputes between MNCs and developing countries from 1960 to 1976 indicates that such disputes are not necessarily politically motivated, but rest on the belief that by asserting her right, the host country can achieve socioeconomic objectives more effectively. The following abstract of Professor Kobrin's study,[11] covering 511 disputes in 23 developing countries, highlights the changing events:

> The findings of this study refute an assertion that forced divestment is simply a manifestation of "economic nationalism," reflecting national pride,

an anti-foreign bias, or political opportunism. On the contrary, it is more often a means than an end. The findings are generally consistent with a view of forced divestment as a policy instrument used to attempt to achieve national political-economic objectives by increasing control over economic actors.

In the vast majority of countries (approximately 89 percent) forced divestment was selective. While political and/or ideological motives were certainly not absent, only a portion of foreign-owned firms was forced to divest. Furthermore, there is sufficient evidence to conclude that the selection of firms forced to divest is far from a random process. Enterprise vulnerability is a function of industrial sector, ownership structure, and behavior.[12]

The author goes on to say:

Certain types of industrial activity are more vulnerable than others. Firms engaged in infrastructure activities essential to national security (such as utilities and mass communication) and in sectors directly affecting economic control (banking) are obviously vulnerable. Extractive investments— which raise basic questions about foreign ownership of national resources, are often poorly integrated into the local economy, and tend to dominate either GDP or exports—are more often the targets of expropriation than firms in manufacturing and trade. Second, the level of technology is important. Firms in industries where technology is mature and diffuse are vulnerable due to perceptions of a decline in the value of their contribution, their bargaining power, and the difficulties likely to be encountered in running the enterprise. Third, wholly-owned subsidiaries are considerably more vulnerable than joint ventures and, particularly, minority joint ventures. The latter are often perceived as more subject to local control, and partial ownership may imply better adaptation to national political, economic, and social systems.[13]

Minor and Manageable Conflicts

The preceding analysis of conflict dealt with serious disputes resulting in the complete takeover of foreign enterprises by the host countries. However, as Fayerweather has remarked, "More common and actually of greater overall importance are a multitude of lesser points of conflict . . . [such as] the share of capital and control foreign governments exercise over foreign operations, and many other facets of overseas businesses."[14]

Similarly, Mikesell has identified the following factors as having the potential for causing conflict between MNCs and host governments, particularly with respect to the mineral and petroleum industries:

1. Division of total net revenues from operations between the foreign country and the host government
2. The control of export prices, output, and the other conditions affecting the level of total revenues

3. The domestic impact of foreign company operations
4. The percentage of foreign ownership[15]

Bergsten has suggested that the differences between the domestic socioeconomic objectives of the host government and the objectives of the foreign investor give rise to conflicts between these two parties. More specifically, he identifies the following issues over which conflicts and tensions are bound to arise:

1. Job quota requirements by the host government; quantitative and qualitative aspects
2. Requirements for the use of local inputs and parts in manufacturing
3. Research and development activities
4. Export requirements
5. Market power of foreign investors; a demand for reduction to promote local enterprises
6. External financing requirement
7. Building up a high-technology enterprise
8. Reduction of imports
9. Ownership requirement: a reduction of foreign share, and an increase in local participation[16]

Microlevel Issues and Conflicts

In a study undertaken from 1974 to 1979 by myself and my colleagues[17] in six developing countries, attempts were made to examine the relationships among certain attributes of the MNCs and the nature and intensity of conflicts between MNCs and host countries. We examined size, ownership, equity holding, type of industries, nature of technology, level of diversification, and the market share. A brief analysis of the results follows.

Equity and Conflicts

One of the most significant types of host country demands, especially from developing countries, is the concern for equity participation by the local nationals in the foreign enterprises. Such demands by the host countries seem to have resulted in conflicts between the MNCs and the governments. Wholly-owned and majority-owned corporations tend to have a significantly greater proportion of conflict as compared to MNCs with only a minority equity at stake. Minority participation did not imply a complete lack of conflict. Minority-owned companies still had to contend with other policy demands, such as proportionate employment of nationals and a reduction in royalties. This indicates that fulfilling one set of the host government's demands does not make the MNC immune to further demands.

Nature of Industry

We saw earlier that the firms in the resource-based industries tend to get involved in higher levels of conflict than those in manufacturing and service. Our findings gave some indications of this sort. The extractive industries were involved in a larger number of interface conflicts than the industries producing nondurable goods. However, the results across the various industries were statistically insignificant.

Nature of Technology

Of the fifty-six cases of conflict observed in technologically advanced firms, 77% were more serious. The comparable figures for intermediate- and low-technology firms were 66% and 53%, respectively. This could be because the advanced firms were questioned about their leverage through the monopolistic powers, pricing policies, and royalty payments, whereas the low-technology firms came under scrutiny with respect to their usefulness and contribution to the host countries' developments.

Visibility

The degree of visibility of an MNC affects the views of citizens and government officials in the host countries positively or negatively. A firm may become visible for any one of the following reasons:

1. Extraordinary contributions to the host country
2. Use of specialized technologies
3. Generating high employment
4. Paying high wages and providing extensive employee training
5. High level of conflict between host and home governments
6. International publicity (e.g., ITT episode in Chile; recent cases of bribes by Gulf and Lockheed Aircraft)
7. Long period of operation in the host country
8. Pervasiveness of endproducts in daily life

The last factor, of course, reflects both the degree of diversification and the frequency of use of the endproducts. Such pervasiveness, achieved through endproduct use, is likely to catch the attention of governmental decision makers and local business competitors, evoking fears of economic domination. Similarly, highly diversified firms, such as ITT, may generate the same fears in the host countries. The diversified MNCs were confronted with a larger number of serious conflicts in the host countries (almost twice as many as those not diversified).

Period of Operation

Frequent stories and newspaper headlines about firms such as United Fruit in Haiti, ITT in Chile and other Latin American countries, International Petroleum, and Cerro de Pasco in Peru lead one to believe that older, well-established firms might have secured favorable concessions and, consequently, attained a significant bargaining power over the host countries. Also, at times, their overt behavior suggests that they have not hesitated to use their powers against their host countries. Critics have argued that the persistence of such behavior by the established MNCs causes high levels of conflict between them and the host countries. On the other hand, the newer firms presumably may be less prone to conflict, because they have come under recent government regulations.

Our results show that, proportionally, the older firms faced more interface conflicts, whereas the newer ones were plagued with a larger number of operational problems. However, these differences between the older and newer firms were not statistically significant.

Size

It has been argued that MNCs operate on a theme of "bigger is better," and the bigness is viewed with hostility by the host governments. To test such a hypothesis, we explored the relationship between MNC size and conflict. MNC size was evaluated in terms of level of capital investment, sales volume, size of employee force, and the executive's perception of the company's size relative to other companies, foreign and local, in a given country. Level of investment and sales volume do not seem to be significantly associated with level of conflict. The number of employees seems to have some relationship with the level of conflict; corporations with a large work force appeared to have a higher level of conflict. This might be because with a large work force the interests of a larger constituency have to be borne in mind; also, with host governments being sensitive to employment levels and labor demands, even small skirmishes with labor easily tend to be escalated into policy and negotiational level conflicts.

Expectation Differences

Psycholinguists, political scientists, and other social scientists concerned with the study of human behavior have argued for quite some time that actual or imaginary differences in expectations between two parties involved in an interaction are likely to result in a breakdown of communication, and might generate tension and even conflict between them.

Our results show that a wide gap existed between the expectations of the MNCs and the host governments. Such breakdowns in understanding of each other have, indeed, created continuous tensions and conflicts in their relationships. Many of the developing countries, to maximize their returns from foreign private investments, have enacted legislation that requires a majority local equity in foreign enterprises, a higher proportion of local nationals in top positions, an increase of exports and foreign exchange earnings, and a reduction of imports of raw materials and spare parts. Such demands by the host countries have, to some extent, constrained the MNCs to rationalize their worldwide productive capacity. To achieve this goal, MNCs have required that the host countries provide them with efficient infrastructural facilities, reduce bureaucratic controls and interference in corporate affairs, and provide favorable labor legislation and more flexible expansion policies.

Market Share

One of the major concerns of host nations about MNCs is that their local industries are being displaced by foreign-owned companies. There is also a fear that the MNCs could become monopolistic powers, beyond the control of national governments.

Thus potentially monopolistic or oligopolistic market powers of the multinationals that could result in a "takeover" of local enterprises are actively resisted, not only by the developing, but also the industrially developed nations. Countries such as Canada, France, West Germany, and the United Kingdom have enacted regulations to discourage such behavior by foreign investors. Even the United States, the champion of the free enterprise system, has shown concern about the adverse impact of foreign investments on her domestic enterprises.

Despite such widespread concern about the adverse impact of the multinationals' market domination in the host countries, our results did not indicate a significant relationship between the MNCs' market share and the nature of conflict in the host countries. Although a large proportion of the MNCs studied indicated that their market share was more than 25%, their problems were in no case different from those faced by companies whose market share was minimal. It appeared that, regardless of market share, they were equally susceptible to similar issues and problems. Among the six countries we studied, only in Malaysia, and to some extent in Brazil, did the MNCs' market share have some impact on the type of problems experienced with the host government. However, the overall relationship between these two variables was less striking. But this lack of a relationship does not imply that either developing or developed countries are unconcerned about issues of economic domination by the multinationals. India, Malaysia, Peru, and Brazil have, in the recent past, imposed industry-wide controls on their petroleum, mining, petrochemical, and pharmaceutical industries.

The United States, Canada, and West Germany all impose restrictions on the kinds of industries in which foreign companies may invest. The United States government, for example, does not permit foreign investment in or control of its coastal shipping and nuclear-related industries. It also has not shown much hesitation in using antitrust legislation to prevent the formation of giant monopolies. On the other hand, the European countries and Japan have either directly or indirectly supported growth or the formation of giant domestic firms to combat the influence of United States MNCs.

Table 2-2 outlines important issues causing conflicts between multinationals and developing countries.

Table 2-2 Issues that caused conflicts between MNCs and the developing countries

Conflicts	*Total*
Equity participation by locals	28
Management control in the hands of local nationals	52
Control of exchange	6
Control of imports	5
Expansion of exports	9
Transfer pricing (pricing policies)	21
Use of local inputs	2
Interference by host government in corporate affairs	5
Contributions to economic plans of host nations	4
Interference with sociocultural norms	4
Interference by the MNCs' home governments with host government's policies	2
Total	138

Source: Interview data reproduced from Anant R. Negandhi and B. R. Baliga, *Quest for Survival and Growth,* New York: Praeger Publishers, Athenaeum Verlag Koenigstein/Ts., W. Germany, 1979, p. 15.

Nature of External Issues Between MNCs and Industrialized Countries

Many of the industrialized countries, operating as "free and open markets," generally are congenial to foreign investors. Lately, however, they too have begun to question the utility of uncheckud foreign investments. Governmental decision makers and other public groups are discovering that national needs, ambitions, and objectives can be at variance with the MNCs' objectives, goals, and strategies. The range, nature, and intensity of these issues, of course, differ considerably from country to country, depending on the prevailing political climate, economic conditions (unemployment, inflation, balance of payments position), and the level of industrial and economic development. A study by David Fry, in West Germany and Belgium, indicates that the issue of worker participation (*Mitbestimmung*) was most prominent in West Germany. In contrast, the Belgian government was more concerned with the MNCs' impact on employment, balance of payments position, research and development activity, and development and use of local resources.[18]

The host government was the second most important source of problems for the multinationals. The specific problems they encountered concerned controls on foreign exchange, pricing, profits, and expansions. Approximately 50% of the multinational companies studied indicated that the government agencies of the host countries created the most obstacles by enacting restrictive legislation and erecting unnecessary bureaucratic barriers.[19]

In Canada, the establishment of the Foreign Investment Review Agency, and the pronouncement contained therein, comes very close to what the developing countries have been demanding from foreign investors.

The analysis of the foreign investment approvals by the Foreign Investment Review Agency gives an indication of the following expectations by the host country for the foreign investors:

1. Compatibility with industrial and economic policies of Canada
2. Improvement of productivity and industrial efficiency
3. Increased employment
4. Canadian participation in top executive positions and boards of directors
5. Increased exports[20]

In Australia, talk of "buying back the farm" and the massive criticism of foreign investors and multinational companies had simmered down after the fall of the Labor Party's government in 1976.[21] Nevertheless, the Australian public, as well as the politicians, remain very uneasy about the heavy dependence on foreign capital. They are painfully aware that 59% of the Australian mining industry, 45% of the insurance industry, and 50% of the banking business is controlled by foreign companies. They are also worried that 55% of the profits of Australian companies are payable overseas, thus creating a heavy burden on local and national economies.[22]

Even during the Conservative Party's regime, which was generally sympathetic to foreign investors, public uproar was created when two United States MNCs, the Ford Motor Company and the Utah Development Company, announced their dividends and remittances to the respective parent companies in the United States. Referring to such public uneasiness over the behavior of the multinationals, the leading Australian newspaper, *The Sydney Morning Herald*, wrote in its editorial page:

> The standard of the current debate on the behaviour of foreign-owned companies leaves much to be desired. . . . Behind the political point-scoring, both sides agree that the Government should set guidelines for foreign investors and that it has the right to impose appropriate levels of taxation on the profits of overseas-owned business. The need is for a much cooler and more informed discussion about what the guidelines ought to be and what levels and forms of taxation are appropriate.[23]

During the same time, the national television network, ABC, telecast a two-hour long program concerning the activities of the Utah Development Company, and asked the following searching questions:

> Without foreign investment, our economic growth and standard of living would fall sharply. But do we have the necessary controls to achieve a proper balance between the interests of foreign companies and the nation as a whole?
> Are Australians in danger of losing control over their own destiny?
> Companies like Utah may claim to be backing Australia, but ultimately, any company must put its corporate interests first.
> There are many experts who believe that unless we realize this and begin some shrewd bargaining, then companies like Utah will continue backing Australia—all the way to the bank.[24]

The program ended with the following satirical song:

> And daddy won't you take me back to Moranbah County
> Down by the green river where paradise lay
> But I'm sorry, my son, that you're too late in asking,
> You see, Utah's coal train has towed it away.[25]

In the United States, organized labor has assumed an adversary role with respect to the outflow of United States capital and technology overseas.

To protect jobs in the United States, the AFL-CIO has criticized the cost-cutting production rationalization moves of United States multinational companies.[26]

As unemployment continues to undermine the people's confidence in national economic conditions, legislators at the state and national levels, and even the Republican administration of President Reagan, have begun to exhibit protectionist sentiments. During the last few years, approximately one half of the fifty states have introduced legislation to restrict foreign investments in agricultural land. Faced with the declining sale of automobiles, all three of the big auto companies have cried out for protection against imports. At the same time, their own subcontractors and labor unions have blamed the auto companies for their extensive import of spare parts. They hold them responsible for high unemployment levels in the United States.[27]

High-level governmental officials in Washington have begun to speak out for a coordinated national industrial policy. For example, Mr. Majak, Staff Director of the Congressional Subcommittee on International Economic Policy and Trade under the Carter administration, emphasized an urgent need for such national policy:

> The 1980s, it appears, may go down in economic history as the decade in which the United States came face-to-face with lagging industrial productivity and innovation as underlying sources of the nation's international economic difficulties. Singled out by government and private experts, worried about the growing U.S. international merchandise trade deficit, illustrated by back-to-back crises in the steel and auto industries, and touted increasingly by the mass media, the hard realities and implications of international economic competition are rapidly being raised in the public consciousness. "Reindustrialization" and "market share" seem about to rival "ecology" and "energy crisis" in popular phraseology.[28]

On the other side of the Atlantic Ocean, West Germany, the model of stability for three decades, is suffering from growing economic and political upheaval. As Ralf Dahrendorf, a leading German sociologist and Director of the London School of Economics, correctly predicted, "Chancellor Schmidt's 'social peace' is in danger."[29] Unemployment has reached a double-digit figure. *The Wall Street Journal* concludes, "Recent developments seem alarming, less than seven years ago the country had practically full employment, with two job openings for every job seeker."[30] The downfall of Schmidt's government exemplifies the seriousness of the socioeconomic problems in West Germany. Everywhere else in industrialized countries, except in Japan, the situation is still worse.

Controlling the Multinationals: Who Should Do It?

All of the preceding discussion boils down to one simple issue: governmental desire to control the activities of the multinational corporations. As Behrman has stated:

> The desire for national control is at the base of almost all concern over foreign investment. Most other fears are symptomatic of this fundamental fear of a loss of sovereignty. This fear is partly psycho-political, in that no country can be wholly independent today. Most governments recognize this fact in myriad daily operations and policy positions. On many occasions, they appear to be more interested in the *evidence* than the *exercise* of sovereignty or control. Therefore, they have taken the opportunity to demonstrate or assert their control publicly, even though they have not actually resorted to it in practice.[31]

But, as Behrman continues:

> In a world of rapidly changing government policy, it is unclear to foreign investors when the letter of the law will be applied in the strictest manner. So they must operate under a calculated risk, unsure of the extent to which the national control will be fully exercised.[32]

Today, practically every country in the world that receives direct foreign investment has imposed or is in the process of levying stringent controls on its foreign firms. This includes big and small countries, industrialized and developing, capitalistic or communistic, ideologically left or right, as well as the home countries of large-scale multinational companies. In other words, few countries any longer ask the simplistic question: Do we want foreign investment? The issue is how to get foreign investment on terms that allow the host countries to achieve their national goals. On the one hand, the host countries are attempting to maximize whatever benefits they derive from foreign investment in their countries. On the other hand, they are becoming increasingly concerned about the ownership and control of the key sectors of their economy by foreign enterprises, the impact of foreign investment on their political sovereignty, and the possibility of adverse effects on the sociocultural values of their societies.

Simultaneously, the home countries of the multinationals have either imposed controls on MNC operations or are currently engaged in a debate on the need for imposing controls, so as to curb the outflow of private investment, and to reduce their adverse impact on domestic employment, the balance of payments position, and the foreign policy of the country.[33]

Motivation to Control

The developing and developed countries may differ in terms of the types of controls they impose, but the overall aim appears to be the same. Besides economic advantages, other gains sought from control of foreign investment are the derivation of psychological benefits and psychological income. As Safarian and Bell have indicated, such controls provide "a sense of well-being, resulting from an increase in national independence and pride; from the perception that the control over decisions that affect the economic environment rest closer to home than somewhere else."[34]

The need for national identity and cultural distinctiveness is felt much stronger by many developing countries, partly because of their previous experiences with colonization, and partly because of the imbalance in economic development and bargaining power between them and the developed world. Political instability in many developing countries further causes restrictive policies on foreign investments. Vernon has argued that "whatever the trend of ideology may be in the less developed world, uncertainty will be the lot of the foreign investor. Whenever one side or another in local political struggles seeks to rally local support, a call for firmness towards the foreign investor is sure to be a useful tactic."[35]

What to Control?

Among the measures taken to regulate foreign private investment are restrictions on equity holding, acquisition or takeovers, intercompany transactions, the selection of directors, the number of expatriate managers permitted, regulations governing the training of personnel, and the location of the plant. The extent of the controls imposed in each of these areas varies among the countries, depending on the state of their economic and social development, as well as on the existing influence of foreign investment in that country. Countries with minimal foreign investment are likely to have only a few controls imposed. At the other extreme, countries with heavy foreign investment might also take a liberal attitude toward foreign investors. Perhaps the most stringent controls on foreign investment are thus levied in countries with intermediate levels of foreign investment and in nations with important natural resources.

Current trends also seem to point out that countries with potentially large markets—e.g., India, Mexico, and Indonesia—are more likely to impose tighter controls than countries with smaller markets. Our study of six developing countries revealed that three countries, India, Malaysia, and Peru, have imposed very stiff controls on foreign investments, particularly concerning the foreign equity participation. By and large, they do not allow 100% foreign equity. Singapore, Thailand, and Brazil, however, still allow 100% foreign equity holding, but in recent years demands for controls on foreign ownership have also been made in those countries. Second, in almost all of the six countries, some sort of sectoral control on the types of industries foreign investors are allowed to enter has been imposed. For example, all of these countries do not permit foreign investment in defense-related industries.

All of the six countries, including the so-called "open" countries such as Brazil and Singapore, now require a specific proportion of local nationals in management positions and they allow only a limited number of expatriate managers. Although explicit policies for training local nationals have not yet been formulated, many governments in developing countries implicitly require foreign investors to train local employees. Brazil, for example, now imposes an "educational tax" on foreign companies that employ locally trained engineers and scientists. The Brazilian government contends that the purpose of this tax is to help finance its educational infrastructure. It is very likely that the Brazilian action may be a prototype for other developing countries.

There was an increasing tendency toward stricter controls on the use of local capital, royalty rates, and the period of remittance. Royalty rates generally have a ceiling of about 7% of net sales, and are limited to the first three to five years of operations. The amount of remittances permitted varies, but is generally fixed to not more than 12% of the net profit. Repatriation of capital is allowed, but controls are imposed, and only gradual repatriation of capital is permitted.[36]

Who Should Control the MNCs' Activities?

In the current debate on controlling the multinationals, it seems that everyone has a pat solution. Suggested solutions vary from no controls at all to the strictest types of controls imposed by an international body, such as the United Nations. Behrman has adopted a position that differing approaches to controlling the multinationals stem from differing assumptions about the multinationals' and host governments' options. He has argued that at least five patterns of world economic order can be distinguished, which in turn give rise to different types of control mechanisms. These patterns include:

1. A pattern of strong national autonomy and concern for national self-sufficiency
2. A move toward regional blocs
3. The perpetuation of a neoclassical system, leaning toward market efficiency as the criterion for determining international economic activity
4. The development of a technoindustrial structure based on the criterion of company efficiency over the world

5. A new pattern of international industrial structure based on distribution of sectoral activities over the world under multiple criteria, including efficiency[37]

These five suggested patterns can broadly be grouped into the following categories:

1. Belief and trust exist in the concept of a free market and market efficiency.
2. Belief exists that the multinational corporations are supranational agencies and are consequently beyond the reach of any nation-state. Accordingly, they should be controlled by international bodies, such as the United Nations.
3. The multinational corporations are sovereign states themselves.
4. Belief exists that multinational corporations are not different from any other business enterprise and must, therefore, conform to and obey the regulations of the countries in which they operate. Accordingly, the nation-states in which the MNCs operate are the most suitable institutions for imposing controls on the activities of the multinationals.

Belief in Free Market and Market Efficiency

The belief in a free market and market efficiency implies the view that the world's resources are best used through unregulated market mechanisms. To a large extent, the industrially developed countries operate within the framework of a free market economy, and even in many of the developing countries some role is granted to private enterprise. The United States can be characterized as the home of the private enterprise system, symbolizing the viability and vitality of the capitalist doctrine. But even there, the Congress and government officials have started to doubt the capability of the private enterprise system to solve the complex socioeconomic problems facing the United States. Thus even staunch believers in the free market doctrine have come to accept that some form of control on MNCs is inevitable. However, they desire that such controls be directed toward correcting deficiencies of the free market system that have developed as a result of the monolithic size of major corporations. Dissolution of the largest MNCs into smaller, competitive units has thus been recommended.[38] Those advocating controls under the free market system are really arguing for control of the home and host countries, rather than of the multinationals. Their basic aim is to remove the distortions in the operation of the free market caused by undue government interference.

Control of MNCs by International Bodies

The belief that the multinational corporation is a supranational power, a sovereign state by itself, and answerable to no one, has led to some international attempts to impose control. Such attempts are not altogether new, however. For example, beginning as early as 1948 (and perhaps even earlier), there have been a number of conferences on controlling international business. The Havana Charter[39] and the Bogota Agreement,[40] formulated in 1948, advocated restraints on foreign private investment by the host governments. But these earlier attempts were directed more at protecting foreign private investment than at protecting the host countries. Similarly, in 1949, the International Chamber of Commerce formulated its own code of conduct, as did the U.S. Council in 1952.[41] Once again, these codes of conduct sought to guide the multinationals only in a very general sense, and simultaneously tried to restrain the host governments from imposing stringent controls on foreign investors.

In recent years, however, the United Nations' involvement in the economic development process of the developing countries has generated an extensive dialogue about controlling the activities of the multinational corporations. In 1972, the United Nations Conference on Trade and Development (UNCTAD) adopted a resolution calling for the "permanent sovereignty" of nation-states over their national resources. This solution reaffirmed the aspirations of many developing countries by advocating the right of nation-states to nationalize any foreign property and to establish controls over their national resources.[42]

In the same year, the International Labor Organization recommended study of the multinational corporations to formulate a social policy to guide their activities. The overall reaction of the business community toward such calls for controls by international agencies, such as the United Nations, has been negative.

Beyond these negative attitudes of the business community toward international control, there are some inherent problems in imposing controls through international agencies. First, at present there is a distinct lack of a powerful international agency that could exercise this control. Even an organization such as the United Nations probably could not develop and enforce control mechanisms that would satisfy the needs of every nation-state.

The goals and objectives of the various nation-states are not necessarily the same. Different stages of economic development require different types of industrial and economic policies to meet the particular needs of a specific country at a particular point in time. For example, a developing country such as India, with a sophisticated petrochemical and nuclear industry, is strikingly different from a country such as Saudi Arabia, which, although wealthy because of her oil resources, possesses a weak industrial base at present. The point being stressed here is that the fundamental needs and objectives of nations differ, not only at a certain point in time, but over time as well. Thus talk of developing and enforcing a uniform control system for MNCs is mostly an academic exercise.

From time to time many countries have supported the idea of control by international agencies. However, such support has primarily been extended in the belief that it would provide greater bargaining power vis-à-vis the multinationals through a united front.

However, what is involved is not a simple problem; it is a complex problem of imbalance in levels of economic development and standards of living around the world. Industrially less developed countries insist they have a right to decide on the sectors of economic priority, as well as on the location of the plants in their quest for self-sufficiency and to ward off outside interference.

Multinational Corporations as Sovereign States

There are some who believe and advocate that the MNCs themselves are a new autonomous force in the world. They contend that the magnitude of resources commanded by the multinationals endows them with substantial political power. In other words, they envisage a world of multinationals replacing the world of nation-states. For example, the late Mr. George W. Ball, former Under Secretary in the U.S. State Department, had argued "the multinational corporation not only promises the most efficient use of world resources, but as an institution, it poses the greatest challenge to the power of nation-states since the temporal position of the Roman Church began its decline in the Fifteenth Century."[43]

Ball believed that if the nation-states were to give up their sovereignty over economic and political decisions, and let the multinationals make decisions for them, this would indeed be the "harbinger of a true world economy." To promote the development of this technoindustrial world, various organizations such as the International Chamber of Commerce, the United Chamber of Commerce, and the Federation of Industries have already begun to formulate codes of conduct that, in effect, limit the role of the nation-states in intervening in the activities of multinational corporations.

However, the current debate over the multinationals, as well as the various disclosures of corruption, misdeeds, and misuse of their powers around the world (e.g., ITT in Chile, bribes by Lockheed Aircraft in Japan and Holland and other European countries, political contributions by Gulf and other oil companies), hardly inspire confidence among nation-states in the ability and willingness of the multinationals to regulate themselves.

To visualize the MNCs as a sovereign state is inconsistent both in theory and by evidence in the world in which we live. Moreover, as Safarian and Bell have pointed out:

such arguments raise expectations that are bound to be disappointing and
that form the basic part of criticisms of multinational enterprise activity.
Any institution that attempts to carry the burden of both international
economic development and political order on its shoulder, will have to tread
softly in this nationalistic age, or better still, accept only the realistic part
of that burden.[44]

A Case for Control by Nation-States

It has been said that "man does not live on bread alone." This is equally true
of nations. Nation-states, in this modern world, have many objectives. The
concept of "nation-state" involves more than economic regulation and providing for the well-being of each citizen. The responsibility of each nation-
state is not only to create social and economic growth, but also to preserve
its sociocultural heritage and political independence. The allied objective is
to distribute the benefits of socioeconomic growth equitably. To achieve these
objectives, some interference with the workings of the free market is not only
inevitable, but necessary. Even those who believe in the private enterprise
system have admitted that although multinational corporations can create
wealth, they have no power or responsibility to distribute wealth equitably.
For example, Mr. Ross R. Millhiser, President of Phillip Morris, Inc., has
argued:

> There has been a muddling of the distinction between the creation of wealth
> and the allocation of the redistribution of wealth. Multinational corporations
> are an instrument, not an economic system. They create wealth for the world.
> Nation-states, with their political and economic systems, determine the
> distribution of wealth within their border.[45]

In short, the home and host countries of the multinationals will continue
to control the inflow and outflow of foreign investment to maximize their national benefits.

Present trends, especially in developing countries, point to an era of increasing nation-state control. It appears that, once the current spate of nationalism in "resource-based" industries has worked itself out, these controls
will be more in the form of constraining and channeling the activities of the
MNCs into certain directions, rather than in more extreme forms of outright
nationalization and expropriation. Rather than the emergence of a universal set of regulatory mechanisms, both the MNCs and the nation-states will
come to recognize and react to each other's position of leverage. Such adaptation might prove crucial to the survival of these institutions. Table 2-3 provides a summary of the changing relationships between multinational corporations and governments.

Table 2-3 Summary of MNC and nation-state relationships

Period	Environmental realities	Interaction modes	Concern	Anticipated outcome Nation	MNCs
1950s–early 1960s	U.S. in dominant bargaining position	MNC-host country's relationships	Sociocultural adaptation	Transmissions of advanced knowledge	Higher profitability
Mid–1960s to 1970	Increasing competition from Europeans and Japanese	MNC-host country's relationships Economic/competitive adaptation	Sociocultural adaptation Economic adaptation	Increasing international trade and investments	More stress on research and development More stress on economies of scale
1973 to 1985	Changing balance of economic and political powers between developed and developing countries	MNC-host country's relationships MNC-home country's relationships Home and host countries' relationships	Economic-political adaptation	Restructuring of industries	Survival criteria important

What Can the Multinationals and Governments Do to Cope with the Changing International Environments?

The Multinational Companies

By and large the multinationals have been slow in recognizing the rapidly changing environments in developing countries. In this regard, relatively speaking, the United States MNCs seem to have the greatest difficulty. Overall, the MNCs are making two basic errors that are likely to prove costly in the long run—

> overemphasizing their bargaining power
> underemphasizing the bargaining power of developing countries

Just as a corporation's objectives change over a period of time, so do the objectives of a nation. Accompanying these changes in objectives are changes in policies, intended to attain these different objectives. Whereas a corporation asserts its right to acquire and dispose of business, to hire and fire workers, to change plant locations and product mixes, depending on its objectives at a particular point in time, it is surprising to find how quickly multinationals cry "foul" when changes in government policies and objectives take place. They invariably perceive such changes as threats to their basic survival. When confronted, they react by threatening to withdraw and to invest in other countries that offer them a "fair deal." As recently as a decade or so ago, the MNC could and did get away with such responses. This, however, has changed because of the increasing bargaining power of the host (developing) nation.

Probably the main factors contributing to the increase of power of the host nations have been:

1. The narrowing of the information gap between MNCs and host countries, leading to increased identification of alternatives
2. Increased availability of alternatives

In the past, host nations and their local private investors were generally not well informed about alternative sources of capital, technology, or knowledge. As a result, they depended largely on the United States multinationals and their subsidiaries. This, however, has changed with the rapid development of Russia, the Western European nations, and Japan following reconstruction after World War II, and the formation of international monetary institutions, such as the IBRD and the IMF. Also, the easing of East-West tensions makes it possible for nations to seek assistance even from nations with conflicting political ideologies. Consequently many developing nations are in much better positions to explore several alternative sources of requisite supplies, technologies, products, and capital needed for their socioeconomic development. This, in turn, has increased the nation-states's bargaining powers vis-à-vis the MNCs'.

This stronger bargaining position of most nation-states has greatly reduced the leverage of the MNCs. Host nations have not hesitated to use their superior bargaining position to extract concessions from the MNCs in such areas as equity holding, management control, localization of top-level management, mandatory export targets, and many related concessions.

Strategic Alternatives Open to MNCs

At the micro level in designing organizations, global rationalization and efficiency considerations must give way to long-term survival and growth criteria. This may necessitate more than the use of participative management, quality control circles, and other techniques propounded by the so-called Japanologists.[46] The MNCs will have to create responsive organizational strategies and policies with increased decentralization for their subsidiaries' managers.

At the macro level, the time has come to recognize fully the changing international environment. The multinationals's management strategies and practices designed for a more or less placid or stable environment are becoming inadequate and obsolete for the present turbulent environment. To cope with the changes, the multinationals have to offer imaginative investment patterns such as joint ventures, partnership with other foreign multinational and national firms to operate in a third country, and partnership with government-owned public enterprises. Also, they must learn to work harmoniously with local, state, and federal governments. In this respect, it may not be too far-fetched to recommend the establishment of United States, Inc. and Germany, Inc. as counterparts to Japan, Inc., to pave the way for systematic national industrial policies.[47] Especially in the United States, it will not only require a long-run vision on the part of the businessmen, governmental officials, union leaders, and other community groups, but also demand political courage and a shift in values and orientations.

Governmental Strategies

The preceding discussion may have conveyed the impression that everything is rosy for the host governments. But there are still areas, such as advanced communication systems, where a few multinationals dominate. Many host governments have had relatively little success in securing favorable concessions from such MNCs. For example, members of the Andean Pact, as well as the Arab countries, have not had uniform success in attracting investors under the provisions of their codes, despite offering relatively captive markets to the potential investor. All this seems to imply that investors in general, and MNCs in particular, can only be pushed to some extent. Beyond this, perceived costs are likely to outweigh benefits, and the MNCs might just decide to stay away from potential problems. Given the magnitude of the gap between the expectations of the host governments and the MNCs, it would appear that both host governments and multinationals could benefit if the host government were to make its expectations known at the time of entry of the multinational. In fact, host governments could alleviate potential conflicts by incorporating their general expectations in the economic and social sectors into their foreign investment policies, and conveying these policies clearly at the time of negotiations with the MNCs. Such clarification would provide a concrete basis for discussion and negotiation in the event differences arise. It would also be useful to list expectations in a chronological sequence, so that unrealistic demands could not be made overnight.

Host governments should make it clear that the MNC's terms of entry constitute a policy decision, and not a promise, and that requirements could change as a result of changes in objectives. At the same time, host governments should provide sufficient assurances that policies would not be changed in an ad hoc manner, and that sufficient safeguards will be present to protect the multinationals in the event such drastic policy changes occurred.

With most attention being paid to the raging debate between the host governments and the multinationals, the implications of this debate for the home countries appear to have taken a backseat position. Nevertheless, the implications are real and crucial for the home countries, too. With the host countries now imposing strict requirements pertaining to capital inflow, outflow, exports, prices paid for technical knowledge, and patents, it is very likely that some home countries are not receiving benefits proportional to their investment. If the home governments do not rapidly draw up policies pertaining to the overseas investments of their larger corporations, it is conceivable that they could be at the wrong end of a zero-sum game. The home countries would be wise to draw up regulations pertaining to the amount that can be invested in a particular year or the amount that has to be repatriated. Rather than opposing such regulations, the MNCs might react favorably because these regulations would provide them with some leverage in their negotiations with the host governments.

Ethics and Social Responsibilities of International Corporations

The preceding discussion on the interactions between international corporations and nation-states mainly dealt with economic and power leverage issues between these two parties.

International corporations, by their very nature, are guests in foreign countries. As guests, they are expected to abide by the norms and values of their host countries. The majority of the international companies meet such requirements, and they have tried hard to become "good corporate citizens" of the countries in which they are operating. However, at times, the demands of the various host and home countries conflict. Consequently they often encounter "no-win situations." In other instances, the "wrong doings" of a few corporations shed doubts on the proper conduct of international corporations as a whole. Thus the issue of the ethics and social responsibilities of international corporations, although serious, has no easy solution.

This section briefly outlines some of the critical and controversial issues on this aspect, and provides some normative and analytical guidelines for seeking solutions to a difficult problem. The issues to be discussed are:

- Illegal payments, bribes, and corrupt practices of international corporations
- Extraterritorial government actions and the rights of multinational corporations
- Social, ethical, and environmental conflicts between international corporations and host and home countries

United States Corrupt Practices Act and Extraterritorial Control

Corrupt practices and illegal payments have been motivated to influence host government decision making to overcome competitive disadvantages and to meet the demands of the host government's officials.[48] Some of the examples of such payments include:

1. Lockheed's $25 million bribes to various governmental officials to win orders for new airplanes
2. Exxon's $28 million for political contributions to Italy
3. United Brand's $1,250,000 payments to a country in Central America
4. R. J. Reynold's $25 million payments to promote its business and political interests

American companies are not alone in being accused of illegal and corrupt practices. European, as well as Japanese, multinational companies also were involved in illegal payments. For example, Imperical Chemical Industries of the United Kingdom and the Marubeni Trading Company of Japan have been found guilty. The U.S. Foreign Corrupt Practices Act prohibits illegal payments by United States corporations to any governmental officials and/or any other persons for soliciting favors. Moreover, these illegal activities are not necessarily immoral. Some authors have argued that illegal payments and bribes should be investigated broadly and in the context of a political relationship between society and productive institutions.

Kobrin,[49] for example, has argued that large-scale bribery is neither an aberration nor a special problem of morality or business ethics. It is rather a manifestation of the oligopolistic market situation in which the powers of a few corporations and governmental officials are concentrated. Bribes or illegal payments thus may be one of the means to secure the desired favorable outcome. It is also argued that, although United States law treats such payments as illegal, it has no right to judge and evaluate the behavior and practices of other countries. Particularly, United States subsidiaries should not be under the jurisdiction of United States laws. Moreover, the United States has applied her laws overseas to control the behavior of United States companies and their subsidiaries to satisfy national policy objectives. A number of cases can be cited where United States laws were applied to the foreign operations and foreign business transactions of United States companies.[50] A few selected examples include:

1. International Machine Union's suit against Organization of Petroleum Exporting Countries (OPEC) under United States antitrust laws in a United States court.
2. The Reagan administration's trade embargo on a number of United States companies: Dressler Industries, Inc.; Smith International (North Sea), Ltd.; Baktu Oil Tools (U.K.), Ltd.; AAF, Ltd. (subsidiary of Allis Chalmers Corp., to supply United States licensed equipment for the Soviet natural gas pipeline project). A similar ban was applied to a wholly-owned British Company, John Brown.
3. A United States court allowing foreign governments and private parties to sue United States companies under United States antitrust laws (in 1974, the Indian government, for example, was allowed to sue private companies in the United States. More recently, the Bhopal tragedy has resulted in a number of cases in the United States against Union Carbide.)

Such extraterritorial applications of United States laws have been resisted equally by United States businesses and by foreign governments. For example, in his survey of 142 United States companies, Luter[51] reported that more than 50% of the respondents claimed to have lost overseas business opportunities because of United States legislations. Commenting on the Corrupt Practices Act, Luter states:

> The Corrupt Practice Act is the United States' most recent move toward moral imperialism. Of all the actions of our government, this is the one most likely to cause serious injury to our world-trade relationships. The so-called "sen-

sitive payments" raise complicated questions, both as to the definition and means of corruption. They should be judged by the laws of and regulations of the host countries. . . .[52]

Many governments in industrialized, as well as developing, countries seem to agree on this view. Britain, Holland, West Germany, Australia, Canada, and France have taken specific legislative or administrative actions to prevent their national companies from complying with United States legal requirements.[53]

In the final analysis, the individual executive who acts for the company has to decide. Although the financial rewards may be rich in the short run, the penalties for defying United States laws are also severe. A number of top-level executives and governmental officials were forced to resign from their positions and some even committed suicide for their actions.

Social Responsibilities and Social Conflicts

Social responsibilities involve not only the corporate philosophy, value, and "culture," but also the managers's beliefs, values, and ethical standards. Those who argue that the "business of business is business" ignore that business does not exist in a vacuum. It is part and parcel of society, and business decision makers are also social creatures.

To whom is business responsible? Customers, employees, stockholders, community, government, suppliers, distributors, or the public at large? The answer is: to all. Moreover, to implement and practice such collective, multifold responsibilities is easier said than done.

Social responsibilities of managers and their intrinsic values receive public attention whenever a corporate scandal or corporate "wrongdoing" hits the news headlines. As Schmidt has aptly put it:

> News of a faulty product, pollution of environment [the Bhopal case], bribery, or some other gross misuse of corporate power causes people to ask "what kind of people are running our companies, anyway?" On those occasions we become aware of the influences personal values have on managers, and how those are expressed in company policies and actions.[54]

Business ethics and values seem to be changing. For example, Russ,[55] in his study of 1,043 major corporations, found that a large number of companies were involved in blatant illegalities and wrongdoings. Similarly, Brenner and Mollander[56] found business executives more cynical about the ethical conduct of their peers than they were fifteen years ago.

In contrast to domestic companies, international companies are operating in unknown and less well-defined situations in which the rules of the game are far more diffuse, contradictory, and at times fast-changing. Under these circumstances, the consequences of social conflicts can be far more severe. Consider, for example, the seven-year long boycott of Nestle's infant formula products in less developed countries. The controversy revolved around the following issues:[57]

1. Physicians working in tropical environments believed that bottle-feeding of infants posed a risk of disease to the infant because of the lack of availability of refrigeration and pure water.
2. Poverty in developing countries may encourage the overdilution of the powdered formula, thereby reducing the level of the child's nutrition.
3. People are too poor to afford infant formula products.
4. Advertising and promotion techniques used by Nestle may distort the real uses of such products.

The infant formula products controversy involved not only professionals, government officials, and church leaders, but also the World Health Organization (WHO) and the United Nations.

The boycott ended after seven years with the development, adoption, and implementation of WHO's international code of marketing for breastmilk substitutes. As Post writes:

> The Nestle boycott has had a major impact on the interpretation of corporate accountability and the reconciliation of human rights and commercial interests.[58] . . . The end of the Nestle boycott brings to a close an important chapter in modern business history. The boycott helped create an awareness about the side effects of normal marketing and promotional practices. . . .It is clear that hospital practices have been altered, promotional practices of industry changed, and public awareness of the benefits of breastfeeding has increased.[59]

The recent tragedy in Bhopal, India (Union Carbide's plant leakage of isocyanate that killed an estimated 2,500 persons) may become another epoch-making chapter in the history of business and society relations.[60]

Gladwin and Walter[61] have examined less serious conflicts that multinationals have encountered around the world. Their analyses of 650 social conflicts indicate that the majority of these conflicts concern human rights, questionable payments, labor relations, and environmental pollution. Contrary to common perception, most of these social conflicts occurred in industrialized countries (the United States and Europe) and not in developing countries. Table 2-4 lists the issues involved in these conflicts. Gladwin and Walter have provided an analytical model to resolve such conflicts. It is outlined next.

Table 2-4 Location of multinational corporate conflict: 1969–1978 (650 conflicts involving Dow, Gulf, ITT, Roche, and RTZ)

Conflicting issues	Region					
	North America	Europe	Latin America	Asia-Oceania	Africa	Middle East
Terrorism	28	40	24	4	0	4
Human rights	81	19	0	0	0	0
Politics	40	8	28	8	8	8
Questionable payments	76	3	13	8	0	0
Marketing	61	33	2	2	2	0
Labor relations	79	19	0	2	0	0
Environment	70	23	1	5	1	0
Technology	41	36	9	14	0	0
Economics/finance	78	6	7	4	1	4

Source: Thomas N. Gladwin and Ingo Walter, *Multinationals Under Fire: Lessons in the Management of Conflict*, New York: John Wiley and Sons, 1979, p. 29. Copyright John Wiley and Sons, 1979.

Analytical Model to Resolve Social Conflicts

The model provides the following five major strategies:

1. Competitive strategy: when an MNC's stakes and power are relatively high, interest interdependence and relations are relatively negative (domination as objective).
2. Avoidance strategy: when the firm's stakes and power are relatively low, interest interdependence and relations are relatively hostile (negligence as objective).
3. Collaborative strategy: when the MNC's stakes and power are relatively high, interest interdependence and relations with the opposition are relatively positive (integration as objective).
4. Accommodative strategy: when the MNC's stakes and power are relatively low, interest interdependence and relations are relatively positive (appeasement as objective).
5. Compromise strategy: when the firm's stakes are moderate and power advantage or disadvantage is slight, interest interdependence and relations are a mixture of positive and negative elements (sharing as objective).

The model is outlined in Figure 2-1.

The authors have argued that if an MNC can separate the large issues (or many interest groups) into smaller or workable ones (groups), the proba-

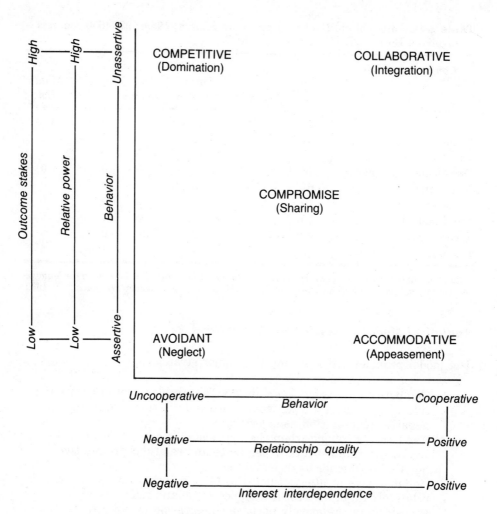

Figure 2-1 Determinants of appropriate-conflict behavior (*Source:* Thomas N. Gladwin and Ingo Walter, "How multinationals can manage social conflict," in Walter H. Goldberg and Anant R. Negandhi, eds., *Governments and Multinationals: The Policy of Control Versus Autonomy,* Cambridge: Oelgeschlager, Gunn & Hain, Publishers, Inc., 1983, p. 90.)

bility of reaching a satisfactory solution would increase. Because the nature of the conflicts is dynamic, the management needs to evaluate carefully the environments over time.

Gladwin and Walter also have recommended the collaboration mode, supplemented by the compromise strategy if possible. However, at the same time, other options also have to be kept in mind as alternatives. The idea is to choose the best combination of alternatives and the path over time, given organizational and environmental constraints.

Summary

This chapter discussed the important issues concerning multinational corporations and governments. Two issues were discussed at some length: (1) divergence in objectives and goals between MNCs and host countries, and (2) controlling the multinational corporations' activities by the host and home countries. This chapter also analyzed the nature and intensity of conflicts and tensions between MNCs and governments. The results of the various studies seem to indicate that local equity and control, using local inputs, earning foreign exchange through exports, and employing surplus labor will continue to be the major issues facing the MNCs in the 1980s and 1990s.

The second part of this chapter discussed the issues of illegal payments, corrupt practices, and the social responsibilities of international corporations. Although the payments to secure favorable outcomes have been declared illegal in the United States, its jurisdiction in foreign countries has been equally criticized by United States businesspeople and foreign government officials.

Social responsibilities involve both corporate policies and "culture," as well as the decision makers' ethical and moral standards. These issues have no easy answers. The analytical model of Gladwin and Walter was provided as a guideline to resolve social conflicts.

Cases

Two cases, given at the end of this chapter, highlight these issues.

The Chrysler UK case suggests how the initiatives taken by the multinational in the negotiation process with the host government can be strategically employed in solving problems of the subsidiary.

The Imperial Tobacco Company case illuminates issues of the changing nature of the local competitive environment and of how a foreign subsidiary that faces a deteriorating bargaining position adapts itself to new environmental demands.

Case 2-1 ══════════════════════════

The Multinational That Wanted to be Nationalised

*Malcolm Crawford and Roger Eglin**

To all outward appearances, the arrangement between the Chrysler Corporation and the UK government which enabled the former to continue manufacturing in Britain, instead of shutting down and liquidating Chrysler UK as John Riccardo, chairman of the parent corporation, threatened to do, was a remarkable achievement on Riccardo's part. The *Detroit News* called it "a triumph of negotiation", which it said "established Riccardo's leadership". The *New York Times* commented that the deal protected Chrysler Corporation from future losses. Chrysler management, in announcing the agreement on December 19, declared that "the agreement is a good one, not just for Chrysler and the people of the United Kingdom, but especially for the employees, dealers, suppliers, and customers of Chrysler UK".

In the end, instead of a liquidation which would have more or less forfeited total assets of £170 mn at book value, plus redundancy payments and other liquidation costs, Chrysler Corporation retains full ownership of the UK subsidiary, subject only to 50-50 sharing of any profits that may be earned in years up to and including 1979. To assist Chrysler UK to return to profitability, it will receive £90 mn in government (or government guaranteed) loans and up to £72.5 mn in grants in aid of losses.

Chrysler's Financial Weakness Gave It Bargaining Strength

It is commonly written that multinational companies threaten the sovereignty of national governments through their financial power, their ability to shift

*Industrial editor of the Sunday Times. © Copyright by Economist Intelligence Unit.

production among countries, and their ability to influence decision makers in the host country. What strikes one immediately in the case of Chrysler's crisis in Britain is that an American multinational company which, while middling large, was financially weak – indeed, in severe straits – succeeded in achieving what it did mainly because of its financial weakness. Had it been in a stronger financial condition, it would not have been able to mount a convincing case for UK government support. It was Chrysler's inability to earn profits either in Britain or in the US that placed the government in the awkward position in which it found itself, and which led it with great reluctance to rescue the firm's UK subsidiary.

Domestic British companies in shaky financial circumstances have also been rescued from disaster. One would not have expected that being part of a foreign owned multinational group enhances a firm's chance of this sort of treatment. Chrysler's multinational character did however affect both the company's objectives in the affair, and the final outcome.

Chrysler UK Has Made More Losses than Profits

Since Chrysler took over the deeply troubled Rootes Motors in 1964, consolidating its ownership in 1967, its financial performance has been erratic, culminating in a sharp deterioration during the recent industry wide crisis. In the ten years to mid 1975, Chrysler UK incurred losses aggregating to £58 mn, while in good years profits totalled only £10 mn (Table 2-5). Even in 1973, the British car market's last boom year, Chrysler could manage a pre tax profit of no more than £3.7 mn (Table 2-6). The report on the motor car industry in the UK published in December by the Central Policy Review Staff (CPRS) (the so called Think Tank) shows that on the measures of return on shareholders' funds, on capital invested and on trading assets, the performance of Chrysler UK was significantly worse than that of any of its major European or Japanese competitors, and much worse than that of Simca, Chrysler's affiliate in France. In terms of market share, between 1971 and December 1975, Chrysler UK's share halved from just over 10 per cent to 5.1 per cent.

Chrysler's output in the UK has never risen to a level sufficiently high to keep the two major car assembly plants, Ryton and Linwood fully employed. Between them these two plants produced 220,079 cars in 1964. It was not until 1970 that production again approached this 1964 total. In an industry growing on a Europe wide basis by as much as 10 per cent or more a year until the recent crisis, Chrysler UK car output was still only 265,000 in 1973 and fell to 227,000 in 1975.

Exports to Iran of cars in CKD form (completely knocked down) have been very important to the company, since 1974. CKD sales in 1974 were some 90,000 units. In 1975, Chrysler exported 102,000 units CKD to Iran alone – underlining Chrysler UK's dependence on this business, which accounted for 10.8 per cent of the total value of British car exports. Chrysler had planned to increase sales to Iran to 220,000 units by 1977. The CPRS has questioned the long term future of this business, however, suggesting that there will be a big increase in local manufactured content and that the Iranian company, INIM, may procure supplies from elsewhere in Europe.

Simca's financial position has been rather better. In recent years, the company has been able to finance its own operations, but both companies have been suffering from an ageing model range and a failure to establish models on an integrated basis, as Ford of Europe has done. The last attempt to achieve this was with the Chrysler 180. Chrysler originally planned to make this in France and Britain. For a variety of reasons, including the poor productivity record in Britain, the idea of UK manufacture was dropped. Again, original plans laid down that the Simca Alpine would be made in the UK and France, and these were shelved, to be resuscitated in the rescue operation, in the form of manufacture in France and assembly in Britain for the UK market.

... And the US Parent Has Been in Financial Trouble

Nor in recent years has the US parent been in a position to underwrite unlimited losses incurred overseas. Last year the US corporation lost $259 mn, following a profit of $52 mn in 1974. Its survival has been openly debated, especially as this is the third financial crisis the US company has undergone since the start of the 1960s—thus promoting speculation that Chrysler is the "marginal" company, capable of making profits only during market upswings. At the end of the third quarter of 1975, Chrysler Corporation's short term debt amounted to $446 mn—better than the $619 mn at the end of 1974, but still worse than the $326 mn debt at the mid point of 1974. The recent labour troubles at Barreiros in Spain and the uncertain future for this plant have aggravated the parent company's present difficulties. Fears about the political stability of Spain appear to have been a significant factor in the Ford decision to produce the Fiesta at other European plants as well as at Valencia, and these considerations may have weighed substantially with Chryslers too in the outcome of its confrontation with the British government.

Chrysler Took the Initiative in
Bringing the Issue to a Head

The first signs of UK government interest in Chrysler's immediate problems came in mid summer 1974. At that time, the company's name was added to the Whitehall list which is intended to give early warning of potential "lame duck" situations. But there is no evidence of any high level contact between the company and the UK government in the period immediately after this. Nor is there any sign that efforts were made to mount contingency plans, either to aid Chrysler in the event of a shut down or to mount an emergency programme of job creation in the Linwood area.

After receiving this amber light signal from Chrysler in the summer 1974, government attention was distracted by the more immediate needs of British

Table 2-5 Chrysler UK financial performance

	Pre tax profit or loss *(£ mn)*	*Pre tax return on net worth* *(%)*
1964[a]	1.6	3.9
1965	−2.5	−4.7
1966	−3.4	−5.8
1967	−10.8	−18.4
1968	3.7	6.2
1969	0.7	1.1
1970	−10.7	−15.3
1971	0.4	0.6
1972	1.6	2.5
1973	3.7	6.3
1974	−17.7	−34.2
1975[b]	−15.9	

[a]Strictly speaking, 1963–64. Only 1974 figures correspond with the calendar year.
[b]Six months.

Leyland. But in January 1975, concern about Chrysler was mounting. Wedgwood Benn, then secretary for industry, wrote to Riccardo asking about his intentions. The next day, Wilson himself dined with Riccardo in London and then flew to Washington where he discussed the position of Chrysler with a surprised President Ford. At this point, Wilson must have felt reasonably optimistic, because he gave a reassuring statement in the Commons on the Friday. But the question of UK government money had already, apparently, been mooted. During the May 1975 strike, Wilson exploded in the Commons: "I am not prepared and the government is not prepared for one moment to contemplate the use of one penny of taxpayers' money, or money borrowed by the government, to gratify that kind of politico industrial ambition."

Again there was a lull until government's expression of surprise at Riccardo's Detroit press conference at the end of October, 1975. On November 3, Riccardo and five other Chrysler directors dined with Wilson, Eric Varley and Edmund Dell at Chequers, a meeting switched from Downing Street because of fears of trade union demonstrations. At this meeting, Chrysler's line was apparently bleak: the company would have to pull out of Britain. It offered the government its UK operations. Riccardo also offered an alternative, whereby Chrysler would retain its UK affiliate, if provided with a substantial sum from the government. Press reports of the figure here ranged from £100 mn, initially, to £450 mn during the subsequent fortnight. Varley asked the Industrial Development Advisory Board (IDAB) to comment. During the next few days, a Cabinet sub committee of ministers and officials was formed by the prime minister to explore the various options.

Table 2-6 Chrysler UK and subsidiaries consolidated statement of net earnings

	13 Months ended Dec. 31, 1973 (£'000)	12 Months ended Dec. 31, 1974 (£'000)
Sales	322,192	313,275
Other income and (deductions), net	223	(1,229)
	322,415	312,046
Cost of products sold, other than items below	294,699	302,730
Selling and administrative expenses	15,191	16,063
Depreciation of property, plant and equipment	5,187	4,176
Amortisation of special tools	1,960	1,719
Exceptional item	(1,103)	–
	315,934	324,688
Operating Loss (1973 profit) before interest and taxation	6,481	(12,642)
Interest paid, less interest received	(2,998)	(6,168)
Non-operating profit	241	1,076
Loss (1973 profit) including minority interest before taxation	3,724	(17,734)
Taxation	(26)	(60)
Minority interest in net earnings of a subsidiary	–	60
Net Loss 1973 profit	3,750	(17,734)

Initially, the Issue Was Withdrawal and How to Cope with It

The discussion, however, still centred mainly on how to cushion the impact of Chrysler's withdrawal. During this period, the possibility of submerging Chrysler UK into British Leyland was explored, and dropped after meeting opposition from BL's senior executives. What hopes remained were at that stage centred on the Iranian contract and the commercial vehicle business, the general presumption (outside Scotland) being that the rest would be allowed to close.

The warning from the IDAB on November 17 that Chrysler UK's prospects looked gloomy did not surprise those involved in the negotiations. Varley was later to tell the select committee, in what was certainly an understatement, that the IDAB "had doubts and reservations and recognised the risks". After another meeting with Riccardo, the government was steeling itself to take a tough line with Chrysler. Wilson warned the Commons on November 25 that "we have a long way to go before we can hope to save any bit of Chrysler".

Scheme B – Chrysler to Manage a State Owned Company

At that time, what came to be known as Scheme B was evolved by the Department of Industry, with some prodding from the Scottish Office. This was a variation on Chrysler's offer to "give" the government Chrysler UK. Under this plan, Chrysler would manage the remnants of a slimmed down operation under a management contract. Chrysler offered to put in £35 mn – against which Varley estimated total liabilities of £170 mn (without deducting realisable assets). This figure implied, incidentally, that Chrysler UK was verging on technical insolvency – or would have been had not Chrysler Corporation just put in £20 mn in fresh capital.

Under Scheme B, the UK company, with car production centred at Linwood, engines being made at Stoke and commercial vehicles in Dunstable, would be nationalised by the government. The attraction of the plan was that it would save the Linwood plant, and most of the profitable commercial vehicle output, and would also save the Iranian contract. And, of course, the act of nationalisation would appeal to Labour's left wing.

Several variations upon Scheme B were considered. One was that Chrysler would retain a 20 per cent interest in Chrysler UK. In terms of capacity to be retained, a shrunken version was considered, which would include only the Iranian contract (presumably concentrated at Stoke, Coventry) and commercial vehicle production. This would have retained a work force of only 6,000 out of 25,000.

Clearly, large sums were required from the government, whether nationalisation or rescue of the operation under existing ownership was the chosen solution. The variants that included saving Linwood as well as Stoke would have involved substantially larger financial commitments from the government than the £100 mn which was the bottom figure leaked early in the negotiations. It is possible that the £100 mn represented the grant or grant equivalent element in a larger package of soft loans and loss funding, however – in which case it closely resembled the deal ultimately agreed.

The Nationalisation Proposal: Doubts about Chrysler Corporation's Likely Methods

The notion of paying Chrysler such sums to induce it to continue in Britain was rejected by the Cabinet in November, mainly out of concern that the money would be applied directly or indirectly to Chrysler's international

Table 2-7 Chrysler UK and subsidiaries consolidated balance sheet

	Dec. 31, 1973 £ '000	£ '000	Dec. 31, 1974 £ '000	£ '000
Property, plant and equipment		37,348		33,141
Unamortised special tools		7,084		6,777
Investments		534		1,296
Current assets				
Balances at bank and cash	3,532		2,509	
Debtors and repayments	22,962		21,015	
Amounts owing by subsidiaries	–		–	
Amounts owing by fellow subsidiaries of Chrysler Corporation	11,879		9,502	
Inventories	77,682		93,635	
	116,055		126,661	
Less				
Current liabilities				
Bank loans and overdrafts	19,285		33,527	
Short term notes payable	1,000		9,000	
Trade creditors and accruing charges	56,263		60,073	
Amounts owing to subsidiaries	–		–	
Amounts owing to Chrysler Corporation and fellow subsidiaries	13,662		6,300	
Current portion of long term debt and deferred liabilities	10,453		6,631	
Accrued interest on long term debt and deferred liabilities	349		325	
Taxation payable	363		121	
Provision for foreign exchange adjustments	132		132	
	101.507		116,109	
		14,548		10,552
Net capital employed		59,514		51,766
Financed by				
Share capital		33,742		33,742
Share premium account		13,330		13,330
Reserves		201		560
Accumulated loss		(4,574)		(22,308)

Table 2-7 Continued

	Dec. 31, 1973		Dec. 31, 1974	
	£ '000	£ '000	£ '000	£ '000
Shareholders' interests		42,699		25,324
Long term debt and deferred liabilities		16,815		26,128
Minor adjustment in net assets of a subsidiary		–		314
		59,514		51,766

solvency problems without assuring a continued presence in the UK on any substantial scale. Negotiations therefore focused on nationalisation, which was in any case politically less repugnant to ministers than supporting an ailing foreign multinational.

Nationalisation within a British Leyland framework was obviously the most attractive formula, and had BL been capable of the job, the precedent of the absorption of Associated Electrical Industries into General Electric in 1967 was encouraging. There were however two fundamental obstacles to BL "doing a Weinstock" on Chrysler UK. One was that BL management was already fully stretched with its own internal problems. Another was that whereas Arnold Weinstock had been free to close AEI's worst plants and re-organise its best ones, Chrysler UK did not readily present such possibilities. The Stoke plant—the least modernised of all the major Chrysler factories—was essential to the Iranian contract, while the top political priority was Linwood which, while fairly modern, had the worst track record in labour relations and (so far as one can tell) of low productivity. Ryton, the most modern car assembly plant in the UK at the time, might have been attractive to BL, but the latter's management refused to consider acquiring even that, for fear of possible repercussions on labour relations in their own plants whose future might consequently be jeopardised.

Nationalisation, with Chrysler continuing to manage whatever remained of its UK affiliate, presented different difficulties—quite apart from the cost to the government in capital outlays. Even with a 20 per cent stake (and even more so with none) Chrysler Corporation would have had little incentive to earn profits in the UK. To maximise group profits, it would have to load the UK end with the least profitable elements of an integrated European business. It would have been provided with powerful incentives to shift profits elsewhere by transfer pricing, and to use its dealership system to sell cars from plants abroad. Its relations with its government partner would have been uneasy at best. The government could had had an unlimited commitment to underwrite losses. That it would have possessed two competing state owned car companies, an objection cited by Varley in testimony to the select committee, was not in itself a serious argument against a state takeover; but the government would thereby have become politically committed to providing continued support to the operation even if the worst happened and losses continued to escalate; and this must have been a critical deterrent.

Civil Service Opposition to a Major Rescue

The Treasury and the Department of Industry were both opposed to any major rescue programme—the Treasury for reasons of expenditure control, and industry officials because they had with some difficulty succeeded (they thought) in shifting the main thrust of industrial policy away from the support of what Peter Carey, the second secretary responsible for the policy, called "permanent pensioners", towards one of selective assistance to firms deemed viable on a criterion of long term profitability. Indeed, it is likely that the government ignored the symptoms of impending collapse (before November) because both the industry department and the National Enterprise Board regarded the demise of Chrysler not only as a necessary reduction in the industry's alleged excess capacity, but also as offering scope for British Leyland to increase its share of the market. The NEB chairman, Lord Ryder, expressed resentment (November 28) when he found that the government was beginning to change its mind.

The Government's Change of Mind

Three principal factors influenced this change. One was the increasing pressure from Scottish MPs, culminating early in December in threats by the secretary of state for Scotland. William Ross, and his parliamentary secretary, Bruce Millan, to resign unless Linwood was rescued. In addition, the Department of Employment prepared estimates of the consequential unemployment of about 50,000 for one year after closure, rather than the 25,000 which ministers had at first assumed to be involved. This higher figure led to an estimate of extra benefit payments of £100 mn to £150 mn falling on the Exchequer. The latter figure, which was the one given publicly, has been disputed (there are, logically, some indirect offsetting effects to consider) but nevertheless they impressed the chancellor, whose conversion to the ranks of ministers in favour of rescue was crucial. Finally, ministers became rather suddenly convinced that closure of Chrysler would cause a wave of imports. The idea that British Leyland would benefit from shutdown of Chrysler UK could no longer be sustained, for the situation in BL was becoming worse; the NEB and BL management were, by the end of November, preparing decisions in response to this, which emerged early in December in the form of a moratorium on new investment. The 850 Chrysler dealers would, it was now felt, go over substantially or wholly to foreign suppliers (including Simca).

On the scenario of Chrysler closing, the industry department put to the Cabinet a plan for import controls for 18 months, along with a recommended running down of Chrysler UK over twelve months. The controls were to be based in such a way as to affect most severely those foreign suppliers which had increased their shipments the most in recent years, notably Japan and to a lesser extent France. Nissan Motors, the manufacturer of Datsun cars, was approached with the suggestion that it take over the Linwood plant, in which context the import controls would be an incentive. Nissan declined the offer.

The chancellor, who had come under considerable pressure from abroad over the import control question, and had given certain commitments, opposed this plan. Harold Lever took a similar view, and also regarded the idea of a twelve month rundown as impracticable, on the ground that Chrysler UK sales would slump even further and therefore the cost of underwriting losses would be impossible to justify, either by Chrysler Corporation or the government. In any case, Riccardo was adamant that if Chrysler UK had to liquidate, December 31, 1975, was the deadline.

The Lever Rescue Package

On December 4, Lever offered an alternative proposal which, after a week of further negotiation (mainly over the loan guarantees and the sharing of losses beyond the first £40 mn) was finally accepted. The contents of the package are now well known, and were published by the government as a Declaration of Intent. The government agreed to meet by outright grant the whole of any loss in 1976 up to £40 mn, and half of losses above that to a maximum of £20 mn (i e. total exposure of £50 mn). Half of any loss is to be similarly met in 1977 up to a loss of £20 mn, in 1978 up to £15 mn, and in 1979 up to £10 mn, making the maximum exposure to loss cover £72.5 mn. The government will share half of any profit in any year up to 1979. It also guarantees a medium term clearing bank loan of £35 mn (for seven years at interest 2 per cent above sterling interbank rate) to fund short term loans already drawn to cover the cash flow deficiency in 1975—towards which the parent company had already injected the £20 mn already mentioned. The government also extended Chrysler UK a loan of £55 mn, of which £28 mn is to be drawn by the end of 1977, and the balance of £27 mn after January 1, 1978. Repayments are in ten equal semi annual instalments after the end of 1985; interest is 12.5 per cent up to 1980, rising thereafter. This £55 mn loan is to finance the introduction of "new models", which we discuss later. Chrysler Corporation guarantees the first £28 mn, but the second tranche will be a charge only on the assets of Chrysler UK. Chrysler does not guarantee to remain in the UK (indeed, Varley said later in testimony to a Commons select committee that it could not possibly have given any such guarantee) but the whole of the £55 mn becomes immediately repayable if Chrysler Corporation reduces its equity interest in its UK subsidiary below 80 percent.

Chrysler also promises to introduce, for assembly at Ryton, a British version of the successful Simca C6 Alpine, imported (as to about 50 per cent of its value) from France. This development is to be financed by the parent company. A mark 2 version of the Avenger is to be produced at Linwood. The government strongly emphasised the fact that this new pattern of production would integrate Chrysler UK much more closely with other Chrysler affiliates (Simca, in point of fact) implying that this, which does certainly mark a change from past production strategy, augurs well for Chrysler's continued presence in Britain.

Reductions in the labour force were agreed, totalling about 8,250. Of these, 3,000 were to occur at Linwood, 2,500 at Ryton, 2,100 at Stoke, and 500 through closure of a small factory at Maidstone. Shortly afterwards Chrysler agreed with the unions at Linwood to reduce the redundancies there to 1,500, making the total layoff about 6,750.

Was Chrysler Serious in Its Threat to Liquidate?

From the beginning of its current troubles, Chrysler management in the US claimed that the currently depressed economic conditions in Britain were the main source of the UK subsidiary's difficulties. This was the main thrust of Riccardo's letter of February 18, 1975, to the then secretary for industry in which he stressed that "the current times are very difficult . . . substantial excess average annual capacity . . . dramatically reduced markets . . . sales of all motor products in the UK are depressed . . ." and so forth. He urged the government to pursue "monetary and taxation policies which will stimulate the purchase of motor vehicles". He also made a thinly veiled reference to price control as a disincentive to investment. Despite a passing reference to productivity, there is little to suggest that Riccardo felt greatly concerned about any serious structural defects in Chrysler UK, either in management or plant. A similar outlook is reflected in press conferences given by Riccardo and the Chrysler president, Eugene Cafiero, on October 29 and on December 19 (after the rescue had been announced). In the latter, Cafiero explained the need for redundancies as follows: "These, really, have to do with the current state of the industry in the UK, which is down to about one million units a year from 1.7 mn in 1973, and the penetration of foreign cars". In another answer, Riccardo emphasised that the main problem was to survive the loss in 1975 and that expected in 1976, while Cafiero pointed to expectations of market recovery thereafter "hopefully to at least the 1973 levels, with some improvement in productivity".

All this must raise doubts, not only about the ability of Chrysler senior management to deal with its non-cyclical problems in Britain—problems of which it is surely aware—but also about the extent to which it seriously intended to liquidate the UK subsidiary. The prime minister was sceptical, on the latter point—as he implicitly revealed in his complaint that his government had been "presented with a pistol to its head".

It was bound to make sweeping changes, but liquidation presented vital problems of its own. A cursory glance at the profit record of Chrysler UK might suggest that its US management would have been not merely serious, but determined, to liquidate its UK subsidiary. It is as certain as anything could be that Chrysler could not have envisaged carrying on Chrysler UK as it was. Model development work had been cut back drastically, so that there were no specifically British models emerging. Any future which Chrysler might have seen for its UK affiliate can only have been as a greatly slimmed down element integrated with Simca, functionally if not in terms of organisation. The Stoke (Coventry) factory, in which little had been invested, was clearly surviving only for the duration of the Iran contract. Doubtless Chrysler wanted to remain in possession of one assembly plant, and to continue making commercial vehicles, which were profitable. But it was undeniably true that it needed financial help to do any of this. And above all, the Iranian contract presented it with a grave problem, for its international reputation would have been irreparably damaged had it repudiated that contract in the course of shutting down in Britain.

Switching this contract to another source was a third possible course. However, the only place in Europe to which the Iranian contract could be re-sourced would be France; and given any recovery in Simca's sales (and these are off to a good start this year) the French affiliate would not have had the capacity, particularly to supply some 70,000 to 80,000 engines to Iran in 1976. Theoretically, the contract could have been re-sourced to the US, but the capital cost would have been very high, as Chrysler does not make car engines in the 1,700 cc range in the US.

Chrysler Corporation would also have faced liquidation costs in the UK. *The Economist* has reported these at about £120 mn. We cannot substantiate this figure, except to estimate as follows. Chrysler's share of redundancy payments would have been rather less than £10 mn. If Varley's estimate of total liabilities (other than to Chrysler Corporation) of £170 mn is correct, one should set against that realisable current assets of about £100 mn (mostly stocks of cars). What the fixed assets would have fetched in liquidation is anybody's guess. Although it has been reported that liquidation losses would have been offsettable against US tax, Chrysler Corporation did not have a federal income tax liability in 1975, and only a small portion could have been recovered against US capital gains tax, if any. The £120 mn appears high, but clearly there would have been a very substantial net cost of liquidation.

Chrysler management could not have been eager to abandon its UK operations, as some press comment declared. In his press conference on December 19, Riccardo indicated that nationalisation by HM government was what he was aiming at. He said: "We hoped that we could make some meaningful arrangement with the government for them to continue the company. We didn't threaten or want to liquidate . . . That was an inescapable conclusion if no other arrangement could be made. But it was our hope that somehow the government could find its way to take over this operation. We pledged our full support, our managerial talent, the technical help, the use of our worldwide distribution network. That's the way the negotiation started, and it took a 180° degree turn to the form that finally evolved."

Nationalisation Would Have Provided a Good Solution for Chrysler

There is every reason to believe that Riccardo was speaking the truth. He would not have offered the government £35 mn from the parent company, in the latter's strained financial condition, to encourage the government to nationalise Chrysler UK, had he not earnestly desired that outcome. The reasons why the government found nationalisation commercially and industrially unattractive made it best from Chrysler's standpoint. Apart from the instant release of £170 mn of debts, one must consider the ongoing possibility of adding to group profits while in partnership with the government, in the ways described above, which would have exceeded the scope offered by the present arrangement. Moreover, Chrysler would have earned a risk free management fee income from an enterprise assured of long term losses.

While Wedgwood Benn was still secretary for industry, Chrysler would have felt reasonably confident that nationalisation would be the government's preferred course. And although the change of policy after his departure became known before October, Chrysler UK management was fully aware too of the force of a threat of almost immediate shutdown, given the UK unemployment situation and the Iranian contract.

From start to finish, these were the two factors which preoccupied ministers the most—though, unforeseeably and almost accidentally, the problem of import controls turned the balance in the end. The prime minister was especially worried about Linwood, right from the beginning. Only a few days after the talks opened, he said in the Commons on November 11:

> "We are paying special attention to the problems of Linwood. I think that the whole House knows—and knew before there was an SNP (Scottish National Party) member in the House—the importance of Linwood . . . . We are certainly bearing that in mind as one of the high priorities in anything that we hope—I use the word 'hope'—may come out of our discussions with the Chrysler Corporation."

And on November 25, when the prospects for a solution appeared at their bleakest:

> "We are striving might and main to save the whole operation, if that is possible, and certainly to save Linwood, because of the high level of unemployment there."

Varley Worried about the Iranian Contract

Varley, although opposed to a rescue on industrial grounds, both as regards the rest of the motor industry and his industrial policy in general, was deeply concerned over the Iranian contract. Both its size as a proportion of total UK car exports, and the possible implications of cancellation upon exports to Iran in general, caused him to seek ways of salvaging this element, in all the various rescue plans he considered. He is even reported to have asked British Leyland to take it over, after BL had refused to take over Chrysler UK. Much of the time spent by his officials on the Chrysler rescue was devoted to the Iranian contract, and the costs and possibilities of re-sourcing it.

The Treasury was rather less convinced of its importance. It does not appear to have believed that the contract was being used to shift profits out of Britain to a co-subsidiary in Switzerland (a charge that has been levelled by Labour left wingers). On the face of it, this view would appear to be correct, because Chrysler UK has no corporation tax liability in the UK to avoid; nor would exchange controls have provided an incentive, assuming that Chrysler Corporation stood ready to meet the debts of its UK affiliate if the worst happened (and the injection of £20 mn of capital by the parent in mid 1975 suggest that it was). However, it is clear that the average price of the CKD units shipped to Iran last year was remarkably low; and the Treasury was aware of this.

On a customs basis, the number of built up cars shipped to Iran last year was 20,000, which agrees with Chrysler's figure for Avengers under the contract. The customs figure for cars shipped CKD was 102,000, compared with Chrysler's figure of 120,000 (scaled down from a target of 150,000). The difference is due to the fact that the customs closes its entries about three weeks before the end of the year. Chrysler is the only UK exporter of cars CKD to Iran. All but an insignificant number (192) of these were in the range of engine capacity 1,600 cc to 2,200 cc, and the average value last year was only £531, compared with £660 for all other exports of cars CKD by the industry in the same range of engine size (mainly Cortinas). Substantially the whole of these were at the lower end of the range, i.e., the same or less than the 1,725 cc Hunter engine, so in this respect the figures are comparable. As the Iran contract was not routed through a foreign intermediary, however, it appears that the low prices realised were the result of the contractual terms agreed with (and highly favourable to) INIM, and that they do not reflect transfer pricing.

The Remarkable Telegram from Teheran

The strange incident of the telegram from Iran, relaying a message from the latter's minister of finance, proves that either Chrysler or the Iranian government (or both) considered Britain to be vulnerable over this contract. The telegram expressed the Iranian government's deep concern over the impact of a possible cancellation of the contract upon financial and industrial relations between the two countries. It is possible that it reflected genuine anxiety on the part of Teheran over disruption of its car import programme—though in that case, it is surprising that it was not sent sooner. It was transmitted on December 10 or 11, just as the Lever solution was being finally accepted in Cabinet. It is also possible that it followed representations in Teheran by Chrysler. In that rather more likely case, it illustrates great concern on the part of Chrysler management over the possibility of having to liquidate its UK affiliate – and perhaps, too, a sense of panic over the government's rejection of scheme B (nationalisation) which it had evidently thought the government would accept.

The telegram came too late to have been decisive in the outcome. The deciding factors were (1) the government's fears that a sudden collapse of Chrysler UK would not only turn 25,000 (or 50,000) workers into the streets (British Leyland had however shed 30,000 workers in a little over a year), (2) even more important, liquidation would increase car imports by perhaps 200,000 a year, and (3) the appearance of a plan which would provide the appearances of reviving Chrysler UK as a going concern, more integrated with the rest of the group, at a cost to the government which compared favourably with the likely cost to the Exchequer of unemployment and other benefit payments. Clearly, in these terms, a solution achieved in December 1975 was more important to the government than one that would be of any lasting benefit.

But Can Chrysler UK Survive?

The Iranian contract is also an important element in the future of Chrysler UK. Owing to delays in Iran in absorbing kits for assembly (partly due to slippage in commissioning plant for making body trim and other parts) and the existence of some 50,000 kits in stock or transit, shipments in 1976 are expected to fall to about 70,000. This is likely to be greatly exceeded in 1977, subject to any further problems at the receiving end. In 1978, however, the outlook becomes complicated by the introduction of a Mark 2 version of the Peykan which will not only have a much larger Iranian component element, but also a new or revamped engine. According to reports in the trade, Chrysler is planning to supply a Simca engine for the Peykan Mark 2. This would leave very little scope for continued operations at Stoke.

Doubts about the Figures

Varley's shadow on the Conservative side, Michael Heseltine, has publicly claimed that the sums required to launch the promised new models in Britain must be at least twice those outlined in the government's Declaration of Intent. He has documented his estimates with obvious signs of expert advice. Timing appears to be the essence of this matter. The bulk of the first £28 mn of the government loan is to be spent at Linwood, on a face lift for the Avenger (which Heseltine puts at £5 mn) and on a replacement for the Imp, to be produced largely from parts supplied from France. The retooling at Ryton for assembly of Alpines will be financed by Chrysler Corporation, which will inject £10–12 mn for this purpose. As the loss estimate for 1976 of £40 mn to £50 mn is described as including the cost of transferring the Avenger work to Linwood, it may be that all expenditure on that model in 1976 is being treated as current. In that case, the £28 mn of new capital is mainly to finance tooling up for the Imp replacement (designated the 424), which appears credible.

The main strain upon the credibility of the government's figures comes after 1977, when the remaining £27 mn is to cover a new car model and a new truck – not to mention more fundamental capital investment, of which there has been very little for more than two years. Chrysler has also to decide this year whether to increase the UK component element in the Alpines (to be made at Ryton) in 1978, at a further cost to Chrysler Corporation estimated at £23 mn.

One rational element in the new production pattern is the elimination of the curious practice hitherto of producing engines and major sub assemblies for the Hunter in Coventry and shipping them to Linwood for assembly, while producing similar sub assemblies for the Avenger in Linwood for assembly in Coventry. On the other hand, the reduction in the labour force at Linwood of only about 20 per cent, while only the Avenger will be fully manufactured there this year, suggests that the labour cutback there reflects plant under utilisation rather than increased labour productivity. Overall capacity of Chrysler UK will be reduced by 25 per cent (Varley has said) whereas the work force is to be cut by about 27 per cent.

... and About Labour Relations

Nor can Chrysler's recent labour relations be seen as an augury of permanence. The firm proposed a participation agreement last spring, which was rejected by the employees. Although a crisis such as that which broke in the autumn might have been expected to place the unions in a weak, almost supine position, there was no evidence that this was so, or that Chrysler was minded to react to it if it was so. One might have thought that a reform of the disputes procedure, ideally one involving compulsory arbitration of disputes (as when the shipbuilders were rescued) would have been sought; but no move was made in that direction. At Linwood, the unions successfully reduced the redundancies from 3,000 to 1,500 (fair enough perhaps since Chrysler expected the other 1,500 to be needed by mid summer) and later staged a plant wide strike over a pay anomaly involving a small number of workers. Don Lander, managing director of Chrysler UK, rebuked the Linwood workers rather lamely, with a warning that they were endangering "the jobs of their colleagues in the Midlands", and the management conceded the claim. Offers of voluntary redundancy at Linwood were heavily oversubscribed, and were fully taken up at Stoke.

The Bristol University motor industry research project, headed by Krish Bhaskar, which last year did an intensive study of the industry, has recently run the Chrysler rescue figures through its computer model a second time, and has concluded that on Chrysler's assumptions about market share (a 10 per cent market share to be achieved in 1977 and maintained thereafter) no profit would appear until 1978. Thereafter, profits would amount to only

£16–17 mn a year in the two best years. Assuming a 7.5 per cent market share (Chrysler's market share in February 1976 was in fact 4.7 per cent, including imports from Simca) losses would persist through 1978, with barely visible profits in the next two years. Both runs are founded on the optimistic assumption that there will be no further recession in the motor industry before 1981.

Incentive to Chrysler to Earn Profits in UK Will Be Impaired

While the incentive provided to Chrysler Corporation to take profits in the UK would be greater under the present arrangement than if it were operating the concern on a fee basis, it will be in its interest to transfer profits elsewhere insofar as the resultant losses in the UK remain within the limits of the 50–50 sharing agreement. If by any chance Chrysler return to profit (and does so in the US also) it will have a tax incentive to shift profits out of Britain. The reason is that the 50 per cent government share in the profit would be more onerous to Chrysler than (say) a 50 per cent tax rate in France on profits of Simca, because the former would not be eligible for credit against US tax, whereas the latter will. While Varley said to the select committee that the two government members on the board of Chrysler UK would watch for any signs that profits were being shifted, this was later contradicted by the Treasury official responsible for industrial policy, Alan Lord, who said that it is not the role of such appointees to channel information to the government. The Treasury board member on Chrysler UK would not be a "government nark" he said.

A Reassessment by 1978?

Besides the fact that loss cover by the government reduces in 1978 to £7.5 mn, that year is of signal importance in other ways. There is, as already mentioned, the Mark 2 Peykan in Iran, which could bring a quick end to supplies from Britain. There is the problem of raising the UK content in Chrysler UK manufacture of the Alpine, the cost of which is to fall on Chrysler Corporation. Replacement of obsolescent equipment, which has been deferred for the past year or more, will either place a strain upon cash flow, or else be further deferred, to the detriment of production. Since the £27 mn second tranche will not be explicitly guaranteed by the parent company, the government will not be eager to urge it to take it up if prospects look poor. Moreover, since all the credit extended by the government becomes immediately repayable if Chrysler reduces its equity in Chrysler UK below 80 per cent, Chrysler is unlikely to draw and spend the £27 mn second tranche without being very confident that the operation will prove a long term success. For, if in 1978 or 1979 Chrysler decided to liquidate (or bring in a joint venture partner), it would at that point be liable to repay a fruitlessly invested £27 mn (plus, in the event of liquidation, up to about £200 mn in existing liabilities). The end of 1977 would be an excellent point at which to reconsider fundamentals.

The Significance of Chrysler's Multinational Dimension

The extent to which Chrysler's position as a multinational company affected the outcome can only be assessed by comparing the position of a British uninational in the same situation. The firm, when under the name of Rootes Motors, had already been rescued twice. Had it remained Rootes Motors in 1975, the political pressures in Scotland, and the awkward industrial logic of fulfilling the Iranian contract from the most antiquated plant, would have been every bit as difficult for the government. The "pistol to its head" aspect of the affair would therefore not have been the least bit different. And since the Iran contract would have been incontestably a UK–Iran matter, the case for a rescue on this account would have been far stronger than it was with the contract between INIM and Chrysler International.

It would not, however, have been possible to save the UK operations by adapting them to assembly of Simca vehicles. This comparatively easy solution would not have been available. Some sort of rescue might have been effected, but the much needed rationalisation could not have been deferred, as it has been. Solutions of problems such as that of Chrysler UK cannot ignore the industry's need for a much greater scale of fully replicative operations. Optimal scale of production is far in excess of the output of any model range in Britain. Bhaskar has concluded that the minimum efficient scale of production in machining operations is a million car equivalents a year (in components machined) and 2 mn in stamping operations. Minimum assembly production is put at 200,000 to 400,000 a year. Assembly operations require less scale than component manufacture, obviously; but, as the CPRS report showed, the British industry compares less favourably with foreign ones in assembly than in component and sub assembly manufacture, probably owing to organisational inefficiency. This does not bode well for a Chrysler solution which reduces component and sub assembly production in the UK while concentrating upon assembly.

Both Parties Have Bought Time

Chrysler Corporation did not get what it wanted. It has secured a stop gap arrangement which will probably cover its losses in 1976 and half of any in 1977 (when it might make a small boom time profit), and has been provided a small interest rate subsidy – not as great, however, as that on loans on concessional terms in developing areas, and not great enough to amount to a serious competitive advantage over other producers (though whatever market share it retains will affect them adversely). The loans must be repaid, and unless the use to which they are put can generate positive cash flow and prof-

Table 2-8 Bristol University Motor Industry Study: Computer projections, March 3, 1976

	1976	1977	1978	1979	1980	1981	1982	1983
Government plans and Chrysler assumptions								
Total UK demand ('000 cars)	1,250	1,400	1,600	1,800	1,900	1,800	1,600	1,800
Total market share (per cent)	8.6	10.0	10.0	10.0	10.0	10.0	10.0	10.0
Total of built up units ('000)	154	198	224	255	265	260	240	260
Profit & loss account:								
Total revenue	298	380	433	436	433	400	376	402
Total trading profits	10	48	66	76	79	73	62	72
Net profit before tax	−44	−6	6	16	17	11	0	6
Government plans and "pessimistic" assumptions								
Total UK demand ('000 cars)	1,250	1,400	1,600	1,800	1,900	1,800	1,600	1,800
Total market share (per cent)	6.2	7.5	7.5	7.5	7.5	7.5	7.5	7.5
Total of built up units ('000)	125	163	184	210	217	215	200	215
Profit & loss account:								
Total revenue	255	334	378	374	367	347	320	339
Total trading profits	1	31	44	52	54	49	40	48
Net profit before tax	−51	−20	−9	3	3	−2	−11	−7

Study project leader: Krish Bhaskar.

its, the loan repayments will in themselves comprise for Chrysler Corporation an unattractive aspect of the deal. Both Chrysler and the government have bought a little time; but it is hard to see that the company, in doing so, has gained any advantage.

The Chrysler UK Updates*

Chrysler UK lost $25 million in 1977 but had a small profit in 1978 in the first quarter. In the second quarter, however, because of a Linwood strike, the company lost nearly $2 million a week. Between 1976 and 1978 Chrysler lost $120 million, of which $97 million was absorbed by the government.

In August of 1978 Chrysler Corporation sold its entire European carmaking operations (France, Britain, and Spain) to Peugeot Citroën SA. The deal included the operations plus $400 million worth of debt for $230 million in cash and a 15% share in the company.

Editor's note (1980): Chrysler Corporation, again in financial difficulty, sold its UK operations to Peugeot Citroën SA in 1979.

*The updated information was provided by Lenore R. Beyer, a student of the MBA class of 1983–1985.

Case 2-2

Imperial Tobacco Company

The India Tobacco Company (ITC), formerly known as the Imperial Tobacco Company, has been in India since the 1920s, dating back to the days of British colonialism. Over the years, ITC has evolved into a profitable, diversified company. ITC is an Indian company with majority foreign shareholding. It is known to have a number of links with British American Tobacco (BAT), a joint venture formed by the Imperial Tobacco Company and American Brands.

The long association with India has sensitized the management at ITC to the changing political, social, and economic environments in India. A year after India gained her independence in 1947, the Industrial Policy Resolution (1948) was passed by Parliament. The provisions of this resolution indicated that the position of a multinational corporation, engaged in the manufacture of nonessential, low-technology products, was rather shaky. ITC responded to this challenge by setting out to create for itself an image of a responsible corporate citizen, which identified with the country in which it was operating.

Twenty-nine years later, in 1977, ITC was faced with yet another challenge. ITC's closest competitor, an Indian company called Golden Tobacco Co. (GTC), was engaged in a campaign to discredit ITC. GTC highlighted that ITC was 95% foreign-owned and claimed that ITC's apparent contributions to India's development efforts were merely a front for its exploitation of India's agricultural and labor resources. The vilification campaign came at a time when ITC was trying to get concessions from the Indian government with reference to the Foreign Exchange Regulation Act (FERA). The FERA required ITC to reduce its foreign-held equity to 40%. An exemption could be arranged under the provisions of FERA if ITC could prove that its operations were either in the high-technology sector or contributed substantially to foreign exchange earnings. ITC was faced with the following possible courses of action. First, it could try to gain concessions from the FERA. Or, it could

Source: Data for this case were collected by Anant R. Negandhi. Ms Rachel Davis assisted in preparing the case. © Copyright by Anant R. Negandhi, 1985.

comply with the FERA and dilute equity. Or, it could fold up its fifty-five-year-old operations.

ITC – "The Good Corporate Citizen"

India is today the second largest producer and exporter of tobacco in the world. ITC takes credit for a substantial contribution to this achievement. ITC introduced "flue-cured Virginia Tobacco" to India. ITC established the Indian Leaf Tobacco Development (ILTD) center, which provides technical assistance, comprehensive "farmer service," and timely inputs with supervision. The ILTD deals directly with 70,000 farmers. Its research centers in Rajamundry and Bangalore are acknowledged as outstanding in the world of tobacco.

ITC directly employs approximately 30,000 persons. In addition, its operations contribute toward the livelihood of another 1.1 million people all over the country.

The company has diversified into fisheries. The activities of its Foods Division are labor intensive, and are located in backward and rural areas. ITC's Hotels Division has set up luxury hotels in major Indian cities to benefit the tourist trade. Both of these activities, along with ITC's primary activity of manufacturing tobacco and tobacco products, are good foreign exchange earners. ITC increased its foreign exchange earning from an average of around Rs 50 million between 1962 and 1966 to over Rs 270 million in 1975–1976, an increase of over 450%.

Imperial Tobacco invested in India primarily to secure a stable source of raw materials for its international operations. Quite unexpectedly, ITC discovered a large and fast developing local market for tobacco products in India. Most of the tobacco exported from India is done through ITC. It is clear that BAT's primary objective would be to continue to secure tobacco supplies from India, and therefore benefit from economies of scale and vertical integration.

ITC has acquired a reputation of having both harmonious labor relations and highly qualified and capable managerial talent.

All of these ITC operations contribute to developmental objectives defined as primary in India's Five Year Plans and Industrial Policy Resolution. These include increasing employment opportunities, contributing to rural development, increasing foreign exchange earnings, and developing world market networks for Indian products.

ITC's efforts should have been sufficient to put the company beyond reproach. However, the perception of a number of Indians, as well as a number of people in other developing countries, was that multinational corporations aim at making extraordinary profits at the expense of host countries; that is, the global spread of these corporations permits the transfer of sums of money across international borders in a manner that cannot be controlled by host governments. This was the aspect of ITC that GTC sought to highlight both to the Indian public and the Indian government.

ITC–"Foreign Monopoly in the Cigarette Industry in India"

The GTC was ITC's nearest competitor. It had a market share of about 15% against ITC's market share of over 50%.

Pratap Narsee, the managing director of GTC, held that ITC was a monopoly that operated to the detriment of the other cigarette manufacturers. (The Monopolies and Restrictive Trade Practices Act defines a monopoly as an undertaking that alone or together with another undertaking controls not less than 50% of the market.)

Pratap Narsee also claimed that ITC and another tobacco company, Vazir Sultan Tobacco, were interconnected companies. Vazir Sultan Tobacco and ITC were said to have common links with British American Tobacco.* The two were also said to have common sales and purchase arrangements. Mr. Narsee was able to show that the two companies had a great deal of overlap in the composition of their boards of directors.

Added to the accusations of ITC's involvement in monopolistic and restrictive trade practices were those claiming ITC's export operations as being less beneficial to the Indian economy than they appeared. Only 10% of ITC's foreign exchange earnings arose from cigarette exports; the rest was earned from the export of leaf tobacco by the ILTD. According to Mr. Narsee, what the ILTD claimed as its export of tobacco was in actuality only the supplies it made to its affiliated cigarette companies. ILTD was therefore, for all practical purposes, a tobacco buying organization for the group. Because of the size and operations of the BAT group (which operates in fifty-five countries), ILTD has been able to establish a monopoly in tobacco leaf trade in India.

These accusations were made by Pratap Narsee at a series of press conferences, aimed at bringing the "activities and operations" of ITC to the attention of the Indian public.

ITC's major problem appears to be the FERA, but GTC is all set to further complicate the issue and place as many obstacles in the way of ITC's continued operations in India as it can.

Appendix 1

Excerpts of the letter, dated September 4, 1970, from *The World Tobacco* (The International Magazine for the Tobacco Industry), John Adam House, London, to Shri Pratap Narsee Thacker, Director, Golden Tobacco Company, Private Limited, Tobacco House, Vile Parle, Bombay.

"In considering what you quote the Chairman of Vazir Sultan as saying about not being inter-connected with ITC or BAT, I imagine that the question turns on what he meant by 'inter-connected'. In our 'World Tobacco Directory', we show various relationships between businesses through the formula 'associated with.' Here, 'associated with' does not mean that one company completely owns or controls another; we sometimes use the formula even

*Refer to Appendix 1.

in cases where the shareholding is less than 50%, but where a business link is for one reason or another of commercial significance greater than that which would arise merely from, for example, a manufacture-under-licence arrangement.

There certainly is a connection between Vazir Sultan and BAT, as BAT's own latest Annual Report, dated September 30, 1969, indicates. It is shown there that 47% of Vazir Sultan's shares are effectively owned by BAT. I say 'effectively' because the link is indirect. That part of Vazir Sultan's shares owned outside of India, being held by one or more holding companies in which BAT has a financial interest, though, does not apparently control 100 percent.

Likewise—and also indirectly, through a holding company or holding companies in which, I would assume, there are at this time no non-BAT shareholders—ITC is connected with BAT. But there is not, so far as we can trace, any shareholding of ITC in Vazir Sultan, or vice versa. Although ITC and Vazir Sultan are, so-to-speak, cousins by both having links with BAT, they do not seem to be financially interconnected, and I have never heard it suggested that way. There has in the past been co-operation between the two companies in technical matters; I do not know whether this still persists."

Appendix 2 Production of Cigarettes in India _____

1947 to 1969	in million pieces
1947	18,880
1948	21,824
1949	21,890
1950	28,629
1951	21,449
1952	20,119
1953	18,424
1954	19,828
1955	22,829
1956	26,303
1957	28,892
1958	29,840
1959	32,166
1960	36,971
1961	39,466
1962	41,124
1963	40,062
1964	46,196
1965	54,033
1966	58,295
1967	54,511
1968	60,430
1969	59,710

Source: "Monthly Statistics of the Production of Selected Industries of India"—Central Statistical Organisation, Cabinet Secretariat, Government of India, Calcutta.

Appendix 3 Cigarette Production by Foreign versus Indian Sector

1948/49 Cigarette production in India was about 20,000 million cigarettes—controlled 75% by foreign monopoly.

1969/70 It was about 60,000 million cigarettes—80% still in the hands of foreigners.

1980 As per the Government's policy declared on the floor of the Parliament on 13th May, 1969 by the Minister for Industrial Development, Internal Trade & Company Affairs that "the Government's policy is to encourage production of cigarettes by Indian-owned firms to take care of the increase demand and the Government is also encouraging establishment of Companies which are 100% Indian-owned", the expected increase 5% to 6% in production would go to wholly Indian-owned companies—still it will be 50% in the hands of foreign-owned/controlled companies.

1990 After 20 years Indian owned companies will have 75% market and hold of the foreign owned companies will go down to 25%.

	Total Production (million cigts.)	Production by Foreign Sector %	Production by Indian Sector %
1948/49	20,000		
1969/70	60,000	80	20
1971		76	24
1972		73	27
1973		69	31
1974		66	34
1975		63	37
1976		60	40
1977		58	42
1978		55	45
1979		52	48
1980		50	50
1981		47	53
1982		44	56
1983		41	59
1984		38	62
1985		35	65
1986		33	67
1987		31	69
1988		29	71
1989		27	73
1990		25	75

Appendix 4 Foreign Shareholding in the Cigarette Industry

The following statement gives information about the percentage of foreign shareholding in the cigarette industry, companywise, and the composition of such foreign holdings.

(1) Imperial Tobacco Co. of India Ltd.

Amount of equity capital	Rs. 1,516.00 lakhs
Non-resident shareholding is:	
Tobacco Manufacturers (India) Ltd., U.K.	Rs. 1,032.19 ”
Tobacco Investments Ltd., U.K.	Rs. 330.11 ”
Carreras Ltd., U.K.	Rs. 53.70 ”
Other non-resident shareholders	Rs. 1.75 ”
	Rs. 1,417.75 ”
Percentage of foreign holding	94% (approx.)

(2) Vazir Sultan Tobacco Co. Ltd.

Amount of equity capital as at 30.9.1965	Rs. 100.00 lakhs
Non-resident shareholding is:	
Raleigh Investment Co. Ltd., U.K.	Rs. 44.19 ”
Tobacco Manufacturers (India) Ltd., U.K.	Rs. 15.61 ”
Tobacco Investments Ltd., U.K.	Rs. 4.99 ”
Carreras Ltd., U.K.	Rs. 0.81 ”
Other non-resident shareholders	Rs. 2.12 ”
	Rs. 67.72 ”
Percentage of foreign holding	67.72%

In 1966 consent for bonus issue of Rs. 100 lakhs was granted which has already been implemented.

(3) Godfrey Philips India Ltd.

Amount of equity capital as at 31.12.1965	Rs. 40.00 lakhs
Non-resident shareholding is:	
Godfrey Philips (Overseas Investments) Ltd., U.K.	Rs. 36.93 ”
Other non-resident shareholders	Rs. 0.13 ”
Percentage of foreign holding	92.65%

A consent was granted in 1967 for capitalisation of reserves of Rs. 20 lahks. This consent has already been implemented.

The Imperial Tobacco Co. of India Ltd. (Now India Tobacco Co. Ltd.)

	Year	Paid-up capital including bonus issues	Good-will	Sales and income	Profit before tax	Net profit after tax	Foreign share-holding percentage	Total drainage of foreign exchange by way of part remittance in form of dividends and remaining a deferred liability for future repatriation
	1959	1,516	490	3,460	287	115	93.4	Rs. 107 lakhs
	1969	1,516	490	12,642	707	359	93.4	Rs. 335 "
Increase percentage				383%	246%	312%		
Projection to	1980			48,419	1,739	1,120	76.0	Rs. 851 "

Between the years 1969 and 1980 the drainage of foreign exchange will jump as mentioned above from Rs. 335 lakhs to Rs. 851 lakhs which averages to Rs. 593 lakhs per year i.e. in 11 years during the period 1969 to 1980 there will be a total estimated foreign exchange drainage of Rs. 6523 lakhs.

The Vazir Sultan Tobacco Co. Ltd.

	Year	Paid-up capital including bonus issues	Good-will	Sales and income	Profit before tax	Net profit after tax	Foreign share-holding percentage	Total drainage of foreign exchange
	1959	129.54	5.81	602	69	29	67.0	Rs. 19 lakhs
	1969	229.54	5.81	3,309	204	82	67.0	Rs. 55 "
Increase percentage				550%	296%	283%		
Projection to	1980			18,200	604	232	67.0	Rs. 155 "

Between the years 1969 and 1980 the drainage of foreign exchange will jump as mentioned above from Rs. 55 lakhs to Rs. 155 lakhs which averages to Rs. 105 lakhs per year i.e. in 11 years during the period 1969 to 1980 there will be a total estimated foreign exchange drainage of Rs. 1155 lakhs.

The India Tobacco Co. Ltd. and the Vazir Sultan Tobacco Co. Ltd., both interconnected undertakings, have produced cigarettes far in excess of their combined approved installed capacity whereas the other six units have a large idle capacity which will be obvious from the following:

		Combined registered installed capacity	Actual production in 1967
		(million cigts.)	
Foreign monopoly excess production	India Tobacco Co. Ltd., Calcutta.		
	The Vazir Sultan Tobacco Co. Ltd., Hyderabad.	33,120	38,211
Six Indian cigarette factories with 70% idle capacity	National Tobacco Co. of India Ltd., Calcutta.		
	D. Macropolo & Co. Ltd., Bombay.		
	Masters Tobacco Co. India, Bombay.		
	Hyderabad Deccan Cigarette Factory, Hyderabad.	16,768	4,963
	Crown Tobacco Co., Bombay.		
	International Tobacco Co. Ltd., Ghaziabad.		

Appendix 5 Comparison between GTC and ITC _____

Comparative Performance of Figures—1960 to 1969 (10 years)

	G. T. C. (Rs. lakhs)	I. T. C. (Rs. lakhs)
Sales	17,579	67,388
Excise duty	9,156	32,950
Net sales	8,423	34,438
Cost of raw materials	5,357	20,736
Wages	362	5,127
Profit before tax	1,653	4,343
Income-tax	1,103	2,389
Profit after tax	550	1,954
Dividends	169	1,415
Foreign-exchange payment for dividends	Nil	1,330 (94% foreign shareholding)

Note:

1. The percentage of raw material value to the net sales value of cigarettes is—GTC 64% and ITC 60%, which shows that the consumer of GTC brands gets 5% more value for the money.

2. Percentage of profit to sales turnover is—GTC 9.5% and ICT 6.4%. It would be interesting to find out why this big monopoly has shown less profitability whereas GTC, a small Company, in spite of heavy odds and cut-throat competition from the monopoly has fared 50% better in profitability.

3. The percentage of income-tax paid to the sales turn-over is: GTC 6.3% and ITC 3.5%. If ITC was 100% Indian-owned Company, it would have worked as efficiently as GTC and in last 10 years the Government of India would have earned additional revenue of Rs. 1887 lakhs by way of Income-tax on ITC's turnover. On the other hand, if GTC had not survived the onslaught of the monopolistic competition, its turn-over would have gone to ITC and the Government of India would have received Rs. 491 lakhs less in Income-tax revenue than what it got from GTC in the last 10 years.

   Is this not enough to justify that foreign monopoly is harmful to the economy of the country?

4. The percentage of dividends declared to the profit after tax is—GTC 30% and ITC 72%; GTC has not frittered away its resources for paying the shareholders as ITC but has ploughed back major portions of its earnings to develop business to fight and get share of the market which would otherwise have been in the foreign sector.

5. Dividends remitted to foreign shareholders of ITC amount to Rs. 1,330 lakhs as against nil in case of GTC. If ITC was 100% Indian-owned Company, this drain on foreign exchange would have been saved. On the other hand, if GTC had not existed, ITC would have been enjoying that share of business and would have paid for additional foreign exchange of Rs. 15 crores in 10 years.

6. In 1970, GTC paid Rs. 83 lakhs as wages to 1350 workers which amount to Rs. 6150 per head per year. ITC paid Rs. 762 lakhs to 12,000 workers which comes to Rs. 6350 per head per year. Keeping in view the size of operations, GTC pays far better than its competitor.

Vazir Sultan Tobacco Company

B.A.T.—London invested less than Rs. 7 lakhs when it bought over VST and by capitalization of profits its equity today stands at Rs. 2 crores—over and above an almost equal amount in reserves and surpluses. Foreign shareholding in VST today is 67% and its assets are worth Rs. 6 crores!

Its profit before tax last year was Rs. 203 lakhs.

VST's registered capacity is 8800 million cigarettes a year, yet in violation of the Industries (Development & Regulation) Act, they have been producing far in excess of this capacity. On top of all this, they now want further expansion of 250%!

Appendix 6 Position of Cigarette Industry in States of India (Based on 1967 figures)

State	Sales (million cigts.)	Production (million cigts.)	Deficit	Sales Value (Rs. million)	Excise (Rs. million)
Assam	1903	nil	1903	9.51	5.71
Gujarat	1631	nil	1631	8.15	4.89
Jammu & Kashmir	1468	nil	1468	5.87	3.52
Kerala	3154	nil	3154	15.77	9.46
Madhya Pradesh	2284	nil	2284	9.14	5.48
Orissa	971	nil	971	3.88	2.33
Punjab	5275	nil	5275	26.37	15.82
Rajasthan	761	nil	761	3.04	1.83
Tamil Nadu	6525	nil	6525	32.62	19.57
Union Territories	3535	nil	3535	17.67	10.60

Appendix 7 Eloquent Facts and Figures on the Cigarette Industry in India

The substantially foreign-owned cigarette monopoly in India, affiliated to a powerful world combine, has wiped out over 200 indigenous cigarette factories in the past four decades—most of them before Independence and the rest thereafter.

During the decade ending 1969, the monopolist's turnover has increased by over 300 per cent as against a meagre 6 per cent increase in the paid-up capital.

The monopolist's production is far in excess of the registered installed capacity whereas the production of most of the indigenous units falls far short of their registered installed capacity.

In Independent India the annual production of cigarettes has phenomenally risen to 300 per cent, the total production being over 6,000 crores of cigarettes and the sales exceeding Rs. 250 crores.

The cigarette industry contributes by way of excise duty to the Central Exchequer Rs. 150 crores representing 60 per cent of the industry's total sales turnover.

Even after 23 years of Independence over 80 per cent of India's cigarette production is controlled by substantially foreign-owned companies, the share of the monopoly alone being as much as 70 per cent.

These companies in India cause a drain on foreign exchange to the tune of Rs. 3.5 crores by way of remittance of dividends in addition to Rs. 18.5

crores by way of deferred liability in the form of reserves and surpluses for future repatriation.

India ranks as the second largest tobacco producer and exporter in the free world–next to the U.S.A.

The excellence of Indian Virginia (cigarette tobacco) has earned an international fame. It is being exported to U.K. and many other European countries.

India earns foreign exchange to the tune of about Rs. 35 crores annually by exporting cigarette tobacco.

The Indian Virginia tobacco trade–both domestic and export–is controlled to the extent of 75 per cent by another foreign monopoly closely affiliated to the world cigarette combine.

In the case of match and soap industries 100 per cent foreign monopolies were reduced (to 50 and 40 per cent respectively) by pegging their production and allowing increase to wholly Indian-owned companies. Unless similar steps are taken, Indian cigarette industry will continue to be dominated by substantially foreign-owned monopoly and will never have its rightful place in our economy.

Increase in cigarette production is 3000 to 5000 million pieces per year, affording scope for more than one factory to be started every year.

In a judicious dispersal of the industry, the 11 States where there are no cigarette factories at present can also have cigarette factories which will increase revenue and employment and also help ancillary industries to come up.

Source: Pratap Narsee, *Foreign Monopoly in Cigarette Industry in India,* New Delhi: Indian Cigarette Manufacturers Association, 1970, pp. 9–12, 23–24, and 55–57.

Discussion Questions

1. What benefits do both the host government and the MNC seek from each other?
2. Discuss the impact of the United States' foreign direct investment on the economy of 1) the host country, and 2) the home country, particularly on trade and employment.
3. What would be the reasons for the host governments to control the MNCs' operations? What kinds of control measures have been used by the industrially developed and developing countries? Are there substantial differences between developed and developing countries in this regard?
4. Give some examples of the MNCs' influence on the sociocultural systems of a host country.
5. What will some of the new threats and opportunities for MNCs be during the 1980s and 1990s compared with the 1970s?
6. What strategies would be available to MNCs to resolve social conflicts in host countries, both industrially developed and developing?

Endnotes

1. U.S. Senate, *Implications of Multinational Firms for World Trade and Investment and for U.S. Trade and Labor*, Report to the Committee on Finance of the U.S. Senate and its Subcommittee on International Trade on investigation no. 332-69, under section 332 of the Tariff Act of 1930, Committee of Finance, February 1973; United Nations, *Multinational Corporations in World Development* (New York: United Nations, 1973).
2. *Multinational Corporations in Developed Countries: A Review of Recent Research and Policy Thinking* (Washington, D.C.: British-North American Research Association, 1974).
3. *U.S. Stake in World Trade and Investment: The Role of Multinational Companies* (New York: National Association of Manufacturers, 1972).
4. *The Impact of U.S. Foreign Direct Investment on U.S. Employment and Trade: An Assessment of Critical Claims and Legislative Proposals* (New York: National Foreign Trade Council, Inc., 1971).
5. Jacques Maisonrouge, quoted by Donald M. Kendal, "The Need for the Multinational Corporation," in *The Multinational Business World of the 1980s*, ed. John K. Ryans, (Kent, Ohio: Center for Business and Economics Research, Kent State University, 1974), p. 22.
6. Kendal, Ibid., p. 23.
7. Emile Benoit, "The Attack on the Multinationals," *Columbia Journal of World Business* 5, 6 (November-December 1970): 15.
8. Frank Shaker, "The Multinational Corporation: The New Imperialism," *Columbia Journal of World Business* 5, 6 (November-December 1970): 84.
9. United Nations, *Multinational Corporations*, p. 2.
10. Robert Hawkins, et al., "Government Takeovers of U.S. Foreign Affiliates," *Journal of International Business* 7, 1 (1976): 9.
11. Stephen J. Kobrin, "Foreign Enterprise and Forced Disinvestment in LDCs," *International Organizations* 34, 1 (Winter 1980): 65–88.
12. Ibid., pp. 85–86.
13. Ibid.
14. John Fayerweather, "Ninteenth Century Ideology and Twentieth Century Reality," *Columbia Journal of World Business* 1, 4 (Winter 1966): 77.
15. Raymond Mikesell, et al., *Foreign Investment In the Petroleum and Mineral Industries* (Baltimore: Johns Hopkins University Press, 1971), p. 30.
16. Fred C. Bergsten, "Coming of Investment Wars?," *Foreign Affairs* 53, 135 (1975): 152.
17. Anant R. Negandhi and B. R. Baliga, *Quest for Survival and Growth* (New York: Praeger Publishers, 1979).
18. David F. Fry, "Multinational Corporations–Host Government Relationships: An Empirical Study of Behavioral Expectations," Doctoral Dissertation, Kent State University, 1977).
19. Anant R. Negandhi and Martin Welge, *Beyond Theory Z: Global Rationalization Strategies of American, German, and Japanese Multinational Companies* (Greenwich Conn.: JAI Press, 1984), pp. 77–113.
20. C. F. Bergsten, et al., *American Multinationals and American Interests* (Washington, D.C.: The Brookings Institution, 1978) pp. 342–344.
21. See "The Raw Economy, Australia: A Survey," *The Economist*, October 31, 1981, pp. 5–26. The Labor Party has regained power; this may change the situation again.

22. "The Takeover of Australia Private Ltd. by the Multinationals," featured in "Four Corners," ABC National Television Public Affairs, November 5, 1977.
23. See "Foreign Backing," *The Sydney Morning Herald*, November 3, 1977, p. 9.
24. "Four Corners," pp. 30–31 of transcript.
25. Ibid.
26. N. Goldfinger, cited in Stanley J. Ruttenberg, *Needed: A Constructive Foreign Trade Policy* (Washington, D.C.: The Industrial Union AFL-CIO, 1972), p. 11.
27. *Wall Street Journal*, May 14, 1981, p. 1.
28. Majak R. Roger, "When all Else Fails, National Industrial Planning," in Mark Winchester, ed., *International Essays for International Decision Makers*, Vol. 5 (Houston: The Center for International Business, 1980), p. 7. For a more comprehensive study on foreign investment policies and the concern of major industrialized countries, see the current study of A. E. Safarian, *Governments and Multinationals: Policies in the Developed Countries* (Washington, D.C.: British-North American Committee, 1983).
29. Quoted from John M. Greddes, "Trouble in Bonn," *Wall Street Journal*, October 30, 1981, pp. 1 and 16.
30. Ibid.
31. Jack N. Behrman, *Decision Criteria for Foreign Direct Investment in Latin America* (New York: Council of the Americas, 1974), p. 47.
32. Ibid.
33. U.S. Senate, *Multinational Corporations and United States Foreign Policy*, Hearings before the Subcommittee on Multinational Corporations of the Committee on Foreign Relations, U.S. Senate (Washington, D.C.: U.S. Government Printing Office, 1976), p. 3.
34. A. E. Safarian and Joel Bell, "Issues Raised by National Control of the Multinational Enterprise," in *Multinational Corporations and Governments: Business-Government Relations in an International Context*, eds. Patrick M. Boarman and Hans Schollhammer (New York: Praeger Publishers, 1975), p. 74.
35. Raymond Vernon, "Multinational: Powers vs. Sovereignty," *Foreign Affairs* 49, 4 (1971): 736–751.
36. Negandhi and Baliga, *Quest for Survival*, 13–41.
37. Jack N. Behrman, "Control of the Multinational Enterprise: Why? What? Who? and How?," in *Multinational Corporations*, eds. Boarman and Schollhammer, p. 22.
38. Neil Jacoby, "Corporate Power and Responsibility," in *Multinational Corporations*, eds. Boarman and Schollhammer, p. 21.
39. USA-BIAC Committee on International Investment and Multinational Enterprise, *A Review of Standards and Guidelines for International Business Conduct* (New York: USA-BIAC), 1973, p. 10.
40. Ibid., p. 11.
41. Ibid.
42. United Nations, "United Nations Conference on Trade and Development," Resolution 56 (III), Foreign Private Investment in its Relationship to Development, adopted on May 19, 1972, *Multinational Corporations in World Development* (New York: United Nations, 1973).
43. George W. Ball, quoted in "Business and Developing Countries," The Liebold Institute, p. 31.
44. Safarian and Bell, "Issues," pp. 82–83.
45. Ross R. Millhiser, "The Multinational Corporation: The Economic Bridge," lecture presented to the Graduate School of Business Administration, Duke Uni-

versity, Durham, NC (New York: Philip Morris, Inc., Communication Department, 1975), p. 4.

46. W. Ouchi, *Theory Z* (Reading, Mass.: Addison-Wesley Publishing Co., 1981).
47. For an account of industrial planning undertaken in Japan and the European countries, see Ezra E. Vogel, "Japan as No. 1: Lessons for America (Cambridge, Mass.: Harvard University Press, 1979), especially Chapter 4, pp. 53–96; and L. G. Franko, *European Industrial Policy: Past, Present and Future* (Brussels: The Conference Board in Europe, 1980).
48. Stephen J. Kobrin, "Morality, Political Power and Illegal Payments by Multinational Corporations," *Columbia Journal of World Business* XI, 4 (Winter 1976): 105–110.
49. Ibid.
50. See Edward R. Luter, "The Tobago Syndrome: The Extraterritorial Application of U.S. Laws and Its Impact on International Trade," in *The International Essays for Business Decision Makers*, ed. Mark E. Winchester (New York: Amacom, 1979), pp. 19–31.
51. Ibid., pp. 33–34.
52. Ibid., pp. 42–43.
53. See "Minding Other People's Business," *The Economist*, August 29, 1977, pp. 20–21; and Robert Mueller and David Brund, "Britain Orders 4 Firms to Defy U.S Pipeline Ban," *Wall Street Journal*, August 3, 1983, p. 30.
54. Warren H. Schmidt, "Values and the American Manger: An Update," *California Management Review* XXVI, 3 (Spring 1984): 202.
55. Irwin Ross, "How Lawless are Big Companies?" *Fortune*, December 1980, pp. 57–63.
56. Steve Brenner and Earl Mollander, "Is the Ethics of Business Changing?" *Harvard Business Review* 55, 1 (January-February 1977): 57–71.
57. James E. Post, "Assessing the Nestle Boycott: Corporate Accountability and Human Rights," *California Management Review* XXVII, 2 (Winter 1985): 113–131.
58. Ibid., p. 113.
59. Ibid., pp. 129–130.
60. "Union Carbide Fights for Its Life," *Business Week*, December 24, 1984, pp. 52–61.
61. Thomas N. Gladwin and Ingo Walter, "How Multinationals Can Manage Social Conflict," in *Governments and Multinationals*, ed. Walter H. Goldberg (Cambridge, Mass.: Oelgeschlager, Gunn & Hain, Publishers, Inc., 1983), pp. 78–101.

Additional Readings

Articles

Graham, John L. "Foreign Corrupt Practices: A Managing Guide." *Columbia Journal of World Business* XIIX, 3 (1983): 89–94.

Johnes, Peter T. "Sanctions, Incentives, and Corporate Behavior." *California Management Review* Vol. XXVII, No. 3 (Spring 1985): 119–131.

Post, James E. "Assessing the Nestle Boycott." *California Management Review* XXVII, 2 (Winter 1985): 113–131.

Vernon, Raymond. "Multinational Enterprise and National Governments: Exploration of an Uneasy Relationship." *Columbia Journal of World Business* XI, 2 (Summer 1976): 9–16.

Books

Goldberg, Walter H., and Negandhi, Anant R. *Governments and Multinationals* (Cambridge, Mass.: Oelgeschlager, Gunn, & Hain Publishers, Inc., 1983).

Negandhi, Anant R., and Baliga, B. R. *Quest for Survival and Growth: A Comparative Study of American, European, and Japanese Multinationals* (New York: Praeger Publishers, 1979).

Vernon, Raymond. *Storm Over the Multinations* (Cambridge, Mass.: Harvard University Press, 1977).

Part II

Strategic Aspects of International Business Corporations

- *Organizational Design and Structure of International Corporations*

- *Policy Making and Control in International Corporations*

- *Decision Making and Headquarters-Subsidiary Relationships in International Corporations*

- *Long-Range Planning and Environmental Scanning in International Corporations*

Chapter 3

Organizational Design and Structure of International Corporations

This chapter will discuss significant issues relating to the organizational design and structural aspects of international operations. The topics to be analyzed in some detail include the following:

- Designing approximate organizational structures
- Theoretical rationales involved in designing structures
- Evolutionary nature of organizational structures
- Organizational structures of United States, European, and Japanese companies
- Multifocused strategies to control and coordinate organizational activities

- Impact of the organizational structure on organizational effectiveness

Preceding the analyses of these aspects, I will briefly explain the meaning and definition of an organization.

Short summaries of the cases pertaining to this chapter's material are provided at the end.

Meaning and Definition of an Organization

Organization theory and management literature contain many definitions of an *organization.* It has been viewed as: (1) a system of communication; (2) a means of facilitating decision making; (3) a social system involving interpersonal relationships; and (4) a managerial function of organizing that involves grouping activities, establishing authority and responsibility relationships, coordinating different functional activities in pursuit of achieving overall organizational objectives and goals, and delegation of authority.[1]

There seems to be a dividing line between the organization theorist and the management theorist regarding how the organization is conceived and studied. Organization theorists place greater emphasis on studying interpersonal relationships among people within a given organization; they use their observations as a "springboard to observe all other activities of an organization."[2] Management theorists advocate multiple functions of management, of which establishing a cooperative interpersonal relationship is only one of many activities. To them, organizational activity or function represents the grouping of activities—departmentalization—providing a system of coordination for different activities, and establishing authority and responsibility relationships among people working in a given organization.[3]

Organization and management theorists, as well as practicing managers, have paid concerted attention to one common issue: the delegation of authority and decentralization in decision making. Particularly in the last three decades or so, management concepts such as "participative or consultative management," "theory Y," "management by objectives," and now "theory Z"[4] have become overused expressions among theorists and practitioners alike. All of these concepts essentially convey the same message: the delegation of authority and decision making power to the lower managerial and nonmanagerial personnel.

This chapter views organization as one of the managerial functions involving structuring tasks, grouping activities, and structuring authority and communications systems within a firm.[5]

Designing Appropriate Structures

There are various organizational design forms available to managers. These include: (1) functional structure, (2) product-based structure, (3) area-based structure, and (4) matrix structure.

A critical issue facing the manager of international corporations is how to choose the appropriate or most organizational structure. There is no clear-cut answer; however, one can deduce some guidelines from the various studies. As shown in Table 3-1, each one of the organizational forms possesses strengths and weaknesses.

1. *Functional structure* (International Division) is useful for deploying specialized skills and training. It fosters professional identity but creates difficulties for coordination among different departments. This structural arrangement is more appropriate for the firm producing standardized products, and is at the early stages of developing international business, having low product and area diversities. Many of the firms in extractive industries (petroleum and mining) use this type of structure because of the standardized products and low geographical and product diversities. Small and medium-sized companies will find this type of structure more suitable.

2. *Product-based structure* simplifies the coordination task, enables growth without losing control, and provides a stronger motivation to divisional heads. It is more suitable for experienced companies in international business with diversified product lines and extensive research and development activities. The main disadvantages of this structure are that it duplicates resources, discourages the development of functional skills (e.g., marketing, finance), and encourages suboptimization among divisions. Many conglomerates such as Gulf and Western and highly diversified firms such as General Electric adopt this type of structure.

3. *Area-based structure* is useful for firms that have a wide geographical spread and mature, standardized products. It also simplifies coordination among different functions, and permits growth without losing control. It enables the firm to respond easily to the environmental and market demands of a given area through minor modifications in product design, pricing, publicity, and packaging. The main disadvantages are the same as those for the product-based structure. Many food, beverage, automobile, and pharmaceutical companies use this type of structure.

4. *Matrix structure* is useful for firms that are both diversified and geographically spread. It is useful to balance the powers of product managers and geographical area managers. Its main disadvantages are a dual authority structure, resulting in time delays,

Table 3-1 Types of organizational structures: attributes, advantages, and disadvantages

Types	Attributes	Strength
Functional Export Dept. (International Division)	1. Divisions according to major tasks of the organization (e.g., production, marketing, personnel)	1. Fosters professional identity and career paths for members 2. Ease of supervision 3. Allows maximum specialization in trained occupational skills 4. Other departments have access to specialized skills
Product	1. Division according to products or services	1. Simplifies coordination among functions 2. Permits growth without loss of control 3. Permits accountability for performance 4. Divisional goals are clear, providing motivation for divisional management 5. Decision authority is moved closer to the problem
Area	1. Division according to end user regions	1. Simplifies coordination among functions 2. Permits growth without loss of control 3. Permits accountability for performance 4. Divisional goals are clear, providing motivation for divisional management 5. Decision authority is moved closer to the problem
Matrix	1. Two complete and simultaneous organizing dimensions 2. Dual reporting responsibilities	1. Enriched flow of information 2. Enhanced control 3. Resource flexibility 4. Attention paid to balance in organization

Types	Characteristics	Strengths
Market-oriented	1. Division according to similar pattern of need, purchasing behavior, or product use	1. Efficiencies in marketing and production 2. Services as an aid to planning
Mixed types	1. Division by two or more dimensions simultaneously; each division only partially complete	1. Permits maximum attention to product, area, and/or functional needs 2. Useful as a transitional structure before implementation of a matrix
Product and area		1. Deals with capital budgeting problem 2. Allows transfer pricing
Function and product		1. Specialization of functions despite product lines
Function and area		1. Specialization for regional markets

Types	*Weaknesses*	*Suitable for*	*Examples*
Functional Export Dept.	1. Creates major differences among departments	Stable company in stable environments	Industries: petroleum aluminum
Product	1. Duplication of resources among departments 2. Reduces specialization in occupational skills 3. Encourages competition among divisions 4. Encourages suboptimization	Growing company with dissimilar product lines	Industries: automobile companies; Gulf & Western; General Motors, Chrysler

Continued

103

Table 3-1 Continued

Types	Weaknesses	Suitable for	Examples
Area	1. Duplication of resources among departments 2. Reduces specialization in occupational skills 3. Encourages competition among divisions 4. Encourages suboptimization	Mature company with narrow product lines	Industries: food, pharmaceuticals, beverage. Companies: AT&T, IRS, Postal Service
Matrix	1. Structurally unstable 2. Conflicts are engendered and/or intensified	Company facing two equally important challenges, e.g., product diversity and need for functional or area expertise	Industries: electronics companies: General Electric, Dow Chemical, Citicorp, Bechtel, Philips
Market-oriented	1. Coordination and control may be difficult	Market-oriented company with good communication networks	Companies: Richardson-Merrill, Ingersol-Rand
Mixed types	1. Coordination and control are difficult 2. Duplication of efforts among departments	Company in transition or company whose products display differing growth patterns	Many companies in initial stage of internationalization
Product and area	1. Coordination problems 2. Doesn't allow functional specialization		

104

Function and product

1. Coordination
2. Doesn't take geography
   into account

Function and area

1. Coordination
2. Doesn't allow product focus

Source: Adapted from Daniel Robey, *Designing Organizations: A Macro Perspective*, Homewood, Ill.: Richard D. Irwin, Inc., 1982, p. 327.

creation of power struggles, and "groupitis" mentalities. Dow Chemical, Philips, Bechtel, and Citicorp are some of the firms that have tried this type of structure.

As indicated in Table 3-1, besides these "pure" types, various hybrid types of organizational structures are used by both domestic and international corporations. Such organizational structures contain elements of two or more bases for designing organizations. Thus they maximize the major advantages and minimize the disadvantages of the given type.

Theoretical and Conceptual Considerations

Chandler's thesis of "structure follows strategy"[6] has been used frequently to explain and predict the evolution of organizational structures of multinational companies.

> Growth without structural adjustment can lead only to economic inefficiency. Unless new structures are developed to meet new administrative needs which result from an expansion of a firm's activities into *new areas, functions,* or *product lines,* the technological, financial, and personnel economies of growth and size cannot be realized. (emphasis added)[7]

The overall contention here is that as the firm expands its activities either through geographical diversification or increased product lines and the end use of the products, the firm, to be effective, must change its structure from a centralized, functional form to a decentralized divisional structure. Chandler's paradigm has been empirically tested both in the United States and abroad. For example, Rumelt, in his longitudinal study of United States firms, found that the proportion of diversified firms had increased significantly since the 1940s, and, correspondingly, the proportion of multidivisionally organized firms had increased during the four decades of the 1940s to the 1970s.[8]

At the international level, the extensive work of the Harvard Multinational Enterprise Project Group, under the direction of Raymond Vernon, used Chandler's paradigm to explain and predict the evolution of organizational structures of United States, European, and Japanese multinational companies.[9]

Evolutionary Nature of the Organizational Structure

In tracing the evolution of the organizational structures of multinational companies, the Harvard Group indicated that a firm's structure would evolve from

Table 3-2 Evolution and growth of international business and corresponding changes in organizational structures and formalizations

Evolution and growth of international business	A. Evolution of organizational structure	B. Other structural characteristics
I. Initial stage	Export dept.	Loose formal relationships
II. Early production stage	Export dept./ international division	More formalized relationships between hq* and sub†
III. Standardization of production process— mature stage few products	International division	Increased formalized relationships
IV. Product innovations and growth through diversification	Product/area bases for structuring of organization	Increased formalization
V. Quest for global rationalization	Product/area bases for structuring/matrix type organization	Increased formalization

*Hq: Headquarters
†Sub: Subsidiaries

the export department to the global structure, as the firm increases its overseas activities. These changes in a firm's international activities, and corresponding changes in the organization structure, are portrayed in Table 3-2.

As one can see from Table 3-2 and Figure 3-1, at the earlier stage of the international business activities, the firm manages its overseas business through the export department, which maintains loose formal relationships with the overseas distributors. By the time the firm has established four to six manufacturing subsidiaries overseas, a more formal linkage with the foreign operations becomes a necessity. Under these circumstances, the international division within the domestic organizational structure is estab-

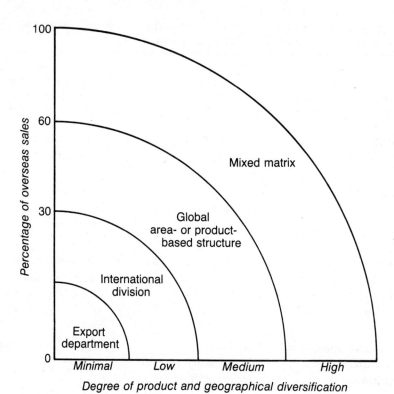

Figure 3-1 Evolution of the organizational structure of multinational companies (*Source:* Adapted from W. Davidson, *Global Strategic Management,* New York: John Wiley and Sons, 1982, p. 274.)

lished to communicate with and coordinate the subsidiaries's operations. In the next stage of expansion of overseas business through production and diversification, the international division becomes extremely overloaded and experiences conflicting demands from the domestic units and the corresponding overseas operations. Its ability to coordinate the subsidiaries's operations becomes insufficient, and some other form of organizational structure to manage the overseas business is now needed. At this point, depending on the nature of the expansion strategies—i.e., either through product diversification or through geographical expansion—will the firm establish a product-based global organization structure or an area-based structure (i.e., North America, Western Europe, Latin America, or Asia).

This discussion of the relationship between strategy and structure is based on a rational, logical model, which assumes that the firm has strong control over its internal and external environmental factors. To put it differently, as indicated in Chapter 1, those using Chandler's theoretical rationale *overemphasize* the internal aspects of organizational policy making and *underemphasize* the impact of external environmental demands, especially from the host countries. Consequently, the actual organizational structure and design of the multinational company may not match the theoretical predictions.

In the following section, I will present empirical evidence concerning the organizational structures of United States, European, and Japanese multinational companies and its impact on the firms's growth and profitability.

Organizational Structures of United States Multinational Companies

The concept of global organizational structure (either product- and/or area-based, or matrix type) is not altogether new. During the 1950s and 1960s, both academic scholars and practicing managers articulated a need for such an organizational structure to manage worldwide business. In 1959, for example, Clee and Discipio,[10] consultants to McKinsey and Company, argued for a global perspective for international and multinational corporations. The essentials for creating such a world corporation included total commitment by the top-level executives in international management, as well as an assumption of full responsibilities for strategic global planning and decision making. However, their own survey of large United States multinational companies revealed that only a handful of companies had adopted a global structure.[11]

Similarly, Clee and Sachtjen,[12] in 1964, indentified three different types of organizational structures used by United States MNCs: (1) international division, (2) area-based global structure, and (3) product-based global structure. The majority of the companies, however, were retaining the international divisions to manage their overseas business. In other words, the evolution of organizational structures was slow in coming despite the fact that the international division form was becoming ineffective in managing the growth of international business activities. Lovell[13] found a similar trend in his survey of 150 United States companies. Only 5% of the companies adopted some sort of a global concept, whereas 85% of the companies assigned responsibility for international activities to one single executive or a single division. The executives surveyed, however, stressed the need for a global structure.

In a large-scale study of 187 United States MNCs, Stopford and Wells[14] found that approximately one half of the companies had already changed their structures, reflecting the global orientation; the other half, still retaining international divisions, were experiencing serious problems of coordination and communication with their overseas subsidiaries.

Table 3-3 Organizational structures of United States, European, and Japanese multinational companies

Nationality of MNCs	Direct reporting (%)	Structural design		Total (%)
		International division (%)	Global structure (%)	
United States	0	67	33	100
European	39	17	44	100
Japanese	13	87	0	100
Total	18	48	34	100

Source: Managing the Multinational Subsidiary by James M. Hulbert and William Brandt. Copyright © 1980 Praeger Publishers. Reprinted by permission of Praeger Publishers.

Recent Studies

Suzman,[15] in his longitudinal study of nine United States companies, observed that only three of them had adopted a global structure, whereas the others were still moving from the export department to the international divisional form. This shift in organizational structure was rather gradual.

Hulbert and Brandt,[16] in their study of United States, European, and Japanese companies, found that only one third of the United States companies surveyed had adopted a global structure; the other two thirds were still maintaining international divisions to manage their worldwide business. This clearly reflects the predominance of a domestic market orientation in the United States companies. In contrast, as shown in Table 3-3, the European companies were much more globally oriented.

Our recent study also does not support the earlier predictions by the Harvard Group. Of the nine large United States MNCs, only one seems to have adopted a global structure, whereas four are retaining their international divisions to coordinate overseas business activities. The other four adopted mixed structures, using their international divisions, overlapping with second organizing dimensions of either product or area concentration. The German MNCs, on the other hand, seem to be operating with the global concept. Three out of eight German MNCs studied used the global structure to manage and coordinate their domestic, as well as their international, business.[17] These results confirm the overall trend reported by Schollhammer[18] almost a decade ago. The German global structure reflects their long-standing commitment to international business and the realities of a small domestic market.

Like many United States companies, the Japanese MNCs operate through their international divisions. Ten out of fourteen companies studied have retained this structural arrangement.

Regional Headquarters

During the mid-1960s and early 1970s, there was a considerable move toward establishing regional centers or headquarters for coordinating the various national markets in a given region. Regionalism seems to be losing its attractiveness as a mode of carrying out global rationalization of production and marketing plans. During the early 1970s, it was estimated that approximately two thirds of the large MNCs maintained some sort of a regional headquarters.[19] However, a current study of thirty-one MNCs reveals that only one third of these companies were coordinating their international business through regional centers. Among these, Japanese MNCs seem to favor regional offices the most, and Germans the least. The regional centers were being used as information posts rather than as decision-making centers.

Tall Versus Flat Structures

In the literature on organizational design and structure, many studies and controversial findings have concerned the effects of "tall" *versus* "flat" structures. Among these, the classical study by Worthy, of Sears, Roebuck and Company,[20] indicates that the "flat" type of organizational structure (meaning a larger number of subordinates) was more effective than the "tall" type (smaller number of subordinates) in terms of employee morale, work satisfaction, and productivity. The underlying rationale for the greater effectiveness of a flat structure seemingly resulted from a higher level of delegation of authority given to the subordinate, or the greater degree of decentralization in decision making. However, in later studies, such conclusions have been challenged on the basis of the complex nature of the relationships among structure and such organizational and personal variables as size, technology, location, skills, and personnel training.[21] Moreover, the existence of tall *versus* flat structures may itself be a poor indicator of the degree of centralization and decentralization in decision making.[22]

Organizational Structure *Versus* Multifocused Strategies

The multinational companies seem to use multifocused strategies to manage their worldwide business. As Bartlett has observed, "changes in formal organization provided only one means of change."[23] To understand the shift toward the global concept, one needs, therefore, to "think of structure in much more complex and subtle terms than the formal organization chart."[24]

To understand the multifocused strategies, an examination of the following aspects may be useful:

- Level of formalization
- Reporting mechanism between the headquarters and the subsidiaries
- Relative decision-making influences of the headquarters and the subsidiaries (see Chapter 5)

Level of Formalization

To study the level of formalization among the United States, German, and Japanese multinational companies, three aspects were examined:

1. The subsidiaries' dependence on manuals, policies, and procedures supplied by the headquarters
2. Use of these policies and procedures for strategic and policy-level decision making
3. The nature and the frequency of reports required by the headquarters[25]

Figure 3-2 shows the extent to which the subsidiaries of United States, German, and Japanese multinational companies depended on the written policies of the headquarters. An overwhelmingly large number of United States subsidiaries (88%) relied on the headquarters' policies. Approximately one third of the German subsidiaries did the same, whereas merely 12% of the Japanese subsidiaries depended on the policies supplied by their headquarters. Conversely, only 6% of the United States, 48% of the German, and 66% of the Japanese subsidiaries indicated a negligible influence of the headquarters's policies on their individual operations.

A similar picture emerged when we examined the influences of the written policies and procedures (whether those supplied by the headquarters or modified by the subsidiaries) on actual strategic and policy-level decisions.

The level of formalization pursued by the United States companies, as compared to the German and the Japanese companies, changed very little. In other words, the United States MNCs' drive toward unification and integration of policies is quite intense, whereas the German and the Japanese MNCs still prefer to operate with more flexible and diffuse policies. Only one third of the German subsidiaries and 12% of the Japanese subsidiaries use the formal manuals and policy guidelines supplied by their headquarters for making strategic and policy-level decisions.

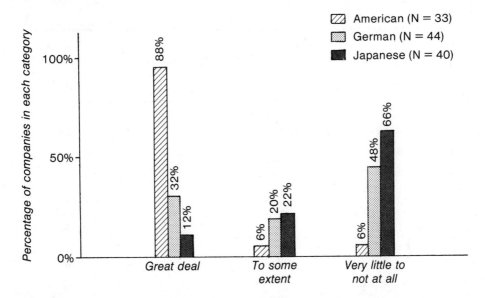

Figure 3-2 Extent to which subsidiaries depend on written policies from headquarters

An earlier comparative study, undertaken from 1968 to 1970, also shows that the majority of United States subsidiaries are highly formalized. They rely on written policies and manuals for such organizational tasks as personnel selection, hiring and dismissal, promotion, accounting, and financial matters. Formalizations and documentations were so detailed that they irritated some of the local employees working in those subsidiaries.[26]

Inkson and his colleagues,[27] in their comparative study of United States and British firms, reported that the former use considerably more formalized procedures than the latter.

The formalization of policies and procedures may indeed be the initial step toward achieving unification and integration into global operations. However, such a high level of formalization is not achieved without stress and a negative impact on the personnel of the subsidiaries.

Further evidence of increasing levels of formalization can be seen from Table 3-4, which reports the data on the types of policy manuals supplied by the headquarters. Here too, the United States leads the way. An overwhelming 88% of United States MNCs supplied multiple policy manuals to the subsidiaries, and they did not differentiate between subsidiaries located in industrially developed *versus* semideveloped countries. These manuals cover such functions as technical and product decisions, sales and marketing, personnel and industrial relations, and accounting and financial matters. In contrast to the United States MNCs, less than one half of the German and

Table 3-4 Types of policy manuals supplied by the headquarters

	(N = 34) United States MNCs 1 (%)	(N = 45) German MNCs 1 (%)	(N = 41) Japanese MNCs 1 (%)
Technical and product designs	03	12	21
Sales/marketing	–	–	08
Personnel-industrial relations	–	09	–
Accounting/financial matters	06	31	13
Manuals for all major functions	88	41	45
No manuals supplied to subsidiaries	03	07	13

Source: A. R. Negandhi and M. Welge, *Beyond Theory Z*, Greenwich, Conn.: JAI Press, Inc., 1984, p. 16.

Japanese MNCs sent formal manuals to their subsidiaries, and those subsidiaries located in semideveloped countries were even less formalized.

Remarking on global rationalization and the resultant higher levels of formalization and reporting requirements, Vernon states: ". . . over the past few decades an increasing proportion of the world's largest firms have tended to favor an organizational structure having the world as its domain . . . [while] differences based on national factors have been obliged to take a second place."[28]

Referring to the differences arising among United States, German, and Japanese MNCs, because of distinctive national histories and national cultures, Vernon goes on to say:

> . . . The Americans can still be counted on to develop unusually elaborate tables of organization, job descriptions, and operating procedures, and to feel uncomfortable in the presence of more ambiguous systems of control; the Germans can still be expected to approach strategic decisions as if they were the sum of a series of technical questions and to give unusually large scope to their technicians to provide the definitive response. . . . For the Japanese, one important purpose of the formal structure is to provide titles and rank . . . the decision-making process itself is more diffuse.[29]

However, these differences in decision making among United States, German, and Japanese MNCs are narrowing fast. The drive for global rationalization and unification of policies seems to be contagious, and the United States was leading the way even before the concept of the multinational enterprise came into vogue.

Reporting Requirements

One can also evaluate the headquarters' relative influences on the subsidiaries' operations by examining the nature and frequency of the reports required from the managers.

As shown in Table 3-5, almost all United States subsidiaries, and approximately two thirds of German and Japanese subsidiaries are required, by their respective headquarters, to provide up-to-date information on balance sheet, profit and loss figures, production output, market share, cash and credit positions, inventory levels, and sales per product. The frequency of reporting is

Table 3-5 Frequency of monthly report required from subsidiaries by the headquarters

Type of Report	United States MNCs (33)	German MNCs (44)	Japanese MNCs (40)
Balance sheet	97	49	42
Profit and loss statements	91	49	42
Production output	94	50	47
Market share	70	48	31
Cash and credit statement	100	41	39
Inventory levels	88	46	38
Sales per product	88	37	44
Performance review of personnel	9	15	2
Report on local economic and political conditions	33	32	12

Source: A. R. Negandhi and M. Welge, *Beyond Theory Z*, Greenwich, Conn.: JAI Press, Inc., 1984, p. 18.

greater for United States (mostly monthly) than for German and Japanese subsidiaries.

It is revealing to note from this table that the subsidiaries are less bothered with performance reviews of their personnel and the local socio-economic and political conditions. In other words, the stress is placed more on those aspects affecting the short-run financial picture of the company rather than on the factors affecting the firm's long-term survival and growth.

The analyses of these aspects of formalization clearly indicate the increasing levels of formalization being introduced by United States multinational companies. And the German and the Japanese MNCs, although maintaining more flexible attitudes, are also attempting to catch up with the United States' modes of operating, especially in industrialized countries, where until now the market forces where the main determinants of organizational practices and managerial behavior.

Similar results on extensive formalization and reporting requirements by multinational enterprises have also been reported by other researchers. For example, with respect to the reporting requirements, Schollhammer,[30] in his study of twelve multinational companies in chemical and phamaceutical industries, found only negligible differences between United States and European MNCs.

There have been some changes in the level of formalization and control policies in European multinational companies. During the 1960s, European firms exercised very little control over their overseas subsidiaries. For example, Rocour,[31] in his study of European MNCs in 1966, found the following situation:

No control excercised by the headquarters	37%
Little direct control	41%
Fairly close supervision	12%
Tight controls	10%
	(N = 52)

The managers of subsidiaries resist high levels of formalization and control by the headquarters. This has been borne out in various studies.[32]

Japanese companies, on the other hand, seem to have mastered the so-called "Z" mode of operation in which organizational members are acculturated and socialized toward a common set of organizational and societal values.[33] Given such an orientation, the headquarters can be less concerned about losing their control, in spite of higher autonomy afforded to the subsidiary operations. The salient attributes of the Japanese organizational structure are portrayed in Table 3-6.

Table 3-6 Japanese management – characteristics of organizational types

Type A (American)	Type J (Japanese)	Type Z (Modified American)
Short-term employment	Lifetime employment	Long-term employment
Individual decision making	Consensual decision making	Consensual decision making
Individual responsibility	Collective responsibility	Individual responsibility
Rapid evaluation and promotion	Slow evaluation and promotion	Slow evaluation and promotion
Explicit, formalized control	Implicit, informal control	Implicit, informal control with explicit, formalized measures
Specialized career path	Nonspecialized career path	Moderately specialized career path
Segmented concern	Holistic concern	Holistic concern, including family

Source: William G. Ouchi and Alfred M. Jaeger, "Type Z Organization: Midst of Mobility," *Academy of Management Review* 21, 3, (September 1978): 308–311.

Organizational Structures of European Multinational Companies

Historically, the European companies' organizational structures used to reflect informal headquarters and subsidiary relationships, higher autonomy of the overseas subsidiary, and direct reporting by the subsidiary's managers to the top management in the home office. The immediate years after World War II, because of the existence of seller's market conditions and earlier practices of cartelization, discouraged long-term planning and policy making. To put it differently, as Hulbert and Brandt have observed,

> In early days of overseas investment, home office executives were not so concerned with managerial control as they were with profitable entrepreneurial venture. Men were sent abroad and were expected to run the business independently, maintaining little more than a profit-remitting relationship with the home office. . . . Managers were told to go with God and send home the profits.[34]

The advent of the European Common Market and the increasing internationalization of European firms changed this picture. Franko,[35] for example, has shown that increasing size and level of geographical and product diversification in European MNCs creates pressure for change in organizational structures. The yesteryear "mother-daughter" relationship between the home office and the overseas subsidiary is being replaced with a more formalized relationship. As shown in Table 3-7, some 70% of 127 large Euro-

Table 3-7 Changes to divisionalized structures by large European organizations (through December 31)

Headquarters	*Companies divisionalized in 1972 (%)*
Switzerland	85
Italy	57
Germany	60
France	48
Holland	84
Belgium and Luxemburg	67
Sweden	71
United Kingdom	80
Total	70

Source: Adapted from Lawrence G. Franko, "The Move Towards a Multi-Divisional Structure in European Organizations," *Administrative Science Quarterly* 20, 4 (December 1975): 494.

pean MNCs had changed their organizational structures to a divisionalized form, based on either global product and/or area.

Similarly, Hulbert and Brandt,[36] in their survey of United States, European, and Japanese companies, found that about 44% of the European companies were using global structures (see Table 3-3). Only a minority (17%) were operating through the international divisional structures.

Overall, it seems that the European MNCs, although maintaining more adaptable strategies and structures than the United States companies, are coming closer to the United States management system of more formalized structures and processes of controls. Hulbert and Brandt have observed that:

> Regardless of the preferences expressed by today's managers, the changes occurring in European firms are likely to continue. Many of the larger and more diversified European multinationals look very much like their American counterparts . . . a process more fundamental than cultural or historical differences may be fostering these changes.[37]

Organizational Structures of Japanese Multinational Companies

Recently, much has been said and written about the effectiveness of Japanese organizations. The adaptive, flexible organizational structure, informal, nonhierarchical authority relationship, nonformalized controls, long-term profit orientations, lifetime employment practices, and deep concern for employee welfare have been singled out as worthwhile attributes in managing organizations.[38]

Indeed, as we will see in succeeding chapters, the Japanese employment practices and their concern for employee welfare are different both for cultural and for strategic reasons. And such practices may have considerable impact on their organizational structures and designs. However, research evidence on the Japanese multinational companies' structures requires some caution in making broad generalizations concerning their practices. Furthermore, it has been argued that the basic differences in the organizational structures of United States and Japanese companies may be the result of the inexperience of the latter in international business.

Although Japanese companies have been exporting since the 1950s, they are still newcomers to overseas manufacturing. For example, until 1966, Japan had invested a total of $200 million in overseas manufacturing, mostly in extractive industries. The Japanese total direct overseas investment in all sectors, including service industries, was $1.5 billion in 1966, compared to $56.6 billion by United States companies. However, during recent years, their foreign investment has increased sharply, to $27 billion in 1979. Such expansion in foreign investments has induced the Japanese companies to take a second look at their organizational arrangements.

As Yoshino's[39] research indicates, Japanese companies are under pressures to modify their structures. They seem to follow a pattern established by the United States firms. At an earlier stage, the export divisions assumed considerable power in managing overseas business activities, including manufacturing. However, by the time the firms were operating four manufacturing subsidiaries abroad, the need for new structural forms became more evident. Yoshino reports that 80% of the fifty Japanese companies he had studied created an international staff to deal directly with the managers of the overseas manufacturing subsidiaries. Similarly, Hulbert and Brandt's[40] study shows that 87% of the Japanese companies they had studied already had adopted some form of international division to manage overseas business. Given the importance of the direct export of goods by Japanese companies, both the export departments and the international divisions coexist. My study of Japanese MNCs indicates that ten out of fourteen companies operated through an international division structure. In addition, the majority of these companies also established regional headquarters to coordinate their overseas activities.

Whether Japanese companies will eventually adopt global organizational structures remains uncertain, although Yoshino argues forcefully that they should. The following paragraph summarizes Yoshino's recommendations:

> Japanese management faces a serious dilemma. In order to undertake major expansion internationally, the Japanese must bring about basic changes in their management system. The extent to which they can achieve such a feat is by no means certain. But, more important, in the process they may well lose those very elements which have made their system so effective internally. The optimist would cite the remarkable ability of the Japanese to achieve what appears impossible through their ingenuity and diligence; he would also point to the great success of the Japanese in selective assimilation of foreign institutions and technology. Clearly, however, what is demanded now of Japanese management is fundamentally different from the adoption of certain elements of foreign cultures into the tight and homogeneous cultural setting. The past offers no assurance in this regard, and the outcome is by no means certain.[41]

Japanese Multinationals and Japanese Trading Companies

No discussion on Japanese multinational companies will be complete without mentioning the role and structure of Japanese trading companies, known as *Sogo Shosha*, originated from *Zaibatsu*, a large conglomerate controlled by powerful families. Because of their large size, they are most effective in handling large megaprojects, turnkey plants, and other major and minor investment projects.

Although around 8,000 Japanese trading companies exist, a large bulk of both domestic and international business is undertaken by the nine largest trading companies. These are: Mitsubishi, Mitsui, C. Itoh, Marubeni, Sumitomo, Nissho-Iwai, Toyo Menka Kaisha, Kanematoh-Gooho, and Nichimun. Together they control 55% of Japanese imports and 48% of the exports.

The vital element of their success is the close, symbiotic relationship with the Japanese government. They are known to coordinate their activities closely with the overall policies laid down by the Ministry of International Trade and Industry (MITI).

Organizational structures of major trading companies are simple, but their communication network is extensive. This is illustrated in Figures 3-3 and 3-4.

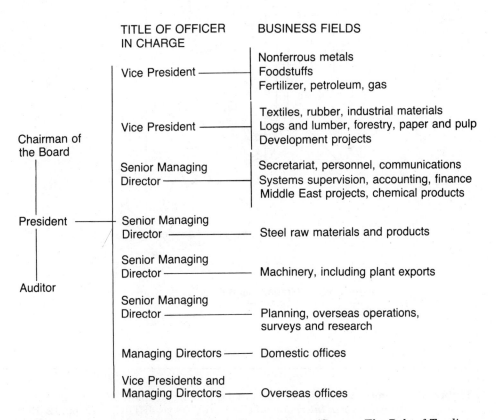

Figure 3-3 Organization of a major trading company (*Source: The Role of Trading Companies In International Commerce,* Tokyo: JETRO, 1976, p. 29.)

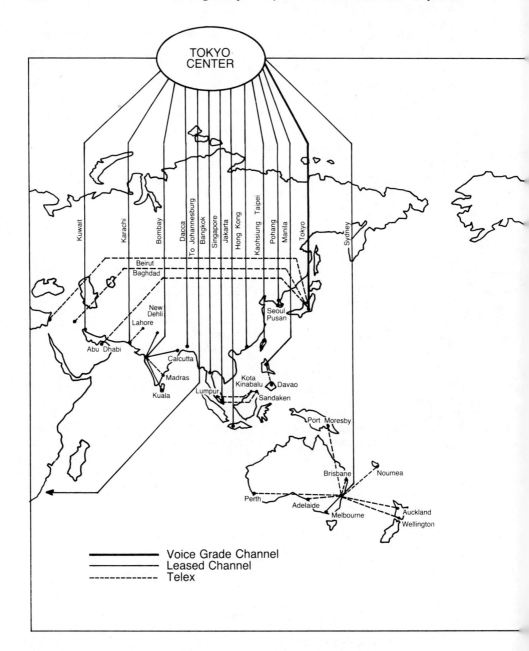

Figure 3-4 Communications system of a major trading company (*Source: The Role of Trading Companies in International Commerce,* Tokyo: JETRO, 1976, pp. 12–13.)

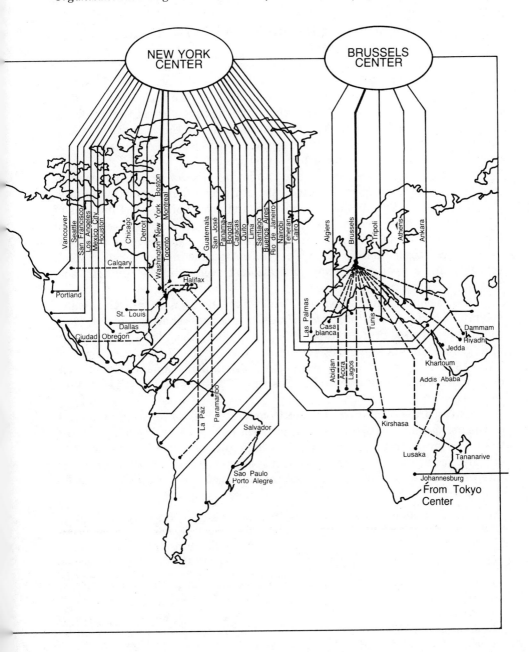

Organizational Structure and Effectiveness

Some have suggested that the global structure is more effective in terms of return on assets, operating return on assets, and return on sales.[42] As shown in Table 3-8, the profitability of the subsidiaries of the multinationals using international divisions and direct reporting was much lower than of those using global structures. Franko also reported that the European firms using direct reporting structures (mother-daughter relationships) experienced lower growth rates than those with other structures.[43]

Research evidence is limited and cannot provide an overall generalization concerning the impact of a given structure on a firm's growth and profitability. This is partially because growth and profitability are functions of many other factors, such as market and economic conditions, political and legal situations, and the firm's monopolistic leverage in the given markets.

The analyses of financial data of *Fortune* magazine indicate a rather weak relationship between the global unification strategy and the financial success of the company.[44]

The least integrated Japanese firms show the highest growth in sales and profits and the most integrated United States firms show the lowest. More specifically, United States multinational companies recorded approximately 18% growth in sales and 19% in profits during the three-year period of 1977–1979. In contrast, German and Japanese multinational companies experienced 25% and 28% growth in sales, and 22% and 49% growth in profits, respectively.

One can draw similar conclusions from a recent study reported by Lecraw on the performance of transnational corporations in the less developed countries. The growth rate for United States companies was much lower than for Japanese companies. Generally speaking, Japanese companies are the least integrated of the three types of multinationals.[45]

Table 3-8 Profitability of subsidiary by structural design of organization

Organization variable	Profitability measure			
	Return on equity (%)	Return on assets (%)	Operating return on assets (%)	Return on sales (%)
Structural design				
Direct reporting	10.5	4.9	26.2	4.1
International division	16.8	9.1	29.0	8.0
Global structure	25.3	10.2	31.5	7.4
Total	19.1	8.7	29.4	7.0

Summary

This chapter discussed the organizational designs and structures of international corporations. Using Alfred Chandler's theoretical paradigm of "structure follows strategy," a number of studies were carried out among the multinational companies. These were reviewed in more detail. The result indicates the following trend:

1. Although the evolutionary nature of the organizational structure of the multinational companies is well articulated, the actual shift in structures has been slow and gradual.
2. Many of the large United States MNCs are still retaining international divisions to coordinate and manage their overseas business operations. The same is true concerning Japanese companies.
3. In contrast, the European MNCs are more inclined to use a global concept in managing their worldwide business.
4. Organizational designs and structures by themselves are not good indicators of unification and integration strategies. The multinational company may use multifocused strategies to unify and integrate its worldwide business.
5. The level of formalization of policies, reporting requirements, and the relative influences of the headquarters and overseas subsidiary in decision making are some of these elements of multifocused strategies.
6. Studies indicate that the level of formalization and reporting requirements are higher in the United States MNCs as compared to European and Japanese MNCs. However, the latter companies are catching up with the United States in these aspects. As we will see in Chapter 5, the United States MNCs are more centralized in decision making than their European and Japanese counterparts, but here also the latter are narrowing the differences.
7. The relationship between organizational structure and organizational effectiveness seems to be less clear-cut. Many other factors seem to have greater impact on organizational effectiveness.

Case

The case in this chapter highlights the evolving structures and their impact on the functioning of international corporations. It focused on how and why an MNC needs to coordinate and integrate its fast-growing overseas business into the domestic operations. The case stresses the importance of not only the organizational structure, but also the strategic orientation of the top management.

Case 3-1

Brown Boveri: Six Years After McKinsey Came

*James McArdle**

Since the Swiss market is so small, Swiss companies of any substantial size are usually multinational. Brown Boveri, the Swiss maker of power generating and other heavy electrical equipment, has long been a classic example. Its German offshoot has for most of its life been larger than its parent, and because of the nationalistic nature of the power generating business, Brown Boveri & Company (BBC) has had to let its foreign affiliates have almost complete autonomy in their national markets. BBC has shown over the years that it is possible for a multinational supplier of power generating equipment to succeed without a large domestic market. Nevertheless, in 1970 a thorough reorganization was started, and those apostles of centralised management control, the McKinsey management consultants, were called in to recommend structural reforms for the Brown Boveri organisation.

The reasons for the reorganization do not leap immediately to the eye from a cursory examination of Brown Boveri's accounts over the years, though it must be said that the interpretation of Swiss company reports raises difficulties at the best of times. BBC management felt that operating results could be better; that the long standing and probably inevitable policy of geographical diversification, which involved production of similar products in affiliates in more than one country, was leading to an unnecessary amount of duplication of investment; that research and development in particular needed to be centralised a good deal more than it was; and that there was in general a complex problem in deciding exactly how to gain what could be gained from the fashionable trend among multinational companies towards

*At the time of writing a consultant with the EIU. © Copyright *The Economist.* Permission of the publisher is greatly acknowledged.

centralised control and structure, in a company whose business and peculiar circumstances defied centralisation.

Whatever was contained in McKinsey's confidential report, it is clear that BBC management imposed characteristics of its own upon the reorganisation. The company was and remains deliberate and slow moving; it took considerable time to implement the McKinsey changes, and is still in the course of evolution. The reasons for this are the very ones that caused BBC to call in McKinsey in the first place: BBC's international marketing problems and strategies.

BBC is a "National" Company in its Various Markets

Fundamentally, Brown Boveri must still be identified as a "national" company in each of the markets in which it operates. Competitors claim that BBC is "foreign" and is therefore a higher risk supplier and a strategic threat to the domestic industry. This can be a powerful disincentive to potential customers, most of whom are government owned or else closely regulated. It is a major reason why BBC's hard won toehold in the US market is under constant threat, and why its share of US business is disproportionately low, given its international standing.

The BBC companies in Germany and France do have strong local identification built up after years of genuine independence of management. In Mannheim the company has been operative since the turn of the century. The French division, Cie electro-Mécanique (CEM) is even older. Both of these companies form autonomous profit centre divisions known confusingly in BBC as Groups, within the new five Group management structure. A third is formed by the Swiss manufacturing base at Baden together with the former Oerlikon artillery engineering company and the Secheron factory. The remaining two are the so called Medium Sized Group, with seven manufacturing bases in Europe and South America, and Brown Boveri International, which encompasses the rest. In terms of products, there are five product subdivisions: power generation, power distribution, electronics, traction and industrial equipment. Thus each of the five Groups contains up to five product divisions, depending on its product range.

BBI Controls Export Marketing

Brown Boveri International also performs the function of controlling all export marketing operations. Orders for export are allocated by BBI in Baden to member subsidiaries according to their capacity, and with a view to maximising overall "Konzern" profitability in the light of tariff barriers, costs, exchange rates, taxation, government incentives, and export finance. Exports are allocated to the Swiss manufacturing division on the same basis as to any other, at least in theory. But, presumably because of the presence of the highly successful international sales and marketing organisation in Baden,

BBC Baden is geared to a level of demand quite unrelated to the size and type of its domestic market, and its production is remarkably stable. Exports for the whole BBC Konzern are somewhat under 30 per cent of sales, but for the last three years the export performance of the Swiss division has been 70, 70 and 80 per cent of sales.

This cross border selling is the key to BBC profitability, being generally more lucrative than domestic orders. Sales within the EEC area account for 60 per cent of the total, with another 20 per cent in other European countries. This indicates a large potential for expansion in the Americas, Africa and Asia. The heart of the business is power distribution and conversion (with 19.5 per cent of the Swfr7.7 bn – £1.75 bn – turnover last year) and power generation (21 per cent of the total). Another 20 odd per cent is accounted for by industrial and transport goods. Household and professional products are a meagre 4.5 per cent.

BBC Damps the Cycle Through Geographical Diversification

Brown Boveri is thus heavily weighted towards the capital investment side of electrical engineering, and therefore must expect to be affected by investment cycles. Geographical diversification rather than product diversification is the key to company stability. Last year the German subsidiary, which accounts for 45.5 per cent of sales and 41 per cent of group employees, increased its sales by 15 per cent and its order book by a huge 55 per cent. None of this improvement was apparent in either the French group or the Spanish subsidiary, both of which lost money in 1975. A good deal of manufacturing overlapping still occurs because of the geographical organisation. This is judged to be inevitable given the political nature of power generation. In the major European markets, substantial domestic capacity is the prerequisite for major contracts. Hence it is possible for different parts of the company to experience quite different trading results. The barometer for the whole organisation, however, is the Swiss division or Group. This had sales in 1975 of Swfr1.76 bn, of which Swfr1.4 bn were exports. This represented a rise of a fifth, but it always has to be borne in mind that the strength of the Swiss franc means that BBC's results are understated. In 1974, sales in Swiss francs registered a rise of only 3 per cent. They would have been 18 per cent higher under a constant exchange rate – that is, if exchange rates in all countries had remained at their 1973 cross rates.

BBC is Prevented from Expanding Employment in Switzerland

This financial peculiarity of Swiss multinationals affects BBC. In 1973 the company was asked by the Swiss government not to expand employment in Switzerland. Major investments in future had to be outside the country. Over

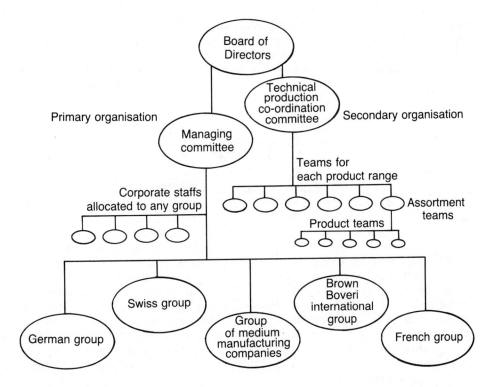

Figure 3-5 Brown Boveri group organization (*Source:* J. McArde, "Brown Boveri: Six years after McKinsey came," *The Economist,* 2, 1976.)

the years this will necessarily increase the weight of the German and French divisions – although under the McKinsey structure they only have one seat each on the six man Konzern Managing Committee (one for each Group, plus a man for corporate strategy) which is now attempting to centralise all power and decision taking in BBC. The other four seats are Swiss, i.e. occupied by Swiss citizens.

The power of BBI in Switzerland lies in its control over exports, although the Swiss manufacturing division is dwarfed by the German subsidiary which is a larger, more integrated and diversified company. In particular the Germany company incorporates BBC's entry into the nuclear power business. The influence that may bring to bear is of course tempered by the fact that this strategic area has not been a conspicuous success. It has 55 per cent of Hochtemperatur Reaktobau in Cologne, but the other 45 per cent is held by Gulf Energy Systems, which is rapidly winding down its business after making massive losses on high temperature reactors. BBC also has 26 per cent of a consortium company with Babcock and Wilcox of the USA specialising in design and construction of nuclear power stations. This cooperation with a US partner is important to BBC, which is under great competitive pressure in the US from Westinghouse and General Electric. BBC has sold generating equipment in the US to some of the largest utilities such as Tennessee Valley, and American Electric. But recently competitiveness has been eroded by the upward revaluations of the key European currencies—not least the Swiss franc—and a US manufacturing base is now an urgent necessity if BBC is to hold on to a share of the market.

How to Tackle the American Market: A Major Problem for BBC

This constitutes a major strategic challenge for BBC. The company does not believe that it can serve a major market without a major local manufacturing base. It has strong ideas about quality control and the need for after sales service to maintain a long term market share. The company has considered opening such a plant in the USA, but the investment is apparently considered prohibitive, and moreover the market has remained relatively depressed, hardly encouraging new entrants. New entry is also made much more difficult by the still unresolved pace of technical change, particularly that associated with nuclear power. Brown Boveri has faced up to this problem many times in the past decade, without finding any obvious solution. In fact the question has been shelved several times, particularly as US competition was pushed back in other world markets. The large new business which has been successfully opened up in the Middle East has provided further grounds for postponement.

In 1968 the stage seemed set for an arrangement with Rockwell for them to manufacture for BBC under licence. Rockwell, heavily committed to space and military programmes, badly needed to diversify. There seemed to be clear benefits on both sides. However, BBC eventually backed away, not liking the financial terms. Rockwell approached BBC again as late as 1973, on hearing that the latter was still studying the possibility of manufacture in the USA, but was rejected. To date there are turbo generator service facilities, but no solution to this key strategic problem of the US market is in sight.

George Kent Provided an Entry Ticket to the UK—

A happier marriage—from BBC's point of view—was the acquisition in 1974 of 49 per cent of the equity of George Kent, a major UK manufacturer of instrumentation and control equipment. The firm's capability in industrial control equipment complements the existing range of BBC products and adds to BBC's all round competitiveness in international markets. It is less obvious, however, whether this will help BBC gain a toehold in the UK heavy electricals market—which is in any case not one of the most attractive world prospects.

The initial agreed bid was announced in August of 1974. This bid involved the transfer of all George Kent assets, but excluding scientific instruments companies in which BBC was not interested. A new company was planned, to be called Brown Boveri Kent. BBC would own a majority, 53 per cent, of the equity of this company, at a cost of £6.1 mn. While this bid was approved by the board of George Kent, it ran into immediate political difficulties, occasioned because the Department of Industry had ownership of almost 25 per cent of the company's equity.

Anthony Wedgwood Benn was secretary of state for industry at that time, and strongly opposed the idea of his department becoming a minority holder in a domestic company possessed of valuable technology but controlled by a foreign multinational. We have previously reported (Multinational Business No. 4–1974) how the department attempted to encourage a counter bid by the UK owned General Electric Company (GEC). GEC would own 50 per cent of George Kent's equity, the government 41 per cent and the remaining major shareholder, the Rank Organisation, 9 per cent. But BBC, and for that matter the board of George Kent, determined to fight and decided that the labour force should express its views. BBC was able to assure George Kent employees that within the context of a multinational organisation there would be massive export orders and possibly even 1,500 more jobs. At the same time BBC increased its offer on a per share basis and opted for a politically more acceptable 49 per cent of the equity. GEC weakly responded to the BBC thrust by promising George Kent employees that there would be no redundancies in the event of the GEC bid being successful, but with a reputation for ruthlessness arising from its takeover of AEI in the 1960s GEC was not believed. Predictably, in retrospect, the vote went overwhelmingly in favour of BBC. Benn observed that the workers had been properly consulted and voted for the BBC offer. GEC withdrew, and shortly afterwards Rank also capitulated.

... And an International Network of Subsidiaries

Prior to the acquisition of a controlling interest in George Kent Limited, the United Kingdom was virtually the only major European economy in which BBC did not have a strong manufacturing base, and consequently BBC was hardly represented in the British market. In addition to acquiring a British presence, BBC has assumed the international network of George Kent subsidiaries. These companies are located throughout Europe, the Americas, Australia, the Far East and Africa. Thus, it should be possible to integrate the international George Kent organisation with that of BBC on a European scale at least. The man much concerned with this problem, and with increasing the profitability of the group, is Erwin Bielinski, former executive chairman of George Kent, former head of corporate planning for BBC, and now head of Brown Boveri International, sitting on the Konzern Managing Committee. Bielinski has been reporting directly to the Konzern Managing Committee. However, as he has now become head of Brown Boveri International, George Kent Limited will be incorporated into the Brown Boveri International division and will report to Bielinski in Baden.

Will Brown Boveri Kent Attain "Group" Status?

The inclusion of George Kent within the BBI division reflects the special role that the company and its various subsidiaries will play in complementing BBC's international capability. Apart from the German, French and Swiss companies which form divisions in their own right, nearly all of the European BBC companies belong to the division of medium manufacturing companies. However, George Kent and its international network require coordination from the centre. Whether Brown Boveri Kent ever develops into a large enough organisation to achieve the status of a BBC division depends upon the policies of expansion and acquisition to be adopted. It is likely that profitability rather than growth is the immediate objective. The post merger strategy of improving productivity and delivery dates is still continuing.

More Acquisitions in Foreign Markets Are Likely

The severe limits imposed on expansion in Switzerland since 1973, the current high exchange value of the Swiss franc, and the trend that customers demand manufacture, in so far as is possible, within their own national territory, points to a continued policy of acquisition in foreign markets. It is only in recent years that BBC has made a serious effort to coordinate its operations between countries. Prior to 1970 there was very little cross border coordination of product or marketing strategies. Member divisions and companies operated within their national territories independent of any central unifying strategy. Thus, BBC amounted to a loose federation of units with an historically built in duplication of resources to a greater extent than might be justified by market or political necessity. Possibly the protected nature of heavy electrical engineering markets resulted in the assumption at BBC that there was no choice but to allow member companies to function autonomously. However, this fragmentation and duplication of resources necessarily limited the scale of operations of the whole organisation at a time when it was realised that massive amounts of new capital would be needed. The new structure is built around the idea of central control of essentials, such as product coordination, while at the same time preserving the identities, and goodwill, of the major European components.

The New Structure

Central to the new structure, following the 1970 McKinsey report, is the concentration of a great deal of power in one executive and policy making body at the summit of the organisation. This body is called the Konzern Managing Committee (KMC). As already mentioned, it is composed of the heads of the five divisions with the addition of one member with special responsibility for strategy. Such a structure may be a McKinsey trade mark but in the case of Brown Boveri it fulfills the additional aim of integrating the jealously independent national subsidiaries into some semblance of a single minded multinational corporation.

Corporate staff departments for research, technical coordination, management development, planning, finance and control, and marketing, supplement the KMC at headquarters. In addition, four Konzern Committees set policy for research, technical strategy, nuclear energy and marketing, but the fact that these committees are each presided over by a member of the KMC probably inhibits their originality and independence.

The KMC is Represented at Lower Levels

The representative of each Group on the KMC is responsible for communicating KMC decisions to the Group concerned. The KMC is represented on the board of each manufacturing company by members or delegates additional to the KMC Group representative. The impression of decisions being handed down in the form of orders is carefully avoided; nevertheless KMC recommendations are usually carried out. It is felt that this is the case not because of the undoubted ability of the KMC to apply pressure, but because it is willing to take a pragmatic view of efficiency within the Konzern and is attuned to the political needs of the subsidiaries.

The management is Swiss dominated. The chairman of the Swiss home subsidiary also heads the six man KMC, which also includes the heads of BBI, the Medium Sized Group, and Brown Boveri technical strategy. These three are also managing directors of the Swiss Group.

A Secondary Organisation Runs Through the Company

A secondary organisation runs horizontally through the company coordinating product specifications. This secondary organisation is three tiered and is made up of individual product teams, teams for each product range, and a technical product coordination body. These teams are horizontal counterbalances to vertical divisions. The principal function of the members of these teams is to obtain clearance for proposals made by their respective companies so that these can be incorporated directly into annual plans and budgets. Given this motivation it seems unlikely that teams would, on their own initiative, produce proposals for the rationalisation of any product throughout the Konzern. This is why the third layer was set up, in 1974, for "technical product coordination". This body is composed of three corporate staff senior executives and its main objective is to promote R & D and production rationalisation efforts in the product and product range teams. While the product coordination and rationalisation process might appear fragmented it does allow very full discussion. However, outside of the very limited scope of accepted local autonomy, all executive action in the field of product coordination and rationalisation is confined to the KMC.

The Divisions Negotiate for Their Share of Exports

All Konzern international marketing activities are centred in Brown Boveri International in Baden. The head of BBI is a member of the Swiss dominated Managing Committee; he also chairs the marketing committee, and all corporate marketing staff come under his jurisdiction. BBI has profit responsibility for all activities outside Germany, France, Switzerland, and the Medium Sized Division. It has split this responsibility into four regions: i. Africa and Asia, ii. Canada and Latin America, iii. Europe (including Eastern Europe), and iv. United States of America.

The prime central activity of BBI is the allocation of export orders to member divisions. Corporate marketing staff within BBI decide to which affiliate an export order should be allocated. Allocation is made on the basis described above. Each division begins the financial year with an export allocation budget based on their own forecasts. The forecasts are discussed at a meeting of the Konzern marketing committee – each marketing manager negotiating for his share of anticipated exports. This avoids dictation from the centre and enhances the autonomy of the affiliates. Over the years export based growth has, however, resulted in Swiss capacity being out of all proportion to the requirements of its diminutive home market. The allocation process permits the Swiss management to ensure that the Swiss operation benefits from available world demand. Exports by BBC Baden rose from 70 to 80 per cent of its total sales last year – a measure of Swiss "control of essentials". The average figure for the whole Konzern was 29 per cent in 1974.

Once an export order or enquiry is allocated it is the responsibility of the chosen affiliate to tender independently for the contract. Orders received by a division from within its own territory are not allocated at BBI's discretion but remain with the receiving group. It is free to subcontract elements of an order to other Konzern companies though there is no obligation to subcontract exclusively within Brown Boveri. It is interesting to note that since Brown Boveri Kent is part of BBI, contracts obtained in the UK for products outside Kent's capability automatically enter the BBI export pool for allocation, without having to be negotiated.

BBC enjoys a reputation for quality and workmanship of the highest order. The company has established a name with major utility companies in the United States, despite the enormous disadvantage of being foreign. When it rejected Rockwell a BBC company spokesman claimed that "US production standards and trade union practices being what they are, neither Rockwell International nor, probably, any other US firm would have been able to fabricate our equipment up to our traditionally high specifications". This attitude has not endeared BBC to North American manufacturers and no punches have been pulled in attempting to keep BBC out of the USA and Canada. Recently, BBC successfully defended a charge of "dumping" circuit breakers on the Canadian market. BBC went on to acquire the Tamper Electrical Division of Canadian Canron Ltd, making electric motors and generators and drive equipment for industrial plant and rail transport.

Research is Centrally Coordinated

Research is carried on at two broad levels: pure research and applied product research. In Group terminology, pure research is not divorced from profitability; however, it is in general concerned with fundamentals rather than with specific products. As might be expected, the main Konzern centre for pure research is in Switzerland. Limited research programmes are carried out by BBC Mannheim in Heidelberg and by CEM in Le Bourget, but the Segelhof centre at Dattwil keeps a firm Swiss hand on BBC's technology. The centre opened at the end of 1972. Its conception coincided with the streamlining of the Group's activities and epitomises central Swiss control of essentials.

Product research is carried out in Switzerland, Germany and France independently of pure research, but it too is subject to central coordination. Product research is normally financed by the specific manufacturing unit. Where the product is single sourced this generalisation is easily applied. Where more than one subsidiary is in a position to benefit, allocation of costs and the location and coordination of research is negotiated through a high level research committee. Pure research is financed according to much the same principle; costs are shared according to agreed central estimates of divisions likely to benefit from a particular programme. Predictably, allocation of costs not geared to immediate profit is seldom a cut and dried issue. However, management philosophy, here as elsewhere, incorporates the principal of negotiation. Conflicts in this as in any other area are settled by discussion of national and Konzern interests. Major decisions involving different national interests are, eventually, unanimous.

The centralisation that took place after 1972 increased the scope and scale of research, and the fund for such spending dropped by over a half in two years. It is replenished by royalties income, which more than doubled over the same period to 4.9 per cent of BBC Baden turnover in 1974.

Areas of research at Dattwil include one dimensional metals, permanent magnets, thyristors for high voltages, silicon in the context of high power electronic devices, high temperature materials, ceramics, lasers, liquid crystals in information displays, plasma physics, automatic control theory and super ionic conductors.

The Reorganised BBC Intends to Remain a World Leader

BBC is determined to remain one of the major manufacturers of heavy electrical engineering equipment in the world. About 6,000 people are engaged in research and development, on which the company spends some Swfr450 mn a year. As a result of heavy research investment the company is technologically advanced and in some areas it is a world leader. One such example is circuit breakers for electrical substations. BBC specifications are probably ahead of any other manufacturer in this field—including the North American giants.

Following reorganisation BBC is more able to view the world market as one large oyster rather than as a collection of separate more or less succulent ones. Cross border production and marketing strategies have been established. Duplication of sales and manufacturing capability in different European markets is inevitable given the importance of being able to compete as a domestic supplier. However, multisourcing imparts great flexibility to the overall marketing function. Export orders can be allocated between subsidiaries to maximise advantage to the Group.

The company has a policy of careful acquisition and purchases are made with integration on an international scale in mind. The acquisition of a controlling holding in George Kent Limited is a good example of systematic expansion, since that company's capability in instrumentation and control equipment complemented the resources of BBC's major European divisions. The company is also able to consider selling out of loss making situations. It went a long way down the road to selling its loss making Italian subsidiary before negotiations stalled. The great question surrounding the future of BBC is whether or not the company will eventually set up manufacturing facilities in the United States, come to a licensing arrangement with a US company, or hope to improve on its modest but significant success with the American utilities from its European base alone. In 1974 sales in North America accounted for only 3.5 per cent of the worldwide total and no advance was made in 1975. Latin America and Africa are each more important, while Europe accounted for about 80 per cent of turnover. BBC recognises the importance of the US market; the board held a press conference to say so in 1973. But following a disappointing year in 1975, continuing overcapacity, and a successful shift to selling a quarter of the export order book to the Opec countries, it seems likely that the long term US strategy will continue to get fairly low priority.

The Brown Boveri Updates* _____

- In 1978, BBC formed a joint venture with Gould, Inc. in the United States.
- In 1980, BBC bought out Gould's 50% stake and owned 100% of equity in the United States.
- In 1982, BBC was one of the top one hundred international corporations outside the United States with $4.7 billion of revenue and 94,000 employees.

*The updated information was compiled from various sources by Mannsoo Shin, a Ph.D. student of the University of Illinois at Champaign.

Questions for Discussion

1. Discuss the four major types of organizational structures.
2. What considerations would be necessary to design an effective organizational structure?
3. Discuss the argument of the evolutionary nature of the organizational structure. Also, test the validity of this concept using some examples.
4. What are the multifocused strategies of control used by the various MNCs?
5. Compare the key global strategies and the organizational structures of United States MNCs with those of Japanese and European MNCs.
6. What is the relationship between the organizational performance measures, such as survival, growth, and profitability, of the United States, Japanese, and European MNCs and their respective organizational structures?

Endnotes

1. See James March and Herbert Simon, *Organizations* (New York: John Wiley and Sons, 1958); and H. Koontz and C. O'Donnell, *Principles of Management*, ed. 4 (New York: McGraw-Hill Book Co., 1968).
2. Simon and March, *Organizations*, pp. 84–111.
3. Koontz and O'Donnell, *Principles*, pp. 24–25.
4. William Ouchi, *Theory Z* (Reading, Mass.: Addison-Wesley Publishing Co., 1981).
5. The analysis of the structural aspect follows Max Weber's model of bureaucracy. Max Weber, *The Theory of Social and Economic Organization*, trans. Henderson, A. M. and Parsons, T. (New York: Oxford University Press, 1947).
6. Alfred D. Chandler, Jr., *Strategy and Structure* (Cambridge, Mass.: MIT Press, 1962).
7. Ibid., p. 60.
8. Richard Rumelt, *Strategy, Structure, and Economic Performance* (Boston: Harvard Business School, Harvard University, 1974).
9. John M. Stopford and Louis T. Wells, *Managing the Multinational Enterprise* (New York: Basic Books, 1972); Lawrence G. Franko, *The European Multinationals* (Stanford, Conn.: Greylock Publishers, 1976); and Michael Yoshino, *Japan's Multinational Enterprises* (Cambridge, Mass.: Harvard University Press, 1976).
10. G. H. Clee and A. Discipio, "Creating a World Enterprise," *Harvard Business Review* 37, 6 (November-December 1959): 77–89.
11. Ibid.
12. G. H. Clee and W. M. Sachtjen, "Organizing a Worldwide Business," *Harvard Business Review* 42, 6 (November-December 1964): 55–67.
13. Enid Baird Lovell, *Organizing Foreign-Based Corporations* (New York: National Industrial Conference Board, 1961).
14. Stopford and Wells, *Managing*.
15. Cedric Suzman, "The Changing Nature of Export Management," *Atlanta Economic Review* 1, 1 (September-October 1975): 15–20.
16. James M. Hulbert and William K. Brandt, *Managing the Multinational Subsidiary* (New York: Holt, Rinehart and Winston, 1980).

17. For more details see Anant R. Neghandi and Martin Welge, *Beyond Theory Z: Global Rationalization Strategies of America, German, and Japanese Multinational Companies* (Greenwich, Conn.: JAI Press, Inc., 1984), Chap. 2, pp. 9–27.
18. Hans Schollhammer, "Organizational Structure of Multinational Corporations," *Academy of Management Journal* 14, 3 (1971): 345–365.
19. David A. Heenan, "The Regional Headquarters Decision: A Comparative Analysis," *Academy of Management Journal* 22, 2 (1979): 410–415.
20. J. Worthy, "Organization Structures and Employee Morale," *American Sociological Review* 15 (1950): 169–179.
21. See Rocco Carzo and John N. Yanquzas, "Effects of Flat and Tall Organization Structure," *Administrative Science Quarterly* 14, 2 (June 1969): 187.
22. Hulbert and Brandt, *Managing*, pp. 10–34.
23. Christopher Bartlett, "Multinational Structural Evolution: The Changing Decision Environment in International Divisions," paper presented at the conference on The Management of Headquarter-Subsidiary Relationships in Transnational Corporations, Stockholm School of Economics, Stockholm, Sweden, June 24, 1980.
24. Ibid.
25. Negandhi and Welge, *Beyond Theory Z*, pp. 13–16.
26. See Anant R. Negandhi and S. Benjamin Prasad, *The Frightening Angels* (Kent, Ohio: Kent State University Press, 1975), Chaps. 4 and 5.
27. J. H. Inkson, et. al., "A Comparison of Organization Structure and Managerial Roles: Ohio (USA), and the Midlands (England)," *Journal of Management Studies* 7, 3 (1970): 347–363.
28. Raymond Vernon, *Storm Over the Multinationals* (Cambridge, Mass.: Harvard University Press, 1977), pp. 31–32.
29. Ibid.
30. Schollhammer, "Organizational Structure," pp. 455–456.
31. Jean-Luc Rocour, "Management of European Subsidiaries in the United States," *Management International* 1 (1966): 13.
32. See Anant R. Negandhi and B. R. Baliga, *Quest for Survival and Growth* (New York: Praeger Publishers, 1979), Chap. 3.
33. Ouchi, *Theory Z*, pp. 39–55.
34. Hulbert and Brandt, *Managing*, p. 17.
35. Franko, *European Multinationals*, pp. 198–201.
36. Hulbert and Brandt, *Managing*, p. 16.
37. Ibid., p. 18.
38. Ouchi, *Theory Z*, p. 58.
39. M. Y. Yoshino, "Emerging Japanese Multinational Enterprises" in *Modern Japanese Organization and Decision-Making*, ed. Ezra F. Vogel (Berkeley: University of California Press, 1975), pp. 146–166.
40. Hulbert and Brandt, *Managing*, p. 19.
41. Yoshino, "Emerging Japanese," p. 166.
42. Hulbert and Brandt, *Managing*, p. 32.
43. Lawrence G. Franko, *European Business Strategies in the United States* (Geneva: Business International, 1971).
44. Negandhi and Welge, *Beyond Theory Z*, pp. 70–75.
45. Donald J. Lecraw, "Performance of Transnational Corporations in Less Diversified Countries," *Journal of International Business Studies* XIV, 1 (Spring/Summer 1983): pp. 15–33.

Additional Readings

Articles

Davis, Stanley M. "Trends in the Organization of Multinational Corporations." *Columbia Journal of World Business* XI, 2 (Summer 1976): 59–71.

Drazin, Robert and Howard, Peter. "Strategy Implementation: A Technique for Organizational Design." *Columbia Journal of World Business* XIX, 2 (Summer 1984): 40–47.

Negandhi, Anant R. "Management Strategies and Policies of American, German, and Japanese Multinational Corporations." *Management Japan* 18, 1 (Spring 1985): 12–20.

Pitts, Robert A., and Daniels, John D. "Aftermath of the Matrix Mania." *Columbia Journal of World Business* XIX, 2 (Summer 1984): 48–55.

Books

Negandhi, Anant R. *Organization Theory in an Open System* (Port Washington, NY: Kennikat Press, 1975).

Negandhi, Anant R., and Welge, Martin. *Beyond Theory Z: Global Rationalization Strategies of American, German, and Japanese Multinational Companies* (Greenwich, Conn.: JAI Press, 1984).

Chapter 4

Policy Making and Control in International Corporations

Organizational structure and design, formalization of strategies, policies, procedures and reporting requirements, and centralization of strategic decision making in the home office are some of the important means through which international corporations integrate their global operations. As discussed in the last chapter, multinational companies (MNCs) are increasingly moving in this direction. To integrate and unify diverse subsidiaries' operations, structural change, undertaken by the MNCs, is the first step, to be followed by other changes in policy making and control devices. The global company usually follows a multifocused strategy to integrate its worldwide operations.

In this and ensuing chapters, I will examine the multifocused strategies, policies, and control devices used by international companies. More specifically, Davidson[1] has identified seven areas that are important to those firms pursuing a global strategy:

1. Ownership or participation policies
2. Market selection
3. Marketing mix management
4. Sourcing or procurement strategy
5. Financial policies
6. Organizational structure and decision making
7. Strategic long-range planning

Other authors have identified additional areas, such as technological transfer policies and human resource policies as control devices.[2]

This chapter will discuss the following aspects of control devices:

- Ownership policies
- Control through expatriate managers and personal contacts
- Control through the selection of entry methods

Preceding the analysis of these control aspects is a brief discussion on the concepts of policy making and control.

Policy Making

Policies are guides to decision making. They reflect and interpret organizational objectives, channel the contributing decisions towards those objectives, and establish the framework of the various functional segments of the business organization. On the one hand are generally company-wide policies; i.e., those likely to have long-term implications, and those formulated by the top management's group. On the other hand are policies related to functional areas. These two sets, however, are interrelated. As Koontz and O'Donnell expressed, these "major policies beget derivative policies to guide the decision-making of subordinate managers."[3] In addition, these policies also serve as mechanisms to control performance. In Ginzberg's words: "The range of actions which management of large organizations can take to control ineffective performance can be viewed in terms of the need to plan, the stability of policies, and the specifics of policies and procedures."[4]

One should also distinguish strategic and operational policy levels. The strategic policies are the overall, primary objectives of the firm. The operational policies refer to the tangible manner through which the strategic policies will be implemented. One should also identify the short-term and

Table 4-1 Sample objectives matrix

Type	Time horizon	
	Short-term	Long-term
Strategic	Increase market share	Attain dominant market share
Operational	Attain 10% of total market one year after introduction	Our share will be 150% of the combined shares of the next two competitors at the end of year four

Source: Managing the Multinational Subsidiary by James M. Hulbert and William Brandt. Copyright © 1980 Praeger Publishers. Reprinted by permission of Praeger Publishers.

long-term policies. The matrix in Table 4-1, provided by Hulbert and Brandt,[5] illustrates these different types of policies.

As mentioned earlier, the strategic and key operational policies are necessary for the international corporation to integrate and unify its diverse subsidiaries operating around the world. Although the policies provide overall guidelines to establish a control mechanism, the concept and operational meaning of control itself should be understood in a much broader perspective.

Concept of Control

The concept of control carries negative, as well as psychological connotations. Negatively, control implies restrictive measures and guidelines about what an individual must or must not do. Psychologically, the exercise of control may be satisfying or frustrating, depending on one's individual position. Those able to exercise control over their own and others' activities may experience satisfaction; those who are unable to exercise control and who, instead, *are being* controlled by others, may be dissatisfied and alienated from their activities.

Nevertheless, some form of control is absolutely necessary for the functioning of any organization, whether domestic or international. As Tannenbaum has stated:

> Organization implies control. A social organization is an ordered arrangement of individual human interactions. Control processes help circumscribe idiosyncratic behaviors and keep them conformant to the rational plan of the organization. Organizations require a certain amount of conformity as well as the integration of diverse activities. It is the function of control to bring about conformance to organizational requirements and achievement of the ultimate purposes of the organization. The coordination and order

created out of the diverse interests and potentially diffuse behaviors of members is largely a function of control. . . . Control is an inevitable correlate of organization.[6]

Control Measures

Various measures of control are suggested in the management organization literature. Evan, for example, has taken a broader perspective and suggests: span of control; the number of levels of hierarchy; the ratio of administrative to production personnel; "time span of discretion" (maximum length of time employees are authorized to make decisions on their own initiative that commit a given amount of resources of the organization); the hierarchical level at which given classes of decisions are made; and the formal limitations that apply to the decision-making authority of management.[7]

Many of these measures are related to the degrees of decentralization and participation in decision making. The organizational structural aspects were discussed in Chapter 3. The decision-making aspect and the relative influences of home office *versus* overseas subsidiary in decision making will be taken up in Chapter 5. Some of the aspects of policy control will be discussed in this chapter.

Although ownership and control of foreign subsidiaries are conceptually two different aspects, the interrelationships are close and at times indistinguishable. As the firm accumulates certain expertise in conducting international business, its desire to integrate and unify overseas units into a global system increases. To accomplish this goal, besides restructuring the organization, the firm will increase its ownership share of the overseas subsidiaries.

In other words, as Stopford and Wells have reported, in their study of 187 United States MNCs, "In most cases in which firms showed strong preference for wholly-owned subsidiaries, the issue of control appeared to be paramount."[8] They further state that "certain strategies demanded tight central controls; others did not. . . . Strategies that are generally extracted through a tightly controlled organization are also usually associated with a strong preference for wholly-owned subsidiaries."[9] Overall, they found that firms emphasizing marketing and advertising techniques, rationalization of production processes, and control over sources of raw materials tend to prefer wholly-owned subsidiaries.

This trend seems quite visible among United States multinational companies. For example, in 1971, Booz, Allen and Hamilton,[10] a consulting firm, observed that approximately 60% of the new United States overseas subsidiaries were wholly owned, and 8% were majority owned. In spite of increased demands by the host countries, especially developing nations, to reduce the share of foreign ownership, majority equity holding in overseas subsidiaries continues.

Data of the Harvard Multinational Enterprise Project indicate that some 63% of the subsidiaries of 187 large United States multinational companies were wholly owned by the parent companies. An additional 14% of the parent companies had majority equity. Less than one fourth of the United States subsidiaries held minority interests.[11] Interestingly, there were no visible differences in the levels of the equity holdings by the parent companies in overseas subsidiaries located in developed *versus* developing countries.[12]

European multinationals are more inclined to enter into joint ventures in developing countries. However, the Europeans seem to prefer wholly-owned subsidiaries in industrialized countries.[13] In his study of European firms operating in the United States, Franko found that over 70% were wholly owned.[14] More recent data on the ownership behavior of German MNCs clearly substantiate a preference for wholly-owned or majority-owned subsidiaries. Kayser, et al., in their study of German subsidiaries in Australia, France, Japan, Canada, and the United States, also found a strong preference for wholly-owned or majority-owned subsidiaries.[15]

Japanese MNCs have shown a preference for joint ownership of their overseas subsidiaries in developing countries. Approximately three fourths of Japanese overseas subsidiaries are jointly owned. However, as the Japanese firms expand their manufacturing activities in industrialized countries, their desire for a greater ownership share in the subsidiaries also increases. For example, Tsurumi's survey of the Japanese subsidiaries in Indonesia reveals that the Japanese parent companies hold over 80% of the equity interests in two thirds of the total of eighty-seven subsidiaries. Commenting on the future trend, Tsurumi states: "Japanese multinational firms, like their U.S.-based counterparts, will also attempt to secure, where and when permitted, effective control of the MNCs' overseas subsidiaries. Long gone are the days when Japanese firms preferred positions of minority-owners while going through trial and error practices of managing their overseas ventures."[16] The majority of Japanese subsidiaries in industrialized countries are wholly owned.

The preference of United States MNCs for wholly-owned and majority-owned overseas subsidiaries reflects their drive for the unification and rationalization of global units. To the United States, ownership means control, and without extensive control over the subsidiaries' activities, unification is harder to achieve. In contrast, European, and particularly the Japanese, companies' willingness to enter into joint ventures reflects their adaptability to the developing countries' demands. It also indicates that, besides 100% ownership, there are other means of control available to international corporations. These include input and output controls and control exercised through technological and personnel transfers.

Evaluation of Ownership As Control Measure

Although integrating subsidiary operations through ownership control seems rational for the multinational companies, its logic has to be reconciled with the demands of the host countries.

As discussed in Chapter 2, ownership is a thorny issue in many developing countries. And recently, even the industrialized countries, such as Canada, Australia, and France, are demanding local equity in foreign enterprises. Generally speaking, countries with minimal foreign investment are likely to allow 100% ownership to foreign investors. The same may be true for countries with heavy foreign investment; however, this is changing in Canada and Australia.

Current trends seem to indicate that the countries with potentially large natural resources and/or large markets—such as India, Mexico, Indonesia, Australia, and Malaysia—are demanding greater local equity participation in foreign enterprises. Table 4-2 illustrates governmental policies on ownership and other restrictions on foreign investors in selected developing and developed countries.

In the face of restrictive environments on ownership control, the global firm is obligated to use other means of control to integrate its subsidiary operations. These include:

1. Technology transfer (throughput controls)
2. Marketing policies (output controls)
3. Procurement policies (input controls)
4. Financial policies
5. Strategic long-range planning
6. Work force policies
7. Use of expatriates
8. Personal visits to overseas units
9. Methods of entry

The last three aspects of controls are discussed in this chapter. The other aspects will be taken up in ensuing chapters.

System Versus Personal Control

Conceptually, one can conceive control in a holistic sense in terms of system control *versus* personal control. System control emphasizes organizational measures, such as authority, formalization, reporting, and standardization of policies and procedures, whereas personal control relies on informal personal contacts, visits, and the "culturalization" of employees concerning organizational goals and objectives.[17]

Table 4-2 Ownership policies and other restrictions on foreign investors in selected countries

	Ownership and management rules	Restricted investment areas
Australia	No specific rules, except in certain areas. However, government usually presses for 50% Australian equity and 50% Australian voting rights on boards of directors for new projects costing A$1 million (A$1:US $1.14) or more.	Foreign investment is not allowed in utilities, media, certain parts of civil aviation industry, and banking. It is closely scrutinized in real estate. By start of production of uranium project, 75% equity must be held by Australians.
Japan	Foreign investors may take up to 100% equity in all areas except where foreign investment is prohibited completely. Investment in mining is limited to 50% equity.	Foreign investment is prohibited in nuclear energy, power and light, gas supply, aircraft, armaments and explosives, and manufacturing.
United States	No controls on the percentage of foreign ownership.	The only restrictions are in areas that are deemed vital to national security, such as coastal shipping and broadcasting.
West Germany	No limitations on foreign equity participation.	Foreign investment is prohibited in weapons and drugs. All other areas are open.
France	No limitation on foreign equity participation.	Restrictions exist in the manufacturing of rolling road material, shipbuilding, aerospace, film, radio, photography, medical, pharmaceutical products, and agriculture.
Portugal	No limitations. Expatriate personnel also allowed. A certain percentage of Portuguese employees plus a training program in technical and administrative positions is required.	Legally, all areas are open except those reserved for the government. But because approval is required, the host country has considerable leeway for decision.

Spain	Foreign participation of more than 50% requires government approval. This is granted fairly easily, except when industry is already foreign-dominated or a monopolistic structure is likely. Exceptions to ownership exist—100% is allowed when (1) certain priority goals—employment, foreign exchange earnings, are positive, and (2) when royalties are surrendered.	Areas that are restricted include defense, public sector, film industry, communications, mining, banks, airlines, and shipping. There are often special conditions for each, limiting ownership to 10%, 15%, or 25%.
Mexico	Varies according to industry type: Extractive—49%; Secondary/Petrochemical—40%; Manufacturing of parts/auto industry—40%. In other cases not specifically covered—foreign investment allowed up to 49%, *provided* they do not dominate the management. This is a key requirement, Government retains the right to refuse even minority holdings on this criterion.	Very detailed and explicit restrictions exist in most areas.
Hong Kong	There are no controls on the percentage of foreign ownership.	No areas are restricted except for some utilities.
India	Firms must have a minimum of 60% Indian equity. Companies in core sector, having sophisticated technology, or exporting over 60% of production, need to have only a minimum 26% Indian equity.	Industries outside the list of "core" sectors, mostly consumer industries and those reserved for public or small- and medium-scale sectors, are generally closed to foreign investors.
Indonesia	In 1974, government announced that all new foreign projects would require 51% local equity. Majority foreign equity participation in pre-1974 investments is to be phased out.	Foreign investment is prohibited in national defense industries and mass media; foreign control is not allowed in transportation, utility, and atomic power sectors.

Continued

Table 4-2 Continued

	Ownership and management rules	Restricted investment areas
Korea	No specific limitation on wholly foreign-owned enterprises, but preference is given to projects with less than 50% foreign equity.	Foreign investments are prohibited in power generation and distribution, railways, gas supply service, coastal fishing, cigarettes, processing of steamed ginseng, water supply, and enterprises established by Japanese reparation fund.
Malaysia	Firms must comply with New Economic Policy equity goals (30% Bumiputra, 40% other Malaysian, 30% foreign) by 1990. These rules have already been imposed on most firms approved since 1972.	Virtually all industries are open to foreign capital, except those reserved for state–utilities and transportation. Foreign investment in newspapers and related fields would probably not be approved.
New Zealand	No specific rules bar up to 100% foreign equity, but all investments involving 25% or more foreign equity must obtain Reserve Bank's approval.	Foreign investment is barred in trading banks, railways, urban transportation systems, telephone and telegraph services, and savings banks.
Pakistan	No legal limits on amount of foreign equity, but government encourages local equity participation.	Foreign investment prohibited in railways, air lines, atomic energy, telephone and telegraph services, arms and ammunition manufacturing, and domestic banking.
Philippines	Foreign equity is limited to 40% (although government often pushes for 30%). Greater foreign participation allowed in priority or pioneer fields with phase out to 40% participation over a fixed term.	Foreign investment is prohibited in ammunitions and armaments manufacturing, hydroelectric and nuclear power, retail trade, rural banking, and mass media.

Country		
Singapore	All industries are open to foreign investment, except public utilities and telecommunications services.	Government does not insist on joint ventures and many foreign companies have set up wholly-owned subsidiaries.
Taiwan	Foreign investment prohibited in government monopolies, public utilities, and "strategic" industries (e.g., petroleum refining). Discouraged in light manufacturing.	No limitations placed on foreign equity participation.
Thailand	No activities are completely off-limits to foreign capital, but Alien Business Law restricts foreign equity in certain activities.	No overall official limitation on the amount of foreign equity, but restriction to minority participation in many investment areas.

Source: Compiled from various government documents.

149

Personal Control

Besides exercising hierarchical control, the multinational firm may exercise control over its subsidiaries by involving the important executives of the overseas units in the headquarters' formal and informal structures.

Studies have shown that European and Japanese companies have successfully integrated their subsidiary managers into corporate decision- and policy-making structures. For example, one study found that 61% of the Japanese subsidiaries' executives were represented in one or more of the strategically important corporate committees. Additionally, 32% were members of the Corporate Board. In contrast, only 17% of the United States and 33% of the German subsidiaries' executives participated in the headquarters's committees.[18]

Galbraith and Edstrom,[19] in their study of European multinational companies, found that these companies have successfully used the home countries' nationals to coordinate, control, and implement the headquarters' policies. Transfer of the home countries' nationals can be used as a high-leverage tool to affect the transmission of verbal information in an organization. The movement of home country nationals "can be an effective way to design verbal information systems, private lateral contacts, and permit local decentralized control and yet maintain overall system integration."[20]

Control Through Personal Visits

It is generally believed that top-level Japanese executives maintain close ties with the managers of their overseas subsidiaries. Through strong personal relationships and extensive socialization the Japanese organizations are able to implement a so-called "Ringi-system," or "bottom-up" decision-making system.[21] Indeed, personal ties among the employees play an important role in Japanese organizations. However, a recent study reveals that only 12% of the Japanese top-level managers are globetrotters; in contrast, 55% of the German and 70% of the United States top-level executives visit their overseas subsidiaries regularly. One third of the Japanese top-level executives, compared to 15% of the United States and 11% of the German, rarely visit their subsidiaries' operations.[22]

The desire to control and coordinate through personal contacts, in addition to formal policies, procedures, and centralized decision making, could also be seen by examining the nature and purpose of these visits. United States executives seem to be the most purposeful and goal-oriented visitors. One study shows that 52% of their visits to the subsidiaries were scheduled meetings to discuss specific matters, as compared to merely 20% of the German and 12% of Japanese executives' visits.[23]

The globetrotting exercises by United States executives are undertaken to reinforce the overall corporate objectives of unification and global rationalization. Their frequent visits to the subsidiaries' operations are not contrived to decentralize decision making. At the same time, fewer visits by German and Japanese top-level executives seem to be a function of travel costs and their increasing abilities to control the subsidiaries' operations through other means.

Similar results are reported by Hulbert and Brandt in their study of United States, European, and Japanese companies in Brazil. United States multinational companies were most devoted to the "personal visits syndrome."[24] Their results show that United States executives visited their subsidiary operations 4.8 times a year. European and Japanese executives did the same 2.6 and 2.7 times a year, respectively.

Likewise, managers of United States subsidiaries visited their home offices 2.2 times a year, as compared to 1.5 visits by European and 1.6 by Japanese managers. Thus the authors concluded that the "intensive visitation patterns are part of an extensive and formal control system adopted by many American companies."[25]

Overall, these results reflect the organizational systems and management styles of each nationality group. As discussed in Chapter 3, the United States style is more formal, objective, and problem-oriented. The Japanese are less formal, unstructured, and goal-oriented. The Europeans seem to incorporate the elements of both the United States and the Japanese styles.

Method of Entry

Entry strategy provides additional means of control. Basically four different options are available to the firm to enter international markets:

1. Exporting from the home country
2. Licensing arrangement with a private or state-owned enterprise in the host country
3. Joint manufacturing venture with a private or state-owned enterprise
4. Acquiring or forming wholly-owned subsidiaries

Those firms desiring substantial control over their international business prefer either the first or fourth options; that is, either exporting from the home base or acquiring or forming a wholly-owned subsidiary. Besides this generalized statement on the relationship between the method of entry and the desirability of control, one can identify several important determinants of the method of entry that also can be conceived as evolutionary steps being followed by the firm as it gains international experience. In the earlier stage of entering the international markets, the firm may start out with exporting goods and services and then progressively move through the other stages of licensing, forming joint manufacturing ventures, and forming wholly-owned subsidiaries. The method of entry is also related to the stages of the product life cycle.[26] Initially, when the firm is still at the innovative stage, it may simply export its technological and marketing knowledge. As the technology matures and the product is standardized, the firm will face intensive competition in both the domestic and overseas markets. It may then be obligated to manufacture overseas either through a joint venture arrangement or by owning overseas subsidiary operations.

Chapter 1 identified the five stages of the product life cycle and its relationship to the method of entry in the international marketplace. These were: (1) developing a product for the domestic market through research and development activities; (2) exporting domestic products to overseas markets; (3) setting up manufacturing facilities in other industrialized countries to cope with increasing competition, exporting goods from these subsidiaries to developing countries; (4) setting up manufacturing facilities in developing countries; and (5) exporting goods to the United States market from the developing countries.[27]

Figure 4-1 shows the relationship between stages in the product life cycle and the firm's method of undertaking international business.

Licensing and Joint Ventures

Tables 4-3 and 4-4 outline the major advantages and disadvantages of licensing and joint ventures.

As can be seen from these tables, smaller firms with limited experience in overseas markets and possession of limited capital and personnel resources may find both the licensing and the joint venture methods more attractive. The same is true with respect to highly diversified firms. These types of enterprises, such as Gulf & Western and Litton Industries, do not possess significant innovations or brand names. Thus they do not need to worry about losing control over these important assets, as well as part of the company's image. Second, highly diversified firms will be unable to generate enough capital and the personnel resources needed to sustain majority or 100% ownership for all of their product lines. Entering overseas markets through licensing or joint venture methods enables these firms to spread their resources more effectively.

The major advantages of licensing and joint ventures are lower political and financial risks, and less need for capital and experienced personnel in international business. It also allows the firm to increase its flow of earn-

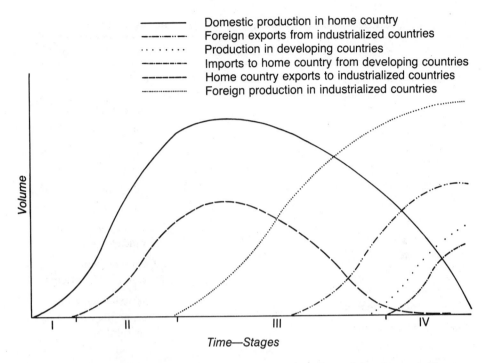

——————— Domestic production in home country
—··—··—·· Foreign exports from industrialized countries
········· Production in developing countries
—·—·—·— Imports to home country from developing countries
——————— Home country exports to industrialized countries
················ Foreign production in industrialized countries

Time—Stages

Figure 4-1 The product life cycle in international trade and investment (*Source: Adapted from J. Fayerweather, International Business Strategy and Administration, Cambridge Mass.: Ballinger Publishing Co., 1978, p. 224.*)

ings without additional capital involvement; that is, recouping some of its earlier investments made for developing products and brand names. At the environmental level, the company is able to adapt to the host country's demand for increasing local participation more effectively.

The major disadvantages of licensing and joint ventures are losing effective control in overseas markets and reduced flexibility for future expansion. For example, Davidson cites a case of Continental Can, which had pursued the licensing method to enter into international markets. By 1965, it had signed fifty-three licensing contracts, whereas its rival, Crown, Cork and Seal, had established majority or wholly-owned subsidiaries in sixteen countries. In the 1970s, when the domestic market growth slowed down, Continental found it difficult to expand overseas because of the market already being preempted by its domestic competitors and by its licensor, Metal Box, of the United Kingdom.[28]

Whatever the advantages and disadvantages of licensing and joint venture methods may be, one cannot ignore the host country's demands and con-

Table 4-3 Advantages and disadvantages of licensing arrangements

Advantages	Disadvantages	Suitable for
Exposure to adverse political and economic events	Creates competitors in overseas markets	Smaller firms with limited capital and personnel resources
Less need for experienced managers in international affairs	Reduces flexibility for future expansions	Highly diversified firms
Less need for capital	Giving away important research and developmental work and other tangible assets of the company	Firms with mature product lines
Increased earnings from already capitalized research and development that was done at the home office	Loss of control of overseas market	Firms averse to taking major risks
Better adaptability to host countries' demands		Firms unwilling to invest overseas
Increasing diversification of product lines without additional research and development expenditure		Countries demanding active local participation
		Countries with high economic and political instability

ditions. Many of the developing countries and the centralized economies of the USSR, East European countries, and now China allow the foreign investors only a minority equity participation. The logic of such demands rests on the presumption that the increased local participation in foreign enterprises provides more effective control over the foreign companies, as well as the needed training to local personnel in managing complex industrial enterprises. Countries such as India, Venezuela, Peru, Taiwan, Mexico, and Turkey prefer licensing and minority ownership arrangements to secure technological and marketing knowledge from the United States companies. Even Japan has pursued this policy of securing needed technological knowledge through licensing and minority equity participation. Until recently, Japan spent more money on buying technological knowledge than she earned through selling her knowledge in other countries.[29] In other words, Japan's national industrial policy prefers domestic control of industries for her economic development plans. Japan's success is now being emulated by other newcomers in the industrial world.

Table 4-4 Advantages and disadvantages of joint ventures in international business

Advantages	Disadvantages	Suitable for
Easier to adapt to host country demands	Loss of control of overseas market	Smaller firms with limited resources
Lower economic and political risks	Less flexibility in integrating global operations	Entrepreneurial firms
Effective use of knowledge and connections of local partner	Creates competitors in the global market	Highly diversified firms
Effective use of available capital and personnel to cover larger segments of the world markets	Potential conflicts with the local partners/host government concerning major strategic and financial policies (sourcing, pricing, export, dividends)	Firms producing mature product lines
		Firms averse to taking political and financial risks
		Firms making investment in their secondary product lines
		Countries demanding active local participation
		Countries with high economic and political instability

Based on various qualitative and quantitative research studies concerning licensing and joint venture decisions, one can formulate the following propositions[30]:

1. The smaller the firm, the greater its propensity to license.
2. The less experienced the firm in international business, the higher the propensity to license.
3. The greater the level of diversification of the firm's products and services, the higher the propensity to license.
4. The more mature the product lines of the firm, the higher the propensity to license, if foreign investment is not possible or desirable.
5. The greater the similarities in market and economic conditions of the home and host countries, the higher the propensity to license (i.e., cross-licensing among industrialized countries).
6. The greater political and economic risks perceived by the firm, the higher the propensity to license.
7. The greater the demands made by the host countries for local participation, the higher the propensity to license.

Although selling technology through licensing is considered to be an in efficient method of using the firm's important technological capabilities, its role in international business is increasing.[31] For example, during the three decades from 1950 to 1980, the United States companies' royalty payments through licensing have increased from $50 million in 1950 to over $1 billion in 1980.[32] The increasing demands from host countries, particularly developing nations, for higher local participation in foreign enterprises point to the significance of licensing in international business.

Joint Venture Decisions

One of the main advantages of joint ventures is that they enable firms to spread the risks—political, economic, and market-related—into various projects. They also provide access to resources, raw materials, capital, and local net income otherwise not available to the firm. Joint ventures also meet the increasing demands for local participation from many developing countries. Table 4-5 shows the countries discouraging or not allowing majority and 100% ownership.

Joint ventures represent a significant change in industry structures and in competitive behavior. They can also be a versatile tool in a highly competitive and turbulent environment. Particularly for industries undergoing rapid technological changes or requiring huge capital investments, joint ventures may be the only means available to the small and medium-sized firms to attain a better position in global markets.[33]

Joint ventures are not without problems. Besides personality and intercultural clashes between foreign and local parties, joint ventures also involve critical business issues. These may include: decisions concerning component sourcing, transfer pricing, assignment of markets, product pricing, annuity control, use of profits for dividends, expansion and diversification, and the evolution of research and development.[34]

Franko's study of joint ventures also indicates that MNCs will eliminate joint ventures for pursuing centralized unification strategies for their global business.[35]

Summary

This chapter discussed policy making and the control aspect in international corporations. First, the general concepts were reviewed briefly. Then, three aspects of policy controls were analyzed: ownership policy, control exercised through expatriate managers, and policy control exercised through selection of entry methods.

Table 4-5 Position of nations on foreign ownership

Percentage of wholly-owned foreign subsidiary of U.S. MNCs	*Country*
1. Over 75%	Canada United Kingdom
2. Less than 75% but more than 50%	Netherlands Argentina Belgium South Africa & Rhodesia Sweden Germany Australia New Zealand Philippines Greece Ecuador Africa (except South Africa & Rhodesia) Mexico Peru Colombia Central America Venezuela Chile Thailand
3. Less than 50% but more than 30%	Taiwan France Indonesia Turkey Spain North Africa Middle East India
4. Less than 30%	Pakistan Japan South Korea

Source: Based on Harvard Multinational Enterprise Project data reported in J. P. Curhan, W. H. Davidson, and R. Suri, *Tracing the Multinationals,* Cambridge, Mass.: Ballinger Publishing Co., 1977, pp. 316–317.

Analysis of the various studies indicate that United States MNCs tend to use ownership of the subsidiary as a control device; consequently, they prefer and secure 100% or majority ownership of overseas subsidiaries. In contrast, Japanese MNCs have opted to use other means of control, such as large numbers of expatriate managers, input controls, and control through technological transfers. They have thus preferred joint ventures and minority equity in overseas operations, especially in developing countries. However, in industrialized countries, they seem to prefer 100% ownership in overseas subsidiaries.

Although European MNCs seem to have more joint ventures in developing countries, their drive for global rationalization is moving them closer to United States practices.

Case

Coca-Cola's operation in India can be characterized as a highly profitable business in the low-priority consumer goods industry. The case highlights the issue of control by MNCs vis-à-vis a national government. Some dynamic aspects of the negotiation processes between the two parties are also examined.

Case 4-1

The Coca-Cola Company

"The activities of the Coca-Cola Company in India during the last 25 years furnish a classic example of how a multinational corporation operating in a low priority, high-profit area in a developing country attains runaway growth and, in the absence of alertness on the part of the government concerned, can stifle the weaker indigenous industry in the process." This statement was made by George Fernandes, the Minister for Industry, Government of India, in August 1977.

It was at this time that the Foreign Exchange Regulation Act (FERA) was being enforced. Under the FERA all multinational companies functioning in India had to dilute their equity so that at least 60% of equity was in the hands of Indian nationals. Furthermore, no changes could be made to existing facilities and technologies while the dilution of equity was being carried out. In addition, the guidelines for transfer of technology into India stipulated that technical knowledge should be fully imparted to the Indian company within a fixed time limit.

The Coca-Cola Company, headquartered in Atlanta, Georgia, had a policy by which subsidiaries that manufactured the soft drink concentrate would be wholly owned by the parent company to protect the confidentiality of its formula, which was a "carefully guarded trade secret." Bottling the soft drink was carried on under franchise agreements with bottlers spead out all over the globe.

Therefore, the situation faced by Coca-Cola in India demanded actions that went contrary to the corporation's strategic and operational policy. Headquarters was faced with the problem of having to decide the fate of the lucrative Indian subsidiary. (The capital of the Indian company had remained stationary at Rs 0.66 mln. The ROI was estimated as being as high as 800% to 1,200%. Pretax profit margins were found to be between 55% and 60%.)

Source: Data for this case were collected by Anant R. Negandhi. Ms. Rachel Davis assisted in preparing the case. © Copyright Anant R. Negandhi, 1985.

Coca-Cola's Foreign Empire

Coca-Cola Export Corp. [CCEC], the overseas operations branch of Coca-Cola, is responsible for over 50% of Coca-Cola's earnings. The CCEC is on the one hand thoroughly decentralized, with as much operational decision making as possible pushed down through a hierarchy of zone, area, and regional offices to the person on the scene. On the other hand, strategic decision making is the concern of those at the top in Georgia.

It was only after World War II that the company made its major thrust into the virtually untapped soft drink market outside the United States. Within a few years, Coca-Cola's rapid growth had prompted the company to adopt the basic overseas strategy it follows to this day. Management was decentralized to make the company appear as local as possible, whereas the drink itself kept its traditional image.

The CCEC, like the domestic company, sells a variety of products, from other soft drinks to freeze-dried coffee. However, the bulk of the profits comes from selling Coca-Cola concentrate to more than 800 overseas bottling plants.

Because most bottlers are local nationals, the company see that it has relatively less to fear from expropriation than most multinational companies. The only substantial production facilities Coca-Cola has abroad are twenty-eight plants that produce its concentrate.

The Coca-Cola Formula

It is widely believed in the southern United States that Coca-Cola once contained a small amount of cocaine from the cocoa leaves that give the cola its distinctive flavor. The cocaine, according to folklore, was a factor in building consumer loyalty to Coca-Cola. It has not been substantively proved that there was cocaine in Coca-Cola. At present, the cola makers extract the cocaine from cocoa leaves before they go into the cola-brewing process. The New Jersey firm that extracts Coca-Cola's cocaine sells more than a ton of the white powder a year under government supervision for use in medicines.

As mentioned earlier, the formula of the Coca-Cola concentrate is a closely guarded secret. The ingredients and the mixing and brewing formula are all locked away in an Atlanta bank vault and are only known to two senior chemists at the company. The vault can only be opened after a special vote of the directors.

Coca-Cola was around long before the existence of government labelling regulations, and therefore was exempt from these regulations. The company concedes even today that most of the ingredients in its formula, especially the composition of 7-X, the company's secret ingredient, are still unknown. (Excerpts from the statement by Mr. George Fernandes, Minister for Industry in the Lok Sabha, on August 8, 1977.)

The Coca-Cola Company entered India in the early 1950s, when four bottling plants were set up at Bombay, Calcutta, Delhi, and Kanpur, based on the import of concentrates worth about Rs 0.8 mln per annum on an actual user basis. In 1958, Coca-Cola was permitted to set up a branch in India to manufacture concentrates from imported raw material. This was done to save foreign exchange spent on importing concentrates by the four Indian bottling plants. Coca-Cola was allowed to manufacture its concentrate in India on the specific condition that the quantum of production would meet the needs of the then existing four plants.

According to Mr. George Fernandes, the manufacture of the concentrate did not require an industrial license and the Registration Certificate did not stipulate any approved capacity. The company expanded its capacity enormously within the next few years, from 0.3 mln kg to 2.6 mln kg of concentrates per annum, without seeking any formal approval from the government. This enabled the company to supply concentrate to twenty-two Indian bottling plants that had come up by 1970 in various parts of the country, and to attain a dominant position in the beverage industry. By 1977, Coca-Cola had 45% of the soft drink market in India. The remaining 55% was divided among a number of competitors, all of them Indian.

The company was enabled to import raw material for the concentrate through a liberal export replenishment entitlement of 20%, even though a subsequent study showed that the import content in the concentrate was only about 4.5%. When the import entitlement was thereafter increased from 20% to 45%, the CCEC said it was unable to feed all twenty-two bottling plants, even though, as pointed out earlier, their manufacture of concentrate was specifically restricted to the four bottling plants.

Another study was carried out in 1973, and the actual user import entitlement of the company was fixed at Rs 1.6 million per annum, on the basis of its performance in that year and in addition to the export replenishment entitlement of 45%. It was decided, however, because of considerable public pressure exerted in the parliament and outside, to scale down the actual user import license by 11% and the export replenishment entitlement by 0.5% every two years from 1973 to 1974.

Export had been stated as another objective for setting up the Indian branch of the CCEC. Export earnings are high on the list of India's economic priorities, and therefore were important in enabling the CCEC to get favorable terms for import when the Indian branch was set up in 1958. The total value of exports of concentrates and other goods during the period 1958–1970 was Rs 111.2 mln. Exports were found to have declined from Rs 15.6 mln in 1971 and 1972, to Rs 10 mln in 1973 and 1974, and finally to Rs 0.18 million in 1976. This decline in exports closely followed the reduction of the CCEC, India's import quota, raising suspicions of transfer pricing.

Foreign exchange is scarce in India and is doled out to industry on the basis of the priority listing of various industries. In 1977, the government of India held that the CCEC had earned profits and made remittances in foreign exchange totally disproportionate to its investment in India. The company's original investment in India by way of cash, plant, and machinery was Rs 0.66 mln. During 1958–1974, it had remitted Rs 68.7 mln in foreign exchange by way of imports, profits, and home office's service charges. The amount claimed by the company as still due to be remitted for the same period is Rs 36.9 mln, making a total of over Rs 100 mln. This sum exceeds the total export earnings of Rs 99.2 mln during the period 1958–1974, resulting in a net outflow of foreign exchange.

In view of the restrictions imposed on the company, the total remittances should not exceed 80% of the total export earnings, and the value of the imports should not exceed 5% of the total exports. In 1977, the government of India refused to issue further import licenses for raw materials to the company.

Problems have also arisen in the use of brand names such as "Coca-Cola." According to the license agreements entered into by the company, no royalty or other "consideration" is payable by the user. It has been held, however, that the restrictive clause in the agreement, confining the user only to the concentrates supplied by the company, would amount to "consideration." It has also been found that the concentrates are sold to the Indian bottler with a very high margin of profit (about 400%), which would include a very large portion of hidden royalties.

In the context of the impact of FERA on Coca-Cola's operations in India, the Minister for Industry stated that because the company was engaged in a low-priority industry, not requiring sophisticated technology, and with little export potential, the Reserve Bank of India issued orders in April 1977, requiring the corporation to convert itself into an Indian company with foreign equity not exceeding 40% within one year; that is, by April 1978.

The CCEC had agreed to form the Indian company, but has qualified its acceptance by proposing that it should be allowed to have a "Quality Control and Liaison Office" of the United States company in India to protect the "confidentiality" of the "carefully guarded trade secrets" of its formulas. This proposal was not in consonance with the provisions of FERA, because the proposed Indian company would not in reality be taking over the operations of the CCEC but would merely function as a selling company of the concentrates that would still be under the manufacturing control of the United States company. Furthermore, this agreement would also militate against the guidelines for transfer of technology into India, which provide that the technical knowledge should be fully imparted to the Indian company within a fixed time limit. The Reserve Bank of India had, therefore, rejected the application by the CCEC in this matter.

The government of India had indicated to Coca-Cola that the matter was completely up to the United States company to decide whether it would fully comply with the provisions of the FERA and transfer to the proposed Indian company all of the present activities, including the technical knowledge and the blending operations of the concentrates, or whether in the alternative the United States company would prefer to close down its operations in India.

Appendix 1 *Excerpts from Parliamentary Debates in Indian Parliament Concerning Coca-Cola, 1976–1980* ____

Who Was Responsible for the Closure of Coca-Cola?

What was the reason for Coca-Cola closing down its operations in India? Was it the Janata decision? or was it George Fernandes who did it? In this hotly debated question, some facts are as mysterious as the much publisised secret Coca-Cola formula.

As per FERA regulation the Company was required to Indianise or close operations by May 5th 1978. Yet, strangely enough, the Company's operations came to a halt in July 1977. On this date the Company had ran out of imported concentrate material. If one can find out why they ran out of this material before the time, the key to solve the mystery will be found.

Some facts are known. In 1972–73, the Balachandran Committee recommended that ad hoc licenses to the extent of 16 lacs per year should be given to the Coca-Cola Company with an annual growth of 5%, provided the company achieves a substantial increase in its next export earnings. The record of ad hoc licenses given and the Company's export earnings is as under:

Year	Ad hoc import license (Rs. in lakhs)
1972	7.0
1973	16.0
1974	Nil
1975	14.25
1976	Nil
1977	Nil

The Export earnings of the company in 1974 were Rs. 129.38 lakhs. In 1975 Rs. 5.52 lakhs and in 1976 Rs. 2.94 lakhs, after which the Export was nil.

The question arises why no ad hoc license was granted by the then Government in 1976. Was it due to Coca-Cola exports declining? Was it a political decision? Was it the FERA regulation. The fact is the Government became stern and rightly refused a license to a foreign company not falling in line with the regulations of the Indian Government.

In March 1977, during the Janata Government the Coca-Cola lobby headed by Sardar Charanjit Singh who later became an M.P. made serious efforts to get an ad hoc license denied to the Company in 1976. Reliable reports indicate that he used his friendship with Nanji Deshmukh, the then Janata party President, to approach Brijlal Verma, Minister of Industry and both Deshmukh and Verma had a common Jan Sangh background. Charanjit Singh reportedly paid Shri Verma substantially more than the ad hoc license value of Rs. 4 lacs which he was seeking for import of concentrate material for Coca-Cola. Shri Verma recommended this license to the Commerce

Minister Mohan Dharia. Shri Mohan Dharia reviewing the case, wanted to know why a license was being recommended by Janata Government in 1977 when in 1976 a similar request was turned down by the previous Government. Apparently as Shri Verma could not advance convincing reason he was replaced by Shri George Fernandes who was projected by the media as "George the Giant killer" when in fact the real evictor of Coca-Cola was the then Congress Government.

The files of the Industry and the Commerce Ministers would contain the reasons as to why in 1974, even though there was an export of 129.38 lacs by Coca-Cola Company no ad hoc license was given. And further why no ad hoc import license was given in 1976, even though as per FERA they were required to Indianise or get out by May 5, 1978.

To a Lok Sabha question dated 28 March 1980 (Unstarred 2275) the answers given are "No license was issued in 1974 as their application was received very late," and "In 1977 no AU ad hoc import license was issued in their favour because the Corporation ceased to manufacture Coca-Cola concentrates in India before a final decision on their application for 1977 could be taken." The fact is that the Corporation stopped their manufacturing because this very same license, was not given.

The question is why? Was it Janata, or was it because in 1976 no ad hoc license was given? These are the questions, which when answered, will solve the mystery.

Appendix 2 Coca-Cola in the Shadow of FERA

One of the most outstanding achievements of the then Congress Government was introduction of Foreign Exchange Regulation Act in 1970 and its enactment in 1973. All but 13 Companies fell in line. Amongst those that chose to close operations in India were IBM and Coca-Cola Company.

The Coca-Cola company's application, made in 1974–75, was reviewed by the Government which decided that the company should not be allowed to have more than 40% foreign shareholding. It was further regulated that Coca-Cola should be restricted to sell Cola extracts not exceeding its export sales and that they should not be allowed to export items other than their drinks.

In December 1975, the group of Secretaries of Economic Ministries decided that capacity restrictions be placed on Company's operations and that an export obligation on part of the Company be made compulsory. A minimum export of Rs. 2 crores of their own products annually was made compulsory. It was also decided that no actual users ad hoc licenses of raw materials be considered for 1974–75, if the export limit of Rs. 2 crores was not met.

In July 1976, a group of Cabinet Ministers met and regulated that no permission would be granted for operating a fully owned Indian Branch of the Foreign Company, namely, The Coca-Cola Export Corporation. The ministers meeting gave the Company one year in which it should Indianise their operations in India i.e. before July 1977. (The Janata Party however extended the July 1977 period to May 1978.) It was further decided that no import of concentrates should be allowed.

In summary, the then Congress Government achievements resulted in regulating the operations of his multinational in the following manner:

- 1972 – Remittances not to exceed 80% of exports.
- 1973 – No new plants to be set up.
- 1974 – No new products to be introduced.
- 1975 – Import licenses to depend upon 1972 export performance.

It was the same Government which had the foresight to ask C.F.T.R.I. in 1973 to prepare a substitute for Coca-Cola. The substitute, which was to later become '77,' was ready in 1976.

There have been some misplaced conceptions about the exit of Coca-Cola from the country. There is a general impression that the exit of Coca-Cola was motivated and finally sealed by the Janata Government as a political vendetta. The facts speak differently.

The Government let by Smt. Gandhi was fully conscious of this problem as far back as 1970, when the Foreign Exchange Regulation Bill was first introduced by her Government. Later, the Bill was to become an Act under the same Government in 1973, regulating the presence of 460 foreign Companies in India. All but 13 companies fell in line with the Government's desire to dilute their foreign equity. These 13 companies, including Coca-Cola and IBM, chose to wind up their operations in India.

To highlight the issue, it would be appropriate to quote excerpts from statements made by various Ministers from 1972 till date. It must be noted that the action to resolve the above issues was initiated during the time of the Congress Government led by Smt. Gandhi.

On 20th December, 1972 in Lok Sabha in reply to a starred question no. 533 the Minister of Industry, said in reference to Coca-Cola;

> . . . This is not an essential commodity. I would rather discourage the taking of Coca-Cola. This is not an essential commodity. The sooner we get rid of it, the better it will be for the country.

Mr. Ghanshyam Oza made the following statement on 4th June, 1971 in Lok Sabha:

> . . . Please be posted with all the facts first. Then you may cast any aspersion that you may choose to do. These bottling plants can be switched on to any other drinks, leave alone Coca-Cola. We have made it very clear while licence for this plant was given to this Company that we do not guarantee that they will be supplied with concentrates. It is not our worry. This condition is put in letter of intent and also in the licence that Government is not

at all committed to providing them with any foreign exchange or supply of concentrate.

On March 5th 1975, in reply to Lok Sabha starred question no. 221, the Minister of Industry stated as under:

> . . . We have issued directive to Coca-Cola Export Corporation not to introduce any new drink. We are seeing that the operations of Coca-Cola Corporation are brought under control by various measures including reducing their capital. The Company is having 100% foreign capital. Now, we are asking them to get it reduced as per the Act of Parliament. They have been given two years time. We are also seeing that within two years those who are bottling Coca-Cola take sufficient steps to be independent of Coca-Cola. I regret that the pressure for allowing this is because of the employment problem that is directly coming up before us. We are trying to contain the activities of the Coca-Cola Corporation precisely because we want indigenous drinks to substitute Coca-Cola drink.

In reply to Lok Sabha starred question no. 212 dated 21st January, 1976, the Minister of State in the Ministry of Industry and Civil Supplies said the following:

> . . . The possibility of Coca-Cola bottlers producing their own drinks is still being explored. The Balachandran Committee has also, inter-alia, stressed the need for developing wholly indigenous drinks by the bottlers. It was in this context that a meeting with the bottlers was held in 1975. There was unanimity about the need for efforts to eliminate imports of ingredients common to all soft drinks manufacturers in the country and the need towards research and development in that direction. The bottlers were also informed that they would get their own brands of soft drinks.
>   . . . The Central Food Technological Research Institute, Mysore is reported to have evolved a formulation which might prove to be a substitute for the Coca-Cola beverage. Government is actively pursuing the matter with the institute with a view to its commercial exploitation in the country.

During the debate in Lok Sabha on the same day, the Minister of Industry added the following:

> . . . One of the most important recommendations was that we must make an effort to have these drinks indigenously; we did refer this to all the scientific laboratories of the CSIR, and I am glad to inform that the CFTRI has come forward with a formula to prepare a drink which resembles very closely Coca-Cola.

However, the Coca-Cola Company was preventing the local Indian Bottlers from manufacturing their own drinks.

On this matter the Minister of Industry further stated as under:

... Whether they are introducing any other drink, Fanta or any other soda, this is because under the contract which the bottlers have, I think, the Company has been forcing them to do it though there are alternatives.

The reason for not allowing the bottlers to make their own drinks was that it would affect the quantum of ad hoc import licences which Coca-Cola company was demanding from the Government. On the subject of ad hoc licences and locally-made drinks, the Balachandran Committee recommendations said as follows:

... The Committee held that it may not be fair to deny these bottling plants their raw materials for building up utilisation of installed plant and equipment to the extent capacity approved by Government. To this extent, it was felt necessary that till such time as these units were able to develop an alternate drink, they be assisted in meeting their requirements of raw materials. At the same time, it had to be borne in mind that this was a non-priority industry, though through its export performance the unit manufacturing the concentrates had earned for itself the priority status. Balancing all the relevant considerations the Coca-Cola Export Corporation should push up their exports substantially in the years to come.

The Minister of Industry stated on 21st January 1976, in Lok Sabha while replying to a starred question no. 212 the following:

... So far as the exports are concerned, the exports of Coca-Cola have been going down. Last year it went down. We are looking into it, because the only reason why Coca-Cola Export Corporation came into existence is based on its export performance. We are looking into it under FERA, why it has been going down, because the basis for its existence was export. If that is knocked out, the very basis of its existence is knocked out.
Exports of Coca-Cola were as follows:

Year 1971	Rs. 156 lacs
1972	Rs. 132 lacs
1973	Rs. 134 lacs
1974	Rs. 100 lacs
1975	Rs. 7 lacs.
Thereafter Nil.	

The Balachandran Committee had also observed during 1972:

... No serious efforts seem to have been made by the bottling plants to develop wholly indigenous drinks similar to what they are manufacturing today. National laboratories like the Central Food Technological Research

Institute, Mysore could be of assistance in this direction in developing flavours like mango, ginger, orange etc. to exploit our national resources and also become self sufficient.

Government's efforts to develop a substitute for Coca-Cola fructified in 1975. On January 21, 1976 the Minister of Industry stated in reply to a starred question no. 212 as follows:

> ... We have evolved a formula for a drink which might be a substitute for Coca-Cola, but we have got to build up a reputation of this with considerable propaganda and convince our people that this is a drink which they will have to take.

Question then arose about Indianising the operations of the Company to be in line with Foreign Exchange Regulations Act, since now the Government was ready to offer a substitute to Coca-Cola. With regards to Indianisation of the company, the Minister of State in the Ministry of Industry, said on 31st March 1976 the following:

> ... They would like to manufacture concentrate and that portion will be 100% foreign owned. So far as this is concerned, this proposal is not wholly in conformity with the guidelines under FERA issued by the Government.

On 5th May 1976, the Minister of Industries said the following:

> ... There is no question of any indulgence at all. Their application under FERA has been received; it is under consideration. But the whole problem is this that as long as we have decided not to ask them to quit completely, if they are willing to subject themselves to any regulations we might impose on them they will still have a chance to be considered provided it is in the interest of the country and the export performance is there. But it is true that the exports made are falling and this will also be taken into consideration and a decision arrived at quickly.

On the same day Shri H.N. Mukherjee M.P. asked;

> ... How long do we have to wait for the resuscitation of our own cola drinks industry, particularly in this part of the country about which we all have personal experience for many years.

to which the Minister of Industries replied:–

> ... Not very long.

Minister of State in the Ministry of Industry stated while replying to starred question no. 327 on 31st March, 1976 in Lok Sabha as under:

. . . They would like to manufacture concentrate and that portion will be 100% foreign owned. So far as this is concerned, this proposal is now wholly in conformity with the guidelines under FERA issued by the Government.

The problem which was facing the then Congress Government was as to what would happen to existing Coca-Cola bottling plants which the Minister of Industry described on 5th May 1976 as follows:

> . . . I can only say that the country is not interested in losing valuable foreign exchange for getting soft drinks introduced into the country. But the facts of life are there. For the last 15 years this industry has been there. Nearly 22 bottling plants have been set-up employing about 20,000 workers and involving an investment of Rs. 6 crores in these bottles. But it is not for the sake of the bottlers and not even for the sake of the consumers that a decision will be taken, but because there have been various demands and pressures brought up as to what will happen to the bottles. Something will have to be done for that. What the Finance Minister said is right. We will certainly take into consideration what is in the best interest of the country.

The anxiety of the Government that there may be unemployment in the bottling plants has now been overcome in that these plants are now successfully marketing Nova Cola, Campa Cola, 77 Cola—all locally made—and some companies have even licensed a number of new bottling plants, specially of Campa brands.

In retrospect, it was the Congress Government who as far back as 1971 had the foresight to develop a substitute for Coca-Cola, anticipating Coca-Cola's refusal to accept Indian equity as required by the Foreign Exchange Regulation Act. Without this foresight, it would not have been possible for the Government to tackle the problems of unemployment and idle plants.

Then on 1st March 1978, in Lok Sabha the Minister of State in the Ministry of Industry, said the following:

> . . . Coca-Cola and IBM concerns were permitted to operate in India with non-resident interest not exceeding 40% in accordance with the provisions of The Foreign Exchange Regulation Act, 1973. However, these two companies decided to wind up their activities in the country in keeping with their corporate policies.

Extract of Parliament Debates on Coca-Cola

Starred question no. 533 dated 20/12/1972 (Minister of Industry)

(1) *This is not an essential commodity.* I would rather discourage the taking of Coca-Cola. This is not an essential commodity. *The sooner we get rid of it, the better it will be for the country.*

Starred question no. 221 dated 5/3/1975 (Minister of Industries)

(2) *We have issued directive to Coca-Cola Export Corporation not to introduce any new drink. We are seeing that the operations of Coca-Cola Corporation are brought under control* by various measures including reducing their capital". " . . . *The company is having 100% foreign capital.* Now, *we are asking them to get it reduced as per* the Act of Parliament. *They have been given two years time". " . . . We are also seeing that within two years those who are bottling Coco-Cola take sufficient steps to be independent of Coca-Cola.* I regret that the pressure for allowing this is because of the employment problem that is directly coming up before us.

. . . *We are trying to contain the activities of the Coca-Cola Corporation precisely because we want indigenous drinks to substitute Coca-Cola drink.*

Starred question no. 212 dated 21/1/1976 (Minister of State in the Ministry of Industry)

(3) . . . The possibility of Coca-Cola bottlers producing their own drinks is still being explored. The Balachandran Committee has also, inter-alia, stressed the need for developing wholly indigenous drinks by the bottlers. It was in this context that a meeting with the bottlers was held in 1975. There was unanimity about the need for efforts to eliminate imports of ingredients common to all soft drinks manufacturers in the country and the need towards research and development in that direction. The bottlers were also informed that they would get all assistance from Government if they proposed to manufacture their own brands of soft drinks.

The Central Food Technological Research Institute, Mysore is reported to have evolved a formulation which might prove to be a substitute for the Coca-Cola beverage. Government is actively pursuing the matter with the Institute with a view to its commercial exploitation in the country.

One of the most important recommendations was that we must make an effort to have these drinks indigenously; we did refer this to all the scientific laboratories of the CSIR, and *I am glad to inform that the CFTRI has come forward with a formula to prepare a drink which resembles very closely Coca-Cola.*

Starred question no. 221 dated 21/1/1976 (Minister of Industry)

(5) . . . Whether they are introducing any other drink, Fanta or any other soda, this is because under the contract which the bottlers have, I think, the Company has been forcing them to do it, though there are alternatives.

Unstarred question no. 2976 dated 12/3/1975 (Minister of State in Min. of Industry)

(6) . . . The Committee felt that it may not be fair to deny these bottling plants their raw materials for building up utilisation of installed plant and equipment to the extent of capacity approved by Government. To this extent, it was felt necessary that till such time as these units were able to develop an alternate drink, they be assisted in meeting their requirements of raw materials. At the same time, *it had to be borne in mind that this was a non-priority industry,* though through its export performance the unit manufacturing the concentrates had earned for itself the priority status. Balancing all the relevant considerations, the *Coca-Cola Export Corporation should push up* their exports substantially in the years to come and the bottling plants should, on the other hand, be provided with raw materials to increase their utilisation of capacity by a reasonable amount each year to reach their approved capacity in a period of 5 to 6 years.

Starred question no. 212 dated 21/1/1976 (Minister of Industry)

(7) . . . *So far as the exports are concerned, the exports of Coca-Cola have been going down. Last year, it went down.* We are looking into *it, because the only reason why Coca-Cola Export Corporation came into existence is based on its export performance. We are looking into it under FERA, why it has been going down, because the basis for its existence was export. If that is knocked out, the very basis of its existence is knocked out.*

Export of Coca-Cola were as follows:

Year 1971	Rs. 156 lacs
1972	Rs. 132 lacs
1973	Rs. 134 lacs
1974	Rs. 100 lacs
1975	Rs. 7 lacs
Thereafter Nil	

Unstarred question no. 2976 dated 12/3/1975 (Minister of State in the Ministry of Industry)

(8) . . . No serious efforts seem to have been made by the bottling plants to develop wholly indigenous drink similar to what they are manufacturing today. National laboratories like the Central Food Technological Research Institute, Mysore could be of assistance in this direction in developing flavours like mango, ginger, orange etc. to exploit our national resources and also become self sufficient.

Starred question no. 212 dated 21/1/1976 (Minister of Industry)

(4) 'B' . . . We have evolved a formula for a drink which might be a substitute for Coca-Cola, but we have got to build up a reputation of this with considerable propaganda and convince our people that this is a drink which they will have to take.

Starred question no. 327 dated 31/3/1976 (Minister of State in the Ministry of Industry)

> (9) . . . *They would like to manufacture concentrate and that portion will be 100% foreign owned. So far as this is concerned, this proposal is not wholly in conformity with the guidelines under FERA issued by the Government.*

Starred question no. 677 dated 5/5/1976 (Minister of Industries)

> (10) . . . There is no question of any indulgence at all. Their application under FERA has been received; it is under consideration. But the whole problem is this that as long as we have decided not to ask them to quit completely, if they are willing to subject themselves to any regulations we might impose on them, they will still have a chance to be considered, provided it is in the interest of the country and the export performance is there. But it is true that the exports made are falling and this will also be taken into consideration and a decision arrived at quickly.

Shri H.N. Mukherjee M.P.

> . . . How long do we have to wait for the resuscitation of our own cold drinks industry, particularly in this part of the country about which we all have personal experience for many years?

Minister of Industries:

> —Not very long.
>   . . . *I can only say that the country is not interested in losing valuable foreign exchange for getting soft drinks introduced into the country.* But the facts of life are there. For the last 15 years this industry has been there. *Nearly 22 bottling plants have been set-up employing about 20,000 workers and involving an investment of Rs. 6 crores in these bottles. But it is not for the sake of the bottlers and not even for the sake of the consumers that a decision will be taken, but because there have been various demands and pressures brought up as to what will happen to the bottles.* Something will have to be done for that. What the Finance Minister said is right. *We will certainly take into consideration what is in the best interest of the country.*

Unstarred question no. 1187 dated 1/3/1978 (Minister of State in the Ministry of Industry)

> (13) *Coca-Cola and IBM* concerns were permitted to operate in India with non-resident interest not exceeding 40% in accordance with the provisions of the Foreign Exchange Regulation Act, 1973. *However, these two companies decided to wind up their activities in the country in keeping with their corporate policies.*

Question (22nd July, 1976)

Application of M/s. Coca-Cola Export Corporation seeking approval under section 29 of the FERA for carrying on manufacturing activities and for use of foreign brand names.

Answer by the Group of the Ministers

 (i) *No permission will be granted for operating a fully owned Indian branch of the Coca-Cola Export Corportation.*
 (ii) The Company may be permitted under Section 29 (2) to continue its activities subject to the conditions that an *Indian Company should be set up within a period of one year with non-resident interest not exceeding 40%.*
 (iii) The use of Trade Mark "Coca-Cola" will be allowed to continue.
 (iv) No Royalty would be paid for the use of this Trade Mark.
 (v) No Import of concentrates would be allowed.
 (vi) Only raw materials for concentrates would be allowed to be imported to the extent of value of 5% of total Exports effected by the Coca-Cola Export Corporation of the New India Company.

Question (22nd February, 1978)

 (a) Whether Government have made an assessment of the investment and profit and loss of Coca-Cola company during last ten years; and
 (b) If so, the foreign exchange saved as a result of the closure of its sale in India? (See table p. 174.)

Answer by the Ministry of Industry

 (a) A statement indicating the Assets and Profits of the Indian Branch of the Coca-Cola Export Corporation for the period from 1967 to 68 and 1976 to 77 is attached.
 (b) After the date of closure of its sale in India there would be no further accrual of profits or other charges for remittances abroad.

Question (1st March, 1978)

 (a) The reasons for the winding up of Coca-Cola and IBM concerns;
 (b) Whether it is a fact that many other concerns with considerable foreign participation are enjoying a virtual lease of life because of administrative tardiness in enforcing the relevant regulations; and
 (c) If so, the reasons therefor and the steps proposed to be taken in this regard?

Answer by the Ministry of Industry

 (a) Coca-Cola and IBM concerns were permitted to operate in India with non-resident interest not exceeding 40% in accordance with the provisions

Statement referred to in reply to part (a) of the above question on the 22nd February, 1978: Assets and Profits of Indian Branch of Coca-Cola Export Corporation

Items	1967–68 (31.12.67)	1968–69 (31.12.68)	1969–70 (31.12.69)	1970–71 (31.12.70)	1971–72 (31.12.71)	1972–73 (31.12.72)	1973–74 (31.12.73)	1974–75 (31.12.74)	1975–76 (31.12.75)	1976–77 (31.12.76)
1. Assets (in India)	123.00	243.71	226.68	271.96	399.39	510.44	555.02	525.82	531.20	615.76
2. Profit before Tax	81.25	156.38	224.12	276.10	334.50	332.78	276.78	262.38	190.81	196.99
3. Profit after Tax	19.65	33.24	44.98	61.10	76.50	81.78	71.78	51.09	44.81	46.99

of the Foreign Exchange Regulations Act, 1973. However, these two companies decided to wind up their activities in the country in keeping with their corporate policies.

(b) No Sir.

(c) Does not arise.

Question (20th December, 1978)

(a) Whether Government are aware that Parley Company had mainly a hand in the closure of Coca-Cola Company, and

(b) The grounds on which Coca-Cola Company was closed?

Answer by the Ministry of Industry

(*a*) No, Sir. The closure of the Coca-Cola Export Corporation was a decision taken by the company itself as a result of its corporate policy and in view of inability to comply with the directives issued under the Foreign Exchange Regulation Act.

(*b*) The Reserve Bank of India issued orders on 29th April, 1977 requiring the Coca-Cola Export Corporation to convert itself into an Indian company with non-resident interest not exceeding 40% within one year from the date of the receipt of the order by the Company, i.e., by 5th May, 1978. *The Company agreed to comply with this order provided the Coca-Cola Company, USA, was permitted to have a quality control-cum-liaison office in India to control the manufacture of Coca-Cola concentrate. After considering the application, the Reserve Bank of India issued orders on 5th August, 1977 rejecting the proposal.* Thereafter, the Coca-Cola Export Corporation made another representation to the Reserve Bank of India stating that they would be unable to manufacture Coca-Cola and Fanta in India since their proposal for having a quality control office of the American Company has been rejected and enquiring whether the proposed Indian Company with 40% foreign equity participation would be permitted to manufacture new beverages other than Coca-Cola and Fanta. This proposal was also rejected by the Reserve Bank of India on 8th November, 1977. The Coca-Cola Export Corporation announced its decision to close down its activities in India within the proposed time limit.

Question (11th March, 1980)

(a) whether Government's attention has been drawn to a news item appeared in the Times of India dated February 27, 1980 regarding multinational Corporations probing the new Governments' mind on their reinduction in the country and

(b) if so, the details thereof and Governments' reaction thereto?

Answer by the Ministry of Law, Justice and Company Affairs

(a) Yes, Sir.
(b) The main points made in the news item are as follows:—
    (i)   Coca-Cola which wound up its business in 1978, after it failed to abide
          by the Janata Government's directive that it should divulge the con-
          tents of the concentrate, has already sent feelers to the new
          Government.
    (ii) The IBM, which had pulled out in 1978 because it did not want to
          dilute its equity, as per FERA regulations, has also been probing
          the Government's mind on their re-entry in the data processing
          business. The core office of IBM in India has been researching the
          possibility of its reinduction not only in the data processing business
          but also in the communication field.
    (iii) Firestone and several other companies which were finding it difficult
          to meet the FERA requirements and had decided to wind up business
          in India are also awaiting the Government policy.

    The Departments of the Government concerned with the matters raised
in the news item have no information in this regard. The question of the
Government's reaction to the news item, therefore, does not arise. There is
no proposal before Government at present for relaxing the provisions of the
Foreign Exchange Regulation Act, 1973.

Question (14th March, 1980)

What was the export of Coca-Cola Export Corporation during the years 1973,
1976 and 1977, what was the total sales during the same years, and what
were the reasons for the decrease in the exports, if any?

Answer by the Minister of Commerce and Civil Supplies

Exports by M/s. Coca-Cola Export Corporation were as follows:—

Year	Quantity (Kg.)	FOB Value (Rs.)
1975	10515.0	4,86,558
1976	5852.0	2,73,025
1977	974.0	43,950

Sales figures of the Company were not maintained by the Government. Government are not aware of the reasons for the decrease in exports of M/s. Coca-Cola
Export Corporation.

Question (19th June, 1980)

(a) Whether Government proposes to re-invite Coca-Cola Company of U.S.A.
    for manufacturing this drink in India; and

(b) Whether an officer of the said company visited India during the last five months in this connection and discussed the matter with Government officials and private businessmen?

Answer by the Ministry of Industry

(*a*) No, Sir.

(*b*) There was no discussion between any representative of the Coca-Cola Company of the U.S.A. and Government officials during the last five months. Government has no information about any such discussion with private businessmen.

Discussion Questions

1. Discuss the relationship among these three concepts: policy making, strategy, and control.
2. Are the two concepts *ownership* and *control* of a foreign subsidiary the same? Discuss the interrelationships between these two concepts.
3. Discuss the following two types of control measures: system control and personal control.
4. What are the control practices of United States, Japanese, and European MNCs?
5. Based on the product life cycle model, at which stages, and in which countries, would exports, licensing agreements, and joint venture manufacturing be likely to occur, respectively? Test the validity of this model by using some global industries.
6. Discuss the advantages and disadvantages of the various entry modes, such as wholly-owned subsidiary, joint venture, and licensing.

Endnotes

1. William H. Davidson, *Global Strategic Management* (New York: John Wiley and Sons, 1982), p. 20.
2. See Anant R. Negandhi and Martin Welge, *Beyond Theory Z* (Greenwich, Conn.: JAI Press, 1984), pp. 29–75.
3. Harold Koontz and Cyril O'Donnell, *Principles of Management* (New York: McGraw-Hill Book Co., 1964), p. 158.
4. Eli Ginzberg, *The Development of Human Resources* (New York: McGraw-Hill Book Co., 1966), p. 206.
5. James M. Hulbert and William K. Brandt, *Managing the Multinational Subsidiary* (New York: Holt, Rinehart and Winston, 1980), p. 66.
6. Arnold S. Tannenbaum, *Control in Organizations* (New York: McGraw-Hill Book Co., 1968), p. 3.
7. William M. Evan, "Indices of the Hierarchical Structure of Industrial Organizations," *Management Science* 9 (April 1963): 468–477.

8. John M. Stopford and Louis T. Wells, Jr., *Managing the Multinational Enterprise* (New York: Basic Books, Inc., 1972), p. 107.
9. Ibid., p. 208.
10. Booz, Allen and Hamilton study reported in *Business Abroad,* June 1971, p. 9.
11. Joan P. Curhan, William H. Davidson, and Rajan Suri, *Tracing the Multinationals* (Cambridge, Mass.: Ballinger Publishing Co., 1977), p. 20.
12. Ibid.
13. Yoshi Tsurumi, *The Japanese are Coming* (Cambridge, Mass.: Ballinger Publishing Co., 1976), p. 203.
14. Lawrence Franko, *European Business Strategies in the U.S.* (Geneva: Business International, 1971).
15. Martin K. Welge, *Management in Deutschen Multinationalen Unternehmungen* (Stuttgart: Poeschel Verlag, 1980), p. 234; and G. Kayser, et al., *Erfahrungen Deutscher Auslands-Investoren in Ausgewaehlten Industrielaendern* (Goettingen: Verlag Otto Schwarz, 1981), p. 31.
16. Tsurumi, *The Japanese,* p. 209.
17. For extensive discussion on this topic see Hulbert and Brandt, *Managing,* pp. 129–131. Japanese companies are using the personal control mode. See William Ouchi, *Theory Z* (Reading, Mass.: Addison-Wesley, 1981), pp. 47–55.
18. Negandhi and Welge, *Beyond Theory Z,* pp. 51–50.
19. Jay R. Galbraith and Anders Edstrom, "Creating Decentralization Through Informal Networks: The Role of Transfer," in *The Management of Organization Design,* ed. R. M. Kilmann, et al., Vol. 2 (New York: North-Holland), pp. 289–310.
20. Ibid., p. 308.
21. Ouchi, *Theory Z,* pp. 43–45; also Michael Yoshino, *Japan's Multinational Enterprises* (Cambridge, Mass.: Harvard University Press, 1976).
22. Negandhi and Welge, *Beyond Theory Z,* pp. 51–54.
23. Ibid.
24. Hulbert and Brandt, *Managing,* pp. 94–97.
25. Ibid., p. 96.
26. For an extensive discussion on the product life cycle theory in international business, see Louid J. Wells, Jr., ed., *The Product Life Cycle and International Trade* (Boston: Division of Research, Harvard University, 1972).
27. Ibid, p. 15.
28. William H. Davidson, *Global Strategic Management* (New York: John Wiley and Sons, 1982), p. 32.
29. See Chapter 2 for a discussion on the demands made by host countries.
30. Davidson, *Global,* p. 24.
31. Jack Baranson, *The Japanese Challenge to U.S. Industry* (Lexington, Mass.: D.C. Heath and Company, 1981), pp. 1–3.
32. Piero Telesio, *Foreign Licensing Policy in Multinational Enterprises* (D.B.A. thesis, Harvard Graduate School of Business Administration, 1977), Chap. 8, pp. 4–6.
33. See Davidson, *Global,* pp. 28–30.
34. National Science Foundation, *Science Indicators,* 1981, quoted ibid., p. 52.
35. For a detailed discussion and specific examples of joint ventures by United States companies, see John I. Reynolds, "The 'Pinched Shoe' Effect of International Joint Ventures," *Columbia Journal of World Business* XIX, 2 (Summer 1984): 7–16.
36. Ibid.
37. Lawrence G. Franko, "Joint Venture Divorce in the Multinational Company," *Columbia Journal of World Business* VI, 3 (May-June 1971): 13–22.

Additional Readings _____

Articles

Baliga, B.R. and Jaeger, Alfred M. "Multinational Corporations: Control Systems and Delegation Issues." *Journal of International Business Studies* XV, 2 (Fall 1984): 25–40.

Contractor, Farok J. "Choosing Between Direct Investment and Licensing: Theoretical Considerations and Empirical Tests." *Journal of International Business Studies* XV, 3 (Winter 1984): 167–188.

Cray, David. "Control and Coordination in Multinational Corporations." *Journal of International Business Studies* XV, 2 (Fall 1984): 85–98.

Harragan, Kathryn Rudie. "Joint Ventures and Global Strategies." *Columbia Journal of World Business* XIX, 2 (Summer 1984): 7–16.

Books

Negandhi, Anant R., and Welge, Martin. *Beyond Theory Z: Global Rationalization Strategies of American, German, and Japanese Multinational Companies.* Greenwich, Conn.: JAI Press, 1984.

Tannenbaum, Arnold S. *Control in Organizations.* New York: McGraw-Hill Book Co., 1968.

Chapter **5**

Decision Making and Headquarters-Subsidiary Relations in International Corporations

This chapter discusses the relative influences of the home office and the overseas subsidiary in strategic and operational decisions. First, the critical issues involved in decision making are identified, and the following aspects are then analyzed:

- Elements and types of decision making
- Factors affecting decision making
- Modes and locus of decisions

• Emprical studies of the locus of decisions among United States, European, and Japanese multinational companies

Critical Issues

Perhaps the most fundamental issues facing the international corporations are: (1) Who should make which decisions? and (2) How should the firm allocate decision-making power between the home office and the overseas subsidiary? Responses to these questions will shape the basic character of the firm and provide the framework for establishing headquarters-subsidiary relationships.

As discussed in Chapter 2, multinational companies are caught between the fast-changing socioeconomic and political conditions around the world. They are hard-put to balance the requirements of efficiency through the global rationalization of production and marketing processes, and to adapt to the home and host countries' demands.[1] The former necessitates centralized control and decision making, whereas the latter calls for a higher level of the overseas subsidiary's autonomy. In other words, as Fayerweather has argued, basically the issue is unification *versus* fragmentation in strategies, policies, and decision making.[2] On the one hand is a large and growing need to integrate the strategies of different units of a multinational company. "The evolution of the environment of multinational companies, and the dynamics of their own evolution, make this integration more necessary."[3] On the other hand, restrictive and hostile environments in developing countries and changing socioeconomic realities in developed countries make such integration more difficult than heretofore.

With respect to the developing countries, Singh has identified the following aspects in which the multinational corporations and the host countries have sharp differences of opinion:

1. The nature of the MNC's investments, including its method of entry and areas of activity
2. The pattern of ownership and the degree of local participation in equity and decision making both for new investments and for existing ones
3. The structure of production envisaged for developing country affiliates, including the extent of downstream activities in resource-based industries and the local content or value added in manufacturing enterprises
4. Pattern of financing and intracompany transactions at various stages of implementation and operation
5. The nature and conditions of the supply of foreign technology and services, including the development of technological and managerial skills and research and development activities[4]

Although industrialized countries have imposed minimal controls on MNCs recently, they too have been revising their policies on foreign investments.[5]

Elements and Types of Decision Making

Decision making is a dynamic process. It involves communication, information flow, and behavioral aspects. It is relatively easy to identify the locus of decisions, but the implementation of decisions is more complex and requires a deeper understanding of behavioral dynamics involved in transmitting decisions. The aspirations, motivations, frustrations, and problems faced by those at the receiving end must be incorporated in any decision-making system.[6] Otherwise, like organization structures and charts, it may become a static phenomenon.

Essentially three options are available to managers in deciding a locus of decisions:

1. Decisions are made at the home office.
2. Decisions are made at the subsidiary level.
3. Joint decision making occurs between the home office and the overseas subsidiary.

The specific choice of a given option is dependent on the managerial orientation, the firm's internal attributes, such as size, technology, product line, commitment to international barriers, and the environmental forces in the home and host countries. The impact of organizational and environmental variables in decision making is portrayed in Table 5-1. I will first analyze the impact of the firm's attributes and environmental forces on the locus of decision making and then discuss the differences among United States, European, and Japanese multinational companies.

Decision-Making Levels

Generally speaking, the financial aspects, research, and developmental activities show the highest degree of the headquarters' direction. Consequently, decisions on these aspects are centralized at the home office. Advertising, promotion, personnel, and routine production decisions are shared equally by home office and subsidiary personnel. Purchasing, product pricing, and marketing research activities are basically within the domain of the subsidiary's managers. Later in the chapter a few research studies are reviewed that support this contention.

Table 5-1 Factors affecting centralization-decentralization in the MNC's system

	Loose coupling of the system (decentralized) *Home Office*
Centralization in decision making Tight coupling of the MNC system *Home Office*	*Very loose coupling of the system (decentralized)* *Home Office*
Factors giving rise to tight coupling: • Large capital investment • Large size • Necessity for achieving • Interdependence of subsystems for parts and raw materials • Technology–R&D intensity • Accountability to stockholders • Marketing and advertising intensity • Competitive pressures • Low level of diversification • Standardized product line • Homogeneous and stable economic and political environment	Factors giving rise to loose coupling, (i.e., decentralization of decision making, higher autonomy of the subsidiary): • Low morale of subsidiary managers • Inability of the subsidiary's managers to cope with environmental demands • Long geographical distance between HQ and subsidiary • Large differences in product design and marketing mix management • Environmental demands (host and home country's demands) • Heterogeneous economic and political environment • Turbulent, dynamic, and complex environment

Source: Compiled by the author, based on a review of the literature. The help of William Emmons and Toshi Asaka is gratefully acknowledged for the preparation of this table.

Factors Affecting Locus of Decision Making

As shown in Table 5-1, the following variables play a significant role in choosing the locus of decision making:

1. *Size of the company:* the larger the size, the greater the need for integration and, consequently, the higher the degree of centralization in decision making.
2. *Capital investment:* the larger the capital involvement made by

the parent company in the overseas operation, the higher the degree of centralization in decision making.

3. *Relative importance of foreign business:* the larger the stake in international business, the more centralized the decision making.

4. *Level of competitive environment:* the more competitive the market conditions, the higher the degree of centralization in decision making. Strictly speaking, the proposition goes against the established contingency theory of the organization. For example, a study by Lawrence and Lorsch indicates that a firm operating in a highly competitive market tends to be more decentralized.[7] However, in the international context, higher competitive pressure means lower gross margins and, consequently, the need to standardize product and marketing decisions to reduce unit cost. This, in turn, calls for a higher level of centralization in policy decisions.

5. *Volume/unit cost relationship:* the stronger the relationship between the volume produced and the cost of a unit, the higher the degree of centralization in decision making. The logic here is to achieve economies of scale by producing optimal volume to reduce unit cost.[8] To do so, the firm will produce standardized products that will have a higher interchangeability of parts and new material among different units of the multinational system. This in turn necessitates centralized sourcing and marketing management policies, strategies, and practices.

6. *Level of technology:* the more sophisticated the technology, the higher the degree of centralization in decision making. The logic here is to protect the firm's valuable technological resources. This proposition also applies to the firm's research and development activities. High research intensity firms will be more centralized than the low research intensity firms[9] (e.g., IBM, DuPont, pharmaceutical firms).

7. *Brand name, patent rights:* the higher the importance attached to brand name and patent rights, the higher the degree of centralization in decision making. The logic is the same—to protect the firm's valuable assets[10] (e.g., Coca-Cola).

8. *Diversification of products:* the higher the level of diversification in products and services offered by the firm, the greater the need for decentralizing the decision-making process (i.e., the higher the subsidiary's autonomy). The logic here is that the firm producing diversified products may lack the capital or technological and human resources needed to provide centralized guidance to subsidiaries. In other words, the bargaining strength of the managers of the subsidiaries manufacturing specialized products and possessing knowledge of local markets and environmental conditions may be stronger than that of the home office personnel.

9. *Heterogeneity:* refers to both the differences in products and services offered by the firm, and the differences in socioeconomic,

political, legal, and cultural environments in the various countries in which the firm is operating. The impact of the heterogeneity of products and services on centralization was outlined earlier. With respect to the environmental differences, research studies have shown that the higher the level of environmental differences between home and host countries, the greater the need for decentralizing the decision-making process.[11] Heterogeneity in the international environment requires more adaptive strategies, policies, and practices. This can be done more effectively at the subsidiary level, thus requiring a higher level of subsidiary autonomy.

10. *Time and distance:* the greater the distance between the home office and the affiliate, the longer the delays in communicating information and transmitting skills and resources, which may necessitate granting higher autonomy to the subsidiary's managers.[12] In general, United States subsidiaries in Latin American countries and Canada are controlled more tightly than those in Japan and Southeast Asian countries. However, the sociocultural diversities between Canada and Southeast Asia may also account for the differences in degree of controls exercised by United States MNCs in those two regions.[13]

11. *Interdependence among units:* the higher degree of interdependence among the different units of the MNC's system may require closer coordination and integration by the home office and, consequently, a higher level of centralization in decision making.[14]

Besides these organizational and environmental factors, other researchers have identified additional factors affecting the decision-making process. These include:

1. *Competence level of managers in host countries.* Less competent subsidiary managers will be more controlled by the home office personnel than more competent subsidiary managers.[15]

2. *Mode of entry.* Subsidiaries established by the home office will be more integrated than those that are acquired.[16] The higher the level of integration, the higher the level of centralization in decision making.

3. *The firm's experience in international business:* the longer the firm has been involved in international business, the higher the degree of centralization.[17]

Many illustrations and research studies show the relationships between these organizational and environmental variables and the level of centralization in decision making. For example, high-technology companies such as IBM require 100% ownership in overseas units for the purpose of establishing substantive control over their overseas subsidiaries. IBM's recent withdrawal from the Indian market was rationalized on this basis. (The Indian Government, through its Foreign Exchange Regulation Act of 1973, asked IBM and other companies to reduce equity to 40%, which IBM refused to do.) Although not in a high-technology industry, Coca-Cola also refused to reduce its equity because of the proprietary nature of its "secret formula" and marketing knowledge. Both IBM and Coca-Cola derive over 50% of their income from overseas investments, indicating the substantial stake each maintains in international business.

Similarly, Stobough,[18] as well as Aylmer,[19] found that only large companies with heavy involvement in international business possess the required knowledge, skills, and competence to exercise stiff controls over their subsidiaries.

Doz's study revealed that the competitive environment created the need to reduce unit cost and to rationalize the production and marketing processes. This resulted in a higher degree of centralization in decision making.[20] To secure the benefits of economies of scale, the Philips Lamp Co. of Holland decided to abandon its highly decentralized structure in favor of centralized control over production and marketing. This change in strategy resulted in increased profit performance.[21]

DeBodinat, in his study of multinational companies, found a strong relationship between the complexity of technology and the high degree of centralization. Similarly, the actual expenditures on research and development activities by United States MNCs indicate that the headquarters exercised substantial control over these activities, and that the subsidiary's autonomy is minimal.[22] For technologically sophisticated products, there is little need for local adaptations and, consequently, the home office influence on manufacturing and marketing policies will be substantial.[23]

Functional Areas and Decision Making

Various studies of multinational companies have shown that the centralization in decision making is highest in such functional areas as finance, research and development, strategic planning, and technological transfer. It is lower in marketing mix management, production scheduling, and personnel and industrial relations. Barlow, for example, found that the home office exercised considerable control over its subsidiaries in areas of product quality, choosing personnel, accounting and financial methods, and expansion of local production. However, in sales planning, labor relations, and local pricing decisions, the subsidiaries were granted a fair degree of autonomy.[24]

Wiechmann, in his study of twenty-seven European companies, found that the decisions concerning research and development activities and product policy were highly centralized, whereas purchasing, marketing research, advertising and promotion, and distribution decisions were decentralized at the subsidiary levels.[25] Franko reported similar results.[26]

Important Determinants

Of the factors affecting the degree of centralization in decision making, the two most important variables seem to be interdependence among the various units of the multinational system and the market share of the given subsidiary. The higher the level of interdependence among units, the higher the level of centralization. The higher the importance of a given subsidiary in terms of sales and revenue generated, the higher the level of centralization in decision making. Conversely, a large subsidiary may create a need for greater autonomy.[27] Such results were obtained in a comparative study of multinational companies.[28]

Changes in Locus of Decision Making

As noted earlier, the decision-making process itself is dynamic and shifts over time. For example, Phahalad and Doz[29] have shown that in the earlier stage, when the home office controls the critical inputs—technology, capital, and managerial and marketing knowledge—major strategic decisions are centralized. As the business matures, the need and ability to control diminishes.[30] To quote the authors:

> The ability of MNCs to use substantive control over subsidiaries is being eroded as businesses mature and as subsidiaries grow in size and sophistication. The nature of tensions imposed by the external environment also reduces the importance of substantive control as the primary tool. MNCs need to rely ever more on administrative context as a strategic control mechanism.[31]

These dynamic shifts in decision making are portrayed in Figure 5-1.

National Origin and Decision Making

Although a number of authors have indicated the impact of national origin of MNCs (United States, European, and Japanese) on the degree of centralization in decision making, few have done systematic comparative studies on decision making in multinational companies. Of these few, studies by Franko concerning European MNCs, Yoshino and Tsurumi of Japanese MNCs, and

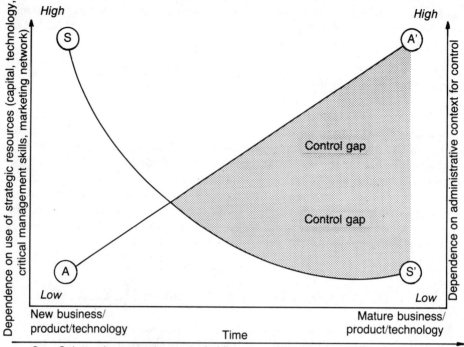

S = Substantive controls over subsidiary operations
A = Administrative control through procedures and policies

Figure 5-1 Schematic representation of shifts in control in headquarters-subsidiary relationships (*Source:* C. K. Prahalad and Yves L. Doz, "Strategic Control–The Dilemma in Headquarters-Subsidiary Relationship," *The Management of Headquarters-Subsidiary Relationships in Multinational Corporations,* ed. Lars Otterbeck (Hampshire, England: Grower, 1981), p. 194.)

Hulbert and Brandt and Sim of subsidiaries of United States, European, and Japanese MNCs in Brazil and Malaysia, respectively, are worth noting.

Franko, in his study of eighty European multinational companies, found considerable autonomy offered to the subsidiaries' managers by their respective home offices.[32] Similarly, in his study of the MNCs' subsidiaries in Western Europe and in the United States, Franko found greater autonomy among these subsidiaries operating in the United States.[33] The relative size of the subsidiaries, distance, and market competitiveness in the United States were considered important factors, leading to a higher autonomy of the subsidiaries in the United States.

Both Yoshino's[34] and Tsurumi's[35] research on Japanese multinational companies, as well as those of Ouchi[36] and Johnson and Ouchi,[37] have indicated a greater degree of decentralization among Japanese MNCs–that is, a higher autonomy of the subsidiary's manager. Tsurumi's observations illustrate this situation:

> The consensus-building practices in the decision-making process of Japanese firms have created two distinct Japanese characteristics: namely, (1) the substantive involvement of middle management (section chiefs to department heads) in making strategic decisions; and (2) the presidential leadership being expected to cope mainly with crisis situations or with abrupt and clear-cut changes in the direction of the firm. Once the general direction of the firm is communicated to the middle management echelon, both operational decisions and incremental changes tend to be entrusted to the initiative of the lower to middle management echelons.[38]

Although Hulbert and Brandt,[39] in their study of United States, European, and Japanese subsidiaries in Brazil, found a higher level of centralization and formalization in the United States subsidiaries as compared to those of the European and the Japanese, they seem to underplay the impact of nationality on decision making. In other words, they are suggesting a convergence thesis. They have argued:

> For the multinational organization today, the increasing comparability of environmental and strategic conditions, embracing almost all the world's major markets and a common set of multinational competitors, encourages the adoption of a more geocentric perspective.[40]

In contrast, Sim's study in Malaysia indicated a higher level of decentralization in the United States subsidiaries, and a lower level in Japanese subsidiaries. He provides the following explanation for the higher level of centralization in Japanese subsidiaries[41]:

1. Japanese firms tended to use operational and managerial control rather than equity ownership to control their subsidiaries. Control was maintained through the use of Japanese personnel in top management or technical positions in the subsidiary and the retention of authority in decision making by head office or Japanese management.
2. Japanese managers in the subsidiaries tended to be autocratic in their management and did not delegate their authority to the extent that the American and British managers did.[42]

Sim's study relates more to operational aspects at the subsidiary level rather than at the policy and strategic levels.

Finally, as discussed in Chapters 3 and 4, Stopford and Wells's[43] study of 187 United States multinational companies clearly indicates a higher level of integration of the subsidiaries and hence, a considerable degree of centralization in decision making at the headquarters. Their results were further reinforced by Egelhoff, in his current study of United States, European, and Japanese multinational companies.[44]

Results of the Current Study

In a recent study of 120 subsidiaries of United States, German, and Japanese multinational companies, the subsidiaries' managers were asked to rate the relative influences of the headquarters and subsidiaries on the following items on a five-point scale (1 = little influence of the subsidiary, 5 = very high influence of the subsidiary):

> Training programs for local employees
> Layoff of operating personnel
> Use of expatriate personnel
> Appointment of chief executive
> Maintenance of production facilities
> Determining aggregate production schedules
> Expansion of production capacity
> Use of local advertising agency
> Servicing of products sold
> Pricing decisions
> Introduction of new product for local market
> Choosing public accountant
> Extensions of credit to major customers
> Use of cash flow by the subsidiary
> Borrowing from local banks

Tables 5-2 and 5-3 provide the raw scores and the difference in means between the subsidiary's and the headquarters' influences on decision making concerning these fifteen items. At first glance, the subsidiaries seem to have at least moderate influence on decision making. Here too, United States subsidiaries possess the least autonomy, the Japanese the most. The German subsidiaries are between those two extremes.[45]

The picture of the greater autonomy of the subsidiary changes as soon as one compares strategic *versus* routine decisions. Table 5-3 shows that the score of the relative influence turns negative for the strategic decisions for all three types of subsidiaries. Figures 5-2 and 5-3 indicate the extent of delegation provided to the subsidiary's management in various areas.

The overall delegation index is fairly low in absolute terms. Despite the headquarters's acknowledgment of a less than perfect understanding of the

Table 5-2 The relative influence of the subsidiary in decision making*
(raw score)

Item	Mean Scores		
	United States MNCs	Japanese MNCs	German MNCs
Personnel training program for your subsidiary	3.8	4.6	4.5
Layoffs of operating personnel	4.4	4.9	4.4
Use of expatriate personnel from headquarters	2.7	3.6	2.4
Appointment of chief executive of your subsidiary	1.5	2.8	1.7
Maintenance of production facilities at your subsidiary	3.3	4.3	4.8
Determining aggregate production schedule	3.2	4.2	4.3
Expansion of your production capacity	2.5	3.5	2.7
Use of local advertising agency	3.9	4.7	4.5
Servicing products sold	4.4	4.7	4.7
Pricing products sold in your local market	3.0	4.5	4.0
Introduction of a new product in your local market	2.6	4.1	3.1
Choice of public accountant	2.7	4.6	4.4
Extension of your credit to one of your major customers	3.7	4.5	4.3
Use of cash flow in your subsidiary	3.2	4.2	3.4
Your borrowing from local banks or financial institutions	3.2	3.6	3.4
Average (means)	3.21	4.19	3.77

*The responses were precoded from "1" for "very little or no influence" to "5" for "very high influence."

Table 5-3 Relative influence over 15 decision areas (mean score differences*)

Item		Differences in Means		
		United States MNCs	Japanese MNCs	German MNCs
Personnel training		1.1	3.1	2.4
Layoffs		2.6	3.3	2.7
Expatriates	(S)	−.7	.2	−1.7
Appointment of CEO	(S)	−3.0	−1.6	−3.0
Maintenance		.1	1.8	2.4
Production schedule		−.1	1.2	1.9
Expansion	(S)	−1.4	−.2	−1.2
Advertising		1.4	2.7	2.7
Servicing		2.5	2.9	3.1
Pricing		−.5	1.9	1.3
New products	S)	−1.2	.8	−.6
Choice of CPA		−.5	1.8	2.4
Credit to customers		1.2	2.4	2.5
Use of cash flow		.1	1.7	.3
Borrowing from banks		.1	.5	.1
Average (means)		.11	1.50	1.02

*The figures in the table represent the differences in means between the rated subsidiary and the headquarters's influence for each of the decision items and the means taken over the companies in the identified country category. A positive number implies a relatively greater influence on the part of the subsidiary, whereas a negative number indicates greater influence by the headquarters.
S = Strategic Issues

subsidiary's operation and its environment, the subsidiary's influence on strategic decision making remained minimal.

A Study in a Single Country

Until now, this analysis of decision-making influences by the headquarters vis-à-vis the overseas subsidiaries was carried out on an aggregate level— combining the data collected from all twelve host countries. Given the differing socioeconomic, market, political, legal, and cultural environments in

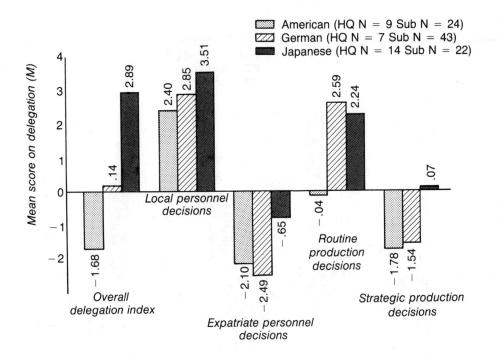

Figure 5-2 Comparison of delegation in the various areas for U.S., German, and Japanese MNCs (*Source:* A. R. Negandhi and M. Welge, *Beyond Theory Z: Global Rationalization Strategies of American, German, and Japanese Multinational Companies* (Greenwich, Conn.: JAI Press, Inc., 1984), p. 23.)

the various countries studied, it is possible that such environmental differences may affect the degree of autonomy granted to the subsidiary. To explore such effects, an analysis of data collected from the German and Japanese subsidiaries in a single country was carried out; namely, the United States.

The results obtained confirm the overall trend toward centralization in decision making, as discussed in the preceding pages. Both the overall delegation index and the decision-making authority of the subsidiaries, with respect to such strategic factors as marketing policies, financial matters, use of expatriate personnel, and decisions on production capacity indicate a fair degree of centralization, especially in the German subsidiaries.[46]

Similar results were also obtained from a study of German subsidiaries operating in France, India, and the United States.[47]

The convergence in organizational practices in general, and decision making in particular, is taking place rapidly. This can be seen from the results

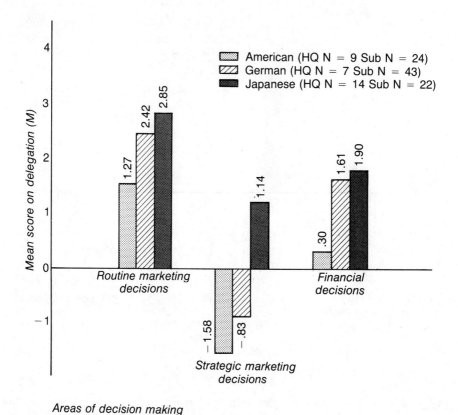

Figure 5-3 Comparison of delegation in the various areas for U.S., German, and Japanese MNCs (*Source:* A. R. Negandhi and M. Welge, *Beyond Theory Z: Global Rationalization Strategies of American, German, and Japanese Multinational Companies* (Greenwich, Conn.: JAI Press, Inc., 1984), p. 23.)

of our recent study of United States, German, British, Japanese, and Swedish multinational companies. The results showed that United States management practices concerning decision making are the norms being followed by other nations. Other countries' practices correlated strongly with those of United States practices. Commenting on such close relationships among different multinationals, Lars Otterbeck stated that although "the fact remains that managements of non-U.S. MNCs seem to grant their subsidiaries higher autonomy than those of U.S. MNCs . . . still they are heavily influenced by American management theory and management education . . . all so-called international business schools teach American management."[48] Summing up, our results concerning the level of formalization, documentation, reporting requirements, and decision making point toward the MNCs' drive for global rationalization and the unification of strategies and policies. The underlying rationale for this drive, of course, is to realize economies of scale and higher operational efficiency. However, the impact of centralization in decision making may have adverse effects on maintaining effective head-quarters-subsidiary relations, morale and motivation of the subsidiary's managers, and providing subsidiary managers the flexibility to cope with the host country's demands.[49]

Summary

This chapter analyzed decision making and headquarters-subsidiary relations in international corporations. Two critical issues were identified: (1) Who should make which decisions? and (2) How should the firm allocate decision-making power between the home office and the overseas subsidiary? These two issues concerned the overall aspects of centralization and decentralization in the organization.

Particularly in international corporations, the centralization-decentralization aspect is a thorny issue at best. On the one hand, the international company needs to integrate its global units via centralized decision making. On the other hand, the required adaptation to the host country's demands necessitates some autonomy on the part of the overseas subsidiary.

This chapter examined the firm-related and environmental-related factors affecting the locus of decision making. The actual decision-making practices of United States, European, and Japanese companies were then reviewed.

Cases

Restructuring an existing organization is sometimes inevitable and even desirable to cope effectively with new environmental changes. The PIA Agricultural Equipment Company case shows the limitations in pursuing a global integration strategy through tight formal controls by the headquarters. Also, economic and noneconomic impacts of a newly centralized reorganization of the subsidiary operations are discussed.

The simplest and most direct form of countervailing forces available to an MNC is the refusal to participate or the decision to divest existing operations. The second case deals with conflicts between the economic decision of IBM and the legal decision of the Indian government. Process and strategy of the negotiation are also investigated in the case.

Case 5-1 ════════════════════════════════

PIA Agricultural Equipment Company (Impact of Reorganization)

A Critical Meeting in New York City in March 1985

As Mr. Hans Schmidt, managing director of the German subsidiary of a United States multinational, was getting ready to board the plane, his mind was preoccupied with the eventual outcome of this important meeting in New York. The meeting for managing directors and other important officials of all important subsidiaries around the world was called by the chairman and chief operating officer, Mr. John Melcher. The purpose of this meeting was to discuss further changes in the organization's structure and the subsidiary's operations to reduce losses and to increase productivity and profitability.

The Company

PIA Agricultural Equipment Company was established in the United States some 150 years ago to manufacture tractors and other farm machinery. The company was a leader and one of the largest in its field. Over the years, it retained its leadership not only in tractors and farm equipment business but also in earth-moving machinery, commerical trucks, and construction equipment. Since 1965, it has been diversifying in related and nonrelated areas,

Table 5-4 Five-year comparison of selected financial data (PIA agricultural equipment) (millions of U.S. dollars, except dividends per share)

	1983	1982	1981	1980	1979
Sales and revenues of continuing operations	$3,960	$4,754	$6,897	$5,762	$7,786
Income (loss) of continuing operations (usual items only)	(477)	(939)	(576)	(231)	–
Income (loss) of discontinued operations & extraordinary income	(586)	(1,454)	(576)	(231)	–
Income (loss) per common share of continuing operations (usual items)	(15.6)	(29.8)	(18.7)	(7.6)	–
Income (loss) per common share of discontinuing operations and extraordinary income	(18.8)	(45.8)	(18.7)	(7.6)	–
Dividends per common share	–	–	0.33	2.75	–
Net assets of year's end	(589)	(116)	1,768	2,174	–

such as steelmaking, power generation, solar energy, computers, and natural gas. Overall, the company was profitable until 1979, when the impact of reorganization plans, announced in 1977, coupled with the forces in the international competitive environment, changed the scene dramatically. For example, from a U.S. $8 billion company in 1979, it was reduced to half that size, approximately U.S. $4 billion, in 1983. Return on stockholder equity was maintained approximately by 10% to 12% throughout the 1970s, which dropped to zero in 1983. Its common stock price fell from $40 in 1979 to $3 in 1982 and recovered to $14 in 1983. To cover the losses, the company was obligated to sell off a number of overseas subsidiaries: the steelmaking, earth-moving, and commercial truck divisions. Important financial data of the company, during 1979 to 1983, are given in Table 5-4.

Settings for Reorganization

Beginning from 1959, when G. H. Clee and A. Discipio wrote the article "Creating a World Enterprise" in the *Harvard Business Review*, (November–December, 1959, pp. 77–79), a number of large United States corporations initiated changes in their organizational structure to reflect global orientations.[1] Research studies on multinational companies by the Harvard Business School and others during the 1960s and 1970s stimulated such changes in organizational structures.[2]

PIA Agricultural Equipment Co.'s chairman, Mr. John Melcher, was under pressure to keep pace with the fundamental organizational changes that were taking place in many United States companies.

In 1974, he hired a Harvard professor, Ken Uhl, first as consultant and subsequently as Vice-President of Strategic Planning and Corporate Policy, to recommend and implement necessary changes in the organizational structure.

After two and one half years of hard work, Professor Uhl presented his recommendations to the chairman and the Board. Based on these recommendations, the chairman announced that the company would change its organizational structure from its divisional concept to five freestanding, worldwide groups. Each group would have its own president and regional functional vice-presidents (e.g., in marketing, finance, and purchasing). The five groups consisted of agricultural machinery, commercial trucks, construction and earth-moving equipment, power generation, and spare parts division.

In announcing the reorganization plan, Mr. Melcher noted that each group was distinct and different with respect to products, markets, and requirements for success. Each group was also large enough to stand alone as a company to compete effectively in domestic and world markets. Each group and its president would be responsible for its entire global market, sourcing, generating needed capital, and use of cash flow and profits. Each group's president would have direct control over domestic and overseas subsidiary operations. Mr. Melcher also indicated that the overall corporate group would be reduced to minimal size, consisting of a strategic planning function, a policy-making group, and a legal and public relations function.

Figures 5-4 and 5-5 provide the old and new organizational structure of the company.

Meeting in New York

The meeting was called to discuss the present financial situation and problems facing the company. As can be seen from Table 5-4, the company had incurred huge losses during the last four years and was obligated to sell off many of its efficient domestic and overseas operations. It was widely held by many senior officers in the overseas subsidiaries that the main cause for

[1]John Stopford and Louis T. Wells, *Managing The Multinational Enterprise: Organization of the Firm and Ownership of the Subsidiaries* (New York: Basic Books, 1972).

[2]Raymond Vernon, *Sovereignty at Bay: The Multinational Spread of U.S. Enterprises* (New York: Basic Books, 1971). Michael Yoshino, *Japan's Multinational Enterprise* (Cambridge: Harvard University Press, 1976). Lawrence Franco, *The European Multinational* (Stamford: Greylock, 1976).

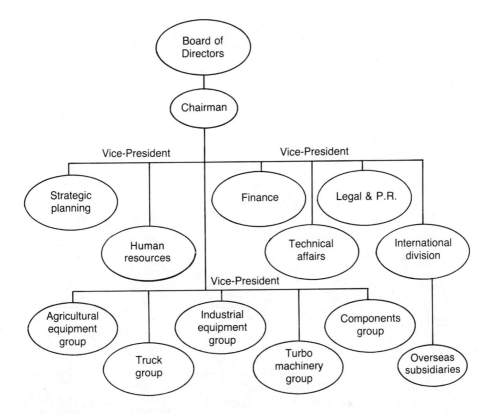

Figure 5-4 Before reorganization

these losses was the implementation of the new organizational structure announced by the chairman in 1977. Of course, the world's market conditions, and particularly Japanese competition, were first thought to be the principal causes of the company's downward economic fate. However, many overseas subsidiaries' managers were not convinced of this argument. Particularly, Mr. Hans Schmidt, managing director of the most efficient and profitable West German subsidiary, strongly believed that the reorganization of the company had much to do with the company's present financial woes.

Before 1977, as a managing director, he was totally responsible for the operations and profitability of the German subsidiary. He then reported to the vice-president of the International Division of the New York headquarters. However, since the reorganization, all of his product managers reported directly to each of the group's president concerned. Mr. Schmidt only got copies of these reports from his own product managers. These changes in reporting requirements and accountability had made the product managers independent and less accountable to the managing director of the subsidiary. Besides

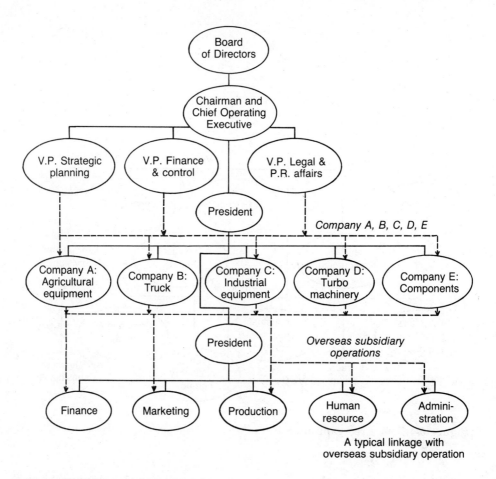

Figure 5-5 After reorganization

losing overall control over the overseas subsidiaries, Mr. Schmidt was experiencing a great deal of interpersonal tension and conflict in dealing with his managers since the reorganization plan was implemented.

His informal conversation with the managing directors of the subsidiaries in Australia, France, Brazil, and Mexico indicated a similar situation prevailing in those subsidiaries.

Thus the New York meeting was considered critical, not only for the survival and health of the overseas subsidiaries, but also for the entire company. Specifically, the main agenda of the meeting was to discuss the various alternatives to review the company's financial strength. Suggested alternatives were:

1. To dismantle the new and adopt the old organizational structure.

2. To sell off the British and Australian subsidiaries that were marginally profitable until 1979, but were losing money since 1980. The selling of these two subsidiaries could generate U.S. $300 million to cover the losses of 1983.
3. To sell off all of the manufacturing activities, except the agricultural equipment division, the service organizations, and the financial credit company, to generate approximately U.S. $2 billion to cover the entire losses incurred during 1981–1983.

Mr. Schmidt and the managing directors of the subsidiaries in Australia, France, Brazil, and Mexico, although in agreement concerning the negative impact of the reorganization, were not sure about the various alternatives they could choose. All of them felt that something needed to be done to cover the losses. However, selling the British and Australian subsidiaries might create a chain reaction for others to follow in case of financial crises. Besides, the British and Australian subsidiaries were the oldest and most established in the international markets. These subsidiaries were considered the "eyes and ears," the window to the expanding markets in Southeast Asia and Africa. The British Commonwealth countries were important for these subsidiaries.

Appendix 1 Facts About the Australian Subsidiary _____

The Australian subsidiary was established in 1935. Until World War II, it was simply involved in selling goods imported from the United Kingdom, West Germany, and the United States.

In 1946, its first manufacturing operation was established to assemble trucks and tractors. By 1970, it operated four facilities, employing about 5,000 persons. In 1983, trucks and tractors constituted 95% of the total revenue, whereas construction equipment amounted to only 5% (Table 5-5).

Table 5-5 Selected financial data of the Australian subsidiary (in U.S. $ millions)

	1979	1980	1981	1982	1983
Sales	200	220	180	140	110
Profits	4.0	3.8	(1.5)	(7.0)	(10.0)
Dividends paid	–	–	–	–	–
Long-term debts	2.0	2.0	2.0	2.0	2.0
Total assets	160	200	220	280	300
Total liabilities	80	85	90	95	150

Appendix 2 Facts About the British Subsidiary _____

Table 5-6 Selected financial data of the British subsidiary

	1979	1980	1981	1982	1983
Sales	250	280	230	200	150
Profits	15.0	10.0	(8.0)	(10.0)	(20.0)
Dividends paid	–	–	–	–	–
Long-term debts	5.0	5.0	8.0	8.0	8.0
Total assets	280	285	250	240	240
Total liabilities	70	75	80	85	90

The PAE started its business in the United Kingdom in 1910. As the volume of the business was getting larger PAE decided to set up a wholly-owned manufacturing subsidiary in 1921. Since then, the main activities of the British subsidiary were to manufacture commercial trucks and farm equipment to serve both domestic and overseas markets (Table 5-6).

In 1983, employing 7,000 workers, the subsidiary had become one of the largest of PAE's overseas production facilities. Agricultural equipment, industrial equipment, and spare parts represented about 60%, 25%, and 15% of its sales, respectively. Roughly one half of its production was directed towards the British market, whereas the rest went to overseas markets.

Case 5-2

International Business Machines (IBM)

History and Background

The year was 1977. IBM was faced with certain problems primarily related to ownership and equity. Iran, Nigeria, Indonesia, Brazil, and India had raised questions concerning IBM operations in their countries. None of these countries accounted for much of IBM's revenues—the company does business in 125 countries. Hoever, the main area of concern for IBM officials was that the company should not set a precedent that could lead to troublesome demands in other countries in the future.

Nationalistic fervor in developing countries may touch off drives toward nationalism in industrial countries. For instance, the French often talk about nationalizing hundreds of businesses. IBM probably gets about 3% of its revenues from France. The French governmental demands may thus create significant problems for IBM.

At corporate headquarters in Armonk, New York, there was a perceived need to evaluate corporate strategy in the light of these developments; the areas to which special attention would have to be given were organization and control.

International Activities

Domestically, IBM has long been the classic growth company. General opinion is that as the leading producer of advanced electronic computing equipment, IBM would certainly seem to be a long way from exhausting its growth potential in the United States market. However, IBM has been cultivating

Source: Data for this case were collected by Anant R. Negandhi. Ms. Rachel Davis assisted in preparing the case. © Copyright by Anant R. Negandhi, 1985.

foreign markets since World War I. One of the mottoes of the late founder, Thomas J. Watson, was: "World peace through world trade."

After World War II, before the Marshall Plan got off the ground, and European economic recovery was still very uncertain, Watson detached IBM's foreign operation from its divisional status and set it up as a wholly-owned but independently administered subsidiary, known as the IBM World Trade Corporation.

The recovery of Western Europe developed a mass market, and along with it, chain stores, time payments, higher wages, and labor shortages. It became essential for European firms to start spending money on increasing efficiency. Increasing human efficiency is exactly IBM's business.

By 1960, IBM World Trade Corporation had operations in eighty-seven countries, thirty-six served by nationally incorporated companies, the rest by branch offices and sales agencies. In 1976, the number of countries in which IBM had operations had risen to 125, with 300,000 employees worldwide, one half of these being overseas employees. Less than 1% of the overseas employees are from the United States. From the mid-60s, foreign business has accounted for roughly 50% of IBM's total revenues and earnings.

IBM's Corporate Philosophy

A healthy respect for governing institutions led IBM very early to adopt an austere hands-off policy towards politics.

Over the years, IBM has developed an elaborate system for managing its dealings with national governments. IBM blends into the background of the countries in which it operates like a chameleon and then makes its appeals to governments based on the national interest rather than IBM's interest. It behaves ethically. No bribery scandals mar its past. Most governments are made aware that "IBM does not make deals." Yet IBM is not above playing one government against another, using its base to its fullest advantage, or bringing into play its own considerable power and resources that stem from its size and its dominance of the market for vital products, usually computers.

IBM has a strict policy towards taxes, one that is sometimes irritating to other companies. It pays them in full. IBM never uses tax havens. The taxes can sometimes be deferred, but never dodged. This gives the company a fine reputation when it wants to enter a new country. This is another legacy of Thomas J. Watson, the founder. He had confidence in his ability to build a great and everlasting company. Thus, he reasoned, why fool around with short-term tax fiddles that could endanger IBM's eternal growth? This basic premise helps every IBM subsidiary behave as a good corporate citizen.

When it comes to moving money around the face of the earth, IBM is similarly law abiding, but less open about the mechanisms. For example, IBM is quite secretive about the royalty and licensing fees paid by the subsidiaries and intracompany pricing of components and products.

Organization and Control

Given strong emphasis on research and development, IBM consistently demanded and secured 100% ownership in its overseas subsidiaries.

IBM's insistence on 100% ownership led to problems in such countries as Japan, India, Indonesia, Nigeria, and Brazil.

In the early 1960s, the Japanese Government demanded that the wholly-owned subsidiary, IBM Japan, be converted to a joint venture with the Japanese holding a majority. IBM was able to use their customers to counter this demand; it was found that IBM customers would continue to deal with IBM, no matter what their government did. With its industry support evaporating rapidly, the government gracefully withdrew its demands. IBM gracefully increased its manufacturing and education facilities in Japan, and continues to do so whenever the stress levels on the issue seem to be rising. IBM now operates two companies in Japan, one 100% owned holding company and the other a joint manufacturing firm.

In 1977, IBM faced challenges from Nigeria, Indonesia, and India concerning its organizational and control practices. Nigeria and India demanded equity participation in the local subsidiaries; Indonesia asked for local control in its marketing operation.

Demands from India

IBM withdrew from India in 1977. Until this time, it has been the only instance of IBM suspending operations in any country. Since its withdrawal from India, there has been a lot of debate as to who, India or IBM, was the loser when IBM pulled out of India.

Economic Background on India

India is a country of paradoxes. Its per capita income is among the lowest in the world, while at the same time its gross industrial output is the tenth largest in the world. This anomaly is explained by the fact that 40% of India's 700 million people live below the poverty line, so there are great disparities in income.

Politically, India has been at the forefront of various international movements initiated by the developing countries. Examples are the Non-aligned Movement and the Group of 77. India has also used her expertise in middle-level technology to transfer technology to developing countries.

Political Background

Under the Foreign Exchange Regulation Act of 1973 (FERA), the government of India required all foreign-owned subsidiaries operating in India to reduce the proportion of ownership held in foreign hands to 40% or below. This directive had been invoked by the then Prime Minister Indira Gandhi in 1973, and was subsequently enacted into law in form of the FERA. Those firms desiring exceptional treatment were to file a request for an exemption of FERA regulations. Exemption was permissible in cases of extraordinary contributions to the Indian economy, such as the transfer of advanced technology, production in a high-priority sector, or operations providing foreign exchange earnings.

In the 1977 elections, there was a swing away from the Congress party for the first time in the thirty years since independence. The Janata Party, which came to power, was composed of members of widely differing political persuasions. The Janata Party represented a coalition of interests rather than a clear and cohesive mandate. It sought to legitimize itself by focusing on social and nationalistic issues. As a result, there was pressure from within the new ruling party, as well as from local pressure groups, to look into the functioning of multinational corporations in India.

IBM and India

Just five years after India won her independence, IBM opened its Indian office. IBM quickly established a superior reputation and market share for typewriters, adding machines, data processing equipment, and computers. Technical superiority, as well as a demonstrated commitment to after-sale service and maintenance, resulted in a 70% share of the Indian office machine market by the early 1970s. However, only the most rudimentary manufacturing took place in the Indian subsidiary. In fact, most of the computers sold by IBM in India were reconditioned machines, brought in from the United States and elsewhere.

Therefore, the presence of IBM was not perceived by the Indian government as providing either advanced technology or access to world markets. Fulfillment of either of these two conditions might have qualified IBM for preferential treatment under the provisions of the FERA. The company, through its global strategy, had located its high-technology and export facilities elsewhere. India was seen primarily as a market for sales and service.

IBM's wholly-owned Indian subsidiary employed only about 1,000 people; the number had fallen to 800 in 1977. The Indian subsidiary contributed only 0.07% of IBM's total net income. During the 1951–1977 period, IBM installed nearly 1,000 computer systems in India, mostly refurbished 1401s. The Bombay plant reconditioned used computers and, at one point, manufactured a medium-sized computer with 20% local content for the domestic market and an inexpensive keypunch machine with 70% local content for export.

Under the FERA, IBM-India qualified as a trading company because it imported and sold computers in the Indian market. However, it had hoped to gain an exemption from the local ownership requirements of the FERA on the grounds that it was selling high-technology items that India badly needed, and therefore qualified as a "priority" producer. Negotiations between IBM and the government of India began in 1975 and continued on and off until November 1977.

IBM's proposal, in response to the government of India's enforcement of the FERA, was prepared in New York. The Indian general manager forwarded all relevant correspondence between the company and the government to the headquarters. The manager also included his own input as to what would be the minimal requirements, what was desirable, and what would have to be done to qualify for "exceptional treatment." The final proposal was developed in New York and then sent to India. The Indian employees were "heavily" involved in terms of follow-up—meetings with government officials and explaining the various aspects of the proposals.

The Proposal

IBM's only publicized offer, made in April 1976, proposed creating two companies. One company would have 40% equity, which would operate IBM's data center (service bureau) operation in India. The second company would be wholly owned by IBM; it would conduct marketing, maintenance, and manufacturing operations. (Under the FERA, companies manufacturing exclusively for export could be fully owned by foreign interests.) IBM's Bombay plant would produce $100 million of data processing equipment, entirely for export, over the following ten years (1976–1986).

Other elements of the IBM proposal included establishing government-operated testing labs, setting up an IBM research center for government use, and making IBM patents available to Indian enterprises.

The company's proposal served as the basis for negotiations that continued for almost a year and a half. Both parties seemed to feel that they had "bent" their negotiating positions as far as possible.

The government did not accept this proposal, primarily because the FERA stipulated that no changes should be made in the existing facilities to get an exemption. The intent here was eventually to transfer the technology to India. After the initial proposal was rejected, IBM's regional vice-president requested a face-to-face meeting with the new Indian Prime Minister, Morarji Desai, whose ministerial portfolio included electronics. The meeting was arranged, and IBM restated its case. The company was not willing to go any further towards compliance, but then neither was the government.

In the words of a senior manager of IBM in India, "IBM-India was sandwiched between IBM and the Indian Government." For the company, it was a "stubborn economic decision," and for the government of India, it was a "stubborn legal decision."

In September 1977, the company was informed verbally by a government official that its proposal had been rejected. The government gave "formal notice" rejecting IBM's proposal in early November; on November 15, IBM announced it would phase out essentially all of its manufacturing, marketing, and maintenance operations over a 180-day period and sell IBM equipment

Table 5-7 Electronics in India

Sector	Production (Rs. mln.)		Growth Rate Percent	
	1979–80 (Actual)	1984–85 (Targets)	1979–80 (Actual)	1984–85 (Targets)
Consumer electronics	1,944	5,225	19.7	22.0
Industrial electronics	1,150	3,500	34.0	25.0
Aerospace and defense equipment	1,915	4,640	5.2	19.4
Computers	165	900	13.0	40.4

Source: Annual report 1980–81, Department of Electronics, Government of India, New Delhi, India.

already on rental. Only a liaison office would remain in India to receive authorized requests for IBM products and services in the future.

The managing director of IBM-India, when asked what would be IBM's reaction to a request from the government of India to return to India at some later date, said that IBM would return and though IBM was disappointed at the Government's current decision, IBM was not "sore."

The Computer Industry in India Post-1977*

The Computer, Control, and Instrumentation Sector achieved a production of Rs. 1,600 million in 1980 as compared to Rs. 1,310 million in 1979. This accounted for a growth rate of 22.1% in 1980 as compared to 10.1% growth rate in 1979 (U.S. $1 = approximately 11.50 Indian Rupees) (see Table 5-7).

During the year 1980–1981, fifty-five major computer systems were approved for import in various application areas such as transport, communication, steel plants, education, science, and research and development. The promotional efforts of the Department of Electronics in appropriate computerization through the Regional Computer Centres were continued.

The National Informatic Centre (NIC), New Delhi, has been expanding the provisions for information system development to various government departments, ministries, and agencies.

Through the assistance of the United Nations Development Program (UNDP), Phase II of the National Centre for Software Development and Computing Techniques, became operational in January 1981. The UNDP has approved assistance on proposals for the Computer Aided Design program and the Computer Aided Management program.

The Department of Electronics is committed to the comprehensive growth of the computer industry. Special emphasis has been placed on the promo-

*Adapted from the Annual Report of 1980–81, Government of India, Department of Electronics, New Delhi, India.

tion of manufacturing activities for computer peripherals ranging from back-up storage devices such as floppy disk drives, magnetic tape drives, hard disk drives; input/output devices such as line printers, matrix printers, desktop printers, plotters, interactive CRT terminals, graphic terminals, and graphic subsystems to make India self-reliant and to keep pace with the latest technology now available in the world. An announcement was made in 1980, inviting parties to come forward with technically sound proposals before the end of 1981.

India has been entering into dialogues with a number of countries to promote scientific and technical cooperation. The USSR, France, Bulgaria, Czechoslovakia, Romania, Hungary, West Germany, Yugoslavia, the United Kingdom, and East Germany are some of the countries with which India has agreements for technical cooperation in computer technology.

The Sixth Five-Year-Plan (1979–1980 to 1984–1985) envisaged a compound growth rate of 23%, amounting to Rs. 18,665 minimum. This compares to 15.5% achieved during the previous five years. The highest growth rate of 40% is projected for the computer industry. The emphasis during the Sixth Five-Year-Plan was on export promotion, import substitution, large volume production of components, and the development of a specialized work force required for the industry.

In spite of India's achievements and confidence in mastering the computer technology, the question is asked, "Who won? Should India invite IBM again with 100% equity to develop its computer industry?"

Appendix 1 Computer Industry in India

Computerization in India started in 1955, when the Indian statistical Institute of Calcutta installed a first-generation computer. The next nine years saw the installation of sixteen computers. This period can be described as a period of the introduction of computers in India. The second phase of computerization started in 1965 and lasted until 1972. During this phase, the rate of computerization was much higher. Organizations in private and public sectors and government and educational institutions acquired computers in increasing numbers. The period from 1955 to 1972 was characterized by the presence of multinationals in India. In 1973, in accordance with the provisions of FERA,* the Indian Government asked IBM to convert its branch into an Indian company and to dilute the foreign equity in that company to 40%. IBM had conveyed their inability to comply with the requirements of the FERA and decided to phase out their operations.

Source: The information in "Computer Industry in India" was compiled by Computer Maintenance Corporation of India, Bombay, India.

*Foreign Exchange Regulation Act of 1973

The post-IBM era proved to be a rapid growth period for the computer industry in the country. Several private sector units such as HCL, DCM, ORG, and ECIL, a public sector unit, were involved in the computer manufacturing industry. Whereas the private sector units concentrated on minicomputers, ECIL continued manufacturing mainframe systems. Toward the end of the 1970s, a number of private units applied for license to manufacture minicomputers. Over a period of two years, that number of manufacturers increased from five to about twenty-five. An annual growth rate of 40% in electronics has been forecast by the Planning Commission.

The first step taken by the government of India to formalize and regulate electronic activities in the country was to set up the Department of Electronics in 1972. The working group formalized a series of policies for the computer industry to foster its growth. The first major event was the 1973 FERA, which saw the expulsion of IBM. Subsequently, the import policy was tightened. One of the main clauses for granting an import license was that "a company can import 100% value of hardware only if it exports 200% value of software." This increased the software generation and expertise in the country to some extent.

Two committees were appointed by the government to look into the strategies for developing a computer industry in India:

1. Committee on Electronics Exports, under the presidency of Prof. H. G. K. Menon
2. Review Committee on Electronics, under Shri Sondhi

The Sondhi and Menon committees gave their reports to the government, which accepted them. The two points to be emphasized are:

1. Immediate measures are necessary to ensure that indigenous production of contemporary computers and peripherals makes rapid strides so that the range of computer systems produced in the country does not continue to be restricted.
2. Strategy for the development of the computer industry should be to give first priority to the minicomputers and microprocessor-based systems, costing not more than Rs. 5 million. The large computer systems will naturally have to take the third priority.

Product Structure

The computer is an information processing system, consisting of various models, vis-à-vis the peripheral units, constituting the input and output devices, the CPU, which is the core of the operating system, and the software compiler that facilitates information processing. It can be considered the total system and involves a high level of technology. Computers are generally identified based on the generation to which they belong, which essentially implies the level of technology incorporated in the product. Rapid growth in the electronic component industry (both in design and manufacturing) has resulted in a reduction in hardware cost, thus enabling wider use and application. Software basically is a set of structured instructions both for the operating system and the user application. Because this essentially involves manual effort of high caliber, the cost has been increasing. Of the cost of a computer system, 30% can be attributed to hardware elements, the balance of 70% to the software packages.

Presently in India the manufacture of computers consists of importing the bulk of the hardware elements and integrating them into a system. The variation in the product characteristic is here limited to the source of the procurement of these elements and the software back-up provided. Therefore, as far as the domestic production is concerned, it is truly not a high technology. However, the cost of developing software and integrating the components involves high technology.

Market Structures

There are about twenty companies in India involved in various aspects of manufacturing, selling, and maintaining computer systems. In addition to this, a large number of firms specialize in software development and consultancy aspects for computers. The main firms are: DCM, HCL, ORG, NELCO, WIPRO, and ECIL. The market structure is oligopolistic. However, because of liberal government policies and a high growth rate, many new firms are venturing into this area.

In recent years, because of technological advancement, there is a big influx of minicomputers that can meet a large portion of customer requirements at a fraction of a mainframe computer cost. Except for ECIL, all of these companies market only minicomputers.

The computer industry is having a high growth rate that is likely to continue into the perceptible future. The growth rate in the past has been on the order of 20%; it is anticipated that this will increase to 40%.

The number of firms at the threshold of computer use has increased substantially in recent years. As compared to the 1960s, when only companies with a turnover of Rs. 20 crores (R$2 million) were experimenting with computers, firms today with a turnover of Rs. 50 lakhs (R$5 million) are contemplating using computers.

The Indian market can be segmented in terms of customer: (1) large manufacturing units, (2) medium-scale industries, and (3) service sectors, such as banking, insurance, transportation, and educational institutions. The type of computer required by each one of them is different and in terms of product segmentation can be classified into minicomputers and mainframe computers.

The benefits derived from this product are mostly intangible (in terms of information processing) and hence, a product usage awareness and a rigorous cost-benefit analysis is a prerequisite for adopting. However, this is not a serious limitation in the Indian context because a professional workforce base exists in India, enabling rapid acceptability and adoption.

The product can be considered as an industrial product in terms of cost, investment, and productivity.

Product Life Cycle

The computer industry is in the growth stage of the product life cycle. This product has been exposed to many of the prospective users and has crossed the awareness state. Developments in the computer field throughout the world indicate that the growth stage is continuously extended by product innovation and technology development, so much though that there has been an exponential growth in the use of computer applications. Other factors contributing to this high growth rate are the declining cost of hardware and the increasing complexity of modern business. This situation is valid for India, too, and in the foreseeable future, the market will continue to grow. In this period of growth, different companies have started product differentiation. Because there is no significant difference in the hardware technology used, the only area for product differentiation is variation in software. Additional features, such as efficient back-up services and system maintenance, are used to enhance product value.

As the product is advancing into the growth stage, new competitors are entering with more sophisticated and larger systems, posing a threat to the existing manufacturers. As a consequence, the existing companies are trying to create new markets for the existing product. This enables them to extend the life of the existing models. In spite of this, the product life cycle for each brand is going to be small because of the rapid development in technology. Because the product life is short, aggressive marketing has to be adopted to recover the cost in a shorter period.

Appendix 2

Details of computer systems or reconfiguration costing over Rs. 0.5 million approved by the Department of Electronics during 1980–81

Sl. No.	Name of the user	Computer system	Purpose
1.	Indian Telephone Industries Ltd., Bangalore	DEC-1091	Scientific and EDP application
2.	Reactor Research Centre, Kalpakkam	CII-HB 266 DPS/05 and mini 6	R&D
3.	Realtime Textile Industries, Bombay	Computer based "colour control system"	R&D activities and to achieve optimum utilisation of scarce colour pigments, etc.
4.	India Meteorological Department, New Delhi	Computer based meteorological data processing equipment	Reception and processing of meteorological data
5.	Defence Research & Development Laboratory, Hyderabad	EAI 2000+PDP 11/34	R&D
6.	Vikram Sarabhai Space Centre, Trivandrum	EAI 2000 + PDP 11/34	R&D
7.	Bhabha Atomic Research Centre, Bombay	EAI 2000	R&D
8.	Indian Tobacco Company Ltd., Delhi, Bangalore, Calcutta, Guntur, Madras, Monghyr	Change of configuration	Production, planning and management
9.	Heavy Vehicles Factory, Madras (Ministry of Defence)	TDC-312 system	Work load details of production, planning and control and cost analysis
10.	Defence Rearch & Development Organization, New Delhi	Prime-750 with two Prime-450 as RJEs and Array Processor	Scientific applications, development of war game techniques

Continued

213

Appendix 2–Continued

Sl. No.	Name of the user	Computer system	Purpose
11.	Bombay Electric Supply and Transport Undertaking/Bombay Municipal Corporation, Bombay	MV-8000 + 150 computer system	Planning, management and commercial
12.	Technical Teacher's Training Institute, Bhopal	Computer equipment based on Hewlett Packard system 1000 Model 45	Development of item bank for the National Education Testing Services for technical education, educational research, building up of the computerised educational management and information system, development of computer aided instructions, teachers training activities, management programmes etc.
13.	Tata Iron & Steel Co. (TISCO) Ltd., Jamshedpur	Change of configuration	Production, planning and management
14.	Steel Authority of India Ltd., (Rourkela Steel Plant), Rourkela	B-6806	Data processing online enquiry operational and management information needs
15.	Indian Telephone Industries Ltd., Naini	VAX-11/780 applicon graphic system	General purpose
16.	Govt. of Uttar Pradesh, Lucknow	Burroughs-3950	To serve the computer centre
17.	Hindustan Spinning and Weaving Mills Ltd., Bombay	Computer based colour control system	Optimum utilisation of colour pigments
18.	Delhi Neurological Research Institute, Delhi	CAT scan equipment ET-4001	Neurological applications for diagnosis purposes

214

No.			
		-do-	-do-
19.	Madras Neurological Research Institute, Madras	-do-	Conducting research and teaching
20.	Govt. Stanlay Hospital & Medical College, Madras	MED 80 data acquisition system	For Trombay Thermal Power Station
21.	Tata Electric Companies, Bombay	Computer based data acquisition system	Maintenance of medical records
22.	Christian Medical College Hospital, Vellore	PDP-11/34	
23.	Patni Computer Systems (P) Limited, Bangalore	Change of configuration of M-600 computer system already approved	Software export
24.	C.M.C., Bombay	AS IS computer system/sub-system (IBM) 1401/ICL 1901	Maintain the IBM/ICL range of computer systems
25.	Electronics Corporation of India Ltd., Hyderabad	Prototype computer system type 211	R&D
26.	Vikram Sarabhai Space Centre, Trivandrum	CDC Cyber 170/730	R&D, test and evaluation of system in the area of space techniques
27.	Thumba Equatorial Rocket Launching Station, Trivandrum	PDP 11/60	Rocket experiments
28.	Tata Engg. & Locomotive Co. (TELCO) Ltd., Jamshedpur	Change of configuration	Production, planning and management
29.	Tata Engg. & Locomotive Co. (TELCO) Ltd., Pune	Change of configuration	Production, planning and management
30.	Vikram Sarabhai Space Research Centre, Trivandrum	SD-1009 D automatic random digital control system	Random vibration testing of sub-assemblies of SLV/PSLV to the test specification for flight acceptance programme

Continued

Appendix 2–Continued

Sl. No.	Name of the user	Computer system	Purpose
31.	Oil & Natural Gas Commission, New Delhi	4 Nos. of PDP 11/34 computer central processors and computer peripheral units	To meet tele-control system requirements of ONGC's offshore oil programme
32.	Smt. Varsha Bhatia	Change of computer system from PDP 11/34 to HP 3000/III	Software export
33.	Aeronautical Development Establishment, Bangalore	VITAL-IV computer generated image system	Development of training simulator for Ajit/Kiran aircraft
34.	Tata Institute of Fundamental Research, Bombay	–CDC 170/730 dual processor –VAX-11/780 –Prime 2 × P-450	Fundamental research work and complex scientific computations
35.	Engineers India Limited, New Delhi	VAX-11/780, graphic terminal, calcomp plotter, printer plotter	Analysis and engineering design and concept of interactive graphic
36.	Regional Engineering College, Rourkela	VAX 11/780	Scientific and technical education and R&D work
37.	National Aeronautical Laboratory, Bangalore	PDP 11/23	Part of advanced high precision materials testing machine
38.	Topiwala National Medical College and BYL Nair Charitable Hospital, Bombay	IMAC-7311 clinical image data processor system	Computer-based clinical human body scanner system

216

No.	Institution	Equipment	Application
39.	Govt. Madras Medical College & Govt. General Hospital, Madras	Hitachi automated axial tomographic scanner model CT-HF	Diagnosis and research of brain disease
40.	Electronics Corporation of India Ltd., Hyderabad	Data acquisition systems (5 Nos.)	Power systems development
41.	National Institute of Hydrology, Roorkee	VAX-11/780	R&D
42.	Electronics Radar & Development Establishment Ministry of Defence, Bangalore	PDP 11/34	Defence R&D
43.	Army Headquarters, New Delhi	CII-HB 64/DPS-4	R&D
44.	Institute of Nuclear Medicine & Allied Sciences, Delhi	Phe/gamma camera ZLC 37 with gamma 11 computer system	Organ imaging and fast dynamic function studies
45.	National Geophysical Research Institute, Hyderabad	DHR-1632 24 channel stacking data acquisition system	Oil & gas exploration, mining/civil engineering
46.	Vikram Sarabhai Space Centre, Trivandrum	Fourier transform high resolution 13C NMR with built in JAC 9808 computer	Ascertain structure of the pre-polymeric binders

Source: Annual Report 1980–81, Government of India, Department of Electronics, New Delhi, 1982.

Appendix 3

Targets of production for the electronics industry (1984–85) (in Rs. million)

Sl. No.	Sector	1979–80 (Actuals)	1984–85 (Targets)	Growth rate %
1.	Consumer Electronics	1,944	5,225	22.0
	(i) Radio receivers	845	1,770	16.0
	(ii) TV receivers	635	1,800	23.0
	(iii) Calculators	105	320	25.0
	(iv) Electronic watches	14	500	102.0
	(v) Others	345	835	19.4
2.	Industrial Electronics	1,150	3,500	25.0
	(i) Instruments (T&M, analytical etc.)	325	1,025	25.8
	(ii) Process control equipment	445	1,225	22.5
	(iii) Power electronics	295	950	26.4
	(iv) Medical electronics	85	300	28.7
3.	Professional Electronics	1,915	4,640	19.4
	(i) Aerospace, etc.	610	1,230	15.0
	(ii) Telecommunication	1,230	3,060	20.0
	(iii) Mass communication	10	50	38.0
	(iv) Two-way communication	65	300	35.8
4.	Computer Systems	165	900	40.4
	(i) CPU and peripherals	130	700	40.0
	(ii) Software	35	200	41.7
5.	Components	1,400	3,950	23.1
6.	Free Trade Zones (including bonded factories)	115	450	31.4

Source: Annual Report 1980–81, Government of India, Department of Electronics, New Delhi, 1982.

Appendix 4

Plan outlays for the schemes and programmes of the Department of Electronics for 1980–85 as agreed by the planning commission (in Rs. million)

Sl. No.	Scheme/programme	Agreed outlay
	A. Ongoing Schemes/Programmes	
1.	Electronics Trade and Technology Development Corporation (ETTDC)	20.0
2.	Computer Maintenance Corporation	40.0
3.	Semiconductor Complex Ltd.	154.3
4.	National Informatics Centre Programme	100.0
5.	Industrial Electronics Promotion Programme	30.0
6.	Headquarters	21.7
7.	National Centre for Software Development and Computing Techniques	–
8.	Standardisation, Testing and Quality Control Programme	148.3
9.	Special Components and Materials Programme	77.4
10.	Special Microwave Products Unit	39.6
11.	System Engineering Cell	100.0
12.	Computer Centres Programme	39.9
13.	Science and Technology Programme	
	(i) Technology Development Council Projects	174.5
	(ii) National Radar Council Projects	148.9
	Sub-total	1,094.6
	B. New Schemes/Programmes	
1.	Software Promotion Programme	72.5
2.	Export and Production Programme of ETTDC	30.0
3.	Electronics R&D Organisation (ERDO)	0.1
4.	Special Manpower Development Programme	60.0
5.	Centre for Electronics Design Technology (Northern, Eastern and Western Units)	25.0
6.	High Power Microwave Tube R&D and Production Unit	50.0
7.	Radar Systems Consultancy and Production Corporation	40.0
8.	Reliability Studies Programme	20.0
9.	Electromagnetic Interference/Electromagnetic Compatibility Studies Programme	20.0
	Sub-Total	317.6
	Total	1,412.2

Source: Annual Report 1980–81, Government of India, Department of Electronics, New Delhi, 1982.

Discussion Questions

1. What would be the advantages and disadvantages of centralization and decentralization in decision making?
2. Compare the decision-making types of United States, Japanese, and European MNCs. Which type of decision making do you think is the most flexible in adapting to today's dynamic environments? Why?
3. What factors affect the level of decentralization in decision making?
4. In many studies it has been suggested that the organizational practices of Japanese and European MNCs appear to be converging to the United States mode of management. Why do many scholars think the United States MNCs should learn the Japanese or European management styles?
5. What types of conflicting issues or tensions are most prevalent in the following relationships:
   1. Headquarters and subsidiary
   2. Headquarters and host govenment
   3. Subsidiary and host government
   4. Headquarters and home government

Endnotes

1. For extensive discussion of this point see Anant R. Negandhi, ed., *Functioning of the Multinational Corporation* (New York: Pergamon, 1980), especially Chap. 13, pp. 273–279.
2. John Fayerweather, *International Business Strategy and Administration* (Cambridge, Mass.: Ballinger Publishing Co., 1978), pp. 7–9.
3. Gunnar Hedlund, "The Role of Foreign Subsidiaries in Strategic Decision-Making in Swedish Multinational Corporations," *Strategic Management Journal* 1 (1980): 23–26.
4. Rana K. D. N. Singh, "Policy Issues and Trends in Parent Affiliate Relationships in Developing Countries," *The Management of Headquarters-Subsidiary Relationships in Multinational Corporations,* ed. Lars Otterbeck (Hampshire, England: Gower, 1981), p. 15.
5. For an extensive discussion see Anant R. Negandhi and Martin K. Welge, *Beyond Theory Z* (Greenwich, Conn.: JAI Press, 1984), Chap. 5, pp. 77–113.
6. See Fayerweather, *International,* pp. 527–543.
7. Paul R. Lawrence and Jay W. Lorsch, *Organization and Environment: Managing Differentiation and Integration* (Boston: Division of Research, Graduate School of Business Administration, Harvard University, 1967), pp. 212–245. Also see, for international and comparative contexts, Anant R. Negandhi, *Organization Theory in an Open System* (New York: Dunellen, 1975), Chap. 5, pp. 106–109, and Anant R. Negandhi and Bernard D. Reimann, "A Contingency Theory of Organization Re-examined in the Context of a Developing Country," *Academy of Management Journal* 15, 2 (June 1972): 137–146.
8. Yves L. Doz, "Managing Manufacturing Rationalization Within Multinational Companies," *Columbia Journal of World Business* 13, 3 (Fall 1978): 85.
9. Raymond Vernon, *Storm Over the Multinationals* (Cambridge, Mass.: Harvard University Press, 1977), Chap. 3, pp. 39–58.

10. Warren J. Keegan, "Multinational Marketing Control," *Journal of International Business Studies* 3, 2 (Fall 1972): 33–47.
11. Gunnar Hedlund, "Autonomy of Subsidiaries and Formalization of Headquarters-Subsidiary Relationships in Swedish MNCs," in Otterbeck, *Management*, p. 43; also see H. de Bodinat, "Influence in the Multinational Corporation: The Case of Manufacturing" (Ph.D. diss., Harvard University School of Business, 1975).
12. John D. Daniels, Ernest W. Ogram, Jr., and Lee H. Radebaugh, *International Business: Environments and Operations* (Reading, Mass.: Addison-Wesley, 1982), p. 467.
13. Negandhi, *Organization Theory*, pp. 256–261.
14. Hedlund, in Otterbeck, *Management*, pp. 40–42, 49–53.
15. Daniels, Ogram, and Radebaugh, *International*, pp. 466–467. Also see Cameron McKenzie, "Incompetent Foreign Managers?," *Business Horizons* 16, 1 (Spring 1966): 83–90.
16. William H. Davidson, *Global Strategic Management* (New York: John Wiley and Sons, 1982), pp. 59–68.
17. William H. Davidson, *Experience Effects in International Investment and Technology Transfer* (Ann Arbor: UMI Research Press, 1980), p. 50.
18. Robert Stobaugh, Jr., "Financing Foreign Subsidiaries of U.S. Controlled Multinational Enterprises," *Journal of International Business Studies* 1, 1 (Summer 1970): 48–55.
19. R. J. Aylmer, "Who Makes Marketing Decisions in the Multinational Firm?" *Journal of Marketing* 34, 4 (October 1970): 27–29.
20. Doz, "Managing," pp. 82–94.
21. From *Business Week*, January 13, 1973, pp. 64–69, cited in Stefan H. Robock, Kenneth Simmonds, and Jack Zwick, *International Business and Multinational Enterprises* (Homewood, Ill.: Irwin, 1977), p. 445.
22. Centre for Development Planning, Projections and Policies of the Department of Economic and Social Affairs of the United Nations Secretariat, based on United States Senate, Committee on Finance, *Implications of Multinational Firms for World Trade and Investment and for United States Trade and Labor* U.S. Government Printing Office (Washington, D.C.: 1973).
23. Keegan, "Multinational"; Daniels, Ogram, and Radebaugh, *International*, p. 467.
24. E. R. Barlow, *Management of Foreign Subsidiaries* (Boston: Harvard Graduate School of Business Administration, 1953), pp. 84–113.
25. Ulrich E. Wiechmann, *Marketing Management in Multinational Firms* (New York: Praeger Publishers, 1976).
26. Lawrence G. Franko, *European Business Strategies in the United States* (Geneva: Business International, 1971).
27. See Anant R. Negandhi and Martin K. Welge, *Beyond Theory Z* (Greenwich, Conn.: JAI Press, 1984), Chap. 4.
28. For a discussion of this point, see Hedlund in Otterbeck, *Management*, pp. 40–43.
29. C. K. Prahalad and Yves L. Doz, "Strategic Control—The Dilemma in Headquarters-Subsidiary Relationship," ibid., pp. 187–203.
30. Ibid., p. 201.
31. Ibid.
32. Lawrence G. Franko, *The European Multinationals* (Stamford, Conn.: Greylock, 1976), especially Chap. 8, pp. 186–212.
33. Franko, *European Business Strategies*.
34. Michael Yoshino, *Japan's Multinational Enterprises* (Cambridge, Mass.: Harvard University Press, 1976).
35. Yoshi Tsurumi, *The Japanese Are Coming* (Cambridge, Mass.: Ballinger Publishing Co., 1976).

36. William Ouchi, *Theory Z* (Reading, Mass.: Addison-Wesley, 1981).
37. Richard T. Johnson and William G. Ouchi, "Made in America (Under Japanese Management)" *Harvard Business Review* 52, 5 (September–October 1974).
38. Tsurumi, *Japanese*, pp. 228–229.
39. James M. Hulbert and William K. Brandt, *Managing the Multinational Subsidiary* (New York: Holt, Rinehart and Winston, 1980).
40. Ibid., p. 34.
41. A. R. Sim, "Decentralized Management of Subsidiaries and their Performance," *Management International Review* 2 (1977): 45–52.
42. Ibid., p. 47.
43. John M. Stopford and Louis T. Wells, *Managing the Multinational Enterprise* (New York: Basic Books, Inc., 1972).
44. William G. Egelhoff, "Strategy and Structure in Multinational Corporations: An Information Processing Approach," *Administrative Science Quarterly* 27, 3 (1982): 435–458.
45. See Negandhi and Welge, *Beyond Theory Z*, Chap. 2.
46. For a detailed discussion, see Anant R. Negandhi and B. R. Baliga, *Tables are Turning, German and Japanese Multinational Companies in the United States* (Cambridge, Mass.: Oelgeschlager, Gunn & Hain, Publishers, Inc., 1981), Chap. 2, pp. 27–38.
47. Martin K. Welge, "The Effective Design of Headquarters-Subsidiary Relationships in German MNCs," in Otterbeck, *Management*, pp. 79–106.
48. Lars Otterbeck, "Concluding Remarks – And A Review of Subsidiary Autonomy," ibid., p. 340.
49. For a detailed discussion on this point, see Anant R. Negandhi and B. R. Baliga, *Quest For Survival and Growth: A Comparable Study of American, European, and Japanese Multinationals*, (New York: Praeger Publishers, 1979), Chap. 2 and 3; and Negandhi and Welge, *Beyond Theory Z*, Chap. 5.

Additional Readings

Articles

Franco, Lawrence G. "The Organization of Multinational Manufacturing." *The European Multinationals.* Stamford, Conn.: Greylock, 1976, Chap. 8.
Yang, Charles Y. "Management Styles: American vis-à-vis Japanese." *California Journal of World Business* XV, 3 (Fall 1977): 23–31.

Books

Leksell, Laurent. *Headquarter-Subsidiary Relations in Multinational Corporations.* Stockholm: Stockholm School of Economics, 1981.
Negandhi, Anant R., ed. *Functioning of the Multinational Corporation.* New York: Pergamon, 1980.
Otterbeck, Lars. *The Management of Headquarter-Subsidiary Relationships in Multinational Corporations.* Hampshire, England: Gower, 1981.

Chapter 6

Long-Range Planning and Environmental Scanning in International Corporations

This chapter will examine long-range planning and environmental scanning functions. Specifically, the following aspects will be discussed:

- Long-range planning: philosophy and definition
- Environmental scanning concepts, issues, and practices
- Factors affecting long-range planning and environmental scanning practices
- Types and focus of long-range planning

- Goals and objectives of long-range planning
- Actual practices of United States, European, and Japanese multi-national companies
- Impact of long-range planning and environmental scanning on organizational effectiveness
- Future outlook: long-range planning and national industrial policies.

In recent years the concept of strategic planning has been widely used. However, the distinction between strategic planning and long-range planning is quite blurred. Accordingly, these concepts will be used interchangeably throughout this chapter.

Although this book is concerned with international business and is focused on comparative management policies and practices of United States, European, and Japanese companies, the various management concepts and practices were developed in large-scale U.S. domestic enterprises. Consequently, in discussing these concepts and practices, I will make reference to the domestic enterprises only to pinpoint their developmental stage. Attempts have been made to incorporate the use of such practices in international business operations.

Long-Range Planning: Philosophy and Definition

Steiner defines strategic long-range planning in terms of the futurity of current decisions, processes, philosophies, and structures. As he has stated, "strategic planning is inextricably interwoven into the entire fabric of management."[1] It "deals with the futurity of current decisions and . . . looks at the chain of cause and effect consequences over time of an actual or intended decision that a manager is going to make."[2] Second, it is a process that "begins with the setting of organizational aims, defines strategies and policies to achieve them, and develops detailed plans to make sure that the strategies are implemented so as to achieve the ends sought."[3] Third, strategic planning is a philosophy, an attitude, and a way of life. It "necessitates dedication to acting on the basis of contemplation of the future."[4] It is "more of a thought process, an intellectual exercise, than a prescribed set of processes, procedures, structures or techniques."[5] Fourth, strategic planning "links three types of plans: strategic plans, medium-range programs and short-range budgets and operating plans."[6]

Planning Modes

Mintzberg has identified three different planning modes prevailing among different organizations depending on their respective philosophy and their organizational and environmental contexts. These are: (1) the entrepreneurial mode, (2) the adaptive mode, and (3) the planning mode. Each mode leads to different assumptions concerning organizational roles and functions and encourages differential planning practices. The following paragraphs summarize the interrelationship between the given mode and planning practices.

In the entrepreneurial mode, strategy making is dominated by the active search for new opportunities. The entrepreneurial organization focuses on opportunities; problems are secondary. Power is centralized in the hands of the chief executive; strategy making is characterized by dramatic leaps forward in the face of uncertainty. Growth is the dominant goal.[7]

In the adaptive mode, clear goals do not exist. Strategy making reflects a division of power among members of the complex organization. The strategy-making process is reactive rather than proactive.

The adaptive organization makes its decisions in incremental, serial steps, because its environment is complex. Disjointed decisions are characteristic of the adaptive organization.[8]

In the planning mode, the analyst plays a major role in strategy making. It focuses on systematic analysis, particularly in assessing the costs and benefits of competing proposals. The emphasis is on the integration of decisions and strategies.[9]

Table 6-1 outlines the attributes of an organization, its environment, and the corresponding practices as described in these three modes.

Strategic long-range planning is not a panacea for solving complex international business problems. As Mintzberg has stated:

> Rather than seeking panaceas, we should recognize that the mode used must fit the situation. An unpredictable environment suggests use of the adaptive mode just as the presence of a powerful leader may enable the organization to best achieve its goals through the entrepreneurial mode. Some situations require no planning, others only limited planning. Often the planning mode can be used only when mixed with the others. *Most important, planners must recognize the need for the manager to remain partially in the adaptive mode at all times.* Crisis and unexpected *events are an important part of every strategy-maker's reality.*[10] (emphasis added)

Planning Focus

Planning focus can be conceptualized in terms of types, time horizon, and formality. Types refer to the basic orientation and can be differentiated into three distinct but interrelated groups: strategic, business unit programming, and operations planning.[11] Strategic planning, as discussed earlier, concerns formulating overall missions, purposes, objectives, goals, and policies. It identifies the major strengths and weaknesses of a company, and deals with the

Table 6-1 Characteristics and conditions of the three modes

Characteristic	Entrepreneurial mode	Adaptive mode	Planning mode
Motive for decisions	Proactive	Reactive	Proactive and reactive
Goals of organization	Growth	Indeterminate	Efficiency and growth
Evaluation of proposals	Judgmental	Judgmental	Analytical
Choices made by	Entrepreneur	Bargaining	Management
Decision horizon	Long-term	Short-term	Long-term
Preferred environment	Uncertainty	Certainty	Risk
Decision linkages	Loosely coupled	Disjointed	Integrated
Flexibility of mode	Flexible	Adaptive	Constrained
Size of moves	Bold decisions	Incremental steps	Global strategies
Vision of direction	General	None	Specific
Condition for use			
Source of power	Entrepreneur	Divided	Management
Objectives of organization	Operational	Nonoperational	Operational
Organizational environment	Yielding	Complex, dynamic	Predictable, stable
Status of organization	Young, small, or strong leadership	Established	Large

assessment of macro and micro environments. The time horizon for strategic planning is five to ten years.

Business unit programming, sometimes referred to in the literature as tactical planning, deals with planning for selected strategic business units and may include selecting markets, product planning, marketing unit strategies, and practices.[12] The time horizon for this type of planning is usually one to three years.

The operation's planning mainly deals with short-term operational activities, such as production planning and scheduling, inventory management, personnel recruitment and selection, and cash management.[13]

Davidson[14] observed that these three planning phases can be conceived of as either fixed or flexible systems, depending on organizational philosophy (culture), size, technology, market conditions, and environmental conditions. If each of the planning phases is conceived as a fixed system, then business unit and operating plans have to follow directly from the macro strategic plans and the planning process will be essentially a one-way system and will be more formalized. If the planning system is conceived as flexible, there will be considerable overlap between the three planning phases and the flow and process will move in both directions. This will require extensive consultation among the different units and will be less formalized. Gluck, Kaufman, and Walleck have identified four phases in planning: (1) financial planning, (2) forecast-based planning, (3) externally oriented planning, and (4) strategic management planning. Figure 6-1 shows the evolution and attributes of these four planning phases.[15]

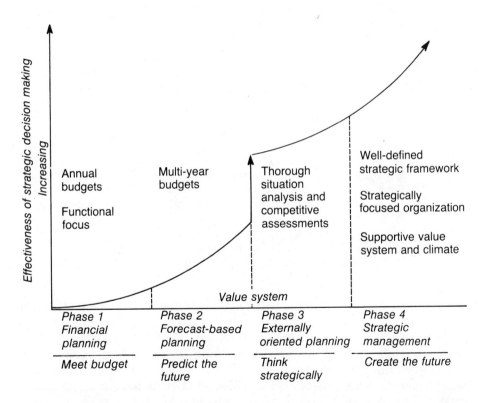

Figure 6-1 Phases in the evolution of strategic decision making (*Source:* Reprinted with permission from: *Journal of Business Strategy*, Winter 1982, Volume 2, Number 3, Copyright © 1982, Warren, Gorham & Lamont, Inc., 210 South Street, Boston, MA. 02111. All Rights Reserved.

Another useful classification of a planning system is based on the locus of decision making in terms of the familiar dichotomy of a centralized *versus* a decentralized system. Vancil and Lorange[16] differentiated such a system as the integrative *versus* the adaptive mode of planning.

Factors Affecting Planning Modes

It has been argued that centralized planning (integrative) is necessary for those firms facing rapid technological changes and intensive market competition in serving their global customers. A decentralized or adaptive planning system is more appropriate for firms producing goods and services for local customers with fewer competitors and operating in stable technological fields. Research evidence to support these arguments is meager and more studies are needed before one can draw definitive conclusions. For example, Lindsay and Rue,[17] in their recent study, attempted to test the following hypotheses:

> Hypothesis 1. As environmental dimensions of complexity and instability increase, the completeness of the long-range planning process will increase.
> Hypothesis 2. As the environmental dimensions of complexity and instability increase, emphasis on components of the long-range planning process will change as follows:
> a. Use of uncertainty-reducing methods, specifically consultants and computer models, will increase.
> b. Use of "open systems" approaches to planning as measured by more participation of lower organization levels, more upward flows of information, and more public information, will increase.
> c. The formal long-range planning process will have been in use for a longer period of time.
> d. Long-range planning time span will be shorter.
> e. Planning review periods will be shorter.
> f. Planning premises will support more immediate and tangible goals, as opposed to longer-range and intangible goals.[18]

Their results supported the first hypothesis that the firms tend to adopt more complete formal long-range planning processes as the complexity and instability of business environments increase. However, they also observed that these findings were moderated when the size of the firm was included as an intervening variable. In other words, any large firm facing a high degree of environmental complexity and instability undertook long-range planning; smaller firms did not under these environmental conditions.[19] Other hypotheses, dealing with the environment and long-range planning, were tested with mixed (inconclusive) results.

My study,[20] undertaken with fifty-six United States subsidiaries and fifty-five comparable local firms in Argentina, Brazil, India, and Philippines, Uruguay, and Taiwan, indicates that the existence of a seller's market, governmental control of prices, availability of raw materials, inflation, and political instability adversely affected the firm's ability to plan for a long duration. There were some differences in rank-order importance of these factors among the different countries. Executives in the Latin American countries, for example, were more worried about political instability and inflation, whereas those in the Far East showed more concern over the existence of the seller's market. Overall, the findings showed that the majority of the executives interviewed (58%) in these countries indicated that the seller's market condition makes planning less necessary for the firms to achieve high profitability. In such a situation all firms are making high profits, regardless of their managerial practices. More or less the same proportion of executives (56%) pointed out that governmental control of prices and the unavailability of raw materials inhibited long-range planning. Inflation, the political situation, and governmental attitudes toward the business community were mentioned as additional factors that discourage planning for the future.

One study, undertaken in developing countries, seems to indicate the following impact of market and environmental factors on long-range planning:

> The greater the degree of competition, the greater will be the need for long-range planning by individual firms.
> The greater the degree of economic and political instability, the lesser the likelihood that private industrial enterprises will undertake systematic long-range planning.
> The greater the degree of governmental control of prices and the availability of raw materials, the lesser the likelihood that the firm will undertake systematic long-range planning.
> The greater the governmental hostility toward the business community, the lesser the likelihood that a firm will undertake systematic long-range planning.[22]

These two studies seem contradictory, but they are not. Both show that a competitive environment has a positive impact on long-range planning, and conversely, that a lack of competition (seller's market) discourages planning. In addition, the study from the developing countries underscores the importance of nonmarket factors affecting the planning process. Environmental factors causing uncertainty seem to discourage long-range planning. In other words, when the future is uncertain and unpredictable, the usual tendency is to operate on a day-to-day or short-term basis. However, a changing but reasonably predictable environment may induce more planning.

Multinational Planning

The multilingual and multicultural environment compounded by differing socioeconomic and political conditions and ideologies, prevailing in the international business arena, prompted one writer to quip, "Multinational planning: Mission Impossible."[22] Table 6-2 outlines the major differences between the domestic and the international planning environment.

In spite of the complexity in the environment, however, the international company needs to chart out its future systematically and to integrate its diverse activities scattered around the world. This calls for more, and not less, planning orientation.

In the following sections, the actual planning practices of international corporations are examined in more detail. Following the comparative focus of this book, attempts have been made to compare and contrast the practices of United States, European, and Japanese multinational companies.

Long-Range Planning in United States Companies

Notwithstanding the current criticism of United States business as short-term profit maximizers, United States companies have been in the forefront in institutionalizing planning. For example, studies undertaken during the 1960s indicate that five- and ten-year plans among large corporations were common features.[23]

A cross-cultural study, which I did during the 1970s, also indicates that some 70% of fifty-six United States MNCs' subsidiaries, located in the Far East and Latin American countries, undertook comprehensive five- to ten-year long-range planning. Their own fifteen parent companies in the United States did the same. Such planning activities involved all major functions, such as finance, sales, production, plant capacity, capital budgeting, and work force. The resulting plans were detailed and systematic. They were reviewed and revised, if necessary, on a quarterly or a yearly basis.[24] Similarly, Steiner and Cannon, in their review of the planning practices of United States and European multinational companies, came to the following conclusions:

1. Planning structures of large companies on both sides of the Atlantic were highly comparable.
2. Just about all larger companies have three-, five-, or seven-year plans.
3. Many subsidiaries of large multinational companies enjoy autonomy in planning (decentralized planning with centralized policy making).
4. Most large multinational companies have established staff units composed of specialists to help top line management with the planning process.
5. The thought processes used in planning are about the same in all companies, even though the initiation of, structure for, and detailed sequential steps governing planning might be different.[25]

Table 6-2 Domestic *versus* international planning

Domestic	International
1. Single language and nationality	1. Multilingual/multinational/multicultural factors
2. Relatively homogeneous market	2. Fragmented and diverse markets
3. Data available, usually accurate and collection easy	3. Data collection a formidable task, requiring significantly higher budgets and personnel allocation
4. Political factors relatively unimportant	4. Political factors frequently vital
5. Relative freedom from government interference	5. Involvement in national economic plans; government influences business decisions
6. Individual corporation has little effect on environment	6. "Gravitational" distortion by large companies
7. Chauvinism helps	7. Chauvinism hinders
8. Relatively stable business environment	8. Multiple environments, many of which are highly unstable (but may be highly profitable)
9. Uniform financial climate	9. Variety of financial climates ranging from overconservative to wildly inflationary
10. Single currency	10. Currencies differing in stability and real value
11. Business "rules of the game" mature and understood	11. Rules diverse, changeable and unclear
12. Management generally accustomed to sharing responsibilities and using financial controls	12. Management frequently autonomous and unfamiliar with budgets and controls

Source: William W. Cain, "International Planning: Mission Impossible," *Columbia Journal of World Business* (July–August 1970): 58. Copyright © 1970 by the Trustees of Columbia University in the City of New York.

Recent Comparative Studies

In a comparative study of United States and Japanese companies, Kono[26] reported that more than 80% of the large United States corporations he surveyed (n = 27) had some kind of long-range plans. The same was also true of large Japanese companies. Kono's overall conclusions are summarized as follows:

> In the U.S., long-range planning is used for integrating the strategies of divisions and to control the divisions. The planning process is more a bottom-up or guide-line and build-up approach.
>
> In Japan, long-range planning is used for improving the strategic decision by top management, so the planning process is more a centralized interactive process.
>
> To cope with uncertainty, American corporations update their plans every year or even over shorter intervals, and adopt contingency plans.
>
> To the same end, Japanese corporations use two time horizon plans which are composed of long-range strategy and a medium-range plan. This system is closely related with system approach.
>
> With respect to follow-up and implementation, American corporations use more closely controlled follow-up. . . . Long-range planning is used to evaluate the managers of the divisions, with the quality of plans and accomplishments being reflected in economic rewards.
>
> Japanese corporations are less inclined to follow up the long-range plan itself, but it is considered as important to implement it through budget and also through the project plan. Project teams are quite frequently used.[27]

Hulbert and Brandt[28], in their study of United States, European, and Japanese subsidiaries operating in Brazil found a similar situation. The annual operating plan was used by all of the companies, except a few Japanese companies, as a starting point for longer range planning. "Most subsidiaries combined their short and long-term plans with a rolling or forward planning system."[29]

Recent studies on the planning behavior of German corporations show very similar results to what has been observed with respect to United States and Japanese corporations. Pausenberger, et al.[30] report that with an increasing degree of internationalization, the necessity for systematic long-range planning is perceived as more important by the majority of the corporations interviewed. Planning activities are more time consuming, and the planning processes become more formalized and standardized to secure the integration of the foreign subsidiaries. Welge[31] reported similar results in an earlier study of German subsidiaries. With respect to the various dimensions of the planning system—degree of formalization, degree of specification, type of integration, factors of planning, and number of levels involved in the planning process—a high degree of unification of the worldwide planning system of German MNCs has been achieved. From the contextual factors analyzed, only the size of the subsidiary correlated strongly with planning dimensions, indicating that larger subsidiaries are more bureaucratic than smaller ones.

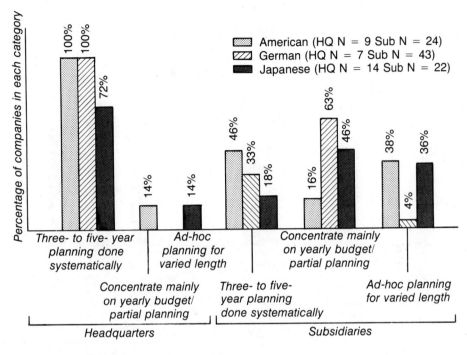

Key: HQ = Headquarters
     Sub = Subsidiaries

Figure 6-2 Long-range planning

A current study of United States, German, and Japanese multinationals confirms these overall trends. As can be seen from Figure 6-2, the U.S. MNCs are the most active among the three types of the MNCs' systems studied in using planning processes as integrating and controlling devices. The majority of the United States companies not only undertook long-range, strategic planning, but also scanned the environments systematically, although the factors examined in the environmental scanning are mainly related to the general economic environments and market conditions.

However, as one can see from Figures 6-2 and 6-3, both the planning and the environmental scanning functions are, to a large extent, headquarters-oriented. The centralization of these two functions is more clearly seen with respect to the communication patterns concerning the planning and environmental scanning processes between the subsidiaries and their respective headquarters. Among the United States MNCs, the nature of communication concerning these two aspects is highly formalized, whereas the German and Japanese companies seem to be moving rapidly in this direction. Moreover,

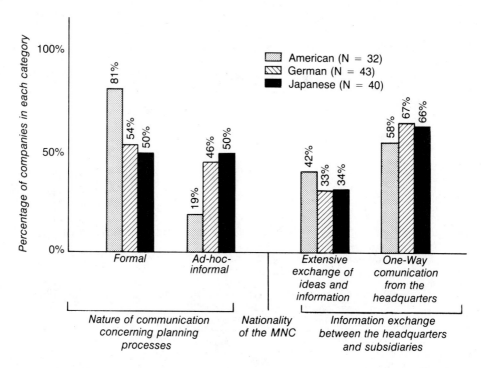

Figure 6-3 Involvement of subsidiaries in environmental scanning and long-range planning processes

these communications are transacted through instructions and imperatives rather than through constructive exchanges of ideas and information. Approximately one third of the subsidiaries surveyed felt that their viewpoints were used by the headquarters in formulating long-range goals and objectives.[32]

Similar results are reported by Hulbert and Brandt, in their study of United States, European, and Japanese multinational companies in Brazil. They state:

> Headquarters of American and Japanese firms played the most directive role in process formalization with specifications for types of information to collect, sequencing of activities, timing, and nature of the approved process. For the annual plan, over 90 percent of American and Japanese firms in the survey followed a standard format specifying the final layout and appearance of the plans. This compares with 73 percent for the European subsidiaries.[33]

To sum up, all three types of MNCs are using strategic long-range planning and environmental scanning as an integrating device to control and coordinate their global activities. Moreover, these functions are largely headquarters-oriented, and overseas subsidiaries seem to play a very marginal role in goals and target-setting even for their own individual operations.

Long-Range Planning and Organizational Effectiveness

Although organizational effectiveness is a function of many complex variables such as size, technology, industry, market, and economic conditions, some researchers have attempted to isolate the impact of formal long-range planning on effectiveness. For example, Thune and House[34], in their study of ninety-two United States firms, found that the formal planners significantly outperform informal planners with respect to five economic measures (growth in sales, earnings per share, stock price, earnings on common equity, and earnings on total capital). They also found that firms facing rapid technological and market changes were more effective when they undertook long-range planning than those operating in stable conditions. Possible economic performance and formal planning were most strongly related among medium-sized companies in the rapidly changing markets. Detailed results of this study are shown in Figures 6-4 and 6-5.

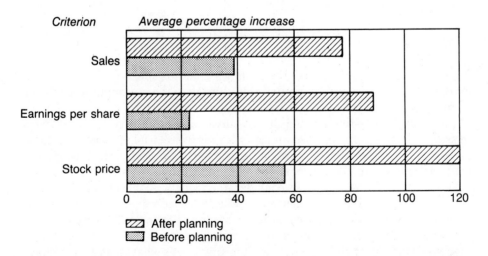

Figure 6-4 Performances of companies before and after formal planning (*Source:* Stanley Thune and Robert J. House, "Where long-range planning pays off" *Business Horizons* XIII, 3 (August 1970): 83–85.)

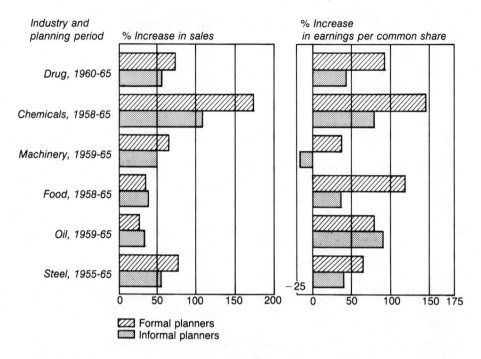

Figure 6-5 Performances of formal and informal planners during planning period (*Source:* Stanley Thune and Robert J. House, "Where long-range planning pays off," *Business Horizons* XIII, 3 (August 1970): 83–85.)

A study by Ansoff et al.[35] also shows that planners do better on an average: they perform more predictably than nonplanners and are effective in managing uncertainty in the environment.

A study of fifty-five United States subsidiaries and fifty-six local firms in six developing countries also indicated a positive relationship between long-range planning and organizational effectiveness. Specifically, the Spearman's rank correlation coefficient between these two variables was 0.60.[36]

These three studies provide considerable evidence concerning the utility of the long-range planning function. Studies also show that the necessity for planning becomes more critical when environmental complexity and instability increase. Thus, for the multinational company, operating in a heterogeneous world environment, the planning function assumes great importance. In the next section, I will briefly review the nature of the environmental uncertainties encountered by the multinational companies and how to cope with these environmental demands.

Environmental Scanning

The main purposes of environmental scanning are as follows:

1. To provide decision-makers with accurate forecasts of trends in competition, regulation, political situation, technological changes, demographic, and sociocultural changes
2. To provide assumptions for long-range planning based on the forecast of these factors[37]

Realizing the importance of environmental scanning for long-range planning, many authors have recommended establishing a corporate-level environmental scanning unit. The purpose of such a unit is, as Stubbart has observed, "to monitor and interpret trends in demographic, social, cultural, political-regulatory, technological and other patterns . . . the unit is to strive for breadth of view, interpretation of interacting trends and a penetration into the distant future."[38]

More specifically, at an international level, Phatak[39] has suggested the importance of the following environmental trends that international management should take into account:

1. Political instability and risk
2. Currency instability
3. Competition from state-owned enterprises
4. Pressures from national governments
5. Nationalism
6. Patent and trademark protection
7. Competition

Prasad and Shetty[40] have recommended an assessment of the following socioeconomic and political conditions in foreign countries in which the firm has made or is considering investments:

1. General economic conditions and trends
2. Stages and rates of economic growth
3. Income size and growth pattern
4. Growth and pattern of world trade
5. International monetary conditions and trends
6. Sensitivity of foreign economies to fluctuations
7. International relations and commercial policy
8. Political environment and stability
9. Government regulation and market structure
10. Incentives and attitudes toward foreign investment
11. Exchange controls and balance of payments situation
12. Population growth and distribution

13. Education and quality of human resources
14. Relative availability of labor, material, and financial resources
15. Technological development relating to the firm's products and operations
16. Worldwide trends in such things as prices and costs.[41]

It is obvious that the firm may not be able to collect, digest, and integrate data on the various socioeconomic, political, and legal conditions systematically. Some sort of selectivity thus may be necessary to reduce the amount of detail work involved in the environmental scanning function.

Empirical Studies

Results of empirical studies concerning environmental scanning practices are mixed. Overall, multinational companies have not paid much attention to this important aspect. For example, Keegan,[42] in his interviews with fifty executives of thirteen United States multinational companies, reported that very few companies were using systematic methods of information scanning. "Computer-based systems were not found . . . and even traditional manual systems of information retrieval were hardly significant as factors in day-to-day information gathering."[43] A majority of the companies used personal sources (word of mouth), for gathering environmental information.

Similarly, Fahey and King's[44] study of twelve large United States companies revealed that environmental scanning was not a well-established corporate function. Their other conclusions were:

1. Environmental scanning was not properly integrated into the long-range planning process.
2. Very few companies gathered useful information on political-regulatory conditions.
3. Most of the firms relied on the ad hoc methods.

On the contrary, both Thomas[45] and Stubbart[46] found some increase in the use of environmental scanning in the long-range planning process. Using an intensive search of published data, Thomas concluded that effective environmental scanning "was permanent, pervasive and multi-level . . . [and] was not a marginal ivory tower exercise."[47]

Stubbart, in his study of the same twelve companies surveyed by Fahey and King, found that three of the twelve companies had moved towards undertaking continuous environmental scanning. Other companies had not moved much further along and continued to scan the environment on an irregular, ad hoc basis.

Political Risk

Political risk has been defined as "loss of control over ownership or loss of benefits of enterprise by government action."[48] The concept of political risk involves:

1. Governmental or sovereign interference with business operations
2. Environmental instability and contraints on operations such as expropriation, discriminatory taxation, and unfair competition from public sector firms[49]

In the same vein, Root[50] has defined political uncertainties in terms of:

1. Transfer—uncertainties about flows of capital payments, technology, and people
2. Operational—uncertainties about policies that directly constrain local operations
3. Ownership control—uncertainties about policies relating to the ownership of subsidiaries.

To assess the political risk, the literature, as Kobrin has observed, "does not provide an analytic framework which can adequately contribute—in either taxonomic or an operational sense—to improved practices."[51]

In identifying the basic problems associated with the realistic operationalization and assessment of political risk, Kobrin isolated the following four factors:

1. Lack of distinction between the political environment directly affecting international business operations and other political events
2. Difficulties in establishing an explicit relationship between political events and the manager's perception of these events
3. Too much emphasis placed on discontinuous, recent, and emotionally charged events while the other elements of the political environment receive only superficial attention
4. Too much emphasis is placed on negative aspects of political or governmental action with implied universality of such events.[52]

Because of such difficulties, as Kobrin has remarked, "most managers' understanding of the concept of political risk, their assessment and evaluation of politics and the manner in which they integrate political information into decision making are all rather general, subjective, and superficial."[53]

Results of various studies support Kobrin's contention. Although the managers ranked political risk as an important factor affecting investment decisions, its assessment is carried out nonsystematically.

Coping with Uncertainties

Given the extreme complexity in the international business environment and the lack of development of integrative analytic models to scan environmental conditions systematically, international managers may continue to use simplified methods. One such example of their methods was uncovered by Mascarenhas.[54] In his study of ten multinational companies, he observed two approaches: *control* and *flexibility*.

The purpose of the control strategy to cope with environmental uncertainty "is to keep the environment from changing in a way that would adversely affect the firm."[55] Some examples of this strategy are: (1) integrating backward and forward to control sources of supply and market, respectively; (2) engagement in lobbying operations to obtain favorable legislation; (3) making questionable and illegal payments to influential parties or persons; and (4) influencing client groups through advertising, promotions, legal contracts, and cartels.[56]

The purpose of a flexible strategy is to increase the firm's adaptability to environmental demands and changes. Some illustrations of this type of strategy to cope with the environmental uncertainty are:

1. Using general purpose equipment to handle multiple inputs and outputs
2. Selling a product in multiple markets
3. Using various methods of entering into the international markets (e.g., exporting, leasing, licensing, and subcontracting)
4. Decentralizing decision making at the unit and subunit levels
5. Maintaining financial cushions through liquid assets, emergency borrowing, and stock issuing power
6. Implementing an intelligence and management information system[57]

The results of Mascarenha's study concerning the strategies used by the ten multinational companies are given in Table 6-3.

National Industrial Policy

Conceptually, national industrial policy could be conceived of as a further extension of environmental analysis. Although the concept of industrial policy at the national and regional levels seems to be a novel idea, it is as old as the founding of the United States of America. Some 200 years ago, Hamilton had argued that "the new American republic needed strong government measures such as protectionist tarriffs, bounties, any premiums to nurture its infant industries."[58] As *Business Week* has stated, "some 200 years later,

Americans are still arguing over whether to have a national industrial policy."[59]

Even a staunch believer in the free market, President Reagan, has created a commission to study this issue. The Organization for Economic Cooperation and Development (OECD, "Rich Man's Club") has been discussing this issue for over a decade. Many European countries have formulated some form of industrial policy to provide a framework for national actions for economic, industrial, and technological developments.

Despite recent denials, the Japanese government has been the most active in formulating industrial policy. All of the Communist Bloc countries, and many of the developing nations have, for decades, used national industrial policies to guide their actions.

The main purpose of a national industrial policy is to:

1. Facilitate economic development
2. Enhance social and economic welfare
3. Provide forecasts of emerging industrial structure trends
4. Provide support to "sunrise industries"
5. Scrap excess capacity
6. Close out "sunset industries"
7. Promote technological development

Table 6-4 provides, in summary form, the activities of selected industrial countries for formulating an industrial policy.

In the decades of the 1980s and 1990s, industrially advanced, as well as developing, countries may rely heavily on national industrial policies to manage their socioeconomic activities. Under these circumstances, managers of international corporations will be obligated to take into account the conditions and framework provided by such industrial policies for corporate planning.

In the United States, the industrial policy issue is indeed very emotional and controversial. Those arguing against the adoption of the industrial policy have pinpointed the following negative aspects:

1. It will stifle economic growth.
2. It will slow down the shift of resources to productive industries through the support of declining industries.
3. It will waste money on "targeted growth" industries that may not have a commercial future.
4. It will create excessive governmental bureaucracy.[60]

Overall, the verdict concerning the usefulness of industrial policy is still out, particularly in the United States. Many of the multinational managers seem to be against a national industrial policy.

Table 6-3 Methods used by ten companies for coping with uncertainty in international business

Company	Type of project	Political uncertainty	Foreign exchange uncertainty	Input uncertainty	Production uncertainty	Output uncertainty
1. Airline	Set up of branch in Kuwait	Operation is internationally integrated. (C) Leased ground-handling equipment. (F) Reciprocal government agreements. (C)	Payment accepted in hard currencies only. (A)	Ability to adjust frequency of flights. (F)	Availability of back-up air craft. (F) Re-scheduling capability of other flights. (F) Ability to transfer passengers to other airlines or accommodate them in a hotel. (F)	Leasing permits firm to terminate or step-up operation quickly. (F)
2. Clothing	Entry into Mexican market	Little commitment of resources. (F)	Money market hedging capability. (F)	Sub-contracted inputs. (F) Used multiple tailors. (F)	Initially tested tailors' capability. (F) Used simple labor-intensive technology. (F)	Undertook a test-market to check if market existed. (F) Ability to produce many different styles using same tailors. (F)
3. Food processor	Set up a dairy plant in Saudi Arabia	Dehydrated compounds imported from firm's plant in Europe. (C)	Payment in hard currency. (A)	Used inventories. (F)	On-site expatriate personnel to maintain and run plants. (C)	Prediction of demand for dairy products using demographic factors. (P)
4. Food processor	Set up of a pineapple plantation in Kenya	Integrated export markets. (C) Duplicate plantations in other countries. (F)	Money market hedging capability. (F)	Developed its own strain of higher yielding and more resistant pineapple seeds. (C)	Existence of plantations in other countries to offset bad crop in one area. (F)	Captive export distribution network downstream. (C)
5. Retailer	Set up of a retail store in Japan	Licensing reduces commitment. (F)	Money market hedging capability. (F)	Multiple suppliers. (F) Buys on specification. (C)	Not applicable.	Use of advertising. (C) Ability to adjust price. (F) Ability to sell different products with existing facilities. (F)

Industry	Project					
6. Pharmaceutical firm	Set up of a pharmaceutical plant in Colombia	Insurance. (I)	Money market hedging capability. (F)	Ability to process multiple inputs. (F)	Uses general-purpose machinery. (F)	Ability to make different drugs from same production facilities. (F)
7. Mining and mineral processor	Smelter in Ghana	Insurance. (I) Integrated upstream and downstream. (C) Substantial prediction efforts. (P)	Metal priced in hard currency on world market. (A) Forward contracts. (C)	Integrated upstream. (C)	Duplicate production lines. (F)	Integrated export markets. (C)
8. Petroleum drilling and production	Oil exploration and production in Indonesia	Insurance. (I) Contracts. (C) Integrated downstream. (C) Substantial prediction efforts. (P)	Petroleum priced in hard currency. (A) Use of forward contracts. (C)	Geological investigation before making substantial commitment required for oil production. (P)	Maintains emergency funds to buy oil in spot market if necessary. (F)	Internationally integrated downstream. (C) Contracts. (C)
9. Construction	Construction of a bridge in Jamaica	Used old equipment to reduce commitment. (F)	Payment guaranteed in hard currency by EX-IM Bank. (A)	Used parent country workers as much as possible. (C)	Covered by a cost-plus agreement. (A)	Bids and contracts. (C)
10. Automotive parts	Set up of a plant in Venezuela	Insurance. (I) Internationally integrated upstream and downstream. (C)	Money market hedging capability. (F)	Copes with labor shortage by training workers to perform multiple functions. (F)	Duplicate production lines. (F)	Integrated downstream. (C) Sells products to multiple countries. (F)

Notation: A = Avoidance C = Control F = Flexibility I = Insurance P = Prediction
Source: Briance Mascarenhas, "Coping with Uncertainty in International Business," *Journal of International Business Studies* (Fall 1982): 92–93.

Table 6-4 Major elements of industrial policy and policymakers' priorities in 1979–1980 for selected industrialized countries

Belgium	Italy	West Germany
Maintain existing promotion instruments (industrial expansion laws)	Apply 3 year plan which has the first comprehensive framework for the state enterprise sector; withdrawal of support of government by the communists has however delayed application and makes future measures unclear	Increase federal funding for research and developing, especially in microelectronics and cooperative European aerospace ventures
To the extent permitted by regional, linguistic and political tensions, restructure the industrial sector along the lines of minister Claes' "New Industrial Policy" by providing administrative assistance in:	Even greater emphasis on investment promotion in the South than in the past	Funding of user firms to promote adoption of new technology (e.g. data processing)
• Locating technology transfer opportunities	Key elements of plan:	Creation of a special joint federal-Lander 5 billion DM fund (spread over 5 years) for the reconversion of the Ruhr region
• Developing exports to nontraditional markets	• Replace short-term loans and current subsidies in state enterprises with large capital contributions (estimated at $3.6 billion in 1978–1981)	Major increase (20% over 1978–79 levels) in public support for R & D in coal liquefaction and gasification; 6 billion DM to be allocated annually
• R & D coordination from concept to application	• Limit further acquisitions by state enterprises to safeguard dynamism of private companies, especially highly successful small and medium sized firms; stated aim of GEPI rescue operations is to return firms to private sector	Continuing subsidies to shipbuilding; loan guarantees for shipowners
• Selective government purchasing	• Large state loans and grants (primarily to state companies) for electronics, telecommunications and data processing development	Support for foreign oil exploration by German companies in the DEMINEX consortium
• Increasing the commercial scale of business	• Continued welcome of joint ventures by state firms with higher technology multinationals	
• Concentrating promotion efforts on selected projects		
For the coordination and implementation of this policy, the creation of:		
• A fund for industrial renewal projects		
• A state secretariat to concert sectorial policies, reinforcing traditional business labor-government cooperation		

244

France	The Netherlands	The United Kingdom
Remove price controls to permit firms to have larger investable surpluses	Continued support of the measures provided for by the 1978 Investment Account Law	New Conservative government emphasizing creation of a "favorable climate" (through anti-inflation monetary stringency, tax changes, elimination of price and exchange control) and officially de-emphasizing microeconomic interventions
Allow bankruptcies (to eliminate inefficient management)	Modest increased government funding especially for development and use of energy saving and environmental protection technologies	Drive to cut public expenditure (hitting mainly sectorially nonselective regional grants – cut by 1/3); subsidies to shipbuilding and steel being phased out, not eliminated; sale of part of equity in profitable state enterprises to the private sector
Legislate to control mergers and promote competition	Promote restructing of, and moves away from, declining sectors by:	Renewed commitment to state supported nuclear power development
Reduce current subsidies	• Increasing the transparency of subsidies	National Enterprise Board venture capital entrepreneurial role downplayed, but a new £30 million NEB investment in titanium production for aircraft approved in absence of willingness to invest by private enterprise
Promote "Sectors of the Future," e.g. nuclear energy, aircraft, energy conservation, electronic data processing, telecommunications by:	• Improving business-labor-government social consensus through the Restructuring Board	
• State investments	Some export promotion (e.g. subsidies and guarantees for preparation of bids on turnkey projects)	
• Government purchasing		
• Low interest loans		
• Subsidies and tax incentives to users		
• Soliciting and giving tax incentives to foreign (especially U.S.) firms to form joint ventures		
• Establishment of special funds for employment creation in troubled regions		
• Employment creation by rebates of social charges to hiring firms		

Continued

Table 6-4 Continued

France	The Netherlands	The United Kingdom
Reorient savings toward industry by tax deductions for share purchases		Proposed competition bill attacks only anti-competitive abuses, not mergers
Increased consultation with labor		Continuation of (small) Labour government schemes to promote adaptation of microprocessor technology by British firms
"Hard line" energy conservation		Autonomous regional (e.g. Scottish) initiatives to promote inward investment by high technology foreign multinationals.

Sweden	Switzerland	The EEC
Ongoing debate between advocates of macroeconomic correctives (e.g. exchange rate devaluation) and those who favor industrial policy other than occasional rescue operations	Cantons have primary responsibility but federal government also ready to facilitate job creation and investment on a case by case basis for companies and regions in difficulty	Press for *open public markets* (reinforced by GATT agreement with non-EEC countries on a public procurement code)
Continued support to shipbuilding, steel, and textiles	Try to avoid too much propping up of uncompetitive industry	Year by year continuation and renegotiation of *steel crisis cartel*
Additional measures to promote labor mobility (moving expenses, job search grants etc.)	Expanded budget allocation to ensure exports against political risks	Promote *transparency* of financial relations between member states and public undertakings (in an effort to make state enterprises more competitive with private companies)
Modest increases in public R & D funding, small business loans, and promotion of large export consortia	Modest expansion for support of applied R & D, quality control, and education in electronics	$30 million subsidy spread over four years to European *computer firms*

A plan to pay *shipowners* to scrap surplus ships in return for their agreeing to order new vessels at discounted prices

Expansion of European Investment Bank loans in 1979 by 40% over 1978 to promote investments in *depressed regions* (especially southern Italy and Ireland)

Source: Adapted from Lawrence Franko, *European Industrial Policy: Past, Present and Future,* 1980, (Brussels, Belgium: The Conference Board in Europe) pp. 5–13.

Summary

This chapter discussed the concept philosophy and orientation of international corporations concerning long-range planning. Then the actual practices of the companies were reviewed through an examination of empirical studies of United States, European, and Japanese multinationals.

Results of the various studies indicated that international corporations do undertake long-range planning of five- to ten-years duration. However, the studies also revealed that those practices were headquarters-(home-office) oriented. That is, policy guidelines, objectives, and goals, as well as strategic operational aspects, were decided by the home office. Overseas subsidiaries participated minimally in decision making. They were simply implementors. Long-range planning seems to have a positive impact on organizational effectiveness. This chapter also reviewed the concept and practices of environmental scanning. Very few companies seem to undertake environmental scanning systematically.

Lastly, the issue of industrial policy and its impact on corporate planning was briefly reviewed. There does not seem to be a consensus in the United States about the usefulness of a national industrial policy. Moreover, Western Europe and Japan seem to be positive about the role of organizational policy in generating economic and industrial growth.

Case

The emergence of the Third World multinational is one of the new trends in international business today. This case discusses the growth strategy of an ASEAN multinational, emphasizing the importance of more systematic long-range planning for stable growth.

Case 6-1

Sime Darby BHD

In May 1981, Tan Siew Sin, Chairman of Sime Darby BHD said:

> "In an uncertain world, it is comforting to know that Sime Darby is resting
> on a solid base. It should be noted that the plantation group is contributing
> less and less to the group's profits. We must, therefore, seriously consider
> a plan to reduce Sime Darby's fortunes so closely linked to world commodity
> (e.g. rubber, oil palm, cocoa) prices."

A Brief History:

Sime Darby, now Malaysia's largest multinational corporation (MNC) had
its beginning in 1910 in Malacca. The original company was started by three
Scotsmen, and its business scope was plantation management of 500 acres
of Radella Rubber Estate. In 1915, the company set up an office in Singapore
to engage in "general trading." As the rubber industry in Malaya flourished,
so did Sime Darby. In 1929, for example, it secured exclusive dealership for
Caterpillar agricultural and construction equipment.

Sime Darby's Business Expansion:

In addition to its core business—plantation management—general trading,
and Caterpillar distributorship—the business of Sime Darby grew over the
years in the fields of engineering, canning, insurance, brokerage, vegetable
oil refinery, and the like. As a consequence of the size of the company and
the scope of its operations, the company was divided up into several groups.
The group (or the multi-division) structure included six groups.

1. Plantation Group employs about 23,000 people. This group's profits before tax amounted to M$110 million, in 1981.
2. Tractors Division employs more than 2,800 people. It has two units: one to handle the Caterpillar distribution, and the other for distribution of Ford agricultural machinery.
3. Commodity Refining Division refines palm oil aimed at markets in Asia, Africa, Europe, and the United States.
4. The Hong Kong Division employs 2,500 people. Engaged in automotive dealerships, property management, insurance and the like, this division contributed $M33 million in 1981.
5. Asean and Pacific Division is based in Singapore.
6. The Western Division, based in The Hague (Netherlands), coordinates operations in the United Kingdom, W. Europe, and the United States.

Emergence of Sime Darby as an ASEAN Multinational

Early in March 1978, the Chairman of Sime Darby announced that the company would shift its domicile from London (U.K.) to Malaysia "to make it a truly ASEAN company." Referring to Sime Darby, Louis Kraar of the *Fortune Magazine*, as "a plantation grown conglomerate", had pointed out that its Chairman Tan Siew Sin adopts the American philosophy of "expand or perish." (Oct. 22, 79)

Expansion in recent years has come, for Sime Darby, in the form of acquisitions and joint-ventures. A widely publicized take-over attempt by Sime Darby involved Guthrie Corp. (Malaysia). Of course, this attempt did not succeed. But Sime Darby's joint ventures with a variety of companies at home (Pernas, for example) and abroad gives a clear indication of the strategies pursued by top management of the company. In many ways, Sime Darby's growth-oriented actions are quite similar to the ways of many U.S. companies (ITT, LTV, to name a few) especially during the 1965–1975 time frame. (See Table 6-5 for a short statistical profile of Sime Darby.)

Changes in Top Management Structure

In April 1981, management structure was altered to reflect the challenges of the 1980s. Tunku Dato' Ahmad Yahya, previously Director of operations, was appointed Joint Group Chief Executive. He has full responsibility for the day-to-day operations of the entire group while J.R. Scott, the other Joint Group Chief Executive devotes his attention toward expansion and innovation in the broadest sense, including strategic corporate planning, new projects and acquisitions. Together Mr. Scott and Tunku Ahmad will co-ordinate the activities of the Sime Darby Group toward achieving its corporate objectives.

Table 6-5 A statistical profile

		1972	*1977*	*1981*
State revenue (turnover)	$M	267.8	1,353.0	2,640.7
Earnings before tax	$M	36.5	151.4	245.4
Total assets	$M	412.8	825.2	1,479.7
Dividends	$M	7.5	19.6	46.4
Number of share holders ('000)		10.7	23.6	31.8

The San Francisco Seminar

In June 1981, the Chairman of Sime Darby organized a seminar in San Francisco, California, for more than 100 leading U.S. business executives. Led by Tunku Ahmad, the outcome demonstrated that the U.S. business community was increasingly receptive to joint venture projects in the ASEAN region. Subsequent to this seminar, Sime Darby was studying a number of preliminary proposals for joint ventures with U.S. companies.

One of the many proposals now under consideration (December, 1981) is a joint venture proposal with a U.S. bio-technology company in California called International Plant Research Company (IPRC). The joint venture, if it materializes, would enter the business of applying the newly evolving genetic engineering technology to tropical crops. The main pros and cons include the following:

Pros

(1) The new joint venture will be the first of its kind participated in by an MNC from the ASEAN region.
(2) In spite of the various trading, manufacturing, and service operations in which Sime Darby is involved, its agriculture-based activities constitute the real backbone of the company.
(3) It is very likely that Sime Darby will be able to grow better strains of crops (perennial plants) with the aid of genetic engineering technology on the 80,940 hectares of plantation property it controls—on most of which rubber, oil-palm, and cocoa are presently cultivated. It is foreseeable that the joint venture will focus on ways to upgrade Sime Darby's main plantation crops.
(4) The company sees opportunities to market the results of the new research in the ASEAN countries (Philippines, Indonesia, Singapore, and Thailand, besides Malaysia).
(5) The joint venture company would be headquartered in Kuala Lumpur, with new scientific equipment as well as scientists brought over from the IPRC (San Francisco).

(6) Sime Darby's initial investment in the joint venture will be about M$1 million generated from within.

Cons

(1) Genetic engineering companies in the U.S. have mushroomed in recent years. These include human genetic engineering, animal genetic engineering, and plant genetic engineering.
(2) Most of these companies, although having demonstrated many scientific advances in the laboratory, are still, like research institutes, headed by scientists. IPRC is no exception.
(3) There is nothing fundamentally wrong about scientists heading commercially-oriented science-based companies. In the past Polaroid was headed (for over 40 years) by the founder, Mr. Edwin Land, who was a physicist. There is a number of companies especially computer hardware and software companies similar in top management-character as Polaroid once was.
(4) However, the main difference between genetic engineering companies (such as Bio Tech, Genetech, IPRC) and other science-based and scientist-led companies is that the latter has a product, whereas the former generally does not. The experience of U.S. genetic engineering firms shows plenty of promise, but only limited delivery as yet. Thus, there is no clear-cut indication that the joint venture at a cost of M$ 1 million plus will bear fruit within a couple of years.
(5) Business Press in Malaysia entertains some doubt if Sime Darby, in spite of its size, scope, and leaders does have a sense of direction to pursue, or whether the company simply evaluates each opportunity as it presents itself in the expanding arena of multinational business.

Sime Darby Update*

The British-owned transnational was taken over by the Malaysian government in 1982. The key figure was Prime Minister *Datuk Seri Dr. Mahathir bin Mohammad,* who had been elected as fourth premier of Malaysia on July 16, 1981.

The acquisition of the huge trading company is part of the "look east" strategy Dr. Mahathir is pursuing. He hopes to *emulate Japanese success* in

*Source: "A Premier's Vision for Building a New Malaysia," *South* (August 1983): 23–26 No. 34.

formulation of industrial policy, as well as leading to the use of the term "Malaysia, Inc."

Discussion Questions

1. Discuss the three types of planning modes.
2. What is strategic long-range planning, and why has it become so important to MNCs today?
3. If you were an auto analyst in Detroit, how would you predict the business environment of the United States auto industry in the 1990s?
4. Discuss the difference in planning practices of United States, Japanese, and European MNCs.
5. In spite of the better planning system of the U.S. MNCs, why do they not perform better than the Japanese MNCs that appear to use more of an ad hoc planning system than the U.S. MNCs?

Endnotes

1. George Steiner, *Strategic Planning* (New York: Free Press, 1979), p. 3.
2. Ibid., p. 13.
3. Ibid., p. 14.
4. Ibid.
5. Ibid.
6. Ibid., p. 15.
7. Henry Mintzberg, "Strategy-Making in Three Modes," *California Management Review* 16, 2 (Winter 1973): 45–46.
8. Ibid., pp. 46–47.
9. Ibid., p. 48.
10. Ibid., pp. 52–53.
11. William H. Davidson, *Global Strategic Management* (New York: John Wiley and Sons, 1982), pp. 322–323.
12. Ibid., p. 323.
13. Ibid.
14. Ibid., pp. 323–325.
15. F. Gluck, S. Kaufman, and A. Walleck, "The Four Phases of Strategic Management," *The Journal of Business Strategy* 2, 3 (Winter 1982): 9–21.
16. R. F. Vancil, and P. Lorange, "Strategic Planning in Diversified Companies," *Harvard Business Review* (January–February 1975): 81–90.
17. William K. Lindsay, and Leslie W. Rue, "Impact of the Organization Environment on the Long-Range Planning Process: A Contingency View," *Academy of Management Journal* 23, 3 (1980).
18. Ibid., p. 394.
19. Ibid., pp. 401–402.
20. Anant R. Negandhi, *Organization Theory in an Open System* (New York: Dunellen, 1975), Chap. 4, pp. 54–86.
21. Ibid., p. 77.

22. William W. Cain, "Multinational Planning: Mission Impossible," *Columbia Journal of World Business* 5, 2 (July–August 1970): 58.

23. P. E. Holden, C. A. Pederson, and G. E. Germane, *Top Management* (New York: McGraw-Hill Book Co., 1968), pp. 3–4. Also see George Steiner, ed., *Managerial Long-Range Planning* (New York: McGraw-Hill Book Co., 1966), pp. 311–326.

24. Negandhi, *Organization Theory*, Chap. 4, pp. 54–86.

25. George Steiner and Warren M. Cannon, *Multinational Corporate Planning* (New York: MacMillan, 1966), pp. 295–314.

26. Toyohiro Kono, "Long Range Planning–Japan-USA–A Comparative Study," *Long Range Planning* 9 (October 1976): 61–71.

27. Ibid., p. 70.

28. James M. Hulbert and William K. Brandt, *Managing the Multinational Subsidiary* (New York: Holt, Rinehart and Winston, 1980), pp. 35–64.

29. Ibid., p. 40.

30. Ehrenfried Pausenberger, et al., "Organisation des Planungsprozesses in international taetigen Unternehmen," *Zeitschrift fuer betriebswirtschaftliche Forschung* 31 (1979): 20.

31. Martin K. Welge, "Planungsprobleme in multinationalen Unternehmungen, *Organization, Planning, Informations-systems*, eds. E. Frese, P. Schmitz, and N. Szypershi (Stuttgart: C. E. Poeschel, 1981), p. 206.

32. For detailed results, see Anant R. Negandhi and Martin K. Welge, *Beyond Theory Z* (Greenwich, Conn.: JAI Press, 1984), Chap. 3, pp. 47–53.

33. Hulbert and Brandt, *Managing*, pp. 48–49.

34. Stanley S. Thune, and Robert J. House, "Where Long-Range Planning Pays Off," *Business Horizons* (August 1970): 81–87. Firms selected were large multinational companies with sales of $75 million or more.

35. H. Igor Ansoff, et al., "Does Planning Pay? The Effect of Planning on Success of Acquisitions in American Firms," *Long Range Planning* (December 1970): 2–7.

36. Negandhi, *Organization Theory*, pp. 79–80.

37. Charles Stubbart, "Are Environmental Scanning Units Effective?" *Long Range Planning* 15, 3 (1982): 139–145.

38. Ibid., p. 139.

39. Arvind V. Phatak, *International Dimensions of Management* (Boston: Kent, 1983), Chap. 3, pp. 39–63.

40. S. B. Prasad, and Y. Krishna Shetty, *An Introduction to Multinational Management* (Englewood Cliffs, NJ: Prentice-Hall, 1976), Chap. 5, pp. 67–83.

41. Ibid., p. 74.

42. Warren J. Keegan, "Multinational Scanning: A Study of the Information Sources Utilized by Headquarter's Executives in Multinational Companies," *Administrative Science Quarterly* 19, 3 (September 1974): 411–421.

43. Ibid., p. 411.

44. Liam Fahey, and W. R. King, "Environmental Scanning for Corporate Planning," *Business Horizons* 20, 4 (August 1977).

45. Philip S. Thomas, "Environmental Scanning–the State of the Art," *Long Range Planning* (February 1980): 20–25.

46. Stubbart, "Evironmental Scanning," p. 142.

47. Thomas quoted ibid., p. 141.

48. Mark Fitzpatrick, "The Definition and Assessment of Political Risk in International Business: A Review of the Literature," *Academy of Management Review* 8, 2 (1983): 249.

49. Stephen J. Kobrin, "Political Risk: A Review and Reconsideration," *Journal of International Business Studies* 10, 1 (Spring/Summer 1979): 67.

50. Franklin R. Root, "Analyzing Political Risks in International Business," in *The Multinational Enterprise in Transition*, eds. Ashok Kapoor and Philip D. Grub (Princeton: Darwin Press, 1972), p. 357.
51. Kobrin, "Political Risk," p. 68.
52. Ibid., pp. 67–80.
53. Ibid., p. 68.
54. Briance Mascarenhas, "Coping with Uncertainty in International Business," *Journal of International Business Studies* XIV, 2 (Fall 1982): 87–98.
55. Ibid., p. 89.
56. Ibid.
57. Ibid.
58. Alexander Hamilton, quoted in "Industrial Policy: Is it the Answer?" *Business Week*, July 4, 1983, p. 54.
59. Ibid., p. 54.
60. Ibid., p. 57.

Additional Readings

Articles

Capon, Noel, et al. "Comparison of Corporate Planning Practice in America and Australian Manufacturing Companies." *Journal of International Business Studies* XV, 2 (Fall 1984): 41–54.

Dymsza, William A. "Global Strategic Planning: A Model and Recent Developments." *Journal of International Business Studies* XV, 2 (Fall 1984): 169–183.

Kennedy, Jr., Charles R. "The External Environment-Strategic Planning Interface: U.S. Multinational Corporate Practices in the 1980s." *Journal of International Business Studies* XV, 2 (Fall 1984): 99–108.

Simon, Jeffery P. "A Theoretical Perspective on Political Risk." *Journal of International Business Studies* XV, 3 (Winter 1984): 123–143.

Books

Hulbert, James M., and Brandt, William K. *Managing the Multinational Subsidiary*. New York: Holt, Rinehart and Winston, 1980.

Negandhi, Anant R. *Organization Theory in an Open System*. Port Washington, NY: Kennikat Press, 1975.

Part III

Functional Aspects of International Business Operations

- *Human Resource Management in International Corporations: Managing the Labor Work Force*

- *Human Resource Management in International Corporations: Managing Managers*

- *International Production and Logistics*

- *Assessing the International Markets and Export Marketing*

- *Managing the Marketing Mix in an International Context*

- *Financial Management in International Corporations*

Chapter 7

Human Resource Management in International Corporations: Managing the Labor Work Force

Of all the factors to be considered in the operation of a business enterprise, the management of human resources is perhaps the most critical. Underscoring its importance, Schultz has argued: "It simply is not possible to have the fruits of modern agriculture and the abundance of modern industry without making large investments in human beings."[1] With respect to the United States he goes on to say: "... the most distinctive feature of our economic system is the growth in human capital. Without it there would be only hard, manual work and poverty ... the man without skills and knowl-

259

edge leaning terrifically against nothing."[2] A similar view is that of a leading business man in the Orient, Mr. Sadao Kumazawa, President of the Oji Paper Company in Japan:

> Human resources should be properly shown in figures as assets on the balance sheet, just as physical assets are, as an indication of corporate strength. . . . Cultivation of human resources offers a scope of promise vastly wider than that of physical resources.[3]

In the same vein, Mr. Michael G. Duerr has stated:

> Virtually any type of international problem, in the final analysis, is either created by people or must be solved by people. Hence, having the right people in the right place at the right time emerges as the key to a company's economic growth. If we are successful in solving that problem, I am confident we can cope with all others."[4]

This and ensuing chapters will discuss various elements of human resource management. This chapter covers important issues involved in managing the labor work force in foreign subsidiaries. The next chapter will discuss the management of managerial personnel.

In discussing human resource management practices and their problems, attempts have been made to examine the situations in both industrialized and developing countries. Although a large percentage of foreign direct investment is in industrialized countries, particularly from the United States and Western European countries (approximately 75% of the total FDC), the sociocultural and environmental factors are more distinct and different between industrialized and developing countries. The problems associated with managing human resources are more pronounced in developing countries. Consequently, a detailed coverage is provided on those countries.

The specific issues discussed in this chapter include:

- Cross-cultural and cross-national similarities and differences in labor's commitment, morale, and productivity
- Human resource planning and the practices of international corporations in foreign countries
- Organization and status of personnel departments in foreign countries
- Job analysis
- Selection and promotion practices
- Impact of environmental factors on human resource practices
- Compensation and motivation practices
- Feasibility and utility of the home country's practices in foreign countries

The Cross-Cultural Perspective

During the last three decades, much was written concerning the cross-cultural and cross-national differences in employees' attitudes, motivations, and commitments. In the following sections, these various viewpoints and perspectives are presented first. A discussion of actual human resource practices will follow.

Employee Morale and Productivity

In his study of industrial workers in India, Ornati observed:

> Indian workers are not interested in factory work; they resist adjustment to the type of life which goes with industrial employment. In the value scheme of the majority of Indians, factory labor does not offer any avenue for the expression of their individual personalities; wage increase and promotions do not operate as stimulants to greater exertion, nor does greater exertion lead to changes in status.[5]

Commenting on the labor commitment in underdeveloped countries, Kerr et al. had this to say:

> Cultural factors (such as religious and ethical valuations, the family system, class, and race) all have a bearing on commitment. . . . The greater the strength of extended family, the slower the commitment of workers to industrial life.[6]

Farmer and Richman, following the work of McClelland, arrived at this conclusion:

> The importance of a country's view of achievement and work as a vital determinant of managerial performance and productivity efficiency must not be understated. . . . Prevailing religious beliefs and cultural values, in connection with parental behavior, child-rearing practices . . . traditional Hinduism, Buddhism, Islam, and even Catholicism are not generally conducive to a high achievement drive in their orthodox followers.[7]

Myrdal's monumental study of South Asia also reveals the impact of tradition, custom, value systems, and attitudes on labor commitment and productivity. Myrdal argues: "in [the] absence of simultaneous changes in institutions and attitudes, the effect on labor utilization and productivity throughout the economy may still be less consequential."[8] Similarly, scholars studying the industrial scene in Latin American countries have argued that the industrial employees in these countries are more interested in maintaining and enhancing their family status and fulfilling obligations to friends and relatives than in increasing their productivity or wages.

Zurcher, Meadow, and Zurcher, in their comparative study of Mexican, Mexican-American, and Anglo-American bank employees, found that Mexicans are more particularistic than Mexican-Americans, who are in turn more particularistic than Anglo-Americans.[9] (Particularism indicates the value orientation toward institutionalized obligations of friendships; in contrast, universalism indicates a value orientation toward obligation to the society and organizations.)

More important, these authors also found that alienation from work was significantly and positively related to particularism and negatively related to job longevity, position level, satisfaction with the position, and plans to continue working in a bank.

Of course not all scholars agree with the contention that prevailing sociocultural factors in the Far East and Latin America have a negative and dominating impact on employee commitment to industrial life. A number of researchers have cast doubts on these assertions.

Morris, for example, has pointed out:

> Much of the literature tends to base interpretation on hypothetical, psychological, and sociological propositions which themselves are highly suspect. The argument typically rests on scattered fragments of evidence taken indiscriminately. . . . It is impossible to generate a satisfactory analysis from this sort of melange.[10]

McMillan's research in Brazil revealed that:

> [South] Americans are under less compulsion to probe the attitude of their workers than they are in the United States. . . . Enlisting the allegiance of workers is easier, and motivating employees, most Americans appear to agree, is not difficult.[11]

In his study, *Social Factors in Economic Development in Argentina*, Fillol observed:

> There is no reason to believe that Argentina workers have basically different attitudes toward their jobs from workers anywhere else in industrialized Western countries. . . . Industrialists in general do not seem to have given any thought to the fact that the productivity, motivation, and cooperation of labor are primarily determined by the management which employs it and not by the more or less enlightened social and economic policies of government.[12]

Finally, in the most comprehensive study, Sirota and Greenwood[13] raise considerable doubts about the prevailing thesis of the impact of sociocultural variables on motivation. They state that such generalizations, although interesting, are "based almost entirely on the subjective impressionistic experiences of the observers."[14] They further state: "Acceptance of these conclusions must therefore depend largely on faith—faith both in the observer's objectivity and in the representativeness of the anecdotal evidence he usually presents as proof of his case."[15]

Empirical Studies

Empirical studies, undertaken in various developing countries, concerning employee commitment, morale, and productivity, seem to support Sirota and Greenwood's, as well as Fillol's, contentions. A few of these studies are reviewed here to provide a perspective on the actual situation in developing countries.

In a large-scale, cross-cultural study in six developing countries, my colleagues and I found that the employees in these countries, like their counterparts in the industrialized countries, desire higher wages, opportunity for advancement, job security, fair treatment, better working conditions and welfare, and a higher standard of living for their children.[16]

Altimus, Richards, and Slocum,[17] in their study of Mexican and United States industrial workers, found that job security, esteem, autonomy, and self-actualization needs were very much in the minds of the Mexican workers.

Automobile and Steel Industries Study.[18] This study sought to evaluate the impact of technology and socioeconomic systems on work attitudes and behavior. The data were collected from India and the United States. Samples of workers in both countries were drawn to represent relatively high and relatively low levels of technologies as used in the steel industry in each country. All work places or major job types in the selected plants were sampled.

Analysis of Research Results. Figure 7-1 presents data for the three worker samples on the extent of their personal concern about ten public issues. Not surprisingly, this is a content area where real national differences seem to exist. The difference in level of concern about each of the ten issues between United States steel workers and Indian steel workers is large (both statistically and practically), and the pattern of responses for the two groups is quite different. The Indian sample indicates a high level of concern with only two issues: the country's economic problems and housing problems. Both issues may well reflect important and elemental needs for basic survival. In contrast, United States steel workers indicate a high level of concern with

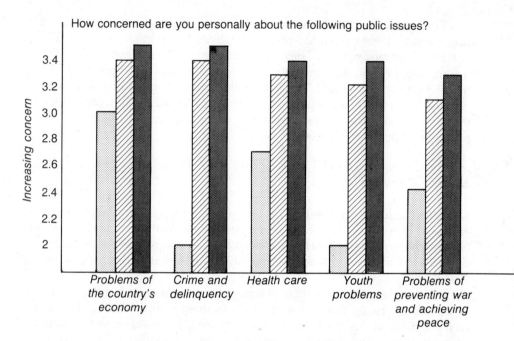

How concerned are you personally about the following public issues?

Increasing concern

3.4
3.2
3.0
2.8
2.6
2.4
2.2
2

Problems of the country's economy   Crime and delinquency   Health care   Youth problems   Problems of preventing war and achieving peace

Figure 7-1 Mean level of concern with public issues (*Source:* G. W. England and A. R. Negandhi, "National Contexts and Technology as Determinants of Employee's Perceptions," in *Organizational Functioning in a Cross-Cultural Perspective,* eds. G. W. England, A. R. Negandhi, and B. Wilpert (Ohio: Kent State University Press: Comparative Administration Research Institute, 1979), p. 178.)

a much wider range of issues. These include elemental needs, as well as more collectively oriented concerns, such as youth problems, problems of war and peace, and pollution.

The contention that these are real national differences is strengthened because the two United States samples show similar levels of concern with each individual issue and almost identical patterns of concerns. In short, the differences between countries in level and pattern of response are large, whereas the intracountry differences are small.[19]

Figure 7-2 compares the three samples of workers in terms of the relative importance of the workers' jobs, containing eight major job areas. Indian steel workers attach greater importance to all eight job facets than do United States steel workers, significantly so on six of the eight items. The establishment of these differences in "work values" as representing real national differences is severely questioned because intracountry differences between the two United States samples are as large or larger than the intercountry differences on four of the eight items. Additionally, the very similar

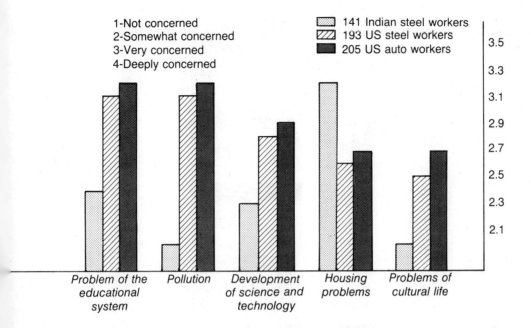

Figure 7-1 (Continued)

patterns of responses (relative ranking of the eight items) among the steel workers in the two countries mitigate against the conclusion that large and meaningful country differences exist in work values across the two countries.

The question of whether there are major national differences in terms of the extent to which the presence of various job facets "explains" or predicts the level of overall or general job satisfaction has attracted considerable attention.[20] The real question centers on the issue of whether there is some small subset of job facets, whose presence or absence is crucial in determining one's satisfaction with the work situation. Conversely, the question has been raised whether the determination of work satisfaction is largely idiosyncratic at the level of individuals and nations.

Several studies seem to have questioned the validity of a second assertion, that is, the existence of vast national differences concerning employee motivation and factors affecting job satisfaction. For example, Holmström, in his study of factory workers, found:

> ... [workers] see factory work as a citadel of security and relative prosperity, which it is; it offers regular work and promotion and predictable rewards, as against the chaos of terrifying dangers of life outside. For every one in-

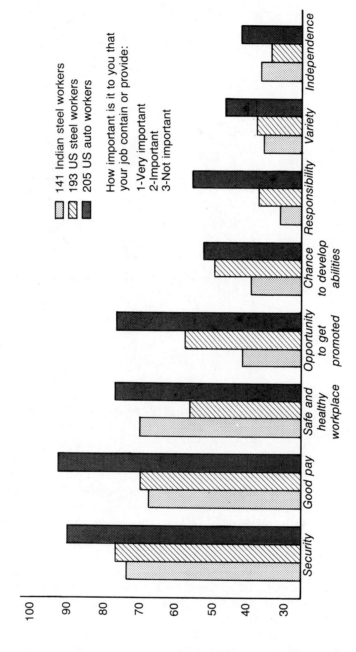

Figure 7-2 Percentage of each group indicating the item is very important (*Source:* G. W. England and A. R. Negandhi, "National Contexts and Technology as Determinants of Employee's Perceptions," in *Organizational Functioning in a Cross-Cultural Perspective,* eds. G. W. England, A. R. Negandhi, and B. Wilpert (Ohio: Kent State University Press: Comparative Administration Research Institute, 1979), p. 180.)

side the citadel, there is a regiment outside trying to scale the walls. Even educated Brahmans will take unskilled, casual factory work in the hope of permanent jobs.[21]

To sum up, the various studies indicate that national differences in worker perceptions existed only on such global issues as pollution, national economy, and housing problems, whereas national differences with respect to job content areas, factors influencing promotions and employees' satisfaction, preferences, and willingness to participate in decision making were marginal at best. In other words, intracountry differences in the employees' perceptions seem to be as large or larger than the intercountry differences.

Human Resource Managment Practices

In the following sections, the actual human resource management practices of United States companies in foreign countries are provided. These are based on a large-scale study, undertaken by me and my colleagues.[22]

Human Resource Planning and Practices

Human resource planning involves (1) anticipating a firm's demands for the different types of skills that will be required to perform future activities, and (2) programming activities for recruiting, selecting, training, and developing individuals to meet anticipated demands.

On the other hand, human resource policies underscore the organizational concern for its human component. Such policies provide guidelines for the following elements of managing human resources:

1. Employment policy—how to obtain suitably qualified and experienced personnel.
2. Training policy—what types of training facilities should be organized, and who should be included in each type of training? Should training be done in-house (on the job or in the classroom) or externally?
3. Wage and salary policy—how should wages and salaries be determined?
4. Staff relations policy—how to establish cooperative relationships among people in a given department and among people in different departments?
5. Welfare and benefits policy—how to ensure the health, safety, and well-being of employees?[23]

The results of the study show that only a few firms in developing countries paid systematic attention to human resource planning and forecasting. Only 12% of the firms (n = 111) undertook human resource planning. There were no appreciable differences between United States subsidiaries and local firms in this regard. Relatively speaking, companies in the Far Eastern region demonstrated more concern than those in Latin America. Why this was so is difficult to discern.

Organization and Status of Personnel Department

A firm's awareness and desire to preserve, develop, and use its human resources can also be seen in examining the organization and hierarchical status of its Personnel Department.

In more than two thirds of the United States subsidiaries studied in the two regions (n = 56), the Personnel Department was organized separately and had two to three specialized units (e.g., training and development, employee benefits, industrial relations, and wage and salary administration). In these companies, the personnel managers were well qualified and in many instances were trained in the United States.

Approximately one half of the local companies (n = 55) had Personnel Departments that were separately organized. However, the personnel manager, although university educated, was not always trained to carry out the personnel function.

Job Analysis

Among the personnel functions, management's initial task is to gather, analyze, and record information on the duties, responsibilities, and qualifications required of persons performing given tasks. In the personnel management literature, these types of activities are subsumed under the term *job analysis*. Briefly, this function is composed of two interrelated activities: (1) *job description*, which records principal duties, responsibilities, and activities involved in specific jobs, and (2) *job specifications*, which outlines special qualifications the individual must possess to perform the assigned tasks in a specific job position.

An inquiry into these functions in Latin American and Far Eastern companies suggests a dismal picture. By and large, neither the United States subsidiaries nor the local firms in Latin America systematically carry on these tasks, and fewer than one fourth of the companies in the Far East undertook job analysis systematically.

A lack of concern for a detailed job analysis is indicative of nonspecialized and undifferentiated tasks of blue-collar employees in developing countries. By and large, lower level employees are unskilled and are used in a variety of tasks—e.g. assembly operations, maintenance, and hauling raw materials and parts. Those undertaking systematic job analysis were large and technologically sophisticated firms.

Selection and Promotion

Management's desire to treat human resources as a critical input in the functioning of an organization can also be discerned by examining a firm's selection and promotion procedures and criteria. As shown in Table 7-1, some 53% of the firms in both regions use a formal and systematic selection process. There were considerable differences between the United States subsidiaries and local firms in this aspect. As can be seen from this table, more than two thirds of the United States subsidiaries had instituted a formal and systematic selection process, as opposed to only a little more than one third of their counterpart local firms.

The informal and ad hoc selection process used by many of the local companies is vividly described by the personnel manager of a large pharmaceutical company. When asked, "How do you select your employees?," he quickly answered:

> I call the prospective employee into my office, ask him to sit down across from my desk, and look straight into his eyes. . . . If his eyes wink frequently, I will not give him a job; if his eyes are steady, he will be employed.

Although this selection practice may seem extreme, an ad hoc selection process existed in two thirds of the local companies in both of the regions studied.

Interviews with executives, governmental officials, and labor leaders pinpointed the following environmental factors affecting human resource management in developing countries[24]:

1. Labor legislation
2. Oversupply of unskilled labor and lack of skilled and trained workers
3. The nature of labor unions (political in nature) and union rivalry

Labor Legislation and Labor Unions

Industrial entrepreneurs in developing countries seem to have taken undue advantage of the labor situation in those countries—oversupply and a high rate of unemployment. As Fillol has remarked with respect to Argentina,

Table 7-1 Summary of results on human resource management practices (percentages)

Item	All companies (n = 111)	Latin American Region			Far Eastern Region		
		U.S. subsidiary (n = 20)	Local firm (n = 17)	Both (n = 37)	U.S. subsidiary (n = 36)	Local firm (n = 38)	Both (n = 74)
Formalized human resource planning	12	5	0	3	19	13	16
Formalized selection process	53	70	41	57	67	37	51
Formalized employee appraisal system	55	60	29	46	72	47	55
Formalized training program (blue-collar employee)	58	—	—	—	50	95	86
Formalized training program (supervisory and technical personnel)	52	—	—	—	81	76	78
Formalized training program (managerial personnel)	40	—	—	—	64	55	59
Formalized managerial succession program	33	60	18	41	42	18	30

Source: Anant R. Negandhi, *Organization Theory in an Open System* (New York: Dunellen, 1975), p. 165. Copyright by A. R. Negandhi.

"Labor tends still to be considered as just another commodity whose services are to be bought as cheaply as possible."[25]

In an attempt to remedy this situation, governments in recent years have modified their existing labor legislation and enacted more liberal labor laws. They have also actively supported trade union activities. This push for liberal labor legislation and the encouragement of aggressive union fronts has resulted in higher wages and has raised expectations among workers. Labor unions in many underdeveloped countries are political; they represent political muscle and political interests instead of the interests of their members. Under such a situation, the managers interviewed felt it was difficult to systematize personnel practices. (The managers of companies without formalized and systematized human resource practices complained more about the environmental constraint than those who were already using advanced human resource practices.)

Compensation and Motivation Practices

Perhaps the most critical question in determining optimal compensation and motivation practices is to ascertain the actual needs, or a need hierarchy, of the industrial worker.

As mentioned earlier, some believe that the industrial employee in developing countries is not interested in money, advancement, or higher achievements. The implications of such assumptions are serious because they leave much less hope for generating economic growth and improving the standard of living for two thirds of the human race living in the less developed part of the world. The actual practices were as follows:

Compensation Level. A large number of United States subsidiaries and local firms in the Far Eastern region instituted a policy of compensating their blue-collar, clerical, supervisory, and managerial personnel at the "market rate," or going rate. Twenty-five percent of the subsidiaries and 16% of the local firms compensated their employees at a higher than market rate, whereas 10% of the former companies and 25% of the latter paid their employees at a lower than market rate.

The practice of paying the market rate indicates the concern of the labor unions and the government to equalize the wages of industrial workers in different industrial enterprises.

Basis for Determining Compensation. Probably more important than the level of compensation is the method for or basis of determining wage and salary rates. Employees want both higher wages and an impartial, objective basis for determining wages and promotions.

Approximately one third of the companies studied in the two regions used some sort of objective basis (e.g. wage surveys or job evaluation) for determining the wage rates of blue-collar employees. This proportion increased to one half with respect to clerical employees but dropped to a marginal 18% in the case of supervisory and managerial personnel.

Overall, a larger number of companies in Latin America used objective methods of determining compensation rates than those in the Far East. Why? We cannot be sure, but our query to the companies in Latin America revealed a greater pressure on the companies by their labor unions to move in that direction.

Regardless of the absolute or relative wage and salary rates, employees in most United States subsidiaries studied felt that they were treated fairly and honestly. Employees in local firms felt they were at the mercy of their immediate supervisors and that their advancement and wage increases depended largely on their supervisors. Many United States companies have attempted to provide their employees with an opportunity for participation in decision making, self-development, use of skills, and initiative in achieving both organizational and individual goals and objectives.[26]

Although the actual practices of the United States industrial enterprises are still short of what many behavioral theorists are advocating, movement toward this goal is more than a facade and represents a genuine desire and interest on the part of individual enterprises in the United States.

Our inquiry into the nature of the motivation practices of the companies studied is discussed next.

Monetary versus *Nonmonetary Rewards.* A large minority of United States subsidiaries and local firms in Latin America and the Far East placed major emphasis on monetary rewards as a way of motivating blue-collar employees. Reliance on monetary devices was stronger in the companies in Latin America compared to Far Eastern companies. Some 92% of the firms studied in Latin America, *versus* 67% in the Far East, placed primary emphasis on monetary rewards.

Similar trends emerged with respect to clerical employees, although the proportion of companies relying solely on monetary rewards was slightly lower.

For supervisory and managerial personnel, this proportion declined further. Overall, approximately one third of the United States subsidiaries studied relied on money for motivating their supervisory and managerial personnel. The local firms, especially in Latin American countries, still relied on monetary rewards.

This is not to say that nonwage benefits were not used by local companies in the two regions. As a matter of fact, historically the industrial employee has received considerable nonwage benefits, such as hospitalization and medical expenses, severence pay, yearly bonuses, dependent allowances, and hous-ing allowances. The local companies in both regions are more paternalistic and welfare-oriented than their United States subsidiary counterparts. How-ever, these nonwage benefits were not conceived as a means to satisfy the higher levels of employee needs. The local companies, although paternalistic in outlook, failed to provide what Herzberg calls "job context hygiene" factors.

The most frequently used nonmonetary incentives in the companies stud-ied were:

1. Good working conditions (e.g. clean factories, air-conditioned work place, good ventilation)
2. Recreation and sports programs
3. Employee counseling programs
4. An opportunity to participate in decision making.[27]

The European MNCs' Practices

Although there are still subtle differences between the basic orientations, management philosophies, and practices of United States European com-panies, the gap between the two with regard to their personnel policies for local employees is narrowing fast. Especially at the levels of unskilled and skilled workers, supervisory personnel, and middle management, there are no substantial differences in wages or in the type of training and promotion opportunities available. The United States and European companies are still somewhat different at the higher technical and managerial levels. However, this topic will be discussed later in the book.

The Japanese MNCs' Practices

Despite the high mark the Japanese companies have been receiving recently concerning their orientations toward employees,[28] our studies in developing, as well as in industrially developed, countries indicate something quite to the contrary.[29] The Japanese seem to have the most severe problems with their employees. They experience the greatest difficulty in attracting, retain-ing, and motivating employees at all levels. Generally, the Japanese MNCs follow two distinctive modes in their personnel policies. One is to practice the Japanese style of management. In this case, an attempt is made to intro-duce the Japanese practices of lifetime employment and promote employees on the basis of seniority. The other mode is to treat the local employees in a manner similar to the way they are treated by domestically owned com-panies. This results in maintenance of the status quo; that is, holding the employees in low esteem as is the custom in many local enterprises and government agencies. However, because of rising expectations and a better understanding of the status of workers in other countries, these policies have resulted in low employee morale and productivity, together with higher absenteeism and turnover rates. Although the expatriate Japanese managers failed to see the causes of their problems, they did admit they had serious human resource and personnel problems, especially in developing countries.

The Modified Local System in Japanese Subsidiaries.[30] Japanese managers who choose to adopt local management practices do so because they are concerned about their lack of familiarity with local culture, practices, and institutions. They may also be wary of the possibility of conflict with local employees. Thus, although Japanese managers retain control over policy formulation and key decisions, administrative duties that involve sensitive and direct contact with the locals and local institutions are delegated to a few trusted local managers.

Given this context, it is hardly surprising that local managers come to interpret their duties as implementing a management system that is as dogmatically "local" as possible. They follow the wage guidelines strictly, and adhere to legal regulations regarding recruitment and dismissal. They play safe by delivering to the Japanese managers a system that follows established rules and policies to the letter.

Legal regulations prescribe only minimal behavior, and in practice, rules are often softened by customs, toleration of minor deviations, and personal considerations. In the case of Japanese overseas subsidiaries, strict adherence to legal regulations results in a system that on the one hand is as dogmatically "local" as possible, and on the other hand is much more bureaucratic, rigid, and insensitive (to the employees' needs) than most local firms actually are.

A comparative study of twenty-seven United States, Japanese, and local companies in Taiwan found the modified local system to be dominant in Japanese companies. The study revealed many similarities between the management practices of Japanese subsidiaries and local firms in Taiwan. Specifically, similarities were observed in the following areas. In contrast to the major United States subsidiaries, the Japanese subsidiaries were quite diffuse in their human resource policies. The study also found decision making more centralized in Japanese and local firms than in the United States subsidiaries. Regarding the leaders' perceptions of their subordinates' abilities, the Japanese local companies' executives seemed to have much less confidence and trust in their subordinates than their United States counterparts in Taiwan. Both Japanese and local managers felt their subordinates needed close watching and guidance and should not be left to function on their own. In other words, Japanese and Chinese managers were autocratic and paternalistic in decision making whereas United States managers used consultative and democratic leadership styles. As far as human resource management is concerned, although the Japanese and local firms appeared to stress the importance of their employees' security and sociopsychological needs, there was no specific management practice to satisfy those needs. In fact, unlike the United States firms, the Japanese subsidiaries and the local companies were unable to attract qualified and trained personnel, and the majority of the executives and technical personnel in these companies were poorly trained. The higher effectiveness of the United States subsidiaries in attracting trained personnel was attributed to such factors as high monetary rewards, opportunity for advancement, individual development, and objective criteria for promotion and rewards.

A recent study of the management practices of twenty United States and Japanese subsidiaries in Singapore also found that the United States companies had been able to transfer successfully many features of their management practices to operations in this country. In contrast, the management style of the Japanese companies there had little resemblance to the "Japanese management system" elsewhere. For example, of a total of ten Japanese companies in the study, only one company used the "ringi" system or the consensus approach to decision making. Further, similar to the findings of the Taiwan study outlined earlier, Japanese companies in Singapore exercised tight control on their operations, and decision making was centralized. Several executives of these companies stated that the statutory requirements of compulsory contributions to the Central Provident and Skills Development Funds, as well as high turnover, were major factors why Japanese companies hesitated to extend some of their home management practices to Singapore.[31]

There are a number of examples of tensions and conflicts between management and local employees of Japanese subsidiaries in both developed and developing countries. In a YKK plant in Italy, workers struck for eighteen months, complaining about the hard-driving ten-man Japanese management team. Although the Japanese managers, to demonstrate their corporate loyalty, attempted to run the machines themselves, a labor magistrate found the company guilty of "anti-union activity" and ordered the managers to keep away from the production line during the strike.[32] Negandhi and Baliga,[33] in a study of 120 United States, European, and Japanese subsidiaries in less developed countries found that the "localized" approach was dominant among the Japanese firms.

Sim's[34] study of United States, British, and Japanese subsidiaries in Malaysia supports the Negandhi and Baliga findings. He found that the extent of participation and information sharing was greatest in the United States subsidiaries and least in the Japanese. In the Japanese subsidiaries, decision making tended to be confined to Japanese executives.

The "modified Japanese system" in its variations has been practiced in the subsidiaries of Japanese firms in developed countries, such as Western

Europe and the United States. Several studies of Japanese subsidiaries in the United States have identified common elements in the management of these companies. These commonalities include some form of job security, and, compared to similar United States companies, more concern for the welfare of their employees, including both blue-collar workers and management.[35] Overall, it seems that Japanese subsidiaries in the developed countries are more successful and encounter fewer management problems than their counterparts in the less developed countries.

Table 7-2 exhibits the comparative motives of United States, Japanese, and the local companies' practices in one developing country, Taiwan.

Human Resource Management Problems in Industrialized Countries

The sociocultural differences between the United States and Western European countries are not as marked as those in the developing countries. However, the differences in work and labor conditions between United States and Europe are considerably different. Some of these differences are discussed in the following section.

Industrial Democracy and Codetermination

Initiated in West European countries, industrial democracy refers to employees' rights to participate in significant management decisions, such as profit sharing, plant expansion and closing, dismissal, wage rates, bonuses, and holiday leaves. These rights are supported by corresponding legislations in many Western European countries. In some countries, such as Germany and Holland, the workers' rights even go further. For example, in Holland, the Works Council has a right to nominate and to veto candidates for the Corporate Board of Directors. Similarly, compulsory profit sharing is required of French business firms employing fifty or more workers. Employers and employees are required by French law to form company "works committees" to select the method by which profits are allocated. Profit sharing is also applicable to subsidiaries of foreign firms operating in France.

Codetermination originally developed in the German coal and steel industries by establishing the Works Constitution Act of 1952, which required 50% directorship from the workers. In 1976, codetermination was extended by law to cover most German employers with one hundred or more workers. Covered under codetermination are not only routine operating issues (e.g., improving working conditions), but also strategic issues, such as plant clos-

Table 7-2 Profiles of management practices and effectiveness of the United States subsidiary, the Japanese subsidiary, and the local firm

Management practices and effectiveness	U.S. subsidiary	Japanese subsidiary	Local firm
Planning	Long-range (5 to 10 years)	Medium- to short-range (1 to 2 years)	Medium- to short-range (1 to 2 years)
Policy making	Formally stated; used as guidelines and control measures	Formally not stated; not used as guidelines and control measures	Formally not stated; not used as guidelines and control measures
Other control devices used	Quality control, cost and budgetary control, maintenance; setting of standards	Quality control; Maintenance	Some cost control, some quality control, some maintenance
Organizational set-up			
Grouping of activities	On functional-area basis	On functional-area basis	On functional-area basis
Number of departments	5 to 7	5 to 7	5 to 7
Use of specialized staff	Some	None	None
Use of service department	Considerable	Some	Some
Authority definition	Clear	Unclear	Unclear
Degree of decentralization	High	Low	Low
Leadership style	Consultative	Autocratic	Paternalistic-autocratic
Managers' attitudes toward leadership style and delegation	Would prefer autocratic style; authority should be held tight at top	Not available	Would prefer consultative type

Continued

Table 7-2 Continued

Management practices and effectiveness	U.S. subsidiary	Japanese subsidiary	Local firm
Human Resource Management Practices			
Human resource policies	Formally stated	Not stated	Not stated
Organization of personnel department	Not separate unit	Not separate unit	Not separate unit
Job evaluation	Done	Done	Done by very few
Development of election and promotion criteria	Formally done	Done by some	Done by some
Training programs	Only for the blue-collar employees	Only for the blue-collar employees	Only for the blue-collar employees
Compensation and motivation	Monetary only	Monetary only	Monetary only
Management Effectiveness			
Employee morale	High	Moderate	Moderate
Absenteeism	Low	Low	Low
Turnover	High	Low	High
Productivity	High	High	High
Ability to attract trained personnel	Able to do so	Somewhat able to do so	Somewhat able to do so

278

	Very cooperative	Somewhat cooperative	Somewhat cooperative
Interdepartmental relationships	Very cooperative	Somewhat cooperative	Somewhat cooperative
Executives' perception of the firm's overall objectives	Systems optimization as an important goal	Subsystems optimization as an important goal	Subsystems optimization as an important goal
Use of high-level workers	Effectively used	Moderate to poor use	Moderate to poor use
Adapting to environmental changes	Able to adapt without much difficulty	Able to adapt with some difficulty	Able to adapt with considerable difficulty
Growth in sales	Phenomenal	Considerable	Considerable to modest

Source: A. R. Negandhi, *Management and Economic Development in Taiwan* (The Hague: Martinus Nijhoff, 1973), pp. 125–127.

ings and industrial policies for workers who have lost their jobs in declining industries.

Initially, managers found that these requirements were restrictive in making critical decisions. For example, Volkswagen experienced considerable difficulties in deciding to manufacture automobiles in the United States. West German workers and their union feared loss of jobs in the home country.

The U.S. multinationals also resisted the codetermination laws that impinge on management authority and decision-making power. However, after some experience with the wording of these laws, United States companies have become accustomed to such labor practices. Codetermination and industrial democracy seem to enhance labor peace and reduce strikes and turnover rates.[36]

Now the concepts of codetermination and industrial democracy are more acceptable practices in principle in some big corporations in the United States and Japan. For example, new labor contracts in steel, auto, rubber, oil, and electrical industries have incorporated some of the aspects of these concepts.

Flextime. Flexible work hours (flextime) are a form of job enrichment that provides greater autonomy to blue-collar workers in the factory. Originating in Germany around 1970, this system allows the individual worker to determine a daily and weekly work schedule. A number of factors has made this system more appropriate today. These are: the rising level of education, growth in the number of women for parttime work, expansion of the service sector, and the growing importance of shift work designed to use the capacity of increasing capital-intensive industries. The flextime system is becoming more popular in many industries and countries, especially in Western European countries.

Labor Organization. Labor organization usually depends on the social values, psychic needs of workers, industrial relations, and the legal framework of a host country. In many cases, the local subsidiary is largely responsible for labor management under the general guidelines of the MNC. One significant issue facing MNCs is the increasing move toward the internationalization of the labor movement, including bargaining and negotiation.

National unions have begun not only to collect and disseminate information about MNCs, but also to consult or coordinate with unions in other countries concerning labor policies and tactics. For example, the International Union of Food and Allied Workers Association initiated the boycott of Coca-Cola in Sweden, Spain, Mexico, and Finland against the antilabor practices by the Coca-Cola subsidiary in Guatemala.

The ten European Community countries are gradually harmonizing their tariffs, taxes, monetary systems, and laws. Many unions have affiliated themselves with either International Trade Secretariats (ITS), or International

Confederation of Free Trade Unions (ICFTU), and the European Trade Union Confederation (ETUC). Also, an information network of the MNCs' wages, benefits, and working conditions was created by such international organizations as the IMF and the ILO.

There are several problems concerning the internationalization of unions. First, there are differences in political motivation, ideological orientation, and economic interests. Second, organizational difficulties and the problem of control and coordination among unions are severe. Third, most MNCs have been reluctant to cooperate with the efforts of international unions, such as the ITS.

United States and European Unions. There are considerable differences in unions among different nations. European unions usually identify with political parties and a socialist ideology. In the United States, however, unionism has been more pragmatic than political, and more concerned with the immediate needs of the workers. Also, labor legislation in the United States mostly confines itself to the framework of collective bargaining, whereas in the United Kingdom, the government's role is more active concerning wages and working conditions. Another significant difference is that in the United States a strike tends to occur at the termination date of a labor contract, after negotiation and a strike vote. This allows the employer time to prepare. However, in Germany and France, wildcat strikes catch everyone unprepared and tend to cause more damage.

Laws and Issues in Industrial Relations. Like labor organizations, labor laws vary substantially among countries, depending not only on the nature of the sociopolitical environment but also on the labor union of the host country. In the United Kingdom the unions are highly organized, quite militant, and a viable political force. In France, many unions are communist, whereas in Germany, the unions are less politicized and enjoy a good working relationship with management.

Substantially influenced by national interests and the global unification drive of MNCs, United States unions have been most concerned over the growth of imports from low-wage countries. In Japan, wages are linked to seniority as opposed to skill, and fringe benefits are provided by companies and not mandated by law. Large companies provide their own medical facilities and low-interest housing loans for employees. Dismissals are rare and are a matter between the employer and the union. In contrast, in Europe, wages are based on skill differentials. Fringe benefits are mandated by law; they represent a considerable part of the workers' income. In West Germany, social insurance and company-provided fringe benefits supplement the wages of workers by about 70%. Dismissal policies are governed by law and are often difficult to implement.

International Compensation Policies

There are marked differences in compensation practices among the developed countries. It is important for an MNC to incorporate the national culture and managerial expectations into its compensation policies. For example, in England, work performance is more emphasized than the potential of an employee. On the contrary, in France, previous educational achievement would be more important than job performance in determining compensation.

Usually, the salaries MNCs pay to the managers of subsidiaries are similar in many European countries. However, individual benefits differ in both range (travel, housing, insurance, and holidays) and amount of benefits, depending on the country. Many benefits are also legally regulated. In Germany, a fired worker may get a salary for up to 18 months. It is difficult, thus, to standardize wages, salaries, and fringe benefits for the entire MNC system.

Summary

This chapter discussed the human resource management practices of international corporations. Emphasis was placed on the human resource management problems in developing countries, a result of the larger sociocultural and environmental differences between these and the industrialized countries.

Many cross-cultural theorists have argued in favor of sociocultural imperatives. However, reviews of the empirical studies on human resource management practices of United States companies caution us not to overemphasize the impact of sociocultural factors on human resource management practices. Results of large-scale studies indicate that more sophisticated management practices concerning employment policy, training, wage and salary policies, selection and promotion policies, and compensation practices were successfully used by the United States subsidiaries abroad. European companies were also using modern methods and policies in their subsidiaries' operations. Only the Japanese companies seem to be using local practices. Studies also show that the local practices were not preferred by the employees and seem to be less effective in motivating them.

This chapter also discussed briefly the differing environmental and labor conditions between the United States and West European countries. In the latter, flextime, codetermination, and industrial democracy policies have taken deep root in labor-management relations. Labor unions are also a more viable, political force than in the United States. The internationalization of unions seems to be gaining momentum, but the problems of control and coordination are severe. However, in the coming decade, multinationalization of the labor union movement is likely to gain more momentum.

Case

Many West German firms had recruited foreign workers during the 1950 to 1970 period. The Siemens case discusses many issues concerning foreign workers, including Siemens's recruitment policy and the socioeconomic problems of the workers.

Case 7-1

Siemens' Foreign Workers

As was the case with most West German firms with the positive upturn in the nation's economy during the 1950/1970 period, Siemens had found it necessary to recruit foreign workers. In 1970 the managers of the firm were saying that regardless of the problems involved, an ever increasing number of foreign workers would be employed.

In 1972, nevertheless, Siemens went through a period of cost consciousness, and the previous policy of recruiting a high number of foreign workers, mainly Turkish and Yugoslavs, was submitted to review. Several top managers were not sure of the analytical rigor of their previous decisions, and decided to review corporate policy concerning foreign workers. In particular, the following questions seemed important to answer:

1. Did Siemens have any choice as between employing and not employing foreign workers?
2. What were the costs and the benefits of employing foreign workers?
3. What should be Siemens' policy regarding the percentage of foreign workers employed, the homogeneity or heterogeneity of foreign workers' nationalities at Siemens, the criteria to be used in selecting one or several given nationalities?
4. How should the firm treat its foreign workers in respect to wages, fringe benefits, housing, promotion, etc.?

The basic material for this case was collected within the Federal Republic of Germany by Ayse Sertel and Yilmaz Özkan during the summer of 1972 and reworked subsequently by Henri de Bodinat under the supervision of Richard D. Robinson. Alfred P. Sloan School of Management, Massachusetts Institute of Technology, 1973. All rights reserved. © Copyright by Richard D. Robinson.

The Company

Siemens, a German-based international firm, was founded in 1947 and had in 1971, 1.2 billion DMs capital, 16 billion DMs standing orders, and 14.7 billion DMs in annual sales.[1]

It occupied the sixth position in the list of world's ten largest firms in electrical equipment production. Of its current production, 4 percent was construction material, 14 percent computers, 31 percent energy production (i.e., measurement and process techniques, energy producing machinery, industrial energy, transportation, and research), 14 percent installation materials and know-how (auto electric, cables, time-equipment, telephone, etc.), 8 percent electrical house equipment, and 4 percent various other products. The firm had 47 branches in different parts of West Germany and numerous other branches in more than 100 countries.

The investments of the firm in 1970–71 amounted to 916 million DMs. As far as sales were concerned, of its 5.9 billion DMs worth of exports, 26 percent was going to EFTA members, 24 percent to member countries of EEC, 13 percent to those European countries outside both EFTA and EEC, 17 percent to the U.S., 12 percent to Asia, and 8 percent to Africa and Australia.

In September 1971, Siemens had 234,000 employees in West Germany, and 72,000 working in different branches of the firm outside the country. Of the employees in the country, 36 percent were women; of those outside Germany, 58 percent.

The German Economy and Foreign Labor

West Germany, one of the major labor-importing European countries, had a population of 61,279,000 in 1971. In the same year, its labor force was 27,414,000 and employment in industry was 12,207,000. The per capita gross national product of this highly industrialized country was $3,370 in 1971, with over 50 percent of the GNP originating in industry. Development of West German key growth variables during post-war cycles is shown in Table 7-3. Some key measures of differences in the employment of foreign and local labor are given in Table 7-4.

Siemens' Foreign Workers

As of September 1971, Siemens employed a total of 25,401 foreign workers within its various operations within the Federal Republic of Germany. This

---

[1]The parity exchange rate in mid-1972 was 3.10 Deutsche marks to U.S. $1.00. By March 1973, the rate had changed to DM 2.9 = U.S. $1.00. The rate prior to May 1971 had been DM 3.66 = U.S. $1.00.

Table 7-3 Development of key growth variables during post-war cycles (annual average rates of change in percent)

Growth cycles	1951 to 1954	1955 to 1958	1959 to 1963	1964 to 1967	1968 to 1972
Real GDP	8.8%	7.1%	5.9%	3.7%	5.1%
Change in capital stock	3.8	5.8	6.4	6.2	5.4
Capital-output ratio	3.8	3.4	3.4	3.6	3.8
Employment	2.4	2.3	1.0	−0.5	0.5
Labor productivity	6.0	5.7	5.6	5.1	5.0
Change in capital intensity	1.4	3.5	5.2	6.8	4.8

Source: OECD Economic Surveys, Germany, 1972, p. 32.

Table 7-4 Wage structure in Germany

Average hourly wage (general average)

DM	**1963**	**1966**	**1972**
	4.00	4.92	9.00

1. *By level of skill*

(1966)	Level of qualification	Percent of labor force	Wages (general average = 100)
	Skilled	43%	114
	Semi-skilled	32	96
	Non-skilled	18	84
	Others (beginners)	7	74
		100%	

2. *By number of years in an enterprise* (general average = 100)

(1966)	2	2–4	5–9	10–19	70
	93	97	103	108	108

3. *By age* (general average = 100)

(1966)	18	18–20	20–24	25–44	45–49	50–54	55–59	60
	57	84	98	103–5	101	99	97	94

4. *By size of firm* (number of workers in the firm, general average = 100)

(1966)	10–1,000	1,000–2,000	2,000–5,000	5,000
	98	100	105	112

5. *Job variances and unemployment index* (1963 = 100) (Figure 7-3)

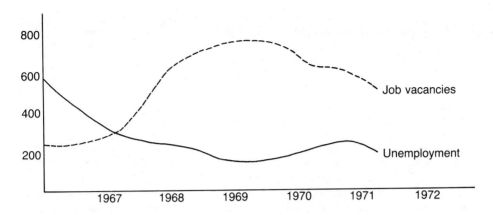

Figure 7-3 Job variances and unemployment index (1963 = 100)

number constituted 20.8 percent of all Siemens' laborers in the country. The breakdown of the foreign workers by nationality was as follows:

Turkish	7,371
Yugoslavian	6,648
Greek	3,498
Spanish	1,507
Italian	1,578
Australian	1,146
Tunisian	451
Other	3,202

A large majority of these workers were between 20 and 39 years of age, while the German workers tended to be somewhat older. The precise age distribution and other social background characteristics of these workers were not known by the Siemens management. It was known, however, that not more than 30 percent of these workers came directly from rural areas. The migration to West Germany was usually a multistep process. This was especially true of the Turkish workers who tended to have some prior industrial work experience within Turkey, even though sometimes brief. Of all the foreign workers coming to West Germany, some 30 percent were classified in their respective countries of origin as skilled workers (though not all worked in this capacity when they arrived in Germany).

The structure of West German population and its projected trend would increasingly necessitate the import of foreign workers. In 1971, the age group over 65 constituted a rather large portion of the overall population. The age group below 14, on the other hand, had been growing very slowly. The size of the working German population relative to total population had been shrinking for the last several decades. The gap between projected demand for manpower and the capacity to fulfill this demand was estimated to be much larger in 1980 than it had been in 1970. In fact, this gap, currently being filled by import of labor, was expected to double within this ten year period.

For the last 11 years the unemployment level in West Germany had been consistently under 1 percent. Such a low level of unemployment, coupled with the current high rate of industrial growth (given the demographic structure) created a labor shortage that could only be fulfilled with labor importation. Although the country did not have a large number of vacancies prior to 1960, with the sudden change in the rate of unemployment in that year, the number of vacancies increased noticeably, reaching 750,000 in 1966. Vacancies still existed in 1972 despite the import of foreign workers. German industrial growth (6.2 percent between 1958 and 1964) called for increasing manpower. Yet the German labor force was expected to remain more or less constant for ten more years.

A recent OECD study had revealed that, taking 1972 as the base year, West Germany's population increased from an index of 100 in 1957 to an index of 112.1 in 1968. However, not all of this increase was natural. Excluding net immigration of foreign labor to the country, the 1968 index was about 107. During the same period, on the other hand, the population of one of the labor exporting countries to West Germany, namely Turkey, increased from an index of 100 to 132.8. This increase was less dramatic in the case of Italy and Spain.

The net flow of foreign labor into West Germany had shown a secular increase over the 1956–72 period. Starting from less than 20,000 in 1956, the migrant labor stock reached a level of 350,000 in 1969 (Tables 7-5 and 7-6). Though the yearly increases had not been uniform, yearly increments of labor before 1960 had been substantially less than those after this period. Although only rough estimates were available, the nature of the inflow reflected a very high labor turnover rate and an increasing mobility of workers between the importing and exporting countries.

The West German economy, being highly industrialized and developing at a fast rate, was dependent on competitive industrial production costs to sustain its exports and to compete with possible imports. In view of the demographic structure and the pressure to hold down costs and sustain a high level of exports, Germany found it imperative to employ foreign workers. Alternatives to the import of foreign workers would be either automation, increasing working hours, or inducing intersectoral labor displacement. As to the first alternative, one must note that Germany is the second most automated country in the world. Secondly, sharp increases in part-time employment as well as in working hours had been evidenced for some time. Nevertheless, the manpower shortage continued. Although intersectoral displacement of labor, or more exactly the transfer of agricultural population to industry, remained a serious alternative to labor importation from abroad, this alternative could be realized only in the long-run.

Table 7-5 Germany: Stock of employed foreign workers by nationality, 1954–69*†

	Total	Italians		Greeks		Portuguese		Spanish		Turks		Yugoslavs	
	All nationalities	Total	% Male	Total	% Male	Total	% Male	Total	% Male	Total	% Male	Total	% Male
1954	72,906	6,509	–	548				411				1,801	
1955	79,607	7,461	–	637				486				2,085	
1956	98,818	18,597	–	953				698				2,297	
1957	108,190	19,096	–	1,822				967				2,778	
1958	127,083	25,609	–	2,838				1,494				4,846	
1959	166,829	48,809	91.0	4,089	87.1			2,150	81.6			7,310	81.0
1960	279,390	121,685	93.6	13,005	88.3	261	85.8	9,454	82.6	2,495	92.0	8,826	81.0
1961	507,419	218,003	–	43,948	–	–		50,976		–		–	
1962	655,463	265,978	91.0	69,146	82.0	1,421	85.8	87,327	75.6	15,318	91.7	23,608	81.0
1963	811,213	299,235	88.7	106,152	67.1	2,284	81.6	117,494	71.6	27,144	89.0	44,428	79.0
1964	932,932	289,252	86.2	143,859	66.8	3,463	77.3	144,256	71.0	69,211	90.0	53,057	79.0
1965	1,164,364	359,773	85.0	181,658	63.8	10,509	84.7	180,572	71.3	121,121	87.2	64,060	77.0
1966	1,314,031	399,154	82.7	196,207	60.4	19,802	83.6	185,336	69.3	157,978	83.5	96,675	73.0
1967	1,023,747	274,249	78.4	146,817	58.1	18,519	76.1	129,126	64.7	137,081	81.5	97,725	67.0
1968	1,014,771	284,440	77.9	136,191	58.0	18,743	72.9	111,982	63.8	139,336	78.3	99,660	63.0
1969	1,372,059	340,244	–	174,348	–	26,379	–	135,546	–	212,951	–	226,290	–
1970 (Jan.)	1,575,072	330,049	75.4	206,812	57.5	32,802	71.2	149,190	68.9	272,423	77.6	296,970	60.0

*In the years 1954–60 all data refer to July, for years after 1960 to June.
†Data refer to wage and salary earners only; i.e., exclude self-employed.
Source: Bundesanstalt fur Arbeit.

Table 7-6 Germany: Inflow of foreign labor by nationality, 1956–69*†

	Greek	Italian	Portuguese	Spanish	Turk	Yugoslav	Other	Total	Net Inflow
1956	738	15,620		475		812	13,944	31,589	19,211
1957	1,550	14,894		736		1,997	26,106	45,283	9,372
1958	1,510	19,460		1,170		3,358	29,079	54,577	18,893
1959	2,479	42,455		1,935		4,189	34,253	85,311	39,746
1960	23,364	141,263		26,745		4,400	63,712	259,484	112,561
1961	36,606	165,793	913	51,183	7,116	9,962	88,918	360,491	228,029
1962	47,559	165,250	1,013	54,958	15,269	24,139	87,379	396,567	148,044
1963	58,009	134,912	1,545	51,715	27,910	19,440	83,969	377,500	155,748
1964	65,130	142,120	3,904	65,872	62,879	17,459	84,899	442,263	121,721
1965	61,822	204,288	11,140	65,146	59,816	30,983	91,705	524,900	231,432
1966	39,742	165,540	9,185	38,634	43,499	50,869	77,318	424,787	149,667
1967	7,605	58,510	1,782	7,785	14,834	15,379	45,999	151,894	−290,281
1968	37,348	130,236	6,709	31,995	62,376	76,782	45,533	390,879	− 8,973
1969	65,126	136,225	13,237	50,086	121,529	192,232	67,644	646,079	357,283

*Including frontier workers.
†Found as the annual increment in the stock of workers.
Source: Bundesanstalt fur Arbeit.

The Social Situation of Foreign Labor in Germany

A recent study undertaken by the *Spiegel Magazine* had provided some insight into the foreign labor phenomena. According to the study, five countries had sent approximately 80 percent of the total. Of the incoming workers one-half had been accompanied by their families, and 77 percent were between 20 and 39 years of age. The percentage of West German workers in this age group was, by way on contrast, only 27 percent of the total. The rate of illiteracy among the migrant group was very low, but they had, nevertheless, a lower education level on average than did indigenous workers in that 64 percent of the foreign workers had had less than eight years of education, which was the minimum required for West Germans. Not surprisingly, foreign workers earned, on the average, less money than indigenous labor. In 1971 the average monthly earnings of the migrant workers was 870 DMs. This amount was, for the same year, 98 DMs less than the average for local workers. Sex-based wage differences were also more visible for the migrant groups. While two-thirds of the female laborers received less than 800 DMs a month, this ratio was only one-fourth for the males. Some 38 percent of the foreign workers lived in public housing, another 38 percent in private houses, and the remaining shared a room or a flat with other workers, again, in private houses. Some 40 percent of the migrants expressed discontent with their living quarters. Of these, only 18 percent indicated high rents as the primary reason for their discontent. They said, in interviews, that it was not the rent but the landlords and the treatment by their West German neighbors that disturbed them most. These workers seemed more pleased with the facilities in West Germany than with its people. They were upset for having been treated badly by the indigenous population. In 1971 more than half of the foreign workers earned enough money for a vacation and 20 percent possessed private cars. Job security, schooling, and health guarantees were among the most pleasing items, while family problems, housing, and climate were among the most disturbing aspects of life in West Germany.

Although they were responsible for about one-fourth of West German production, foreign workers did not have much job security. During the 1966–67 economic recession, some 600,000 foreign workers lost their jobs and were forced to return home. Although it might seem that there was not much difference between German and guest workers with respect to employer-employee relations, working conditions, and ability to change jobs freely, in practice there were important differences.

Foreign workers were brought to Germany on the basis of a one-year contract. No matter how unpleasant the working conditions might be, this contract could not be terminated short of a one-year period by the workers. Otherwise they would be sent back to their respective countries immediately. The salary specified in the contract was almost always the minimum set forth for the job in question. Although the same scale was used both for German and for foreign workers, German workers almost never started at the very bottom of the scale as did the foreigners. Thus, an automatic wage difference between the two groups was created from the beginning.

Moreover, the vocational training offered to the foreign workers in their own countries, and their definition of skilled workers, differed from those of the Germans. Therefore, even a qualified foreign laborer working in Germany in a skilled capacity often received a wage equivalent to that of a semi-skilled worker and was classified in such manner. Although this classification might change as the worker remained in his job for several years, the lower classification would hold true almost without exception for the duration of the first year's contract.

Current statutes regulating the behavior of foreigners required that every foreign worker obtain a residence permit from the German employment office. The newly arrived foreign workers obtained, by showing their contracts, a year's working permit, and consequently, a year's residence permit. These legalities made it impossible for workers to change jobs no matter how unpleasant the conditions might be. In case the worker wished, at the end of the first year, to renew his work and residence permit without renewing his contract, he was required to find a new job, obtain a favorable recommendation from his previous employer, and to leave the boarding house (*heim*) of his previous employer. Provided that he met these conditions, he could acquire a new work and residence permit. This new permit, too, was valid only for one year. The city police could refuse a permit, without which employment was not allowed. As was the case during the 1966–67 economic crises, the police would come up with rather abstract reasons for denying an application for residence. This same mechanism might force workers to remain in their former jobs under undesirable conditions. The threat to be sent back to his own country hung over the head of every foreign worker.

Every firm offering employment to foreign workers was under an obligation to provide housing. This obligation has been included in the bilateral agreements signed between Germany and the labor-exporting countries. Current statutes specified the minimum conditions of acceptability for workers' housing. Accordingly, no room could contain more than eight persons; women and men must live in separate quarters; every worker must be supplied with ten cubic meters air, wardrobe, a chair, and adequate table space. In addition, he must have facilities to dry his laundry and to cook. The bedrooms must at least be 2.30 meters high and the floors must be covered with some material to keep the workers' feet warm. At the most, five workers might share a wash basin and ten workers, a toilet. But even these minimum requirements were rarely satisfied. Only the largest firms, such as Siemens, had *heims* (boarding houses) with the above stated specifications. Control of the smaller firms was difficult to enforce. More importantly, rent control over the houses satisfying these specifications was almost impossible. Those firms with more or less acceptable housing facilities frequently were charging what seemed to be unduly high rents.

The German mass media frequently and critically reported these miserable housing conditions and the ineffectiveness of the attempts to better them. An example was *Brigitte* (September 1971, no. 18), which described the plight of an Italian family with six children. The family, it was claimed, was living in a house without running water, heat, or toilet and paid 235

DMs for a 25-square-meter apartment. The magazine claimed that miserable housing conditions and high rents characterized the living conditions of millions of foreign workers in West Germany. Caritas, an organization formed to help Catholic foreign workers, reported that although it was offering free legal assistance to the workers to improve their housing conditions, the workers, frightened by the threat of being forced to leave Germany or at least of being evicted from their apartments, were abstaining from legal action against the landlords. Despite the high frequency of these reports and research findings, West German officials did not seem to be reacting rapidly.

As noted, foreign workers were placed in *heims* upon their arrival to West Germany, but they soon started to search for private housing. Many workers found it difficult to live with six other persons in a room and felt that the rent was too high for such communal living. Even when the occupants were of the same country, they varied at least in respect to age, place of birth, custom, and socio-economic status. Such differences, needless to say, resulted in frictions. These frictions, when added to high rents and variations in work and sleeping hours, induced many to seek private housing regardless of conditions. Local landlords, fully cognizant of the workers' reasoning, felt quite confident in charging high rents. It was not considered unusual for landlords to ask for 2500 DMs as an *abstand* (guarantee deposit) from incoming tenants. The control of conditions in privately-owned residences, it should be added, was not an accustomed practice in West Germany.

Moreover, foreign workers were required to stay in West Germany for at least a year before they could have their wives join them. In order to get together with his family, a worker was required to leave the factory *heim*. The helplessness of the worker in this regard was also well known and exploited by the landlords.

The fact that workers, as long as they lived in *heims*, were not permitted to have visitors (of both sexes after a certain hour and of the opposite sex categorically) tended to force even the bachelors to look for private housing.

Still another factor inducing workers to search for private housing was their shift from one job to another upon completion of the first year of their contract. Once a worker started a new job he could no longer stay in the *heim* of his original firm. To gain flexibility in looking for better opportunities, some foreign workers found it advantageous to move into private apartments despite deplorable conditions and high cost.

Local prejudice directed toward the foreign workers caused further problems. There were frequently signs on bars and restaurants explicitly restricting entry of foreign workers. The aggression of local German youth against foreign workers in small towns was reported frequently in the newspapers, even some killings. As can be understood from various reference terms used for foreign workers (e.g., *Makkaronifresser, Kameltreiber, Messerstecher*), many of the indigenous population considered the migrants second class citizens.

The children of foreign workers, of which there were an estimated 400,000, also constituted a problem. In accordance with the West German laws, these children had to remain in school until age 18. But, due to shortage of personnel and other educational facilities, this law was not being as strictly enforced for the children of migrants as it was for the indigenous population. After the death of two ten-year old children in the mines in 1970, West German authorities found 97,800 children working illegally. A control week in Berlin resulted in the fining of 98 firms for employing a total of 285 youths under 18 years of age. The West German Trade union had estimated the total number of illegally employed children to be around 1,000,000. The government found it difficult to enforce the obligatory schooling requirements in the absence of sufficient facilities, and many of the migrant parents, highly motivated to save, preferred to send their children to work. Moreover, due to a shortage of kindergartens, even for the indigenous population, migrant parents, if both were working, preferred to keep their older children at home to take care of the younger. This young migrant population, being separated both from their homeland and from the rest of the children in West Germany, constituted a totally alienated group.

Situation of Foreign Workers at Siemens

Siemens, as many other firms employing foreign workers in great numbers, was forced to incur a number of expenditures. First, there was the cost of recruiting and of transporting the workers from their homelands to West Germany. The transportation cost, of course, accrued only in the case of workers recruited directly from their respective countries and not if they were already employed elsewhere in Germany. Up until the first of 1972 a flat transportation payment of 165 DMs had been made to the foreign workers. Subsequently the payment was 300 DMs. This amount was paid directly to *Arbeitsamt*[2] and covered the recruitment costs incurred by this organization. In addition, every foreign worker was entitled to 200 DMs of vacation allowance upon the completion of his second year in the company. Those workers brought directly from their homeland who chose to return directly from the company also received 150 DMs as return travel allowance. There were, however, few foreign workers who did so. For example, it was estimated that only about five percent of the foreign workers in Siemens returned home directly from the company. Since the company was obliged to advertise any job opening in the German press should it decide to employ workers from within West Germany, the cost involved in such advertisement should be subtracted from the 300 DMs recruitment cost of the foreign workers brought directly from their homelands. The Munich branch of Siemens estimated that the initial training costs averaged 450 DMs for a West German worker and 500 DMs for the foreign. The respective figures reported by the management of the Berlin branch of the company were much higher: 593 and 820. The reason for these different estimates was unclear.

    In addition to the above mentioned-costs involved in the employment of foreign workers, the company, under the provisions of German labor law, was

[2]Refers to the branch offices of BAFA.

forced to provide housing facilities. Several million DMs were spent in the building of boarding houses (*heims*). Seimens' *heims,* compared to those of many other firms, were well-kept and comfortable. The monthly rental of a four-person room was around 65 DMs per person (780 DMs per year).

It should be noted, however, that these *heims* were not really some sort of subsidy for the foreign workers. Given the stresses involved in sharing a room with four to six strangers with different habits and working hours, the rental was substantial. If the *heims* were to be filled most of the time, the firm could very well make a profit, but some beds were known to remain empty, sometimes for long periods of time. A study undertaken by the Munich branch of the firm estimated the average yearly cost of a bed to be around 888 DMs. (This figure was obtained by dividing the total cost of beds, empty and occupied, by the total number of foreign workers). The management of the Berlin branch estimated 1380 DMs. It was believed by independent researchers that those figures were unduly high if used to calculate the extra cost of foreign workers in that a number of steps could be taken to fill empty beds, especially in West Berlin. The *heims* were not meant to house only foreign workers, and many West German laborers in fact lived in them. Thus, housing cost per worker could not be viewed as an extra cost of foreign workers. This point needed to be stressed, as many of the current studies viewed the construction of these *heims,* not as another prospective business for the firm, but as an extra cost of labor.

A genuinely important cost of the foreign workers to the company resulted from the organizational changes that had to be made to accommodate the newcomers and to provide a communication link between managers and workers. In the Berlin branch of the firm there was a department in charge of the numerous problems of foreign workers. Staffed by three administrators and several translators, this department handled housing and schooling problems of foreign workers and their families as well as any other problems that the migrant workers might have. There, through the intermediacy of an interpreter, the problems were recorded and hopefully solved. The administrators in charge of this office were deeply concerned with the problems of foreign workers and were tring to find equitable solutions for the problems brought to them. However, to the extent that many of the problems required a more systematic solution by the West German authorities, such as those relating to the schooling of workers' children and to housing, satisfactory answers were not always possible. Nevertheless the proximity and accessibility of the administrators to the workers were important.

Regardless of the extra costs cited above, employment of foreign workers was inevitable so long as Siemens maintained its current level of production. This was so because of several reasons. First, as explained above, the extra cost of foreign labor did not amount to a significant figure. Second, the indigenous labor stock had been exhausted and even during the 1966–67 recession Siemens had been forced to keep many of its foreign workers. There simply was no West German labor to replace the foreigners, especially in those categories of employment in which foreigners were working. One heard from all sources, including company managers, that German labor would under no circumstances do what the foreign workers were doing. Thirdly, it was a known fact that foreign labor was relatively cheap. Even if replacement of foreign workers with the West Germans were possible, equivalent wages would not have been offered to the latter. And as already noted, foreign and indigenous workers started from different points of the same pay scale, and a constant wage differential existed between equivalent quality of workers of these different stocks.

Foreign Worker Recruitment by Siemens

The control and administration of foreign labor recruitment in West Germany was handled by an autonomous public agency, Bundesanstalt fur Arbeit (BAFA).[3] It was headquartered in Nuremberg and had many branches throughout the country. BAFA was concerned not only with foreign labor but also with the administration of the social security system.

The major methods of foreign labor recruitment were three. Of these, the first was through BAFA, which accounted for about 70 percent of total recruitment. BAFA had established offices in those countries with which West Germany has signed labor agreements. BAFA was first informed of the need for labor by the German employer. It responded by making known to the employer the specifications of the available stock of registered potential workers. If the employer were satisfied with what was available, the necessary paper work would be completed, and BAFA contacted its representatives in the appropriate countries. The formalities following this last step varied, both in time and in procedure, in different countries. The second method of recruitment differed from the first in that the application might be made directly by the worker to the firm. BAFA still controlled permits for entry and final documentation as to employment. Although West German visas were in fact issued by the local German Consulate, this was done only after clearance with BAFA. The third method, only applicable in the case of Moroccan and Tunisian workers, consisted of recruitment by BAFA missions in the labor exporting countries. Companies might also obtain BAFA's permission to recruit directly on their own behalf in these two countries. Of these methods, the first two were most frequently used by Siemens.

Arrival Procedures at Siemens

Foreign workers usually came to Siemens in large groups. Upon their arrival in Germany, they were met at the airport or railroad station by representatives of the West German employment office and by representatives and a translator from the firm. They were then taken immediately to the factory and shown around. A brief explanation of their job and pay was given and they were then taken to their living quarters, usually the firm's *heim*. Those

---

[3]Federal Institute for Labor.

who came with families and who had made other housing arrangements were also offered help in locating their quarters. The workers were then given a day to report to their jobs.

During their first day at work, a foreman or an engineer accompanied by an interpreter explained to them what was to be done. The training period varied considerably with the nature of the job, from two or three hours to two or three months.

There seemed to be a discrepancy between the length of the training period as perceived by managers and by workers. This was apparently due to the fact that the management identified a "training period" as the period during which laborers were not working at full productivity. Even for a low-skilled job, training might thus, in this sense, last one or two months. On the other hand, the training as perceived by labor often consisted of a foreman or an experienced worker's showing the foreigner what to do for one hour or so. In training for more complicated jobs, the nationality of the worker was quite irrelevant; no matter from where they had come, several weeks were often needed to acquire the skills if they were new on the job.

Labor Turnover at Siemens

A recent study conducted in the Munich branch of the Siemens company had established a 54 percent turnover rate for foreign workers and 27 percent for the indigenous ones. Another study covering all departments of the Berlin branch had come up with a 113 percent fluctuation rate for foreigners and 37 percent for the West Germans.[4]

Foreign workers' jobs were being changed by the firm quite frequently. Those workers brought from their countries at minimum wages were generally first assigned to those jobs requiring nearly no training. After having worked in this job for several weeks, the workers adjusted to the work conditions of the firm. This adjustment was eased by their high motivation to earn and save and by the perceived threat of loss of employment in West Germany. Managerial complaints in regard to foreign workers' maladjustment to work were few. In fact company managers emphasized their satisfaction with these workers.

At the end of this adjustment period, the workers were likely to be assigned to a somewhat more complicated job. After having worked in several such tasks, the workers became eligible to work in a piece-rate job. The piece-rate was considerably higher than the hourly wage offered to the workers. If any particular worker were on a piece-rate he either produced the set minimum or norm and received a payment substantially above his hourly wage-level or he fell below this level and received his hourly wage. It had been typical for the foreign workers to exceed the minimum levels. For that reason these levels had been changed periodically in many industries with the result

---

[4]Calculated by dividing all interdepartmental shifts and all departures by the total number of workers and multiplying the result by 100.

that a number of West German workers voiced their unhappiness with the presence of the foreign workers. Because the foreigners were so highly motivated to make as much money as possible in a short period of time, they concentrated very hard at least to achieve minimum production, if not to exceed it. As in other firms, the minimum levels were being set jointly by management and labor. Still, many German workers claimed that these levels were too high and the relevant pay levels were too low.

Workers received a substantial bonus for producing over the specified norm. For instance, by producing 850 when the norm was 800 the workers might receive 1–1.30 DM extra for every hour they worked for that particular day. Since labor costs increased considerably if workers were to exceed the minimum levels consistently, not only did these levels have to be set very carefully but also the over-productive workers were shifted periodically from one task to another. For this reason many piece-rate workers were shifted within the firm among different piece-rate jobs. The discontent arising from such practices had been expressed by many workers. In general, task shifts were *intra* departmental to avoid union interferences (the union could intervene in cases of inter-departmental shifts).

The overall turnover rate for foreign workers in West Germany was 22.5 percent and 11 percent for indigenous labor. When these figures were compared with those of the Munich branch of Siemens (54 and 27 percent, respectively) it became apparent that the average for foreign workers in the firm was 2.5 times the national average. It had been suggested that the following were the principal causes for this differential:

(1) It had been the policy of the firm to maintain a certain level of labor turn-over. The workers brought directly from different countries were being employed at minimum wages for the first year. At the end of this period the contract could be renewed only by mutual consent and by a raise in salary in consideration of the worker's experience. The company, at this point, seemed to prefer to terminate the contract rather than raise salary.

(2) It took a year for foreign workers to acquire basic knowledge of the language and of the work conditions in other parts of West Germany. During their first year, foreign workers were extremely obedient and hard working. They even refrained from membership in trade unions, and in all labor activity. At the end of their first contract year, however, many bargained with the firm for a wage raise and became cognizant of their rights to demand such a raise. Needless to say, these were undesirable demands from the viewpoint of the firm. Less problem-prone labor, fresh from foreign lands, was preferred.

Opinions Voiced by Siemens' Workers

The interview of a limited sample of 20 workers who had already left the company and of another 20 currently employed may be summed up as follows.

First and most important, was the view of the piece-rate workers. As explained by these workers, their jobs consisted of producing a given number of units within a work day. If they should fall below the specified number they received a cut in wage. If, on the other hand, they should prove to be more efficient, they were not allowed to continue that particular task for too long. Almost every one of the workers from Siemens and many other workers employed by other firms claimed that they found it very difficult to maintain the specified level of production on a daily basis. A young woman, for instance, said she could only finish about 1/3 of the specified number of units, and all the other women that worked within the same department as she did were in the same position. "A giant-like, strong Turkish woman" was the only exception. While the young girl received approximately 500 DMs a month for the amount she produced, the "strong" workers, regularly working above the norm, recieved over 800 DMs. The young girl was forced to leave Siemens at the end of the third month of her arrival, in breach of her one-year contract. After two months of delay, the firm finally agreed to give her a clearance to seek other employment.

Many workers claimed that as they became more experienced in their jobs, the level of unit production specified by the firm was increased. In other words, if they were asked to produce only 100 units within the first 3–4 months of their experience in the firm, this number was raised to 110 for the next several months and perhaps higher later. A labor leader observed, "Of course, it would be to the advantage of the firm if every worker produced just 99 units when the specification is 100. This is why unit production is being kept at such an unrealistic level.

Workers also compained about the job conditions. Many said the work they performed was extremely heavy and dirty, and that they had to sweat for long hours in front of oily, steamy machinery. The words of a young woman perhaps best characterized these conditions:

> *When I first came to Germany I started in Siemens. We were many women in one large room. There was tremendous noise. Nobody smiled, nobody talked for we could not hear each other. I was in charge of a big machine which vomited oil and soapy water. Out of it came other machines which I was supposed to take out and put aside. As they came out I fed new materials into the machine. We were asked to cover our hair so that the machine would not catch it. We put gloves on our hands. All day we stood. We had an hour's lunch break, but nobody talked. When I went home, I did not have the power to say "hello" to my brother. I went directly to bed. Since my brother was living with me I could not live in the* heim. *It took me a full hour to travel from home to the factory. I had to get up at 3:30 in the morning and leave home at four to be at my work in time. This was in 1966 and I was getting approximately 400 DMs a month. Finally I found another job in a cleaning firm. That was more of a disaster.*

Another worker expressed his complaint as follows:

> *I worked in Siemens for six years. Every day was more of a torture than the previous one. It was killing to get up so early in the morning, run out of the*

house to catch the train. Until the 9:30 coffee break I worked half asleep. I was then assigned to one of the heims *as a* heim *director. That was a good job. But the conditions of the workers, the inhuman manner in which they lived in these crowded quarters was heart breaking. Then came the recession and the* heim *was closed. I was forced to go back to my old job. But this time I just could not take it any more. Bodily exhaustion was not so much the problem. It was sleeplessness that got to me. Finally I had an offer from this office to be a consultant to Turkish workers. This job has its own problems, but compared to the old one I feel I am in heaven.*

The first made a rather clear cut point: when workers were forced, for one reason or another, to move out of the firm *heims,* which tended to be fairly near the factories, they sometimes ended up in neighborhoods very far from their work place.

Hours spent travelling from home to job became a clear addition to work hours. However, given recent legal changes, workers were no longer compensated for the hours spent travelling to their jobs. This consideration might apply to any one of the 4,700 foreign workers living outside the company *heims.* A shift in job occurred when a worker heard of a job opportunity nearer his home, provided he was promised a wage at least equal to that in Siemens.

Many workers, after having moved out of the *heims,* were known to have returned, having found the conditions of private houses intolerable. This meant, on the other hand, deprivation of wives and children. Final departures on the grounds of family reunion were frequent, especially in the case of Turkish labor, a very large percentage of whom were married. Problems relating to the schooling of children, especially in cases where both wife and husband were working, were also mentioned frequently by workers as among the reasons for leaving the firm. It was uncertain, in such cases, however, whether the workers took employment in some other firm, or in some other part of West Germany, or simply returned home. Solution to baby-sitting and schooling problems varied from termination of the wife's employment to bringing a close relative from the home country. There was a tendency for families to refrain from sending their older children to school and to either find them a job or have them baby-sit for the rest of their siblings. German law required that all children under 18 be in school, and workers were being constantly advised by the relevant authorities not to act in this manner.

Management-labor relations and the absence of opportunities for promotion did not appear to be important considerations for the foreign workers. They tended to be extremely obedient toward the foremen and managerial personnel and viewed their work environment less as a social milieu than as a place to earn a living. Workers were also very pessimistic about upward mobility in their jobs; they seemed to believe that as foreigners they were not entitled to such privileges. This was especially true for piece-rate workers. As one laborer expressed it:

There is no such thing as promotion for us. You might work for ten years on the same task. If you produce the specified number of units you get your money;

otherwise you get less or lose your job. Of course, there are exceptional cases. But I know them too. They came here as skilled workers but were employed as unskilled. When finally their industriousness and skills were appreciated they were given a position which they deserved many years ago anyway. There is no such thing as a better or worse position; there are jobs with more salary and those with less. If you put up with more and heavier work you get more.

Yet another worker said:

After six years of work in Siemens I was the most qualified in the department to be the foreman. I was fluent in German and was even offering courses to Turkish workers. We had a mixed department. I don't remember it exactly, but there might have been more Germans than foreigners. Although I deserved it, I could not have been made the foreman. They explained to me at that time that if I were to be selected for such a position it would anger the Germans. This is still true. Only in those departments employing foreign workers exclusively does a foreigner have a chance to get promoted.

Table 7-7 prepared by Siemens gives a list of reasons offered by workers and management for the departure of foreign workers from the Berlin branch of Siemens. As will be noted, 50.3 percent of the male and 50.1 percent of the female workers left the firm of their own choice. Some 34 percent of the former and 36 percent of the latter group, on the other hand, were asked to leave by the company administration.

Interview of the Turkish Attaché in Berlin

"The German labor laws do not discriminate betwen German and foreign workers. However, in case of disputes the laws regulating the activities of foreign nationals play a largely restrictive role. Although it can be argued that the employers do not discriminate against the foreign workers, this does not change the fact that most of the foreign workers do what the German workers refuse to do. Today, not even the most uneducated, unqualified German would clean the bathrooms and sweep the floors.

"The contribution of the foreign workers to the German economy cannot be overlooked. Today, a worker who earns 800 DMs per month spends about 200 for his housing, anywhere between 300 and 350 for his food and clothing. He can send only about 15 percent of his monthly savings to Turkey, or, in other words, he cannot save more than 150 DMs a month to take out of the German economy. His spending from his own earnings in Germany no doubt strengthens the German economy. Moreover, foreign workers, like the Germans, are now entitled to retirement compensation, and every month each worker pays, in proportion to his income, a certain amount of money as his contribution to retirement compensation. This monthly payment required of foreign workers augments the strength of the German social insurance organization. Many workers, as they go back to their country, withdraw these

Table 7-7 Reasons given by workers and management for departure of foreign workers from the Siemens plant in Berlin

	Male		Female	
From the workers' viewpoint				
Dislike for the job	41	8.6%	73	6.6%
Job is too far	–	–	7	0.6
Low payment	84	17.7	102	9.2
Change in occupation	40	8.4	95	8.6
Sickness	4	0.8	37	3.4
Desire to attend a school	17	3.6	6	0.5
Desire to go to West Germany	11	2.3	51	4.6
Desire to return to West Germany	–	–	–	–
Desire to work in a different country	42	8.9	107	9.7
Need to care for young children	–	–	70	6.3
Marriage	–	–	4	0.4
Need to care for some other family member	–	–	19	1.7
Desire to quit working	–	–	6	0.5
From the viewpoint of the firm				
Inappropriate for the job	38	8.0	41	3.7
Sickness	4	0.8	14	1.3
Inattendance and inefficiency	44	9.3	100	9.1
Lack of appropriate work	10	2.1	16	1.4
Activities in breach of contract	–	1.3	44	4.0
End of contract period	35	7.4	122	11.0
Disgraceful dismissals	26	5.5	62	5.6
Other				
Termination of the contract by mutual consent	51	10.7	118	10.7
Retirement	2	0.4	–	–
Shifts to office work	–	–	1	0.1
Appointment to some other branch of the company	19	4.0	9	0.8
Death	1	0.2	2	0.2
Total	475	100 %	1,106	100 %

forced savings (without interest). Retirement savings accumulated in Germany can, if the worker so wishes, be counted towards his retirement benefits in his own country. Increasingly, a growing number of foreign workers grasp the advantage of not withdrawing their retirement funds from Germany on their return home.

"Many workers find it difficult to live in their country of origin after their return from European employment. Whether or not a worker applics for reemployment in Germany depends upon his socioeconomic status and his previous level of savings abroad. Also, not all of the workers return home voluntarily. For instance, during the 1967 recession thousands of workers were forced to leave Germany. Many of these then reapplied to come back to Germany, and both the government and the German representatives gave their demands a priority.

"The trade unions in Germany are open to every worker. Membership, however, is not obligatory. For many years only a few Turkish workers were willing to join the unions. Gradually, they considered the pros and cons of membership and now a majority pay their union fees regularly.

"The problems of foreign workers are many and much can be done to improve their conditions. The responsibility falls on both the receiving and the sending countries. What needs to be done changes from one country to another. Common to all foreign workers, however, is a problem of housing, schooling, and language and an immediate solution to these problems is a must."

Interview of Head of the DGB[5] Department in Charge of Foreign Labor Affairs

"The German economy needs foreign workers. Our own population does not expand as rapidly as our industry requires. We are unable to meet our manpower needs from within ourselves. Especially after 1961, with the construction of the wall, the manpower shortage in Berlin became acute. Before then every day around 60,000 workers were coming from the East to work in the West. Until 1965 we tried to close at least part of this gap through attracting new labor from within West Germany. But even then the West was unable to meet its own labor requirements. After 1965 it became clear that unless foreign labor were brought to Berlin, continuation of our growth could not be attained. By 1972 the number of foreign workers in Berlin reached 78,000. The number of family members and tourist (illegal) workers together double this figure.

"DGB does not hesitate to give every possible assistance to the tourist (illegal) workers. However, only a very small percentage of such workers ever come to this organization for help. The estimates of the total number of such workers in Berlin fluctuates between 12,000 and 20,000.

"It would have been possible to satisfy the labor needs of West Berlin through the employment of more foreign workers. However, due to the special circumstances of Berlin we are unable to bring in as many foreign workers as we need. The most important of the many problems that face the foreign workers are the following:

[5]Deutscher Gewerkschaftsbund, usually referred to as the German Trade Union Federation. It is the top-level organization consisting of 16 member unions organized along industrial lines.

"*Housing.* The employer is obliged to guarantee housing for those foreign workers brought in through the intermediacy of Arbeitsamt. Generally, the firms prepare *heims* for this purpose. In these *heims* at least four persons live in one room and despite this the price they pay for a single bed is rather high. The firms improve conditions of these *heims* only when there are complaints. This is why many of them deteriorate into unbearable living quarters. When the schedules of four or six workers sleeping in one room do not coordinate with each other, each gets to be extremely disturbed in a matter of just a few days. *Heims* also have strange rules regulating visitors, which adds to the laborers' discontent. To move out of these *heims* is also difficult for there is a rather acute housing shortage in Berlin. Thus, the housing shortage forces us to limit the import of foreign labor into Berlin.

"*The problem of language:* Because foreign workers do not speak German, systematic assistance needs to be given to them. Such assistance, however, is rather costly. The expenditures of the Berlin Senate in this regard are very high compared to similar expenditures in other areas of West Germany. There are many consulting agencies for employment-employee problems. The Senate's yearly housing expense averages four million marks. Land owners frequently refuse to rent apartments to foreign workers, and certain elements of the press stimulate this tendency. Differences in mentality and mutual prejudices cause relationships to deteriorate. DGB has been trying to establish an atmosphere of mutual understanding. We bring in foreign labor only because our industry needs it.

"The firms do offer to help the workers in respect to language training. Recently, the Berlin Senate appointed 80 Turkish teachers to instruct Turkish children. It is very costly to provide occupational training for children of foreign workers for they first must learn the language. Now we are planning a one-year language training program in cooperation with Landesarbeitsamt. This too is a matter of budgeting. There are certain occupational gaps in the German economy. If we had enough money we would establish intensive language and vocational training centers in different parts of the country for the children of these workers.

"Foreign workers arrive here without any prior knowledge about trade unions, social insurance, and other topics relating to working conditions. They show little interest in the information offered to them in their own countries before departure. When they first arrive here they maintain a passive orientation towards the unions. In time some become active and seek membership. Those who come to their respective country's consulting personnel here in DGB continue their contact with us. If they receive sufficient aid from us in their dealings with the courts, their attachment to the union strengthens.

"All foreign workers are informed, via pamphlets prepared in their own language, of their rights and of the services they may receive from the union. Once they become union members, foreign workers—especially the Turks— function extremely positively. Yugoslavs, on the other hand, perhaps due to their forced membership in unions in their own country, are rather disinterested in union activities altogether. The Spanish and Greek workers have the opposite problem. In their countries union membership is forbidden, and government representatives from these countries in Germany pressure their workers and discourage them from taking part in unions. This is why Spanish and Greek union members are very few. Italians, on the other hand, belong to the European Common Market. Unlike other foreign workers, they do not require a residence permit and are well integrated into the local society.

"Today DGB has 6.5 million members, of which some five or six hundred thousand are foreign workers. A more precise estimate is difficult to make. DGB does not differentiate between foreign and German workers. The rights and forms of membership are the same for both. I can say, however, that only about one-third of all Turkish workers, one-fifth of Yugoslav and Greek workers in Berlin are union members. In firms with well organized labor associations more foreign workers join the unions. However, because in some firms union membership is seen as undesirable, pressures are exerted on the workers. This tendency, too, decreases the number of union members.

"At the moment it seems impossible to solve the problem of tourist (illegal) workers in Berlin. This problem cannot be solved even if we give legal rights to all workers living and working illegally in Berlin, because the illegal workers will continue to come to Germany bringing with them a number of problems, the most acute of which is housing.

"In DGB we believe that a rather radical change in the laws regulating the life of foreigners in Germany must be brought about. When the law was modified in 1965 the phenomenon of guest workers was still being treated as a temporary phenomenon. Now this law must be softened. Such a modification, needless to say, would have been easier if SPD were in power. It is now impossible to allow a free movement of labor without solving the problems of education, schooling, housing, etc.

"The West Berlin Senate has established a commission to examine the projected needs of the region for guest workers. It is estimated that by 1978 the number of guest workers in Berlin alone will exceed 100,000.

"It is my personal opinion that the guest workers must participate in local elections. This is, of course, a legal matter. There is a small scale of participation now in West Berlin. In some locales guest workers, though not allowed to vote, participate in local administration in a consulting capacity. These representatives are elected by the trade unions. Although some of the Greek and Spanish organizations and the religiously oriented Turkish organizations have objected to the unions' interference in this matter the Berlin Senate recognizes DGB's right in the matter. DGB believes that under certain conditions (relating to the length of residence, etc.), guest workers must obtain the right to vote and be encouraged to vote. However, this is an issue which will receive little attention for the years to come and will be one of the last problems to be solved in relation to foreign workers."

Discussion Questions

1. What are the differences in labor problems between a subsidiary in an industrialized country and a subsidiary in a developing country?

2. Many people think that productivity increase in many United States firms has been much lower than in other industrialized countries. What are the main reasons, and what would you suggest to improve the productivity of the United States businesses?

3. Many United States firms have been criticized by the union leaders for seeking lower labor costs by establishing manufacturing facilities in many developing countries. Union leaders strongly argue that this will result in a negative impact on the United States economy, as well as in severe unemployment problems. How would you evaluate this statement, and what would you recommend to solve the problem, if you are:
   a. A manager of a United States MNC?
   b. A union leader?
   c. A United States government official?

4. Discuss the differences in labor practices among United States, Japanese, and European MNCs.

5. There appear to be increasing efforts to internationalize the labor union. What would the potential problems be of doing so?

6. Discuss the impact of sociocultural factors on employee morale, work ethics, and productivity.

Endnotes

1. T. W. Schultz, "Investment in Human Capital," *American Economic Review* 51 (March 1951): 1–17, reprinted in B. F. Kiber, *Investment in Human Capital* (Columbia, SC: University of South Carolina Press, 1971), p. 20.
2. Ibid.
3. Sadao Kumazawa, "Future Management: Effective Use of Human Resources," *Management Japan* 5, 3 (July-September 1971): 5.
4. Michael G. Duerr, "International Business Management: Its Four Tasks," *Conference Board Record* 5, 10 (October 1968): 43, quoted in Stefan H. Robock and Kenneth Simmonds, *International Business and Multinational Enterprises* (Homewood, Ill.: Irwin, 1983), p. 554.
5. Oscar A. Ornati, *Jobs and Workers in India* (Ithaca, NY: Institute of International Industrial Relations, Cornell University, 1955), p. 55.
6. Clark Kerr, et al., *Industrialism and Industrial Man* (Cambridge, Mass.: Harvard University Press, 1960), p. 97.
7. Richard N. Farmer and Barry M. Richman, *Comparative Management and Economic Progress* (Homewood, Ill.: Irwin, 1965), pp. 154–159.
8. Gunnar Myrdal, *Asian Drama: An Inquiry into the Poverty of Nations* (New York: The Twentieth Century Fund, 1968), p. 1150.
9. L. A. Zurcher, Jr., A. Meadow, and S. E. Zurcher, "Value Orientation, Role Conflicts, and Alienation from Work: Cross-Cultural Study," *American Sociological Review* 30 (August 1965): 539–548.
10. Morris David Morris, *The Emergence of an Industrial Labor Force in India: A Study of the Bombay Cotton Mills, 1859–1947* (Berkeley: University of California Press, 1965), p. 4.
11. Claude McMillan, Jr., "The American Businessman in Brazil," *Business Topics* 13, 2 (Spring 1965), reprinted in *International Dimensions in Business* (East

Lansing: Graduate School of Business Administration, Michigan State University, 1966), p. 103.

12. Thomas R. Fillol, *Social Factors in Economic Development: The Argentine Case* (Cambridge, Mass.: MIT Press, 1963), p. 76.

13. David Sirota and J. M. Greenwood, "Understand Your Overseas Work Force," *Harvard Business Review* 49, 1 (January-February 1971): 53–60.

14. Ibid., p. 53.

15. Ibid.

16. See Anant R. Negandhi and S. B. Prasad, *Comparative Management* (New York: Appleton-Century-Crofts, 1971), and Anant R. Negandhi, *Organization Theory in the Open System* (New York: Dunellen, 1975).

17. C. Altimus, Jr., et al., "Cross-Cultural Perspectives on Need Deficiencies of Blue-Collar Workers," *Quarterly Journal of Management Development* 2, 1 (June 1971): 91–103.

18. George W. England and Anant R. Negandhi, "National Contexts and Technology as Determinants of Employee's Perceptions," in *Organizational Functioning in a Cross-Cultural Perspective*, eds. G. W. England, A. R. Negandhi, and B. Wilpert, (Kent, Ohio: Kent State University Press, 1979), pp. 175–190.

19. Comparable differences in concerns were found between national samples of the two countries twenty-five years ago, in the pioneering work of Hadley Cantril, as reported in *The Pattern of Human Concerns* (New Brunswick, NJ: Rutgers University Press, 1965), Chap. 4 and 5.

20. G. Hofstede, A. I. Kraut, and S. H. Simonetti, "The Development of a Core Attitude Survey Questionnaire for Internal Use," Working Paper 76-17 (Brussels: European Institute for Advanced Studies, 1976).

21. Holmström, M., *South Indian Factory Workers—Their Life and Their World* (Cambridge, Eng.: Cambridge University Press, 1976), p. 137. See also D. G. Mandelbaum, *Society in India: Change and Continuity, II* (Berkeley: University of California Press, 1970), p. 645.

22. Negandhi and Prasad, *Comparative*; Negandhi, *Organization*.

23. James M. Walker, "Forecasting Manpower Needs," *Harvard Business Review* 47 (March-April 1969): 152–168.

24. Negandhi, *Organization*, pp. 194–222.

25. Fillol, *Social Factors*, p. 73.

26. F. Herzberg, *Work and the Nature of Man* (Cleveland: World Publishing Co., 1966).

27. For detailed results, see Negandhi, *Organization*, pp. 245–273.

28. William Ouchi, *Theory Z* (Reading, Mass.: Addison-Wesley, 1981).

29. Anant R. Negandhi and B. R. Baliga, *Quest for Survival and Growth* (New York: Praeger Publishing Co., 1979); and Anant R. Negandhi, *Management and Economic Development: The Case of Taiwan* (The Hague: Martinus Nijhoff, 1973).

30. Discussion in this section is drawn from Negandhi, *Organization*, and a recent paper by A. R. Negandhi, G. S. Eshghi, and E. C. Yuen, "Localization of Japanese Subsidiaries Overseas: Issues, Facts, and Fictions," (mimeo). University of Illinois, 1985.

31. J. R. Putti, and M. Chong, "American and Japanese Management Practices in Their Singapore Subsidiaries," Faculty working paper, School of Management, National University of Singapore, Singapore, 1984.

32. J. S. McClenanthen, "Cultural Hybrids: Japanese Plants in the U.S.," *Industry Week*, February 19, 1979, pp. 73–75.

33. Negandhi and Baliga, *Quest*, pp. 54–57.

34. A. B. Sim, "Performance of Decentrally Managed International Subsidiaries," *Management International Review* 17, 2 (1977): 45–52.

35. R. T. Johnson, "Success and Failure of Japanese Subsidiaries in America," *Columbia Journal of World Business* XII, 1 (Spring 1977): 30–37; R. Johnson and W. Ouchi, "Made in America, Under Japanese Management," *Harvard Business Review* 52, 1 (1974): 61–69.
36. For a detailed discussion on industrial democracy and codetermination and their impact on labor productivity, see B. W. Wilpert and Arndt Sorge, *International Yearbook of Organizational Democracy* (London: John Wiley and Sons, 1984). The book contains twenty-six scholarly papers on these topics.

Additional Readings

Articles

Denise, Malcolm L. "Industrial Relations and the Multinational Corporation, The Ford Experience." In *Bargaining Without Boundaries.* Eds. Robert J. Flanagan and Arnold R. Weber. Chicago: University of Chicago Press, 1974.

Farmer, R. N., and Richman, B. M. "A Model for Research in Comparative Management." *California Management Review* VII, 2 (Winter 1964): 55–68.

Johnson, R. T. "Success and Failure of Japanese Subsidiaries in America." *Columbia Journal of World Business* XII, 1 (Spring 1977): 30–37.

McIsaac, George S., and Henzler, Hubert. "Codetermination, A Hidden Noose for MNCs." *Columbia Journal of World Business* XI, 4 (Winter 1974): 16–20.

Negandhi, Anant R. "Comparative Management and Organization Theory: A Marriage Needed." *Academy of Management Journal* 18, 2 (1975): 334–343.

Negandhi, Anant R. "Management in the Third World." *Asia Pacific Journal of Management* 1, 1 (September 1983): 15–25.

Negandhi, Anant R., and Estafen, D. B. "A Research Model to Determine the Applicability of American Management Know-How in Different Cultures and/or Environments." *Academy of Management Journal* 8, 4 (1965): 309–318.

Northrup, Herbert R., and Rowan, Richard L. "Multinational Union-Management Consultation: The European Experience." *International Labor Review* 116, 2 (September-October 1977): 118–124.

Books

Fernandez-Kelly, Maria Patricia. *For We are Sold, I and My People, Woman and Industry in Mexico's Frontier.* Albany: State University of New York Press, 1983.

Negandhi, Anant R. *Organization Theory in an Open System.* Port Washington, NY: Kennikat Press, 1975.

Negandhi, Anant R., and Prasad, S.B. *Comparative Management.* New York: Appleton-Century-Crofts, 1971.

Chapter 8

Human Resource Management in International Corporations: Managing Managers

This chapter examines the managerial aspects of human resource management practices. Specific elements discussed are:

- Sources of recruitment for overseas managers
- Determining alternatives between the home, host, and third country nationals
- Using the home country's managerial practices in foreign subsidiaries

- Utility and transferability of advanced management practices and knowledge
- Comparative analysis of human resource management practices of United States, European, and Japanese multinational companies
- Recruitment, selection, and training of managers for the headquarters' international operation
- Future outlook on human resource management in international corporations.

Sources of Recruitment

Basically three sources are available to international corporations for recruiting managers: (1) the home country nationals; (2) the host country nationals; and (3) the third country nationals. The first category consists of citizens of the country from which the multinational company originated; the second group consists of the citizens of countries where subsidiaries of multinational companies are located; and the third country nationals are the citizens of some other countries other than the home and host countries of the multinationals (e.g., a British national working for a United States subsidiary in Malaysia).

Advantages and Disadvantages of Alternative Sources

Home Country Nationals

In the early phase of the internationalization of business, the firm is likely to recruit managers for overseas subsidiaries either from its own home office or from the home country. The rationales for using these sources are: (1) familiarity with the home office's goals, objectives, policies, and practices; (2) technical and managerial competence; (3) effective liaison with the home office personnel; and (4) easier exercise of control over the subsidiary's operation.

     The main disadvantages of employing home country nationals for overseas positions are: (1) difficulties in adapting to the foreign language and the socioeconomic, political, and legal environment; (2) excessive cost of selecting, training, and maintaining expatriate managers and their families overseas[1]; (3) the host countries' pressures for localizing operations and promoting local nationals in top positions in foreign subsidiaries; and (4) family adjustment problems, especially concerning nonworking spouses of managers.

Host Country Nationals

The main advantages of employing host country nationals are: (1) familiarity with the socioeconomic, political, and legal environment and business practices of the country; (2) less costly to maintain; (3) provides the possibilities of advancement and promotion to local nationals and, consequently, increases their commitment and motivation; and (4) responds effectively to the host country's demands for localization of the subsidiary's operation.

The disadvantages of hiring host country nationals are: (1) difficulties in exercising effective control over the subsidiary's operation; (2) communication difficulties in dealing with the home office personnel; and (3) lack of opportunities for the home country's nationals to gain international and cross-cultural experience.

The Third Country Nationals

The third country nationals offer perhaps the best possible compromise in terms of securing needed technical and managerial expertise and adapting to a foreign socioeconomic and cultural environment. Usually, the third country nationals are career, international business managers. They are also relatively less expensive to maintain than home country nationals. The main disadvantage of recruiting third country nationals is the host country's sensitivity with respect to the nationals of specific countries.

As Phatak has observed, "in certain parts of the world, animosities of national characters exist between neighboring countries—for example, India and Pakistan, Greece and Turkey."[2] Consequently, the employment of third country nationals should take into consideration intercountry relations and sensitivity. The second disadvantage of third country nationals is the hindrance created for the local nationals to upgrade their own ranks and assume responsible positions in the multinational subsidiaries. In many developing countries, home country nationals may be more acceptable than third country nationals.

Present Trends

During the 1960s and early 1970s, United States multinational companies used to send a large number of expatriate managers overseas to manage subsidiary operations. For example, in one survey, it was reported that some 150,000 United States nationals were working abroad, of whom approximately two thirds were managers of United States subsidiaries.[3] Similarly, a 1972 study by the Conference Board revealed that 268 United States companies employed some 3,455 of her own citizens abroad. By 1975 this total had increased to 5,300.[4] However, there is a declining preference for sending United States nationals overseas. For example, *Business Abroad* reported that about 70% of the managing directors of United States subsidiaries in Europe were local nationals.[5] Baker and Ivancevich, in 1970, also reported a declining trend.[6] In her study of United States multinational companies,

Table 8-1 Extent of localization of top-level management by MNCs

Percentage localization of top-level management	MNC Ownership		
	U.S.	European	Japanese
	(n = 44)	(n = 33)	(n = 19)
	%	%	%
100	27.3	9.1	0
75–99	31.8	39.4	0
51–74	15.9	12.1	10.5
1–50	22.7	24.2	10.5
0	2.3	15.2	78.9

Source: Anant R. Negandhi and B. R. Baliga, *Quest Survival and Growth*, New York: Praeger Publishers, 1979, p. 54.

Tung found that they used host country nationals as senior managers in greater numbers in industrialized countries than in the less developed nations.[7]

United States MNCs were the first to deal with the widespread demand of the developing countries to localize the management of foreign companies. In our earlier study of fifty-six United States subsidiaries in six developing countries,[8] we found that less than two dozen expatriate United States managers were working in these companies. In the 1974–1976 study, we observed a continuation of this trend in the declining use of expatriate managers by United States multinationals.[9]

As shown in Table 8-1, the majority of the top-level executive positions in United States subsidiaries were filled with local nationals. In fact, only one company did not have any national in a top-level position. In contrast, fifteen Japanese multinationals (78.9%) did not even employ one single national in the top-level management ranks. The table indicates that European MNCs had localized their operations considerably more than the Japanese, though to a lesser extent than the United States MNCs.

The study also indicated that Japanese multinationals employed Japanese personnel even at the supervisory levels. Such practices resulted in tensions and conflicts between expatriate managers and local nationals.[10]

Similar results were reported by Brandt and Hulbert, in their study of more than sixty United States, European, and Japanese subsidiaries operating in Brazil.[11] Specifically, their study showed that 24% of the chief executives in United States subsidiaries were local nationals. In European MNCs, only 8% of the chief executives were local nationals. Japanese MNCs simply did not employ locals as chief executives in their subsidiaries' operations in Brazil.

Table 8-2 Evolution and growth of international business and corresponding changes in staffing policies

Evolution and growth of international business	A. Evolution of organizational structure	B. Staffing policies
I. Initial stage	Export dept.	Host country nationals in charge
II. Early production stage	Export dept./international division	Home country nationals in charge
III. Standardization of production process— mature stage few products	International division	Host country nationals in charge
IV. Product innovations and growth through diversification	Product/area bases for structuring of organization	Home country or third country nationals in charge
V. Quest for global rationalization	Product/area bases for structuring/matrix type organization	Host country nationals in charge

Choosing Among the Three Alternatives

Franko's[12] study shows that in the recruitment of overseas managers, the firm usually follows a predictable pattern. As shown in Table 8-2, in earlier stages of entering into the international marketplace via exporting or licensing, the firm mostly used host country nationals. Once the firm has started manufacturing abroad, the need for home country personnel will arise to provide technical and managerial knowledge. Once the production process has been standardized, host country nationals will be trained and entrusted with major operational responsibilities. Consequently, at this stage very few expatriate managers will be kept overseas. In further expansion of international business via product innovation and diversification, a larger number of expatriate managers or third country nationals will be needed to provide technical and managerial expertise. At the final stage of the internationalization of the business, the firm will strive for rationalizing its production and marketing processes to achieve economies of scale. At this juncture, major strategic and policy-level decisions will be centralized at the home office, and the operational methods, techniques, and practices will be highly standardized. Consequently, technical and managerial transfers will take place through training host country nationals, and the need for expatriates and third country nationals will be diminished.

Selection and Training of Overseas Executives

The declining trend in the numbers of U.S. nationals being sent to manage overseas subsidiaries has reduced the need for selecting and training executives for overseas assignments. However, for smaller and medium-sized companies entering into international manufacturing ventures abroad for the first time, the selection and training issue may still be relevant.

Needed Qualities [13]

An executive who accepts an assignment overseas should be adaptable to the sociocultural environment of the host country. He or she is viewed not only as a representative of the parent company but also as an ambassador without portfolio. The person bears triple responsibilities: to the company as an employee, to the home country as an ambassador, and to the host country as a temporary citizen.

To carry out these varied responsibilities, the executive should not only have the technical and managerial competence of the domestic executive, but should also possess special skills of critical importance. Much has been written concerning the qualities desired. For example, Cleveland, Mangone, and Adams [14] recommend five necessary attributes the overseas executive should possess: technical skill, belief in mission, cultural empathy, a sense of politics, and organizational ability. Fayerweather states that the effective overseas executive should be objective, open-minded, tolerant, and well versed in the history and culture of his host country. [15]

The accommodation by the executive's spouse to a foreign culture is also considered critical for the success of the overseas executive. Cleveland asserts that "[the] wife will cast the deciding vote on whether to stay, and in many cases she will make or break her husband's career."[16]

To some, the special skills are more important than conventional qualifications as determinants of success for the executive. Collectively, these special attributes have been referred to as *Factor X*, a term that defies precise definition but implies many things to many writers. To Stiglitz[17] it is cultural flexibility, Cleveland[18] considers it the "sense of politics," and to Shearer[19] it is friendliness, a lack of racial or religious prejudice, adaptability, cultural empathy, and overall ability to achieve the firm's goals through acceptance and cooperation.

Results of a Survey

In a large-scale study of United States overseas executives, 2,391 executives in forty countries were invited to answer three open-ended questions concerning the following issues:

1. Their views concerning the desirable quality of Factor X
2. The circumstances that influenced their decision to accept overseas assignments
3. Advantages and disadvantages of overseas assignments[20]

The Expatriate Defines Factor X

To learn how the expatriates would define the elusive factor, they were asked what background and qualities they would seek when selecting executives for foreign assignments. Their answers are exhibited in Table 8-3. One must be impressed by the lack of consensus. It should be pointed out that job knowledge or experience was not undervalued by the group but was assumed to be present before all other considerations were weighed. Assuming the person is technically qualified, the most frequently raised question concerned *adaptability* and *tolerance*. These two qualities were variously described as a talent for getting along with others, the ability of the executive and family to live in a foreign country, a liking for people, respect for customs and beliefs of others, and flexibility. Obviously, the overseas executive has as much difficulty articulating the nature of Factor X as the academicians.

Three qualifications of an expatriate can be measured: professional capability, education, and previous experience in living abroad. Many executives specified these in the order given. Many insisted that the prospective expatriate be well educated in the most liberal sense of the word. Considering

Table 8-3 Ideal background for an overseas career

Background	Percentage
Wife and family adaptable	20
Leadership stability	19
Knowledge of job	14
Knowledge of language of host country	13
Well-educated	13
Respect for laws and people of host country	12
Previous overseas experience	4
Desire to serve overseas	4
Miscellaneous	1
Total	100

Source: Richard F. Gonzalez and Anant R. Negandhi, *The United States Overseas Executive: His Orientations and Career Patterns*, East Lansing, Mich.: Institute for International Business and Economic Development Studies, 1967, p. 113.

the strata in which the expatriate lives and works overseas, he or she needs impressive credentials to hold on. Education is perhaps the most tangible of credentials in this sense.

Adaptability of the spouse and children was the factor not only mentioned the most, but also the one for which very specific advice was offered. If the selection of overseas personnel were left entirely to those in the subsidiaries, one could conclude from their responses that more than lip service would be given to the idea that the spouse should be interviewed and tested to determine fitness for life overseas. Adaptability was also defined to mean the willingness to change one's mode of life graciously. Many mentioned the need to participate in a variety of religious and political ceremonies, to entertain lavishly, and to match the appetites for food and drink of one's hosts, although they may, by our definition, be excessive. Adaptability of the spouse also means that she or he must not have abnormally strong ties to parents or other family that may necessitate frequent home leave.

Consensus holds that special problems exist when the expatriates' family includes teenage children. Schooling becomes a critical problem for executives with younger children.

Influential Circumstances

Why would people like to locate overseas? The most frequent response was the opportunity for advancement and recognition. Many respondents stated that working in the foreign country was a real test of their abilities. The foreign situation could prove early in one's career the stuff one was made of. The expatriate manager is not only a nonconformist, but also a young person in a hurry. Many respondents indicated that "the fastest promotions are possible in foreign operations."

Many expatriates stated they were determined not only to prove themselves in international business activity, but also to prove the merit of the United States way of life, including the way of doing business. A sense of mission and love of country were expressed by the majority. Paradoxically, when weighing advantages and disadvantages of the foreign life, the respondents admitted there were many things about the United States way of life that they deplored, but apparently they could separate these from the basic structure and tenets of United States society.

A still greater paradox is represented, on the one hand, by the love of country and desire to serve, and on the other hand by the need to lose one's identity as a United States citizen to a point that successful accommodation in the host's culture may be achieved. These conflicting demands imposed on the expatriate are not clearly recognized nor understood at home. The executive is asked to walk a fine line, and a marked variance is cause for immediate criticism. If expatriates are unyielding and committed to everything in their home country, they are criticized not only by the host but by their own colleagues. If accommodation is complete and the expatriates have gone native, judgment will be made that they no longer can carry out their complex role as representatives of the firm and the country.

The opportunity for advancement was cited by a substantial number of executives who implied that they accepted their first overseas assignment simply because it was the only opportunity available at the time.

Given that the quest for advancement and recognition is subject to several interpretations, predominant was the response to challenge and the drive to be involved in a test situation early in the career. In one way or another, most of the respondents stressed the importance and future potential of the overseas market. International business activities, they believed, are the means to several ends—personal rewards and satisfaction, economic objectives of the firm, and economic development in the host country. These are biased views. The expatriates' behavior is understandable only when one accepts the sincerity and firmness with which these views are held.

The second most frequently cited reason for accepting overseas life concerns the desire to travel and to make a life abroad for the family. A variety of reasons are grouped under this heading. At the one extreme is the desire for adventure, the glamour of living in a foreign country, and the desire to meet and know other peoples. Some expatriates indicated that their tastes for this type of life were whetted during extended military tours of duty. This, however, must be regarded as the exception rather than the rule. At the other extreme, the desire to travel or to live abroad represented a reaction to the respondents' view of life in the United States. The pace, regimentation, job routinization, and the impersonality of United States society were repeatedly mentioned.

A desire for an overseas career was mentioned by 13% of those who had answered the questions. Included were some who acknowledged such a decision early in life, specifically during high school, to enter foreign service whether in a public or private business. For some, the decision was reinforced by overseas service during World War II. The respondents followed up by attending the School of Foreign Service at Georgetown University, and then exercised careful judgment in selecting a firm that would eventually provide an overseas position.

Financial reward, including tax advantage, was named by 13% as the principal inducement to go abroad. One might argue that financial rewards should be classified as advancement and recognition.

Advantages and Disadvantages of Foreign Assignments

Advantages of an Overseas Assignment

The most frequently mentioned advantages were higher pay and tax benefits. Advantages that may be identified with career—broader experience and responsibility, more rapid advancement, avenue to top executive jobs—were ranked as most important by one third of the group. On this score, there is a correspondence between expectation and experience. Most saw the potential and challenge of overseas operations in terms of personal career goals. This supports the conclusion that expatriates do not consider the foreign assignment an end in itself, but hope to make their marks early and demonstrate to the home office that they are ready for advancement at home.

Overall, the expatriate managers view themselves as generalists rather than specialists. They conceive of themselves as general managers preparing for top positions in the corporate hierarchy. Not all make it, because of their attitudes, perceptions, and aspirations. In United States corporations the realities are quite different. However, in European and Japanese companies, overseas experience is considered a necessary stepping stone for the corporate's top position.

The remaining advantages of overseas assignments may conveniently be subsumed under the heading, "the better life." This includes all of the well-publicized pleasures that are associated with foreign assignments, particularly in Western Europe. There are, however, less exotic aspects of a better life that were thoughtfully discussed by the expatriates. They expressed the thought that they were learning to become citizens of the world in various ways and, from the vantage point of many thousands of miles away, were gaining new insights and balanced perspectives about their own country. "You begin to judge people and situations with a wider scope of knowledge . . . you begin to compare the situation with various countries, you begin to see the depth of the situation."

One final recurring theme is the advantage typically described as the big frog in a small pond situation. It is difficult to classify this advantage strictly as personal or professional in kind. The status enjoyed by the top executive of a foreign subsidiary has a significant social dimension, but most executives who spoke of this advantage related it to their careers. They saw the distance from their home office as an advantage that permitted them to operate independently; they also considered the relatively small scale of operation of the subsidiary to be an advantage. Scale encouraged the growth of generalized skills and a much earlier appreciation of the total rather than the functional view of the operation.

Disadvantages of an Overseas Assignment

The most frequently mentioned disadvantage concerned personal comfort, safety, and the concern for one's children. When speaking of the *modern* way of life, the respondent invariably meant the availability and reliability of a number of conditions that one takes for granted in the United States— utilities, transportation, communications, as well as many other personal services. The apparent contradiction between desire for a better life overseas and the comfortably secure modern life at home was implicit in the response. Although the expatriates have made the decision to live abroad, what they are expressing is the irritating set of circumstances one encounters in unfamiliar places.

Closely related in meaning, if not in the manner in which they were expressed, are the disadvantages of distance from home and the concern about schooling for their children. Again, a paradox is very evident—identify with the nationals of the host country and develop empathy, but (where one's children are concerned) do not go too far. In various ways, a concern was expressed about the lack of identification of the expatriate's children with the United States and her culture. This seemed to be the real concern when respondents spoke of the time or distance that separated them and their families from the United States. The usual expression was: "We want our children to grow up as Americans, but as we stay, year by year, they take on more of the culture of the resident country." Worded differently but expressing the same sentiment, ". . . there is one disadvantage that everyone with children abroad has, and that is the effect on children. Although they probably see more and do more than they would at home, they do not grow up as Americans. They grow up as foreigners, and if they are not brought home frequently they never get to feel at home in the United States."[21]

Only 12% of the executives mentioned disadvantages relating to their business careers. A few mentioned that the limited scale of operation of the subsidiary precluded the opportunity for promotion. To some, the methods and procedures employed in foreign operations did not match those of the stateside organization; the expatriates were acquiring skills and experiences not marketable at home. Three percent mentioned growing out of touch with the home office. This suggests that for a few executives the overseas assignment meant, by design, being placed on the shelf.

Almost as important as what the executives said is the manner in which they reported. One concludes they seemed to have a need to be heard by their superiors at home, as well as by their countrymen. Better life and financial rewards are not sufficient inducements.

Managing Managers of Foreign Subsidiaries

The following section will examine two critical issues with respect to the management of high-level managers in foreign subsidiaries:

1. Cross-cultural and cross-national differences in management practices
2. The feasibility and utility of transferring the home country's practices to foreign operations

In analyzing these two questions, I will rely on empirical studies rather than normative judgments.

Cross-Cultural and Cross-National Differences

During the last twenty-five years or so, much has been written on the impact of sociocultural variables on management practices and effectiveness. In spite of the voluminous writings, there is as yet no clear-cut answer to the specific impact of sociocultural factors on management. Accordingly, the issues of applicability, transferability, and utility of advanced management knowledge and practices have remained cloudy, if not controversial. It is beyond the scope of this book to discuss the subject in detail.[22] However, to provide some perspective on this issue, the findings of a few important cross-cultural management studies will be reviewed.

Brief Review of Cross-Cultural Studies

1. Employees in Brazil preferred the participative democratic style of leadership, whereas in Japan, employees preferred more au-

thoritarian leaders. Overall, IBM employees in some forty-five countries preferred consultative-type leadership.[23]

2. There are definite culture differences in supervisory preferences and style. India has been found an authoritarian country as compared with other countries.[24] Morale and productivity were higher under authoritarian than under democratic leadership in India; the results in the United States show opposite effects.[25]

3. Managers projected their own judgments onto others; they saw differences in a very specific way. For example, Indian managers projected their values mostly on others and were also least accurate in rating other colleagues. But they did not disparage others. In contrast, British managers projected almost as much as Indian managers but negated others. The Danish, Norwegian, Italian, and Spanish were similar in both empathy and projection, but the Danish and Spanish were higher on negation than Italian and Norwegian managers.[26]

4. There seems to be a significant difference among managers from the various countries both in their problem solving and their listing of corporate objectives. Tentative data indicate that economic factors seem to be more important than cultural variables in this regard. For example, Indian and Colombian managers put less emphasis on meeting competition than United States, British, and Dutch managers. In general, managers in developed countries stress objectives of growth and competition, whereas their counterparts in the developing countries are satisfied with the usual maintenance of their operations.[27]

5. Managers from developed countries give the poor performer less than average money in terms of increments as against the manager from the developing countries who does not differentiate salary increments between poor and average performers.[28]

6. Indian managers prefer high risk and ideal outcomes whereas United States managers prefer moderate risk with moderate outcome.[29]

7. In terms of value systems, the majority of the managers in each country are pragmatically oriented. Although there are similarities in the managers' orientation, the cultural factors do make a difference.[30]

8. Anglo-Americans tend to regard work as an important end in itself, whereas the same concept of work is largely alien to the Mexican culture.[31]

9. Use of a scientific method is second nature to United States managers; Mexican managers hold no such regard and respect for the scientific method.[32]

10. Whereas United States managers can be characterized as being "prodelegation," Mexican managers can be characterized as being "antidelegation." Participative management embodies a threat to the Mexican manager's role and image as others see it, and is incompatible with the role as he or she perceives it.[33]

More recently, Hofstede,[34] in his study of a single large multinational company (nevertheless a truly monumental and ambitious study), attempted to demonstrate the strong influence of sociocultural variables on authority distribution and the boss-subordinate relationship. Using the concept of "power distance" between the superordinate and subordinate, he has shown that the power distance between the boss and the subordinate is larger in developing countries than in developed nations. (The larger the power distance, the more authoritative or autocratic the leadership style.) Power distance was defined by Hofstede "as the difference between the extent to which A can determine the behaviour of B and the extent to which B can determine the behaviour of A." Besides the formal authority or hierarchy, the "power distance" is dependent on such factors as economic well-being, expertise knowledge, and social status of the parties involved. Table 8-4 shows the power distance values in selected countries.

Based on the theory of cognition applied in cross-cultural settings, Reddings and Martyn-Johns[35] found the following situations in Southeast Asian countries:

1. Oriental* companies used either less formal planning systems, and/or planning systems with fewer variables than equivalent Western companies.
2. In Oriental companies, the degree of formal organization (in terms of defined differentiation of functions, integrating control mechanisms, and coordinating processes) was less than in an equivalent Western company.
3. In Oriental companies the staffing function was less programmed and contained less formal training than in equivalent Western companies.
4. Oriental managers made promotion decisions using less objective data than equivalent Western managers.
5. The style of leadership employed by Oriental managers relied less on interpersonal confrontations with subordinates than is the case with Western managers.
6. Managerial decisions in Oriental companies took greater account of effects on the relative status of other people than in Western companies.

---

*For the sake of simplicity, the word "Oriental" was used as an umbrella phrase for the context being studied here. It is meant to embrace Hong Kong, Singapore, Malaysia, Indonesia, Thailand, the Philippines (and originally, South Vietnam). Japan was omitted from the list because of her special cultural nature, and because of the degree of Westernization that has taken place there, but some of the ideas still apply there.

Table 8-4 Power distance index values in selected developed and developing countries

Country	Power distance index* (actual)	Country	Power distance index (Actual)
Philippines	94	South Africa	49
Mexico	81	Argentina	49
Venezuela	81	USA	40
India	77	Canada	39
Singapore	74	Netherlands	38
Brazil	69	Australia	36
Hong Kong	68	West Germany	35
France	68	Great Britain	35
Colombia	67	Switzerland	34
Turkey	66	Finland	33
Belgium	65	Norway	31
Peru	64	Sweden	31
Thailand	64	Ireland	28
Chile	63	New Zealand	22
Portugal	63	Denmark	18
Greece	60	Israel	13
Iran	58	Austria	11
Taiwan	58	Mean of 39 countries	51
Spain	57	(multinational	
Pakistan	55	organization)	
Japan	54	Yugoslavia	76
Italy	50	(same industry)	

*The higher the index number, the higher will be the power distance and autocratic relationship between the superordinates and the subordinates.
Source: Geert Hofstede "Hierarchical Power Distance in Forty Countries," *Organizations Alike and Unlike,* eds. C. T. Lammers and D. J. Hickson, London: Routledge and Kegan Paul, 1979, p. 105.

7. The control of performance in Oriental companies was less formal, using less information and a shorter time span of discretion than in the Western equivalent.
8. Oriental managers displayed less precision and less urgency in matters such as timekeeping, scheduling, and completion of programs than Western equivalents.

To recap, the review of cross-cultural management studies indicates the following:

1. There is no single-way of doing things. The principle of equifinality applies to the functioning of social, as well as business, organizations. Managers may achieve given objectives through various methods.
2. There is no universal applicability of either authoritarian or participative democratic management styles. In general, the United States can best be characterized as using a participative democratic management style, while Germany, France, and most of the developing countries are authoritarian in their style. Authoritarian style is not necessarily dysfunctional in developing countries. This, perhaps, may be the "right type" of leadership.
3. More objective measures are brought to bear in making managerial decisions with respect to compensation, objectives, and goal-settings in the developed countries, whereas much subjective judgment (emotions, religious beliefs) enters the decision-making processes in developing countries.
4. There are enough similarities and differences among managers around the world. Similarities are explained in terms of industrialization or industrial subculture. Differences are explained in terms of cultural variables. Cultural factors are considered as the most important influencing variables.

I shall return later in this chapter to argue against the cultural imperative hypothesis. Preceding this discussion, I will provide realistic perspectives on the actual management practices used by United States subsidiaries in selected developing countries.

Transferring Advanced Management Practices[36]

In the study reported on later, the main purpose is to examine the applicability and transferability of advanced management practices and knowledge from industrialized nations to developing countries. The study was undertaken in six developing countries: Argentina, Brazil, India, The Philippines, Taiwan, and Uruguay. It was a comparative study of United States subsidiaries and comparable local companies in those countries.

Space limitations preclude a discussion of the findings of the study in detail. The interested reader is urged to refer to previously published work.[37]

A summary of the findings of the study is as follows. First, the overall profile of organizational practices and effectiveness of United States subsidiaries and comparable local firms in the six developing countries studied is outlined. Second, the impact of sociocultural factors on practices and effectiveness is discussed.

Profiles of United States Subsidiaries and Local Firms

The profile of management practices and effectiveness, outlined later, includes the firm's orientation toward planning, policy making, control devices, leadership style, human resource management practices, and management effectiveness.

United States Subsidiary

Long-range planning with a time span ranging from five to ten years was common practice in the United States subsidiaries in the six developing countries. The typical U.S. subsidiary also formulated its long-range plans in considerable detail; it involved all levels of managerial, technical, and supervisory personnel in the planning process. The policy-making task was taken quite seriously by this type of firm. Efforts were made to use major policies effectively, both as guidelines and as instruments for overall control to achieve the firm's objectives. Major policies were formulated by the top-level executives but, in their formulation, all levels of managerial and technical personnel were consulted and their views considered. These policies were generally concentrated in the areas of pricing, personnel selection, plant investment, and salary and wage standards.

Employee training, employee relations, purchasing, acquisition, and expansion received much less emphasis, however. Other control devices used by the subsidiary included cost and budgetary controls, quality control, equipment maintenance, and setting work standards for blue-collar, supervisory, clerical, and managerial personnel. Such techniques as periodic management audit systems, however, were only used by a few of the subsidiaries.

The subsidiary was organized on the basis of major business functions (e.g., production, sales, accounting, and finance). A typical firm had five to seven departments. Specialized staff personnel were found frequently. Service and maintenance departments were well organized.

Authority definition was clear for each position in the organization. The degree of decentralization in decision making was greater in the United States subsidiaries than in the local firms. Attitudes of the executives in the subsidiaries regarding decentralization were only partially consistent with their practices.

The leadership style used in the United States subsidiary can best be characterized as democratic or consultative. Executives of the subsidiary manifested a great deal of trust and confidence in their subordinates. The attitudes of the executives of the subsidiary were not totally consistent with their leadership styles.

Human resource management practices were well developed. The Personnel Department was organized as a separate unit with a specialized, trained personnel manager. Human resource management policies were formally stated. Such personnel techniques as job evaluation, development of selection and promotion criteria for managerial and technical personnel, and training programs for blue-collar employees were widely used. However, there was not much sophistication in compensation and motivational techniques and practices.

Managerial effectiveness, in terms of handling human resources, was found "excellent" in some aspects and "poor" in others. For example, whereas the typical United States subsidiary did not find it difficult to attain high employee morale, it experienced difficulties in motivating its employees. Particularly, absenteeism was a problem. Employee productivity was average, and scrap loss was higher as compared to the United States parent companies.

With regard to high-level managers, the United States subsidiary was able to attract and retain trained managerial and technical personnel and was able to achieve cooperative departmental relationships. It also effectively used its high-level managers and adapted and responded to environmental changes without much difficulty. By and large, the United States subsidiary made good profits and was expanding its sales considerably.

The Local Firm*

The planning orientation of a typical local firm can best be characterized as being medium to short range. The typical firm in this category planned for a span of one or two years. The resulting plans were less comprehensive and detailed. Review procedures, as well as strict adherence to planned targets, were taken less seriously than in the United States subsidiary. There was relatively less participation of other echelons of managers in the planning activities.

Policy making was less formalized and generally not documented. No serious attempts were made to use major policies as guidelines or control mechanisms; however, some other forms of control devices were used. They included quality control, cost control, and equipment maintenance.

The organizational set-up in this type of firm was not very different from that of the United States subsidiary. For example, the various divisions and departments within the firm were organized on the basis of such major

---

*The local firm and the United States subsidiary were comparable in size, technology, and product lines.

business functions as production, sales, and purchasing. Similar to the United States subsidiary, the local firm had five to seven departments. The departmental lines were not clear-cut, however. The local firm generally did not use specialized staff personnel, although a service department was used to some extent.

Authority definition was very unclear and diffuse. The degree of decentralization was low as compared to the United States subsidiary. The leadership style could best be characterized as paternalistic. Trust and confidence in subordinates was low.

Human resource management practices were least developed. The Personnel Department itself was not organized as a separate unit, and a qualified and trained personnel manager was not employed. No attempts were made to formulate human resource policies.

Job evaluation techniques, however, were used in some form or another. Some attempts were also made to formulate selection and promotion criteria. Training and development programs were poor and used only for blue-collar employees. Compensation and motivational techniques used were simple and mainly monetary in nature.

Management effectiveness in the local firm was poor compared to the United States subsidiary. For example, employee morale in this firm was moderate, absenteeism high, turnover low, and productivity low.

In terms of high-level managers, the local firm was less successful in attracting and retaining trained managerial and technical personnel. Interdepartmental relationships among different departments ranged from "somewhat cooperative" to "poor." Managers of this type of firm seemed to stress optimization of the departmental goals in contrast to the firm's overall goals and objectives. Also, the typical local firm was not effectively using its high-level managers and was experiencing considerable difficulties in adapting to environmental changes. Growth in sales and profits, however, was average in this type of firm.

This overall profile of management practices and effectiveness of the United States subsidiary and the local firm is outlined in Table 8-5.

As one can note from this table, the local companies are more traditional, "sleeper-like,"* whereas the United States subsidiaries exhibit more modern, "thruster-like" characteristics. Why so? It is tempting to provide a cultural

---

*This terminology is derived from Gater, et al.'s study of British firms. For a comparison of the results of their study with the present study, see Anant R. Negandhi, "Convergence in Organizational Practices: An Empirical Study of Industrial Enterprises in Developing Countries," *Organizations Alike and Unlike*, eds. C. J. Lammers and D. J. Hickson (London: Routledge and Kegan Paul, 1979), pp. 323–345. For Gater's study see A. D. Gater, et al., *Attitudes in British Management: A PEP Report* (Harmondsworth, England: Penguin, 1964).

Table 8-5 Profiles of management practices and effectiveness of the United States subsidiary and the local firm

Elements of management practices and effectiveness	United States subsidiary	Local firm
1. Recruitment of potential managers	Formally and systematically done. Open-minded on all potential sources for managerial personnel.	Done on ad hoc basis. Restricted to small group of family members or relatives and friends.
2. Recruitment of middle and senior managers	Formally and systematically done. Provided opportunity for advancement within the firm.	Done on ad hoc basis. No systematic attempt at providing opportunity for advancement within the firm.
3. Management education	Formally done. Regularly used outside training courses or personnel.	Done on irregular or ad hoc basis.
4. Attitudes toward management development	Visualized as necessary element in company's growth and survival.	Considered as unnecessary expense.
5. Treatment of existing management	Continuous evaluation. Ready to demote or fire second-rate and promote young and qualified.	Little or no evaluation. Adherence to seniority.
6. Delegation by senior management	Delegate authority to subordinates.	Unwilling to delegate authority.
7. Management structure	Decentralized: individual positions are well defined and specified. Organization charts and manuals used.	Centralized: individual positions are not well defined; authority line diffused. Organization charts not widely used.
8. Management communication	Free flow of communication encouraged and demanded.	A great deal of secrecy and hoarding of information at all levels.
9. Use of management consultants	Used frequently.	Not used.
10. Interfirm comparison at home and overseas	Done on regular basis.	Not done at all or done on ad hoc basis.
11. Market share	Constant awareness of market share.	Not much concern.

Table 8-5 Continued

Elements of management practices and effectiveness	United States subsidiary	Local firm
12. Objective of firm	Growth and profits.	Profits.
13. Assessment of performance	Measured in terms of growth, long-term potential, human resources, profits, assets, and sales.	Measured in terms of short-term profits.
14. Diversification	Considered as desired objectives.	Undertaken as necessary evil.
15. Future of firm	Evaluated on long-term basis.	Evaluated on short-term or medium-term basis.
16. Long-range planning	Five- or ten-year spans. Systematic and formalized.	One- or two-year spans. Done on ad hoc basis.
17. Use of budgetary control	Used with considerable emphasis on its importance to the firm.	Done haphazardly with less emphasis on its importance for the firm.
18. Review of operations	Regularly undertaken with feedback mechanism well developed.	Done on ad hoc basis with no feedback mechanism.
19. Capital budgeting	Regularly done.	Done on ad hoc basis or not done at all.
20. Relationship of sales to production	Production facilities are planned on creating greater demands for the goods.	Production is based on serving short-supply market conditions (seller's market).
21. Advertising and public relations	Seen as useful in creating public image of the company.	Used only as a necessary evil.
22. Capacity, efficiency, and productivity	Assessed on regular basis.	No regular assessment.
23. Plant capacity	Used at the fullest possible level; regular maintenance.	Used as seems appropriate by top executive without objective assessment. Irregular maintenance.

Continued

Table 8-5 Continued

Elements of management practices and effectiveness	United States subsidiary	Local firm
24. Buying function	Conceived as managerial function.	Conceived as clerical function.
25. Suppliers	Conceived as partners in progress.	Conceived as a necessary evil.
26. Operational research techniques	Uses various techniques to optimize plant capacity.	Regards various techniques as status symbols.
27. Creation of positive labor relations	Conceived as management responsibility.	Conceived as government/labor union responsibility.
28. Assessment of good labor relations	Done on regular and systematic basis.	Done on ad hoc basis.
29. Grievance procedure	Carefully worked out, agreed by all parties and adhered to.	Roughly drawn up and not always followed.
30. Unions	Conceived as having constructive role to play.	Conceived as a nuisance.
31. Workers' output	Belief that employees will give their best when treated as being responsible.	Belief that employees are lazy.
32. Personnel function	Conceived as top priority.	Conceived as clerical chaos.
33. Training and education of work force	Conceived as necessary element of organizational activities; variety of training.	Conceived as a necessary evil. Mostly on-the-job training for the blue-collar employee.
34. Shortage of skilled labor and/or other labor	Not taken for granted. Action to train up semi-skilled and unskilled personnel.	Acceptance of shortage of skilled employees as limiting factor.
35. Method of payment	Based on objective criteria. Attempts to pay higher than market rate.	Based on what they can get by with the minimum.
36. Employees	Conceived as a resource.	Conceived as a necessary evil.

Table 8-5 Continued

Elements of management practices and effectiveness	United States subsidiary	Local firm
37. Relationship of Research Department to production	Close cooperation between two units.	Research Department usually nonexistent, or if it exists operates as separate unit.
38. Problems of firm	Conceived as an opportunity to undertake cost efficiency.	Conceived as fault of others—government, labor union, competition.
39. Unprofitable products	Ready to drop unless found useful for the long-range growth.	Unable to find out in the first place.
40. Competition	Conceived as healthy and necessary.	Conceived as unfair and destructive.

Source: A. R. Negandhi, *Organization Theory in an Open System*, New York: Dunellen, 1975, pp. 250–255.

explanation for the differences in management practices between developed and underdeveloped countries. However, the study shows that the economic and political factors were far more important as determinants of managerial practices. This is illustrated by referring to the impact of external factors on planning and on decision making. In cross-cultural management studies, the relationships among economic, political, and legal conditions, on the one hand, and planning in firms, on the other, have been hinted at by a number of scholars. Davis,[38] in his study of Chile, Lauterbach,[39] in his study of a number of Latin American countries, and Lauter,[40] in Turkey, have indicated a relationship between economic, political, and legal conditions and the planning function. Davis reports: "In answer to the question 'How far into the future does formal planning in your enterprise extend?' more than half of the interviewed answered: 'that depends on how long it is before the next election.'"[41]

To inquire about the impact of economic, political, and legal factors on planning, the executives were asked to identify the most important environmental variables affecting their long-range planning activities.

A seller's market, governmental control of prices, the availability of raw materials, inflation, and the political situation were mentioned frequently by these executives. There were some differences in the rank-order of importance of these factors among the different countries. Executives in Latin American countries, for example, were worried about political instability and inflation, whereas those in the Far East showed more concern over the existence of a seller's market. Overall, the findings show that the majority of the executives interviewed in Argentina, Brazil, India, The Philippines, Taiwan, and Uruguay indicate that the seller's market condition in those countries makes planning less necessary for firms to achieve high profitability. In such a situation all firms make high profits regardless of their managerial practices.

As to decision making, many writers affirm that the authority structure of industrial enterprises (and, for that matter, governmental agencies and other social organizations) in developing countries is highly centralized.

In our interviews with top-, middle-, and lower-level executives in United States subsidiaries and local companies in the six developing countries studied, the impact of the following factors on centralization was frequently mentioned: the owner-manager situation; the seller's market condition; the governmental interference and controls on imports of raw materials, machinery, and foreign exchange; and the lack of experience with the delegation of authority.

The typical mentality of an owner-manager is well expressed by an executive in Uruguay: "I do not believe in anybody having anything to do with management except my own family. There is a clear distinction in my organization. My family is on one side, and the rest of the salaried and hourly personnel are on the other side."

Coupled with the owner-manager situation, the seller's market provides much less incentive to the owner-manager to delegate authority to specialized and qualified employees. Under such a condition, huge profits are made regardless of the cost and quality of products. However, the owner-manager takes this positive profit picture as a sign of success as a manager or decision maker. And why not? After all, in a capitalist economy we preach that the primary role of the business enterprise is to "serve" its stockholders (the owner). As a sole stockholder, the owner-manager does exactly this. The owner-manager's only mistake is that he or she has not learned to distinguish between short-run and long-term profitability. Unfortunately, the seller's market itself seems to be a "long-term" proposition in many of the developing countries. In this matter, it is doubtful that, under a similar (seller's) market condition, the counterpart owner-manager in industrially developed countries will be able to distinguish between short-term and long-term objectives.

Impact of Sociocultural Factors on Management

Although a number of studies have underscored the importance of sociocultural factors, the actual empirical evidence on the impact of these factors on management practices and effectiveness is less clear-cut. On the other hand, the similarities in management practices seem to be more striking. This is not to say that environmental and sociocultural variables do not influence management practices and effectiveness. However, research in a number of developing and developed countries suggests a necessity for rethinking this issue at this stage. Although these studies revealed some impact of sociocultural variables on employee morale and interpersonal relationships, it also indicated that many of the elements of management practices, such as planning, organizational decision making, and controlling were both under the purview of management control and constrained only by technological and market conditions. And these technological and environmental factors are themselves becoming similar in the shrinking technological world, giving further impetus to convergence in organizational practices.

Studies also reveal that the similarities in management practices lead to similar organizational effectiveness. For example, the findings indicated that the differences in a firm's effectiveness could largely be explained by the differences in their management practices. More specifically, Spearman's rank correlation between management practices and effectiveness was 0.81; decentralization in decision making and effectiveness was 0.91; and human resources management practices and effectiveness was 0.63.[42]

Such relationships compel one to support the convergence thesis. In this respect, it is appropriate to conclude this section by quoting two of the pioneering cross-cultural management researchers who were largely instrumental in highlighting the *difference* and nonconvergence thesis, and who express hope for future convergence.

First, Harbison and Myers, in studying the management development processes in twelve countries, had echoed that "Organization building has its logic . . . which rests upon the development of management . . . and there is a general logic of management development which has applicability both to advanced and industrializing countries in the modern world."[43] Second, almost three decades ago, Farmer and Richman echoed:

> We began this book by observing differences in management between nations. . . . As the general similarity of men everywhere is recognized, and as managerial and technological necessity presses all types of culture toward a common road, nations everywhere become more similar. Not all countries will arrive at the end of the trip at the same time, . . . but those who make the journey may, to their own surprise, discover that the road of others was not so different after all. Studies in comparative management at the time will be largely obsolete. . . . Instead of differences, we shall find similarities, because the logic of technology and management will lead all to the same general position.[44]

Although the road may be becoming one, it may be necessary to examine the changing contextual and environmental conditions and their implications on the transferability of management practices and knowledge.

Need for a New Focus

Earlier studies of management in cross-cultural settings used the focus of transferring advanced management practices, techniques, methods, and knowledge from industrialized to developing countries. The logic here was to accelerate and hasten the economic and industrial developments in developing countries. As discussed earlier, this pragmatic orientation attracted many scholars to undertake cross-cultural management studies. However, this focus requires some rethinking.

During the 1950s and 1960s, our orientation for transferring management practices was conceived as a one-way street from developed to developing countries, particularly from the United States to elsewhere. As shown in Figure 8-1, the focus was from here to there and from us to them.

A decade of recession, soaring inflation, near-depression levels of unemployment, the deteriorating competitiveness of many industries, sliding labor productivity, and the painful adjustment to the powers of the oil-producing countries have raised serious questions concerning the superiority of United States management practices and knowledge. The recent popularity of the Japanese management system and the rise of Japanese pundits exemplify this point.[45] Consequently, the focus needs to be enlarged. As shown in Figure 8-2, we need to conceive the transfer process in multiple

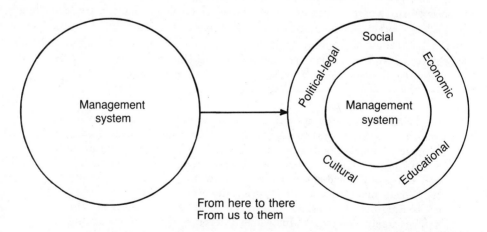

Figure 8-1 Transfer of the management of knowledge issues: Yesteryear orientation

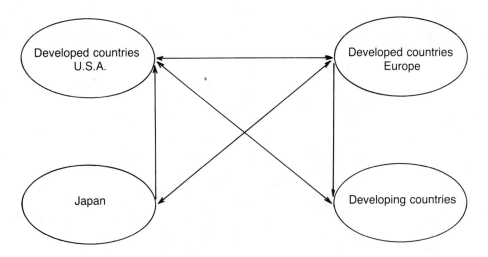

Figure 8-2 Transfer process–Multiple directions

directions–from the United States to other developed countries and vice versa; from the United States to Japan and vice versa; and from developed countries to developing countries and vice versa. Obviously, it will be a more complicated model than the previous one. But this is the reality we need to face if we are interested in undertaking socially useful and relevant research.

To simplify our task, perhaps, we may need to draw up some clear-cut demarcation lines concerning management practices. It may be useful to divide organizational and management practices into three distinct layers[46]:

1. Technical core activities (e.g., planning and control)
2. Social system (e.g., interpersonal relationships)
3. Institutional or external relationships (e.g., establishing legitimacy)

As shown in Figure 8-3, technical core activities of organizations are greatly influenced by contextual variables, economic conditions, and managerial policies; the social system within the organization may be dependent on sociocultural factors, whereas the institutional or external activities may be more influenced by political, legal, and economic conditions. Conceived in this manner, one can argue that the United States' management practices at technical core activities are more advanced, and others may benefit by learning from them. With respect to the institutional or external relationship of organizations with the outside public, Japan, Europe, and even the developing countries may have some useful lessons for the United States. Managing the social system within the organization is indeed a twilight zone

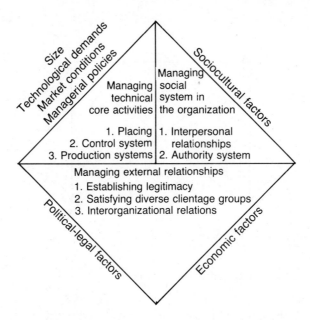

Figure 8-3 Transfer process—System model

where much research is needed before one can talk about transferring management practices.

International Managers for the Home Office[47]

As noted earlier, the internationalization of United States businesses has resulted in two different phenomena: (1) decline in the number of expatriate managers sent overseas, and (2) the need for the internationalization of the domestic managers to deal with overseas business operations. How to develop globally oriented, domestic managers is, thus, a critical question for many companies. Kobrin's study provides the following guidelines.

Sensitivity and Learning a Foreign Language

First, it would be important to develop a sensitivity and understanding to operate effectively in a wide variety of environments. This international expertise could be developed through personal experience, travel, or overseas assignments. Overseas assignments would probably be the most effective, because it will help language competency and an understanding of foreign values.

Besides knowledge of the country or information about economic, political, and social environments abroad, managers will need to develop a sensitivity to time and place. Specifically, they will have to understand how to operate overseas, and how to deal effectively with and communicate to a wide variety of people. To familiarize the above skills, probably one would have to first recognize the differences and similarities between the home country and the rest of the world, then learn specific dimensions of the culture, social customs, business practices, and political and economic organizations. In a practical sense, a good way to start to develop international expertise is to learn the language.

How Important Is International Expertise?

The economic development stage, as well as the cultural difference, largely determine the level of difficulty in adapting to local environments or mastering international expertise. However, managerial and technical capabilities also appear to be important. In spite of the importance of international expertise, it is not a substitute for basic technical, functional, and managerial skills.

Therefore, the real issue is how important the incremental contributions made by international expertise are. One needs to consider international expertise as a part of international competitiveness. For example, the recent declining competitiveness of many United States industries in the international market, compared with those of either European and Japanese firms, can be explained in two ways: (1) narrowing the technological gap, and (2) a lack of international expertise of United States firms relative to their competitors. Both European and Japanese companies have made considerably more efforts in acquiring international expertise than have United States firms.

Adequate preparation for both functional skills and for international expertise are required to become a successful international manager in the future. Three particular recommendations are suggested for students who wish managerial careers in large MNCs: (1) having some language competency; (2) developing an unbiased understanding of the differences in political, economic, social, and cultural systems through taking a wide range of courses, such as comparative politics, economics, and anthropology; and (3) developing an ability to analyze and synthesize creatively these differences on one's own.

Summary

This chapter discussed the management of managers for international corporations. The topics analyzed were sources of recruitments for overseas managers, using the home country's managerial practices in foreign subsidiaries, and training domestic managers for global business.

The research studies reviewed indicated the critical importance of having a knowledge of foreign language, the society's culture, and the business practices of the host countries.

With respect to using the home country's management practices, studies show a trend toward convergence in organizational practices.

The internationalization of business will necessitate preparing domestic managers who are globally oriented.

Case

The Amin Ball Bearing Company case explores the issue of promoting a foreign local personnel in a top management position of the subsidiary. For a Japanese company, this is the most difficult problem because of its organizational culture and control system. The case highlights the pros and cons of promoting a local national.

Case 8-1 ═══════════════════════════════════

Amin Ball Bearing Company

As Japan Airlines Flight 443 took off from Frankfurt, West Germany, for
Tokyo, Japan, Mr. Toshihara Asaka, Managing Director of the German subsidiary, settled down and began daydreaming about the critical proposal he
was to present to the Chairman and the Board of the parent company in
Tokyo.

The issue was to promote the German citizen, Mr. Alfons Tressel, to the
position of Managing Director. Currently, Mr. Tressel is a manager responsible for personnel and public relations functions.

The main reason for promoting Mr. Tressel to the top executive's position in the largest subsidiary in Western Europe was to defend the company
effectively before the European Common Market Commission. The firm has
been sued by various European countries, mainly West Germany, France,
and Sweden, for dumping its products in E.E.C. countries. Although the current cases are being handled by individual national courts, the European Common Market Commission decided to initiate an inquiry concerning the dumping of products by several Japanese companies, particularly electronics and
ball bearing firms. It was widely believed that this inquiry would influence
considerably the subsequent court's deliberations on this issue.

Mr. Asaka has appeared before the commission to defend the charge of
dumping. Although he was fluent in both English and German, and provided
enough cost and pricing data, he was not sure about his personal rapport and
the credibility of his arguments. He was now firmly convinced that Japanese
expatriate managers will not be effective in defending this and other cases
against the company in Europe.

The material for this case was collected by the author and Professor Martin Welge
for their studies on multinational companies, reported in *Beyond Theory Z: Global
Rationalization Strategies of American, German, and Japanese Multinational Companies* (Greenwich, Conn.: JAI Press, 1984). Although the material used in the case
is factual, the actual company's and the persons' names are changed to preserve confidentiality. © Copyright by Anant R. Negandhi, 1985.

As the jet climbed up to its normal altitude of 35,000 feet, Mr. Asaka was in deep contemplation of weighing the pros and cons of recommending the promotion of Mr. Alfons Tressel to the Chairman and the Board.

In terms of advantages, he felt that a German citizen, with his native language and understanding of the European culture, environment, and business practices, would have more rapport and credibility with the European Commission and other officials of national governments.

He would also be able to collect the relevant data and required information concerning local competitors through various sources.

In addition, by promoting Mr. Tressel to the top position in the German subsidiary, he would be able to set the stage to internationalize the company's overseas operations.

The main disadvantage of promoting a local citizen to the top position in an overseas subsidiary concerns the question of confidentiality and loyalty of a foreign person to the Japanese firm. Mr. Asaka kept murmuring to himself, "To what extent can the foreigner be trusted with the company's technological secrets and strategic moves?" He was not sure how to answer this question and was worried about facing the Chairman and the Board on this matter.

He was also concerned that the pressures from the European Commission and government officials may weaken the ability and motivation of Mr. Tressel to defend the company's case.

He was further worried that Mr. Tressel may not be able to resist a better offer from local competitors, thus deserting the company midway in their serious fight with the local competitors.

Lastly, Mr. Asaka, by promoting Mr. Tressel, was uncertain about the snowball impact on other European, Canadian, United States, and Australian subsidiaries. If the other subsidiaries were to promote local persons to top positions, the headquarters may lose control over the subsidiaries.[1]

Thinking about these problems, Mr. Asaka fell asleep and was dreaming about presenting his proposal to the Chairman and the Board. When he was awakened for dinner by a flight attendant, asking him whether he would like Terriyaki beef or curry chicken, he exclaimed, "Mr. Tressel!"

---

[1] A number of studies have clearly demonstrated that the Japanese companies send proportionally a much greater number of Japanese expatriates to manage their subsidiaries overseas as compared to their counterparts, the Americans and Europeans. This means that the *informal* and *personal* control, in contrast to *formal* and *impersonal* control, is more important to the Japanese companies. For further information on the personnel policies of Japanese companies, see:

(A) Anant R. Negandhi, *Management and Economic Development: The Case of Taiwan* (The Hague: Martinus Nijhoff, 1973), pp. 77–97.
(B) Anant R. Negandhi with B. R. Baliga, *Quest for Survival and Growth: A Comparative Study of American, European, and Japanese Multinationals* (New York: Praeger Publishers, 1979), pp. 54–61.
(C) Anant R. Negandhi, G. S. Eshghi and E. C. Yuen, 'Management Practices of Japanese Subsidiaries Overseas," *California Management Review*, Vol. XXVII, Summer 1985, pp. 93–105.

About the Company

Amin Ball Bearing (ABB) Company operates six ball bearing plants overseas, which serve international markets, and maintains seven overseas sales subsidiaries and six representative offices. These offices are engaged in sales of the company's products that are either imported from Japan or manufactured in overseas plants. The underlying management orientation of internationalization has resulted in increasing overseas investment and in growing international operations.

At the end of 1984, ABB operated one plant each in Australia, Brazil, and the United Kingdom. The Australian and Brazilian plants started operation in 1970 and 1972, respectively. In 1974, ABB entered a joint venture with a United States ball bearing company, and in 1976, ABB acquired all of the shares in this company from its United States partner. To the two existing plants of the United States Amin Ball Bearing Companies, ABB added a third, in Iowa, in late 1977. The Iowa plant employs nearly 250 people. In May 1978, another plant, located in Bradford in the United Kingdom, was acquired, employing about 200 people. These overseas plants have experienced a steady increase in demand for their products.

To strengthen the sales activities of their offices in Europe, ABB built a fully computerized warehouse in Ratingen, West Germany. This new facility would permit ABB to become even more responsive to user needs and enhance the reliability of deliveries. In its operations overseas, the ABB Company employs a total of nearly 2,300 local people. Operating in close coordination with the main plants in Japan, ABB plants and offices abroad are trying to respond quickly and flexibly to user needs with competitively priced products. The long-range objective of ABB is to continue to expand its investments overseas and work toward consolidating its position as an international enterprise.

As ABB's overseas operations have continued to expand, the company has moved to use overseas sources of capital to an increasing degree. Financial requirements include short-term finance for purchasing inventories and other working capital, financing for plant exports, and funds for overseas investments. ABB's goal is to acquire the flexibility needed to raise required funds from the most advantageous sources around the world. ABB's first issue of guaranteed notes, amounting to U.S. $20 million, was made in the Euromarket, in September 1976. Another issue for SFr 30 million was made in February 1978.

As far as technology development is concerned, ABB's research and development activities have been centered on:

1. Developing new product technologies
2. Developing production technologies to improve productivity
3. Using computer systems in product design, inventory control, and distribution

In product and technology development, ABB has established a strong reputation because of its close working relationship with end users. Pur-

Table 8-6 Selected financial data of Amin Ball Bearing Company (thousands of US $)

	1984	*1983*
Sales	672,734	599,568
Net income	6,283	5,460
Cash dividends	7,358	6,412
Total assets	872,823	857,554
Shareholders' equity	180,556	175,633
Paid in capital	63,289	55,912

chasers of ABB products buy not only ball bearings and other "hardware" products of the company, but also, frequently, a complete package of technical service and advice, or "software." Some specific examples of the results of ABB's research and development activities in the past have been the development of a high-precision ball bearing and grease for use in videotape recording (VTR) units. VTR bearings require a high degree of precision to assure operation with a minimum of variation in speed under any operating condition and, thus, prevent distortion of the video image. Development of VTR bearings is expected to continue to contribute to sales growth. (See Table 8-6 for additional financial data on Amin Ball Bearing Company.)

Discussion Questions

1. What are the sources of recruitment for overseas assignments? Discuss the advantages and disadvantages of each alternative.
2. Compare and contrast the Japanese management style with the United States management style. Also discuss the strengths and weaknesses of each style.
3. Today, some cross-cultural studies suggest that management style and organizational effectiveness are heavily influenced by the local sociocultural environments. Also, many large firms in developing countries make more profits than the similarly sized United States firms with better management practices and a scientific planning system. Why is that so?
4. Discuss the multiple transfer process in transferring management practices internationally? Give some examples of multiple transfer processes.

Endnotes

1. See, for example, "*Worldwide Executive Compensation*," Business International, New York, 1967.
2. Arvind V. Phatak, *International Dimensions of Management* (Boston: Kent Publishing Company, 1983), p. 92.

3. James S. Byrne, "Who Will Save the Boodle Boys?" *Forbes*, February 6, 1977, p. 34. Quoted in John D. Daniels, Ernest W. Ogran, Jr., and Lee H. Radebaugh, *International Business: Environments and Operations* (Reading, Mass.: Addison-Wesley, 1982), p. 614.

4. Burton W. League, *Selecting and Orienting Staff for Service Overseas* (New York: The Conference Board, 1976), p. 2.

5. "What It Costs to Hire Good Executive Talent for U.S. Subsidiaries Overseas," *Business Abroad*, November 27, 1967 pp. 18–22.

6. James C. Baker, and John N. Ivancevich, "Multinational Management with American Expatriates," *Economic and Business Bulletin* 23, 1 (Fall 1970): 36.

7. Rosalie L. Tung, "U.S. Multinationals: A Study of Their Selection and Training Procedures for Overseas Assignments," *Academy of Management Proceedings* (1979): 298.

8. Anant R. Negandhi, and S. Benjamin Prasad, *Comparative Management* (New York: Appleton-Century-Crofts, 1971).

9. Anant R. Negandhi, and B. R. Baliga, *Quest for Survival and Growth* (New York: Praeger Publishers, 1979), pp. 53–57.

10. For details on operational problems of Japanese multinationals, see ibid., pp. 18–20.

11. W. K. Brandt, and James N. Hulbert, *A Empresa Multinational No Brasil* (Rio de Janeiro: Zahan Editors, 1977), p. 45.

12. Lawrence G. Franko, "Who Manages Multinational Enterprises?" *Columbia Journal of World Business* 8, 2 (Summer 1973): 30–42.

13. This section is drawn from our earlier work, Richard F. Gonzalez, and Anant R. Negandhi, *The United States Overseas Executive: His Orientations and Career Patterns* (East Lansing, Mich.: Institute for International Business and Economic Development Studies, 1967), and from Anant R. Negandhi, "Profile of the American Overseas Executive," *California Management Review* 9, 2 (1966): 57–64.

14. H. Cleveland, G. J. Mangone, and J. Clarke Adams, *The Overseas Americans* (New York: McGraw-Hill Book Co., 1960), p. 124.

15. John Fayerweather, *The Executive Overseas* (Syracuse, NY: Syracuse University Press, 1959), pp. 179–182.

16. Harlen Cleveland, "The Pretty Americans: How Wives Behave Abroad," *Harper's Magazine*, March 1959.

17. Harold Stiglitz, "Effective Performance Overseas," *International Executive* 5, 2 (Spring 1963): 9–10. See also Paul H. Kiernan, "What it Takes to be a Successful International Manager," *International Executive* 5, 4 (Fall 1963): 3–4.

18. Cleveland, Mangone, and Adams, *Overseas*, pp. 99–102.

19. John C. Shearer, *High-Level Manpower in Overseas Subsidiaries* (Princeton, NJ: Industrial Relations Section, Princeton University, 1960), pp. 73–74.

20. Gonzalez and Negandhi, *United States*, pp. 102–104.

21. Ibid., p. 111.

22. Among others, my colleagues and I have done considerable work in this area. See Negandhi and Prasad, *Comparative Management* (New York: Appleton-Century-Crofts, 1971); Anant R. Negandhi, *Management and Economic Development: The Case of Taiwan* (The Hague: Martinus Nijhoff, 1973); Anant R. Negandhi, *Organization Theory in an Open System* (New York: Dunellen, 1975); Bernard D. Estafen, "An Empirical Experiment in Comparative Management: A Study of the Transferability of American Management Policies and Practices into Firms Operating in Chile" (Ph.D. diss., University of California at Los Angeles, 1967); Andrew J. Papageorge, "Transferability of Management: A Case Study of

the United States and Greece" (Ph.D. diss., University of California at Los Angeles, 1967); Filemon C. Flores, Jr., "The Applicability of American Management Know-How to Developing Countries: The Philippines" (Ph.D. diss., University of California at Los Angeles, 1968); Floyd G. Boseman, "Transfer of Management Process: A Case Study of Industrial Enterprises in Mexico," (Ph.D. diss., Kent State University, 1972); and Jack L. Simonetti, "Transfer of Management Process: A Case Study of Industrial Enterprises in Italy," (Ph.D. diss., Kent State University, 1972).

23. R. D. Meade, and J. D. Whittaker, "A Cross-Cultural Study of Authoritarianism," *Journal of Social Psychology* LXXII (1967): 3–7.

24. R. D. Meade, "An Experimental Study of Leadership in India," *Journal of Social Psychology* LXXII (1967): 35–43.

25. G. V. Barrett, and E. C. Ryterband, "Life Goals of United States and European Managers," *Proceedings, XVIth International Congress of Applied Psychology* (Amsterdam: Swets & Zeitlinger, 1969), pp. 413–418.

26. M. H. R. Hoekstra, "Corporate Objectives: A Cross-Cultural Study of Simulated Managerial Behavior," *Proceedings, XVIth International Congress of Applied Psychology* (Amsterdam: Swets & Zeitlinger, 1969), pp. 429–435.

27. K. M. Thiagarajan, *A Cross-Cultural Study of the Relationships Between Personal Values and Managerial Behavior* (Technical Report 23, NONR N00014-67-A, Rochester, New York: University of Rochester, Management Research Center, 1968).

28. K. M. Thiagarajan, and B. M. Bass, "Differential Preferences for Long vs. Short-Term Payoffs in India and the United States," *Proceedings, XVIth International Congress of Applied Psychology* (Amsterdam: Swets & Zeitlinger, 1969), pp. 440–446.

29. *Ibid.*

30. G. W. England, "Personal Value Systems of American Managers," *Academy of Management Journal* X, 1 (1967) 53–68; G. W. England, and R. Koike, "Personal Value Systems of Japanese Managers," *Journal of Cross-Cultural Psychology* I (1970): 21–40; G. W. England, "Personal Value System Analysis as an Aid to Understanding Organizational Behavior: A Comparative Study in Japan, Korea and the United States" (paper presented at Exchange Seminar on Comparative Organizations, Amsterdam, The Netherlands, March 23–27, 1970).

31. Eugene McCann, "An Aspect of Management Philosophy in the United States and Latin America," *Academy of Management Journal* VII, 2 (1964): 149–152.

32. Eugene McCann, "Anglo-American and Mexican Management Philosophies," *MSU Business Topics* XVIII 3 (1970): 28–38.

33. *Ibid.*

34. Geert Hofstede, "Hierarchical Power Distance in Forty Countries," in *Organizations Alike and Unlike*, eds. C. J. Lammers and D. J. Hickson (London: Routledge and Kegan Paul 1979), pp. 97–119.

35. S. G. Reading and T. A. Martyn-Johns, "Paradigm Differences and Their Relation to Management, with Reference to South-East Asia," in *Organizational Functioning in a Cross-Cultural Perspective*, eds. G. W. England, A. R. Negandhi and B. Wilpert (The Kent State University Press: Comparative Administration Research Institute, 1979), pp. 103–125.

36. The material in this section is drawn from Negandhi, *Organization.*

37. Ibid.; Negandhi and Prasad, *Comparative Management*; Negandhi, *Management.*

38. Stanley M. Davis, "The Politics of Organizational Undevelopment: Chile," *Industrial and Labor Relations Review* 24, 1 (October 1970): 23–83.

39. Albert Lauterbach, *Enterprise in Latin America* (Ithaca, NY: Cornell University Press, 1966).

40. G. Peter Lauter, (1970), "Advanced Management Processes in Developing Countries: Planning in Turkey," *California Management Review* 13, 3 (Spring 1970): 7–12.
41. Stanley M. Davis, (1971b), "Politics and Organizational Underdevelopment in Chile," *Comparative Management*, ed. Stanley M. Davis (Englewood Cliffs, NJ: Prentice-Hall, 1971), pp. 173–187.
42. Negandhi, *Organization*, p. 268.
43. F. H. Harbison and C. A. Myers, *Management in the Industrial World* (New York: McGraw-Hill Book Co., 1959), p. 117.
44. R. N. Farmer and B. M. Richman, *Comparative Management and Economic Progress* (Homewood, Ill.: Irwin, 1965), p. 400.
45. William Ouchi, *Theory Z* (Reading, Mass.: Addison-Wesley, 1981).
46. Talcott Parsons, "Suggestions for a Sociological Approach to the Theory of Organizations," *Administrative Science Quarterly* 1, 1 (June 1956): 63–85.
47. This section is heavily drawn from recent a study by Stephen J. Kobrin, *International Expertise in American Business: How to Learn to Play with the Kids on the Street* (New York: Institute of International Education, 1984).

Additional Readings

Articles

England, George W. "Japanese and American Management: Theory Z and Beyond." *Journal of International Business Studies* XIV, 2 (Fall 1983): 131–142.

Kanungo, Rabindra N., and Wright, Richard W. "A Cross-Cultural Comparative Study of Managerial Job Attitudes." *Journal of International Business Studies* XIV, 2 (Fall 1983): 115–129.

Pucik, Vladimir. "White Collar Human Resource Management: A Comparison of the U.S. and Japanese Automobile Industries." *Columbia Journal of World Business* XIX, 3 (Fall 1984): 87–94.

Tung, Rosalie L. "Human Resource Planning in Japanese Multinationals: A Model for U.S. Firms?" *Journal of International Business Studies* XV, 2 (Fall 1984): 139–149.

Books

Kobrin, Stephen J. *International Expertise in American Business: How to Learn to Play with the Kids on the Street.* New York: Institute of International Education, 1984.

Ouchi, William. *Theory Z.* Reading, Mass.: Addison-Wesley, 1981.

Chapter 9

International Production and Logistics

This chapter will discuss the following major aspects and issues concerning the international production and logistics systems:

- The choice between exporting from the home country *versus* manufacturing overseas
- The important determinants of foreign direct investment: why do companies invest overseas?
- The choice of the level of technology to be transferred and used in overseas manufacturing operations
- Plant design and location decisions
- Decisions concerning the sourcing of raw materials, spare parts, and finished goods

In analyzing these issues, I will provide a comparative profile of United States, European, and Japanese practices.

Exporting *Versus* Manufacturing Overseas

In the years before World War II, international business was equated with international trade, in contrast to international investment in manufacturing operations. Even today, the international debate and dialogue for stabilizing world economic and financial conditions and for establishing economic balance between industrially developed and developing countries are being carried out within the framework of increasing and encouraging international trade.[1]

However, since World War II the character of international business has been changing rapidly. In the coming decades, the role and function of international investment is likely to assume a more significant position in international economic relations among the nations of the world. For many developing countries, the quest for economic progress has become the main preoccupation. Industrialization has been singled out as the most effective instrument for achieving such progress. Industrial development in the developing countries will require a massive transfer of technology and capital investment from the developed countries.[2]

At the same time, intensive competitive pressures in developed countries will necessitate the rationalization of production to reduce unit cost and increase efficiency. However, increasing unemployment and a concern for preserving and expanding jobs in industrialized countries may compel both the domestic and the foreign firms to manufacture locally in a given market. This will further increase intercountry investments in manufacturing operations. For example, a study by Buckley and Pearce shows that United States firms have very low ratios of exports compared to the total parent firm's production, because of the large United States market and the commitment to supply foreign markets through production abroad. In contrast, Swiss, Dutch, and Belgian firms manufactured goods in significantly higher proportion outside of their parent countries because of the small domestic markets and a lack of local resources. Japanese firms export more and produce less abroad.[3] However, a balance of payments surplus in Japan and chronic deficits in the United States and elsewhere, coupled with high unemployment in those countries, are forcing Japanese companies to establish manufacturing subsidiaries in developed countries. As indicated in Chapter 1, the foreign direct investment of developed countries has tripled between 1970 and 1980. The Japanese firms' direct foreign investment has increased twelvefold during 1970 to 1979, from a mere $3.3 billion to $38.9 billion. Among the leading foreign countries investing in the United States, West Germany and Japan recorded the highest growth. The number of West German firms operating in the United States increased from 203 in 1974 to 710 in 1978. The number of Japanese firms also grew, from 48 in 1976 to 203 in 1978.[4]

To sum up, the drive for industrialization in developing countries and intensive pressures to preserve and expand jobs in developed countries have compelled many international companies to either shift or to start additional production facilities abroad.

Research Studies on Foreign Direct Investment Decisions

Franko's study of European multinational companies shows that the majority of companies invested overseas to jump trade barriers[5] (i.e., governmental restrictions on imports). His study of European firms in the United States indicates that the companies were motivated to invest in the United States because of the competitive environments and the stimuli for succeeding in the world market.[6]

Yoshino's study of Japanese companies reveals that the main reasons for Japanese investment in developing countries were the import substitution policies of those countries that threatened Japanese exports.[7] Since the late 1960s, Japanese, as well as European and United States companies have been investing in Southeast Asia (Korea, Hong Kong, Singapore, Malaysia, and Taiwan) to take advantage of lower labor cost and to use these investments as "export platforms." As mentioned earlier, Japanese companies have recently invested in the United States and other developed countries to avoid protectionist sentiments and to reduce the balance of trade and payment surplus of Japan.

Crookell[8] classified the foreign investment by United States, European, and Japanese companies in developing countries into three categories:

1. Export-oriented
2. Market development
3. Import substitution

Export-oriented investment was intended to take advantage of lower labor costs for serving external markets. This type of investment was the most profitable and created fewer problems with host governments. Some examples of such investment include the major electronics firms from the United States, Europe, and Japan investing in Southeast Asia to assemble televisions, radios, and other electronic goods for exporting to the developed countries.

Market development investment was intended to gain an initial footing in potential future markets. This investment is conceived of in a long-term perspective and, consequently, short-term payoffs are minimal.

The import substitution investments are basically government initiated to achieve self-sufficiency for economic development. Those types of investment recorded good profitability and the highest rates of reinvestment because of the protected markets and the host governments' subsidies.

Product Life Cycle Model

Perhaps the most refined conceptual model to explain foreign direct investment is the one proposed by Professor Raymond Vernon and his colleagues at Harvard University.[9] The Product Life Cycle Theory (PLC) was discussed in Chapter 1. Briefly, it sought to explain the evolutionary nature of the firm's strategies from exporting from the home-based parent companies to manufacturing in and exporting from developing countries to the home countries and third countries' markets.

These five evolutionary stages were identified as follows:

1. Development of a product for the domestic market through research and development activities
2. Export of domestic products to overseas markets
3. Setting up manufacturing facilities in other industrialized countries to cope with increasing competition; export of goods from these subsidiaries to developing countries
4. Setting up manufacturing subsidiaries in developing countries
5. Export of goods to the United States and other markets in developed countries from the developing countries

The PLC model was helpful in explaining United States firms' foreign direct investment from the early 1950s to the mid-1970s. Since the 1973 oil crisis, the international environment has become more dynamic and complex; the PLC model is now less useful in explaining the outflow of foreign investments.[10] The European and Japanese investments in the United States and other developed countries are more defensive in nature and are being used as "counterthreats" to United States investments in their respective countries.[11]

Internalization of a Firm's Advantages and Strengths

Somewhat similar to the PLC theory, the internalization theory, refined by Dunnng et al.,[12] argues that the firm going overseas must have some important advantage and strength to compete successfully with local firms in the host countries. These strengths and advantages may be found in terms of capital resources, managerial and manufacturing knowledge, patent and copyrights on products and processes, and in the marketing network. Market conditions and socioeconomic, political, and legal environments play an important role in generating the specific advantages of multinational firms from various countries. For example, the high labor cost in the United States led many United States companies to innovate products and manufacturing processes that will be capital-intensive. In contrast, the traditionally lower labor costs and higher material costs in Japan and Europe have induced the firms to innovate products and processes that are material-saving and labor-intensive.[13]

Using the logic of this theory, Wells recently attempted to explain the foreign investments of firms from developing countries. The advantages of these firms lie in terms of their smaller size, scaled-down or "appropriate technology," lower overhead costs, and acceptance of local partners and lower profit margins.[14]

Lastly, Fayerweather's unification-fragmentation paradigm seeks to explain foreign direct investment on the basis of economic rationality and host government demands. Under the unification strategy, the firm attempts to achieve economies of scale by concentrating its production facilities at one or a few important centers. The efficiency criterion becomes the central focus for the unification strategy. Under the fragmentation strategy, the firm may forego the advantages of economies of scale and the efficiency criterion to satisfy the host government's demands for local manufacturing.[15]

However, as Fayerweather himself has pointed out, the unification-fragmentation theory has received very minimal attention from international business scholars. Although the economies of scale argument is relevant for a global perspective, very few firms seem to be thinking in terms of global markets. The global perspective requires product standardization. Given the differing consumers' tastes, preferences, and living standards in different countries, extreme standardization is a difficult, if not impossible, proposition for many consumer products. Some industrial products and machinery can be more easily standardized, but here also the socioeconomic and market differences are stumbling blocks for a worldwide standardization of products. In addition, the managerial task of coordinating a worldwide centralized product system is a nightmare, to say the least. Added to these problems are the increasing demands from the host countries for local manufacturing and exporting. Consequently, in the foreseeable future, we will find many international companies partially rationalizing production and logistics systems and partially manufacturing locally to satisfy those markets.

To summarize, no single theory can explain fully why foreign investments take place. There are a number of motivations for foreign investment. These include: (1) market opportunities, (2) tariff and import restrictions, (3) financial profitability in overseas markets, (4) sourcing considerations, (5) low cost of labor and raw materials, and (6) subjective preference for locating in a given country.[16]

Choice of Technology: The Issues At Stake

Once the international firm has made the decision to manufacture its products abroad, it faces a critical choice of deciding the nature of the technology to be transferred to overseas operations. As discussed earlier, one of the prime motives for many firms to go overseas is to exploit their specific advantages in technological and managerial knowledge. This rationale tends to favor the use and transfer of the firm's existing technology to overseas operations. As we will see in succeeding sections, many United States, European, and Japanese multinational companies have done exactly this, and for that matter, successfully. Multinational companies do not face many critical problems in transferring their home-based technology to industrialized countries. Even in the less developed countries (LDCs), governments are requiring the multinationals to bring the most modern technology. Their logic is to hasten industrial and economic development. However, faced with a high level of unemployment and surplus labor, the developing countries have begun to make ambivalent and contradictory demands for generating employment and, at the same time, demanding capital-intensive, sophisticated technology from foreign investors.

To put it simply, those who are concerned with employment (e.g., the Labor Minister) demand labor-intensive technology, whereas those who are concerned with industrial and economic development, balance of payment problems, and exports (e.g., Industry, Finance, and Commerce Ministers) opt for capital-intensive technologies. Obviously, as Wells has observed:

> The foreign investor designing a plant in a less-developed country has faced such conflicting pressures. Typically, his response has been to go ahead with the kind of plant he prefers to operate, i.e., one usually more automated than his domestic counterparts run.[17]

In making such a decision, he may be right, if the industry, commerce, and finance ministries are in a dominating position in the country. He may turn out to be dead wrong, if the top national authority (e.g., Prime Minister, President, or military ruler) is in favor of providing employment for the masses.

Thus, the technological choice is complex and controversial. In recent years, much has been written on this subject. In the following section, I will highlight the important aspects concerning this issue and pinpoint some practical solutions. In discussing this subject, the following elements are covered:

1. Determinants of technological choice
2. Impact of environmental factors on technological choice

3. Type of industry and technological choice
4. Actual practices of United States, European, and Japanese companies
5. Policy implications of choosing alternative technologies
6. Some practical solutions to this complex problem

Determinants of Choice of Technology

The literature and discussions on "appropriate technology" are concerned with two different aspects:

1. Scale of operation (small, medium, large)
2. Factor costs, particularly capital and labor costs in a given country

The scale argument is directly related to the size of the market, both domestic and international. The larger the market, the larger will be the plant, and vice versa. In a larger plant, there will be a greater possibility of using a production technique that is more capital-intensive, unless a larger plant consists of many smaller, identical machines. In this case, the firm will have a choice of using more labor and less capital. Morley and Smith's [18] intensive study in Brazil indicates that the size of the market is the most important determinant of a choice of production technique. Scale of output or market size will become a dominant factor under the following situations:

1. Production technique in which labor is an unimportant factor in production. For example, process technology, such as petrochemical and chemical industries, where machinery and technology are more or less given and substitutibility of labor for capital is minimal (except in handling of material and maintenance functions, more labor could be used).
2. Machines and processes, in which additions to capacity are discontinuous and involve large increments in capital cost; e.g., increasing production capacity for a petrochemical plant or automobile factory.
3. Economies of scale are reached at a very high level of output, but it is necessary to reach this point to manufacture a product at a reasonable price (e.g., automobile factory and many of the consumer durable goods).

The relative factor cost of labor *versus* capital will become more dominant under the following conditions:

1. Countries in which the labor cost is cheaper and cost of capital is higher. There will be a higher possibility of substituting capital

for labor, if the technological process is of "unit or batch type." That is, the product is produced in a small quantity and more or less custom designed (e.g., industrial machinery).

2. Whenever material handling and maintenance activities are proportionately higher than the actual production of goods, capital could be substituted for labor in countries in which labor costs are cheaper[19] (e.g., textile manufacturing, electronic goods assembly, clothing manufacturing in Southeast Asia and Latin American countries).

The scale and factor cost arguments are illustrated by following the actual practices of the multinational companies.

Although razor blade manufacturing involved capital-intensive technology, the Gillette Company, when threatened by the Malaysian government's policy concerning import restrictions, designed a "miniplant" that was less automated than the company's plants elsewhere. In so doing, it satisfied the need of the Malaysian government to employ more workers. In such a miniplant much of the packing is done by hand. Labor costs in Malaysia are cheap enough to keep costs comparable to larger plants. The company's experiment in Malaysia was so successful that the firm was encouraged to put up similar plants in The Philippines, Indonesia, Morocco, and Kenya.[20]

Similarly, the Dutch electronic company, Philips, designed a pilot plant for its foreign subsidiaries, which is small and less automated, to accommodate smaller markets and higher employment.

Industry Type and Choice of Technology

Types of industries play an important role in exercising options available to foreign investors in choosing technology. In some industries, such as textiles, footware, woodworking, pharmaceutical, and food processing, choices between labor- *versus* capital-intensive technology are possible. In certain other industries, such as petrochemicals, fertilizers, electric equipment, and heavy machinery, however, the choice to use labor-intensive technology is limited.[21] This suggests that a certain technology is "fixed" and cannot be changed.

Other Factors

If the factor prices are distorted, either by artificially increasing the labor wages through fringe and social benefits or reduced cost of capital by low interest loans, the international corporations are likely to use more automated technology, in spite of worker surplus. In the early 1960s, many of the developing countries, to attract foreign investment and sophisticated technology, were competing with each other to provide low-interest loans, subsidies, and tax exemptions.[22]

Empirical Studies

Sellers' markets and imperfect market conditions tend to distort the cost-price relationship. Under these conditions, foreign and local enterprises do not need to design an appropriate technology. Yeoman,[23] for example, found little difference between plants in developing and developed countries with respect to the amount of capital used per worker. Particularly, if there is a greater differentiation in products, either because of market power or advertising, there will be lower price-cost relationships. In such cases, the firm is more likely to use home-based technology. Yeoman found few technological adaptations in pharmaceutical firms and higher adaptation in home appliance firms. The former are found to be in imperfect market conditions, whereas the latter are in competitive market conditions. He observed that if the gains of reengineering and technological adaptation are fewer and the factor price conditions are distorted because of government subsidies, the multinational companies are likely to transfer home-based technologies intact.

Morley and Smith's study in Brazil indicates that in metalworking industries, although alternative techniques were available to foreign investors, the companies used capital-intensive technologies, because of the high cost of searching for labor-intensive technologies. The authors' overall conclusions are summarized as follows:

> Although there were substantial differences between multinational firms and their subsidiaries with respect to the capital used per employee, proportion of nonautomatic machinery and overall production methods, these differences arose because of the *scale* differentials (smaller plants in Brazil) rather than lower cost of labor.
>
> Most of the firms indicated that they would use the home country production techniques if the output levels in Brazil and the United States were the same. This choice will be made despite the fact that the cost of labor in Brazil is only one fifth of the United States labor cost.[24]

Similarly, Mason, in his studies of United States subsidiaries in Mexico and The Philippines, found little adaptation of the home-based technologies to suit local conditions. He also observed that the comparable local firms were likewise using high technology.[25] He argued that the multinational firms are not at fault in using advanced technology in developing countries. In his words:

> The foreign investor, unless he has a complete monopoly, still must face competition from either local firms or other foreign firms; consequently, selec-

tion of technology and the factor proportions available can be ignored at one's peril. Selection of technologies that are inappropriate seem to be rooted in distorted market conditions rather than an inability to substitute labor for capital (technology fixity) or an ignorance of differing market conditions on the part of investing firms.[26]

In a recent study of 120 subsidiaries of United States, German, and Japanese MNCs, four types of information concerning technology were obtained.[27]

1. The level of sophisticated technologies used by the subsidiary
2. The relative technology of the foreign subsidiaries compared to other firms in respective countries
3. The extent of technological transfers from the headquarters to subsidiaries and from subsidiaries to the headquarters
4. Research and development activities

The results on these four aspects of technology indicated a heavy reliance of the overseas subsidiaries on their respective headquarters. The subsidiaries are not only initially borrowing technology from their headquarters, but they are also depending on the headquarters' new technological knowledge. In other words, very minimal research and development activities are being carried out at the subsidiary levels. Some 60%, 80%, and 78% of the United States, German, and Japanese subsidiaries, respectively, did not spend significant amounts of money on this account. Among the three types of MNCs, a greater number of United States MNCs have begun to decentralize their research and development activities (some 40% of the United States subsidiaries claimed to spend between U.S. \$1 to 10 million on such activities, as compared to 11% and 23% by the German and Japanese subsidiaries). When one considers that the majority of the subsidiaries were located in highly industrialized countries, this amount of expenditure on research and development does not look impressive. Few subsidiaries have matured enough to transfer technological knowledge to their headquarters. Here also, the United States MNCs are the forerunners. About 11% of their overseas subsidiaries are involved in the reverse flow of technology. However, at the same time, overwhelmingly large proportions of their subsidiaries (88%) secure technologies from their headquarters (Figures 9-1 and 9-2).

Appropriate Technology: Debate and Advice

The debate on appropriate technology will continue as long as vast economic and technological differences exist between developed and developing countries. Multinational companies, by and large, will be using the home-based,

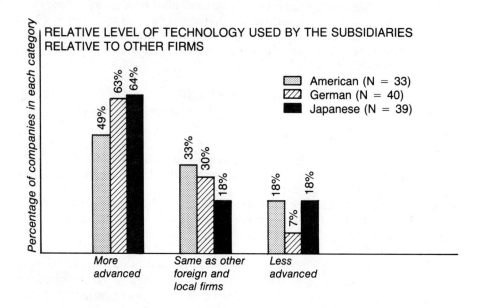

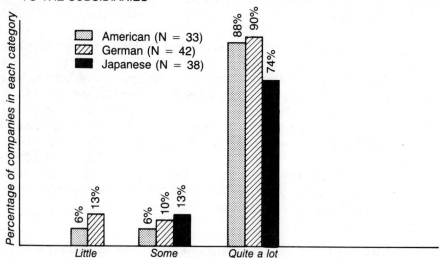

Figure 9-1 Subsidiary technology (*Source:* A. R. Negandhi, and M. Welge, *Beyond Theory Z* (Greenwich, Conn.: JAI Press, 1984), pp. 43–44.)

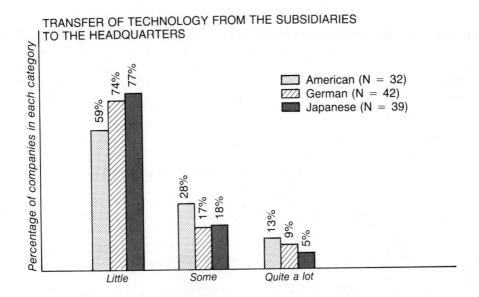

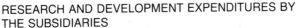

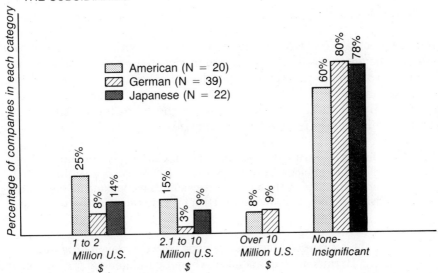

Figure 9-2 Subsidiary technology (*Source:* A. R. Negandhi, and M. Welge, *Beyond Theory Z* (Greenwich, Conn.: JAI Press, 1984), pp. 43–44.)

capital-intensive technologies, whereas the developing countries will be making ambivalent and contradictory demands for securing advanced technologies, and at the same time expecting foreign investors to generate high employment. In other words, the LDC would like to have its cake and eat it too. What is the solution? Research studies seem to offer two types of policy recommendations.

To The Developing Countries (LDCs)

1. Reduce imperfections in market conditions and distortions in factor prices
2. Do not increase labor costs by encouraging excessive social and welfare activities (e.g., housing, unemployment, and health care expenses)
3. Choose the products that are more labor-intensive (e.g., textile, woodworking, furniture, consumer products)

These recommendations, if followed, tend to keep LDCs in a dependent status and steps behind industrially developed countries in technological and industrial spheres. Consequently, such a dependency status will be a less acceptable formula for the majority of developing countries.

To Multinational Companies

A number of other researchers, and those concerned with rapid economic and industrial development in developing countries, have recommended a more acceptable solution to this complex problem of choosing technology. Among others, Baranson[28] and Wells[29] seem to represent many other such scholars and economic planners. Baranson came to the following conclusion in a number of his studies in developing countries:

> For developing countries, it is not an either/or choice between automation and handicraft technology. Technology should be viewed as a continuum of production techniques, with the choice depending on one hand on the scale and precision of production, and on the other on wage rates relative to capital cost.[30]

To avert the continuous technology gaps between developing and developed countries, Baranson recommends developing indigenous production and engineering systems.

These developments seem to be occurring already in a number of developing countries, such as Mexico, Argentina, Brazil, and India. As we saw in

Chapter 1, the rise of multinationals from these countries is largely the result of such indigenous developments in production techniques.

In a similar vein, Wells[31] recommended to the multinational companies not to overautomate their manufacturing plants in developing countries. To avoid doing so, the foreign investors should watch the following:

Engineers' bias. Usually, engineers, like any other professionals, are a self-perpetuating breed. They like to create their own "masterpieces" regardless of a given need. They would prefer machines to humans to produce consistent and high quality products. However, in so doing, the author warns ". . . the engineering mentality often creates a plant that is highly automated and, thus, inappropriate to a country with low wages and high unemployment."[32] To avoid such bias, management should insist on feasibility analyses of alternative technologies and production techniques.

Use labor intensive methods for material handling and transportation. In some industries, such as chemicals and petrochemicals, the technology is "given" and the firm may not have much choice but to use capital intensive techniques. However, here also material handling and transportation activities may be independent of production systems. In such cases capital could be substituted for by labor to create employment.

Innovate new types of reporting systems. Many multinational companies used uniform reporting systems, requiring foreign subsidiaries to provide data on a number of workers per unit of output to evaluate and compare the subsidiaries' efficiency. This type of evaluation is biased against labor-based techniques. To avoid such bias the firm should rather compare profitability and profits per capital invested.

Use machinery from developing countries. As mentioned earlier, many advanced developing countries, such as Korea, Brazil, Mexico, India, and Argentina have developed indigenous capabilities to design and manufacture machinery that is more appropriate for labor surplus countries. The foreign investors may be able to use such adaptable machinery without sacrificing quality standards of the products. As discussed earlier, companies such as Union Carbide, Gillette, and Philips have actively sought to use these sources for designing plants in developing countries.

To sum up, as Robinson has observed:

There is no generalizable objective function to determine appropriateness, just as there is no generalizable objective function determining how a nation should allocate its resources. Appropriateness depends upon the priority of objectives, whether they be maximum employment, technical efficiency, income equality, export development, national autarky or whatever. The phrase "appropriate technology," standing outside of a politically determined priority of objectives, is meaningless. Management should be mindful to this truth.[33]

Plant Design, Size, and Export Processing Zones

Decisions concerning the nature of plant design are directly related to the nature of the technology a firm is using in overseas manufacturing facilities. Usually, in capital-intensive industries and process-type manufacturing (e.g., petrochemicals, synthetic fibers, chemicals), the nature of the technology used will be more or less the same as the facilities in the home country. Consequently, there will be few variations in plant design and layout between the home country and the subsidiary abroad. However, if the time lag between the home country's facility and overseas plants is considerable, there will be a greater tendency to use more modern technology, probably including more automatic machinery, in the overseas plants.

As discussed in Chapter 1, the large bulk of foreign direct investment flow from the United States, Europe, and Japan took place after World War II. Consequently, the manufacturing facilities abroad are relatively new as compared to the home-based plants. Overall, the United States plants are twenty years old; the average age of plants in West Germany and Japan is twelve and ten years, respectively.[34]

More sophisticated plant designs and layouts were observed in comparative studies of 300 United States, European, and Japanese subsidiaries in a number of industrially developed and developing countries.[35] The major differences in plant design and layout between developed and developing countries were found in materials handling and transportation activities.

It was also observed that the Japanese factories in the United States and Western Europe were more automated than those in the developing countries. In many of the Southeast Asian countries (Singapore, Malaysia, Taiwan, Thailand), Japanese plants were less technologically advanced and more labor-intensive. Plant design and layout were comparable to local counterparts; that is, outmoded and clumsy, to say the least. Only in the last ten years or so have these plants been renovated to facilitate exporting to world markets. Such major differences in plant design, layout, and technology used by the Japanese MNCs in developed and developing countries reflect the influence of market conditions in those countries.

Plant Size

Plant size is basically a function of: (1) the market, (2) the firm's policy towards integration and achieving economies of scale, and (3) governmental attitudes and policies.

Markets in Singapore, Malaysia, and Colombia will obviously require smaller plants than in Mexico, India, Brazil, and the United States. However, if the former countries are used as "export platforms" for exporting goods to the home or third countries, then the plants in these countries may be even larger than those in big markets such as India or the United States. In the 1960s, many of the electronics firms from the United States, Europe, and Japan actively used many of the low-wage countries in Southeast Asia and Latin America as export platforms. Even today, many United States, European, and Japanese electronics firms, such as General Electric, General Instruments, Matsushita (Panasonic), Sony, and Telephonika (West Germany) have plants in Southeast Asian countries as large as or larger than those in their home countries. The emergence of export processing zones and their role and function are briefly summarized in the following section.

Export Processing Zones

In explaining the emergence of export processing zones (EPZs), Nash and Kelley state:

> The mode of integration of underdeveloped countries into the international economy has shifted from a base relying exclusively on the exploitation of primary resources and labor to one in which manufacturers have gained preponderance . . . more than a uniformly defined or geographically delimited concept, the export-processing zone provides a series of incentives and loosened restrictions for multinational companies by developing countries in their effort to attract foreign investment in export-oriented manufacturing.[36]

The authors go on to say:

> While the importance of export-processing zones is still reduced in the international context, they are important for what they suggest will become the norm in the organization of production.[37]

The following statistics may illustrate the phenomenon of export processing zones. There are over 600 foreign-owned plants operating in Mexico's border zone. United States, European, and Japanese companies are increasingly attracted to Mexico's wage rate of $1.00 to $1.50 per hour, compared to $8.00 to $10.00 in their home countries.[38]

Turning to the Southeast Asian countries, by 1970, Taiwan, South Korea, and Singapore each had attracted over U.S. $1 billion compared to less than U.S. $300 million in India. The combined domestic markets in the former countries are less than 10% of the Indian market. Obviously, the huge United States investments in the former countries were made to be used as "export platforms."

The United Nations' Industrial Development Organization reports the existence of 120 export processing zones, located in various parts of the world.

Approximately 2 million people are currently employed in EPZ plants, and many more are affected directly or indirectly by their existence. Recently, even China has joined the race by opening several export processing zones. Thus far, China has attracted U.S. $1 billion in foreign investment, mostly by overseas Chinese.[39]

Besides Southeast Asian and Latin American countries, Ireland, under her Industrial Development Act of 1969, has opened the door to encourage such foreign investments. The Industrial Development Agency maintains offices in many principal cities of industrialized countries to attract foreign investments. By 1980, there were 215 United States subsidiaries with a total investment of $2 billion.[40]

To sum up, the emergence and expansion of the export processing zones around the world reflect the multinational companies' desire to integrate and rationalize production systems and to achieve economies of scale. The expansion of production facilities in EPZs may also be a defensive strategy to protect the firm's home market. In other words, offshore manufacturing subsidiaries are formed in export processing zones to preserve the firm's competitive strength in world markets. Moxon's study in Southeast Asian countries, for example, indicates that the United States firms' investments in EPZs of these countries were stimulated to offset Japanese competition in the United States. His study also shows that the labor-intensive industries were more likely candidates for such investments.[41]

Plant Location Decision

Basically two types of decisions need to be made with respect to the site selection for a proposed manufacturing plant:

1. Choosing a country
2. Choosing a site within a country

Although there is a well-developed body of theoretical and empirical literature on location decisions in general, studies undertaken in the international business context are few. Overall, studies on location decisions have uncovered the following influential factors affecting location decision making:

1. Proximity to consumers
2. Cost of production factors (e.g., labor, capital, land)
3. Tariff rates
4. Availability and restrictions on foreign exchange
5. Governmental subsidies
6. Infrastructure development in a given country (e.g., telephone, housing, transport, power, water)

    7. Availability of raw material
    8. Availability of skilled and unskilled workers
    9. Availability of technical and managerial personnel
  10. Political and economic conditions

Ideally, in making location decisions, the firm should not only take into consideration these factors, but should also assign appropriate weights to each of these elements. Some of the leading multinational companies undertake such an exercise. International Business Machines (IBM), for example, has pursued a general policy of manufacturing abroad. In selecting a specific country or location for manufacturing, the firm will assign weights to different factors (Table 9-1).[42]

Not many multinational companies use such a detailed evaluation method for deciding the location of overseas plants. Available studies suggest that the plant decisions are ad hoc, unsystematic, and subjective. For example, Schollhammer's study of 140 United States, European, and Japanese companies indicates that location decisions are made randomly. They are made on "incomplete and preconceived investigation of the consequences of a particular locational choice rather than on the basis of a comprehensive and systematic evaluation of locational alternatives on a global scale."[43]

Kobrin's study also indicates that few market-related factors dominated decision making, whereas other environmental factors such as governmental subsidies, infrastructure in a country, and political and economic stability played only a minor role.[44]

A classic study by Aharoni on the foreign investment decision-making process also reveals that it is rather subjective and unsystematic.[45]

One study indicates that the managers spend more time and effort in selecting a site within a country than in selecting the country. The author states:

> Although both decisions [selection of national site and local site] are made formally at the top of the company . . . , they have rather different characteristics. While the decision to invest in a country is often unstructured, the selection . . . of a specific location is more formalized since it is embedded in the formal procedure for approval of funds. Funds do not seem to be granted merely for an investment opportunity, but only to a specific project at a specific location. There, it is possible that the final and formal decision to invest at all is coupled with the location decision. This does not seem logical, and one of the executives explained, "In our company, the overall analysis for an investment opportunity in a foreign country is not done as carefully as the comparative analysis of potential locations, which is largely formalized."[46]

Given the increasing interdependence of nation-states in economic relations, uncertainties in political and economic conditions, the increasing role

Table 9-1 The weighted criteria method for plant location decisions
(a case of IBM)

Criteria	Assigned maximum value	Sites					
		A	B	C	D	E	F
Living conditions[a]	100	70	40	45	50	60	60
Accessibility[b]	75	55	35	20	60	70	70
Industrialization[c]	60	40	50	55	35	35	30
Labor availability[d]	35	30	10	10	30	35	35
Economics[e]	35	15	15	15	15	25	15
Community capability and attitude[f]	30	25	20	10	15	25	15
Prestige effect on company reputation[g]	35	25	20	10	15	25	15
Total	370	260	180	165	225	280	265

Source: E. S. Groo, "Choosing Foreign Locations: One Company's Experience," *The Columbia Journal of World Business* VI, 5 (September–October 1971): 77.

[a] General appearance of community, availability of housing, community services and education facilities, attractiveness of climate and environment, freedom from disruptive problems, living costs for transferred employees.

[b] Accessibility to markets, suppliers, services and other company facilities, quality of local transportation and of facilities for visitors, availability of communication networks.

[c] Level of industrialization, desirability of industrial and nonindustrial neighbors, potential for area's industrial growth.

[d] Wage rates, population within commuting radius, size of local labor force and level of employment, availability of skills and training programs, history of local labor problems.

[e] Relative cost of construction and site development, local costs of doing business, e.g., corporate and personal tax structure, utility rates.

[f] Quality and types of schools, adequacy of public services, local issues, attitudes toward industry and possible effect of introducing new facility into community, evidence of community planning for future growth.

[g] General reputation of area, especially, reputation which may relate to the type of facility planned, freedom from special problems which would create unfavorable reputation; desire of community to welcome type of activity planned.

of governments in economic matters, and intensive market competition in the world marketplace, the international firm will be compelled to pay more attention to strategic long-range planning, investment decisions, and plant location decisions. The current popularity of the Boston Consulting Group's Strategic Business Unit Analysis and other strategy models points toward such a systematic approach to decision making.[47] At the practical level, a number of organizations, such as the Industrial Conference Board, Business International, and Industrial Development publish checklists for site selections; they report the factors companies use to make location decisions.

Procurement and Sourcing Strategy

Two fundamental issues are involved in formulating and implementing procurement and sourcing strategies and practices:

1. Centralized *versus* decentralized modes to secure needed raw materials, semifinished, and finished goods for serving the world markets
2. "Make-Buy" decisions; i.e., whether to buy or subcontract the needed goods, or to manufacture with the firm's own facilities

To establish a centralized source (or sources) to procure goods for world markets is directly related to the firm's desire to rationalize its production and market process. The main advantages of such rationalizations are:

1. Lower production costs through economies of scale
2. Elimination and reduction of costly scheduling problems
3. Rapid start-up on new products
4. Reduction of inventories.

Some of the disadvantages of the centralized system are:

1. Inability to meet the host government's demands on local manufacturing, and the danger of losing such markets
2. Reduced flexibility of responding to changing market conditions and the consumers' preferences
3. Vulnerability to socioeconomic and political events in a given country in which major plants are located (e.g., strikes and political turmoil)[48]

Not all firms are able to centralize sourcing activities. The most favorable conditions for a centralized system are where there is a high relationship between the unit cost and the volume produced (the larger the volume, the lower the unit cost), and where the production system is using a continuous-process type of manufacturing technology. Additionally, large export incentives offered by host country may be influential in centralizing sourcing facilities.

As discussed in the previous section, export processing zones have become major sourcing points for many United States, European, and Japanese firms, partly because of governmental subsidies and lower labor costs.

The Harvard Multinational Enterprise Project estimated that five countries (Mexico, Ireland, Taiwan, Hong Kong, and Singapore) accounted for 22% of 362 export plants. These, along with another five countries (Canada, Belgium, Netherlands, the United Kingdom, and Italy) claimed 33% of such plants. All of these countries offer substantial incentives to foreign investors.[49]

The choice between centralized *versus* decentralized sourcing is not of the either/or type. The firm may choose both alternatives. High tariff rates, transportation costs, and foreign exchange fluctuations tend to discourage centralized sourcing. In certain parts of the world, and for certain products, the firm may use centralized sourcing; in other parts of the world and for other products, it may use a decentralized system. For example, Dow Chemical Company has established large chemical manufacturing units in West Germany and The Netherlands to supply chemical and petrochemical products for entire European markets, but its consumer-oriented products are manufactured in various countries to meet local demands. Similarly, Philips, of the Netherlands, rationalized its production facilities in Europe in the early 1970s to reduce unit and inventory costs. However, its production facilities in developing countries continue to be local.

Such hybrid or mixed strategies of the partial rationalization of production and marketing facilities and partial local manufacturing reflect the influence of the following factors:

1. *Technology:* capital-intensive industries tend to provide economies of scale at much higher volume through reduction of overhead costs and, consequently, are more likely candidates for production rationalization.
2. *Market competitiveness:* intensive competition in a given market requires lowering unit cost and consequently, production and marketing rationalization become a necessity.
3. *Interchangeability of parts:* unless the products are standardized, rationalizing production facilities for manufacturing parts and other supplies will become a very difficult proposition. Consequently, products at the mature stage of their product life cycle are more likely candidates for production rationalization.[50]
4. *Governmental demands and pressures:* As discussed in previous sections, many developing countries, to achieve self-sufficiency and to generate economic and industrial growth, require multinational companies to manufacture locally. For example, such countries as India, Indonesia, Malaysia, Brazil, and Peru not only require local manufacturing, but also impose stiff duties and penalties on goods imported from other countries.[51]

United States, European, and Japanese Practices

The Harvard Multinational Enterprise Project indicates that United States companies tend to favor decentralized sourcing. Of 3,733 foreign manufacturing subsidiaries, only 9.4% reported intrasystem transactions amounting to more than 50% of their revenues. The larger subsidiaries exhibited higher rates of intrasystem sales.[52]

Overall, the European and Japanese companies have rationalized their production systems more than the United States companies. Japanese firms, until recently, preferred to export from Japan or their offshore facilities in low-wage countries. Their abilities to achieve economies of scale and lower unit cost largely explain their successes in the international marketplace. Competition from Japanese and European firms has compelled many United States firms to rationalize production and marketing systems. For example, a U.S. Department of Commerce study shows that 40% of United States exports and 45% of their imports were intrafirm transactions.[53]

The United Nations' statistics also show that some 23% of sales by United States affiliates were intracompany transactions. Such intracompany trade is higher in the mining and petroleum industries than in the manufacturing sector. They are also more significant for the affiliates located in developing than in developed countries. In contrast, European and Japanese multinational firms claim to use local inputs in large proportions both to satisfy the host government's demands and to grant higher degrees of autonomy to their overseas subsidiaries. This is especially true in developing countries where such demands are most intensive.[54]

Results of a comparative study of United States, German, and Japanese multinational companies, however, show a great deal of convergence in sourcing policies and practices of these three types of multinational companies. Approximately two thirds of the United States, German, and Japanese subsidiaries purchased more than one quarter of their requirements of raw materials, semifinished, and finished goods from their respective parent organizations (Figure 9-3).[55]

Controlling and coordinating the sourcing for the required input is perhaps the first step toward global integration. Ford Motor Company probably was one of the first among the large MNCs to realize the need for such integrated sourcing policies. Stressing this need for integration, Mr. Lee Iacocca, then President of the Ford Motor Company, stated:

> In 1967, we established Ford of Europe to coordinate the activities of our national companies throughout Europe so that our car and truck business could be conducted on a more integrated basis. . . . Through this multinational sourcing, we avoid duplication of tooling costs, maximize product quality by limiting the number of industrial processes for which each affiliate is responsible, and achieve lower unit costs through higher volume production. The consumer benefits, we benefit. And the economies of the host nations benefit most of all.[56]

Through integrated sourcing policies, the firm may indeed be able to reduce the cost and perhaps the price of goods, but whether it equally benefits

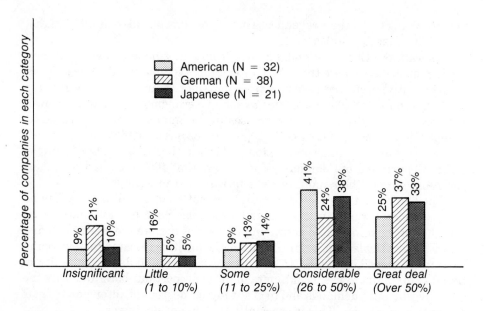

Figure 9-3 Subsidiaries' purchases of inputs from parent company, (*Source:* A. R. Negandhi, and M. Welge, *Beyond Theory Z* (Greenwich, Conn.: JAI Press, 1984), p. 46.)

the home and the host countries is highly questionable. If anything, it limits national hegemony and undermines the ability of both the home and the host countries to achieve their own national policy objectives. It also creates opportunities for transfer pricing manipulation. Such intrafirm flows may be responsible for the current protectionist trend in many industrialized countries.

"Make-Buy" Decisions

"Make-buy" decisions are basically choosing between alternatives of internal *versus* external sources for procuring needed inputs and finished goods to serve the world markets. They involve a cost-benefit analysis. If the cost of acquiring inputs and goods from outside is cheaper than to manufacture in the firm's own facilities, the economic choice will be to buy from the outside. However, beyond economic rationality, the firm is obligated to take into consideration some noneconomic factors. These are:

1. Reliability of Supply: The availability of a consistent supply of required inputs and goods, particularly if they are critical to a firm's survival and profitability, is a major factor in choosing alternatives

of manufacturing or buying from outside sources. In many of the developing countries, multinational firms have integrated their operations vertically and horizontally to assure consistent supplies of inputs. For example, Unilever of the United Kingdom and Holland has gone as far as manufacturing packaging materials and boxes in India to obtain supplies of these inputs. Similarly, many oil refining companies, until the 1973 oil crisis, owned oil wells in foreign countries. Even today the major oil companies have entered into long-term contracts with the oil producing nations to secure supplies. Many of the United States, European, and Japanese electronics firms have integrated vertically for the same reasons. Off-shore plants in export processing zones in Mexico, Taiwan, South Korea, Hong Kong, Malaysia, and Singapore have been established to secure regular supplies of critical inputs and finished goods to serve the world markets.

2. Technological Factor: Firms operating in capital-intensive industries and using continuous-process technology are more likely to use internal sources to obtain critical inputs, because disrupted supplies can create major bottlenecks. Chemical industries are the prime examples of such cases.

Table 9-2 outlines, in summary form, the circumstances favoring internal *versus* external sources.[57]

Table 9-2 Circumstances suitable for internal *versus* external sources

Circumstances	*Manufacture in the firm's own facilities*	*Buy from outside sources*
Economies of scale are reached at high volume (capital-intensive industries)		X
Few suppliers of important inputs in the marketplace	X	
Large number of required inputs		X
Rapid technological changes in manufacturing of critical inputs		X
Few buyers of critical inputs and large number of sellers		X
Few sellers and large number of buyers of critical inputs	X	

Source: Adapted from W. H. Davidson, *Global Strategic Management* (New York: John Wiley and Sons, 1982), p. 208.

In addition to these economic and noneconomic factors influencing sourcing practices, managerial preferences seem to play an important role in choosing alternatives. Generally speaking, United States and European companies are more likely to use internal sources than are their Japanese counterparts. However, as Davidson[58] has pointed out, Japanese companies have powerful nonequity ties with external suppliers, probably through long-term contracts, which permit them to secure needed inputs without much concern for quality, delivery, or inventory problems. In other situations, "Japanese firms collaborate in owning a common producer of components. Fujitsu and Hitachi (for example), jointly own a captive producer of computer peripheral equipment."[59]

Summary

This chapter analyzed the following major issues in international production and logistics activities of multinational companies:

1. Export *versus* manufacturing abroad
2. Determinants of foreign direct investment decisions
3. Plant design and location decisions
4. Sourcing of important inputs and finished goods
5. Technological transfer policy.

In analyzing these issues, my concern was to highlight both the theoretical rationales and the actual practices of United States, European, and Japanese companies. Analyses of empirical studies and case histories of the firms' practices showed that both economic considerations and governmental policies influenced managerial decision making.

Specifically, the decision to manufacture abroad is influenced by the competitive market environment and the host government's demand to produce locally. The plant's design and location decisions are influenced by economies of scale considerations. Sourcing important inputs and finished goods have dual influences of governmental demands and economies of scale.

The technological transfer issue has generated a considerable debate. The developing countries are found to be particularly ambivalent on this issue by demanding both an "appropriate scaled-down technology" and advanced technology. Multinationals on their part have based their decisions on cost-benefit analyses and have transferred mostly home-based technologies. However, to meet increasing demands from the governments, a more creative solution will be needed in the future on this issue.

Case

This case discusses a Japanese tire company's expansion strategy to the United States. Bridgestone has been exporting its high quality products to overseas markets. One of the key issues is how the company evaluates the competitive, regulatory environments of the United States market.

Case 9-1 ==================================

Bridgestone Corporation

On January 5, 1980, Chairman Kanchiro Ishibashi met with the foreign dignitaries visiting the Bridgestone Museum of Art adjacent to the corporate headquarters of Bridgestone Corporation. As the guests were led to the reception area, President Shigemichi Shibamoto also joined them, and as they strolled, Shibamoto mentioned to Chairman Ishibashi that he would ask Mr. Hattori to report on whether Bridgestone should consider the issue of direct investment in the United States. "My feeling," he said, "is that we can't wait too long," to which Chairman Ishibashi nodded in agreement.

The executive vice president of Bridgestone, Mr. K. Hattori, called for a preliminary meeting of the senior managing directors to consider the possibility of more active and direct participation in the United States passenger car and truck tire market. American business journalists had long speculated that, with mounting concern over car and truck imports from Japan, Japanese car manufacturers such as Toyota, Honda, and Nissan had to consider direct investment in the United States. Speculation about Bridgestone considering direct investment was highlighted in a column in *Business Week* (1980).[1]

At the meeting, among various other important matters, Mr. Hattori suggested to K. Ishikure, senior managing director (international operations), that he develop a preliminary strategic analysis of manufacturing in the United States. He was to look at the competitive, regulatory, and production environments and the labor situation. Mr. Hattori had seen the December 1, 1980 issue of *Business Week* which reported that Michelin (Compagnie Générale des Establissements Michelin), the giant French tire company, had developed critical problems in its United States operations. Mr. Ishikure re-

---

[1]"Japan–Why a Tiremaker Wants a U.S. Base." *Business Week*, January 14, 1980, p. 40.

Source: Prepared by Professor S. B. Prasad, Ohio University, on the basis of published information and is meant for the purpose of discussion only. Factual numerical data are drawn primarily from Bridgestone's *Annual Report*, 1980 and 1981. © Copyright by S. B. Prasad, 1983.

sponded that he would immediately ask one of the planning assistants, a recent M.B.A. graduate from Purdue University, to prepare such a report.

Company Profile

The company is named after the founder, Ishibashi, whose name means "stone bridge." Shojiro Ishibashi founded Bridgestone in 1931 in Kurume, Japan, to produce tires using domestic capital and technology. In the years since, two principles have consistently guided the conduct of Bridgestone's business in both tires and chemical and industrial products. The first is an unswerving commitment to "enhancing the quality of life," a commitment served by the second, "serving society with products of superior quality." Bridgestone attributes its growth in large part to this emphasis on quality. The company exercises strict control over every aspect of tire production, from the manufacture of cords to the finishing process.[2]

In 1978, Bridgestone reached a landmark: total production topped 500 million tires, a first for Japanese tire makers. Today Bridgestone operates twelve factories in Japan. It is also the only Japanese tire maker to manufacture tires abroad, with four overseas plants in operation. Bridgestone leads the Japanese rubber industry in sales and has climbed to sixth place among rubber-product manufacturers around the world. Corporate data as of March 1980 are shown in Table 9-3.

Domestic Economy

In 1979, the Japanese economy was faced with rising costs of raw materials because of sharply higher crude oil prices and lower value of the yen on foreign exchange markets. Even so, strong personal consumption and public sector investment combined to boost the gross national product by a healthy measure. In this climate, Bridgestone intensified its sales efforts in order to lift overall corporate performance. The company also pursued ongoing programs to develop innovative new products, raise productivity, and contain costs.

The results were excellent. Total consolidated sales rose to 579.7 billion yen (U.S. $2,645.1 million), up 16 percent over 1978. Before-tax income amounted to 69.9 billion yen (U.S. $318.9 million), 68 percent over 1978, and net earnings reached 29.1 billion yen (U.S. $132.8 million), a 72 percent advance. These unprecedented returns far exceeded the targets for the year.

---

[2]"Serving society with superior products" has served as an enduring guiding principle in the case of Bridgestone and other Japanese enterprises. Interested readers may refer to *Watashi no Ayumi* (in Japanese) by Shojiro Ishibashi, founder of Bridgestone. The philosophy of Konosuke Matsushita, the founder of the giant Matsushita Industrial Electric Company can be discerned from a reading of Rowland Gould, *The Matsushita Phenomenon* (Tokyo: Diamond Sha, 1970).

Table 9-3 Corporate data (as of March 1980)

Established	1931
Chairman	Mr. Kanieniro Ishibashi
President	Mr. Shigemichi Shibamoto
Capital	¥20.5 Thousand Million (US$93.5 Million) (US$ = ¥219.17)
Employees	30,059
Annual Sales (1979)	¥579.7 Thousand Million (US$2,645.0 Million) (US$ = ¥219.17)
	¥434.3 Thousand Million (US$1,981.6 Million) (US$ = ¥219.17)
	(Non-Consolidated Basis).

Organization:	*Domestic*	*Overseas*	*Total*
Branches, Rep. Offices	8	10	18
Factories	12	4	16
Subsidiary Sales Companies	96	11	107
Products	Tires and Tubes (all types), Conveyer Belts, Industrial & Marine Houses, Marine Fenders, Oil Fences, Shock-Absorbing Rubber, Air Springs, Golf Balls, Foam Rubber and Polyurethane Products, etc.		

Tire sales grew especially because of higher demand both in Japan and overseas. Steel-belted radial tires for automobiles sold well because of the economic recovery and brisk automobile production. The company stepped up marketing activities and introduced new products, such as the Super Filler radial tire (RD-207 STEEL), to achieve solid gains both in the original-equipment and replacement-tire markets. Sales of truck tires also advanced. Exports were up significantly as the company focused on sales of steel radials and large tires for mining and construction vehicles, particularly to North America, the Middle East, and Europe. The drop in the value of the yen had a positive effect on exports.

The company invested 40.2 billion yen (U.S. $167.7 million) in plant and equipment on a consolidated basis in 1979. Priority went to increasing capacity for producing steel-belted radial tires. Recreational and welfare facilities also were expanded, and a data management system for domestic sales was enlarged.

The company actively cultivated overseas markets. It marketed the Super Filler radial in West Germany and Australia. Eastern Airlines and Frontier Airlines in the United States adopted Bridgestone aircraft tires. Exports ac-

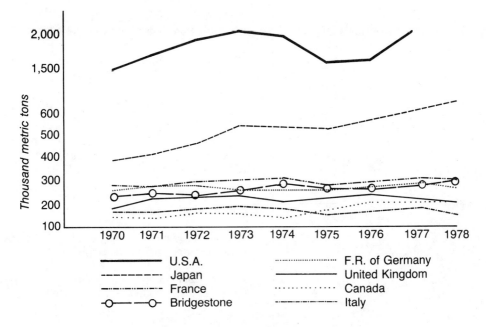

Figure 9-4 Consumption of new rubber in major countries

counted for more than 23 percent of total sales, with the Overseas Division reporting its highest sales on record. Vigorous overseas demand and the decline of the yen by nearly 10 percent were contributing factors. Among overseas factories, Thai Bridgestone Co., Ltd., hailed the tenth anniversary of its founding by expanding its production facilities. Consumption of new rubber in major countries is depicted in Figure 9-4.

Research and Development

The company's R&D policy is aimed at developing new products and technologies for the diverse needs of today's society. R&D developed the comfortably riding Super Filler radial tire and the U-Lug 2 tire for trucks and buses, the latter featuring a new construction. Efforts over the year to find ways to use waste tires culminated in a highly efficient recycling system with great promise for the future. In chemical and industrial products, large-bore, floating-sleeve hoses and floating-wave absorbers, made of Bridgestone Laboratories' glass-fiber-reinforced plastic, are at work in industry. For industrial products, the planned Yokohama Research Center will soon be serving Bridgestone's development programs.

Technological progress and innovation have been central aims of Bridgestone since its founding. The company wants its processes, materials, and

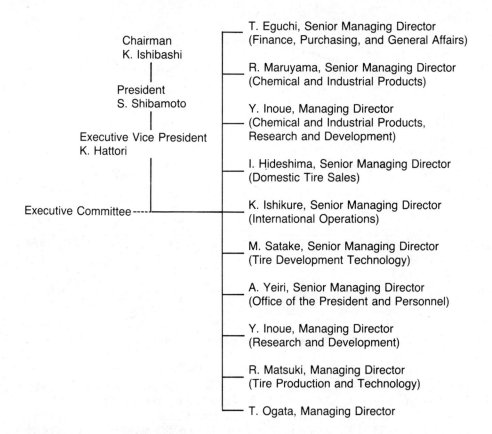

Figure 9-5 Corporate management structure of Bridgestone Corporation, 1980

products to remain in the technological vanguard. Its management structure is shown in Figure 9-5.

In Bridgestone's Technical Center in Tokyo, 1,300 engineers and technicians work in modern facilities. They conduct basic research as well as R&D projects in a wide range of fields. The world's largest tire for heavy mining vehicles, mammoth 200-ton trucks, was designed by a team at the Technical Center. The Center has created tires for the Linear Motor Car, the ground transportation system being developed by the Japan National Railways as a successor to the Shinkansen trains.

Kuroiso City, in Tochigi Prefecture, is the home of Japan's largest tire proving ground. Here, Bridgestone has some of the most up-to-date facilities in the world. Thirty types of road surface, including cobblestone pavement imported from Belgium, extend over a vast site. Reproducing road conditions found throughout the world, these facilities permit comprehensive, meticulous testing for every Bridgestone tire design. Testing data go to the Technical

Center, a feedback process essential to Bridgestone's strategy for providing unsurpassed tire quality.

Because materials and the construction of new products are becoming ever more complex, Bridgestone continues its efforts to maintain productivity superior to that of its competitors. Production facilities were bolstered, and labor-saving programs were implemented at Bridgestone factories in 1979. Labor-swapping between factories was instituted for greater efficiency. Energy-saving measures were also stepped up. Fuel consumption in fiscal 1979 was only 85 percent of that in 1978, and the company succeeded in cutting power consumption overall by 5 percent. The Tokyo factory achieved outstanding results in rationalizing power consumption. In 1979, it received an award from the Minister of International Trade and Industry as the Outstanding Enterprise of the Japan Electric Association for Rationalizing the Utilization of Electricity. The energy-saving measures at the plant were implemented even as production increased.

Expanding Diversification

Major companies have been established to add talent and ability to the corporate family. These subsidiaries produce liquid propane gas (LPG), bicycles, golf balls, and other products that mesh with Bridgestone's main products and technology.

Bridgestone Liquefied Gas Co., Ltd.

Bridgestone has undertaken a significant role in transporting and supplying liquid propane gas by launching the S.S. *Bridgestone*, the world's first giant LPG tanker.

Bridgestone Cycle Co., Ltd.

Japan's leading bicycle maker, with an annual capacity of 1.5 million units, is rated as one of the three largest bicycle manufacturers in the world.

Japan Synthetic Rubber Co., Ltd.

In accordance with the government's policy on the domestic production of synthetic rubber, this company was established by joint investments from the rubber industry, especially Bridgestone Tire Co., Ltd., the petrochemical industry, and the government. Today it is a totally private firm, the top producer in Japan and the third-largest in the world.

Bridgestone Boshingomu Co., Ltd.

Specializing in vibration-damping rubber parts, this company is producing extra durable bushings, engine mounts, shock absorbers, and other components for safe, comfortable riding in an age of high-speed transportation.

Bridgestone Bekaert Steel Cord Co., Ltd.

Bekaert of Belgium is the world's largest steel cord manufacturer. In a joint venture with Bridgestone, its remarkable steel cord is used extensively in tires and conveyor belts and is sold to other tire manufacturers as well. Construction of a second factory in Saga Prefecture to augment the output of Tochigi factory was on schedule in 1980.

Fukuda Industries Co., Ltd.

Established in 1972, this company has received praise for its recovery of the "good life" and preservation of the natural environment. It supplies trees and shrubs for reforestation projects. The company also aids private and public corporations and local governments in preserving and beautifying the landscape.

Bridgestone Machinery Co., Ltd.

This company is a natural outgrowth of Bridgestone's acknowledged leadership in machinery for processing rubber for industry.

Bridgestone Sports Co., Ltd.

Specializing in the manufacture of golf clubs bearing the world-famous "Spalding" name, this company also produces other golfing items and apparel. It is branching out to import and sell a wide variety of sports and recreational products.

Bridgestone Imperial Co., Ltd.

This company, a joint venture with Gould, Inc., produces and sells various oil pressure hoses such as high pressure rubber hoses and plastic hoses, metal parts (B 1 coupler, swivel joint) and bent tubes (oil pressure steel pipe).

Figures 9-6 through 9-8 provide comparative statistics, while Tables 9-4 and 9-5 contain consolidated income and balance sheet data.

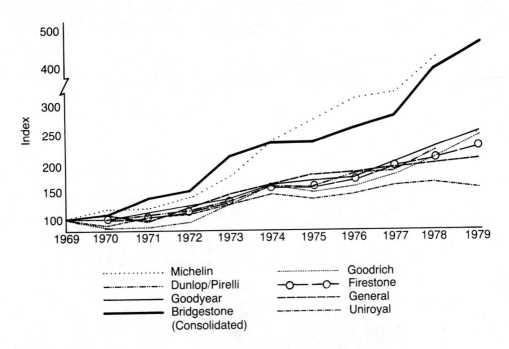

Figure 9-6 Rate of sales growth of world's eight largest manufacturers

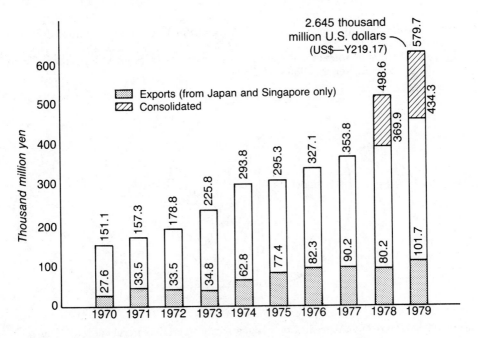

Figure 9-7 Bridgestone's annual sales, 1970–1979

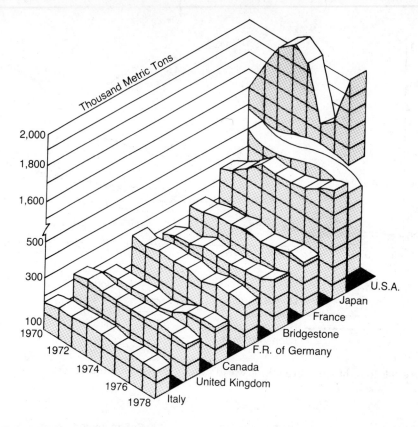

Figure 9-8 Expanding capacity (*Source:* Bridgestone Tire Co. Ltd., Annual Report 1980 and 1981.)

Figure 9-8A Consumption of new rubber in major countries (*Source:* Bridgestone Tire Co. Ltd., Annual Report 1980 and 1981.)

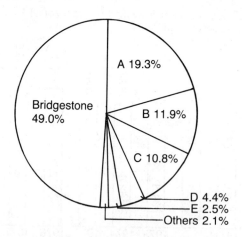

Figure 9-8B Share of total production in Japan by brands (1979 in rubber tons) (*Source:* Bridgestone Tire Co. Ltd., Annual Report 1980 and 1981.)

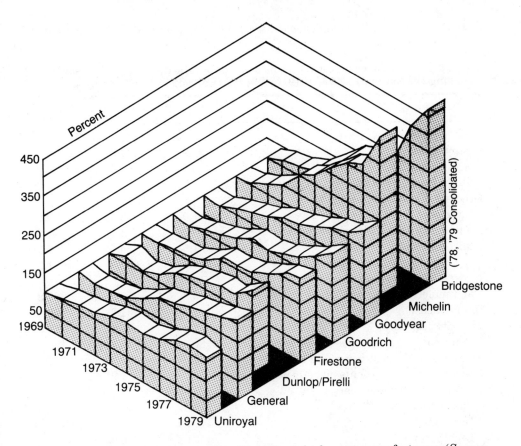

Figure 9-8C Rate of sales growth of world's eight largest manufacturers (*Source:* Bridgestone Tire Co., Ltd., Annual Report 1980 and 1981.)

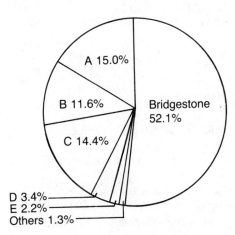

Figure 9-8D Share of total exports in Japan brands (1979 in rubber tons) (*Source:* Bridgestone Tire Co., Ltd., Annual Report 1980 and 1981.)

Table 9-4 Consolidated statement of income and retained earnings (for years ending December 31, 1978, 1979, and 1980, U.S. dollars in millions)

	1978*	1979**	1980*
Sales	$2,369.1	$2,645.1	$3,002.5
Cost of sales	1,592.9	1,717.5	2,073.5
Gross profit	776.2	927.7	929.0
Selling, general & administrative expenses	547.7	599.2	639.0
Other income (deductions):			
Interest, net	(17.5)	(19.6)	(19.2)
Foreign currency accounts adjustments	–	(5.7)	14.9
Miscellaneous	(21.8)	(5.5)	(17.9)
	587.0	629.9	661.2
Income before income taxes and minority interests	189.2	297.7	267.8
Income taxes	101.2	151.3	129.6
Minority interests	7.4	13.6	12.7
Net income	80.6	132.8	125.5
Retained earnings at beginning of year	501.3	539.3	632.6
Foreign currency accounts adjustments	–	1.9	(4.0)
Appropriation for the year:			
Cash dividends	(19.4)	(18.7)	(18.1)
Directors' bonuses	(0.9)	(0.8)	(0.9)
Legal reserve	(0.02)	(0.03)	(0.1)
Retained earnings at end of year	$ 561.6	$ 654.5	$ 735.0

Source: Bridgestone Tire Co. Ltd., Annual Report 1980 and 1981.
**JMF Average exchange rate: 1978 = ¥210.17; 1979 = ¥219.17; 1980 = ¥226.75

Discussion Questions

1. What are the motives for foreign direct investments in industrialized and developing countries? Give some examples.
2. Compare the United States' foreign direct investment method with the Japanese method.
3. Compare and contrast the product life cycle model, Dunning's internationalization model, and Fayerweather's unification-fragmentation model.
4. Discuss the differences in the sourcing policies among United States, Japanese, and European MNCs.
5. Why is sourcing raw material, semifinished, and finished products important for MNCs as a control device?

Table 9-5 Consolidated balance sheet (as of December 31, 1978, 1979, and 1980, U.S. dollars in millions)

Assets	1978*	1979*	1980**
Current assets:			
Cash	$ 181.4	$ 226.1	$ 313.5
Marketable securities	103.6	166.0	77.9
Trade receivables	540.0	668.9	851.5
Less allowance for bad debts	(13.4)	(15.4)	(17.9)
Inventories	260.2	365.5	592.8
Other current assets	34.9	57.0	76.8
Total current assets	1,106.7	1,468.1	1,894.6
Property, plant and equipment, at cost:			
Land	75.6	84.6	119.7
Buildings, Machinery, and equipment	1,136.4	1,336.2	1,887.4
Construction in progress	16.7	23.4	67.2
Less accumulated depreciation	(752.6)	(877.8)	(1,179.4)
Total property, plant and equipment	476.1	566.4	894.9
Investment and other assets:			
Investments in securities	68.6	83.7	105.2
Long-term loans receivable	37.1	38.4	47.6
Less allowance for bad debts	(0.6)	(0.5)	(0.6)
Other assets	21.9	26.3	36.3
Total investments and other assets	127.1	147.9	188.5
Total assets	$1,709.8	$2,182.4	$2,978.0

Liabilities and stockholders' equity	1978*	1979*	1980**
Current liabilities:			
Short-term borrowings	$ 238.9	$ 271.2	$ 372.7
Trade payables	341.9	468.7	661.4
Accrued expenses	48.6	56.2	77.2
Income taxes and other current liabilities	222.8	351.7	413.2
Total current liabilities	852.2	1,147.9	1,524.5
Long-term liabilities:			
Long-term borrowing	78.2	68.4	88.6
Liabilities for severance benefits	145.8	172.5	226.6
Other long-term liabilities	4.9	0.3	6.8
Total long-term liabilities	228.9	241.2	322.0
Special allowances	17.0	18.1	21.8
Deferred profit on translation of foreign currency accounts	–	12.6	16.3
Minority interest	35.0	46.7	79.5
Stockholders' equity:			
Capital stock	80.8	85.6	106.4
Additional paid-in capital	9.6	10.5	61.2
Legal reserve	20.2	21.4	25.3
Retained earnings	466.2	598.4	821.0
Total stockholders' equity	576.8	715.9	1,013.9
Total liabilities and stockholders' equity	$1,709.8	$2,182.4	$2,978.0

*IMF Year-end exchange rate: 1978 = ¥253.52; 1979 = ¥239.70; 1980 = ¥203.00

**Source: Bridgestone Tire Co. Ltd., Annual Report 1980 and 1981.

383

Endnotes

1. For a detailed discussion on this topic, see Judd Polk, "The New International Production," in Mark B Winchester (ed.) *International Essays for Business Decision Makers*, III, (Dallas: The Center for International Business, 1978): 16–28.
2. See A. R. Negandhi, "Foreign Private Investment and Economic Development," in *International Dimensions of Business: Readings from Business Topics* (East Lansing, Mich.: Division of Research, Graduate School of Business Administration, Michigan State University, 1970), pp. 281–293. For a detailed case study of India, see A. R. Negandhi, *Foreign Private Investment Climate in India* (East Lansing, Mich.: Division of Research, Graduate School of Business Administration, Michigan State University, 1966).
3. Peter J. Buckley, and Richard D. Pearce, "Overseas Production and Exporting by the World's Largest Enterprises: A Study in Sourcing Policy," *Journal of International Business Studies* X, 1 (Spring/Summer 1979): 11–13.
4. "Foreign Direct Investment in the United States," *Survey of Current Business* 59, 8 (August 1979).
5. Lawrence G. Franko, *The European Multinationals* (Stamford, Conn.: Greylock Publishers, 1976).
6. Lawrence G. Franko, *European Business Strategies In The United States* (Geneva: Business International, 1971).
7. Michael Y. Yoshino, *Japan's Multinational Enterprises* (Cambridge, Mass.: Harvard University Press, 1976); Yoshi Tsurumi, *The Japanese Are Coming* (Cambridge, Mass.: Ballinger Publishing Co., 1976).
8. Harold Crookell, "Investing in Development: A Corporate View," *Columbia Journal of World Business* X, 1 (Spring 1975): 80–88.
9. Louis T. Wells, Jr., ed., *The Product Life Cycle and International Trade* (Cambridge, Mass.: Harvard University Press, 1972).
10. Yoshi Tsurumi and Hiroki Tsurumi, "A Revised Theory of the Product Life Cycle (PLC)," *Pacific Basin Quarterly* 10 (Summer/Fall 1982): 14.
11. Raymond Vernon, *Storm Over The Multinationals: The Real Issues* (Cambridge, Mass.: Harvard University Press, 1977), pp. 151–172.
12. P. J. Buckley and M. C. Casson, *The Future of the Multinational Enterprise.* (New York: Holmes and Meier, 1976).
13. For more detailed discussion on this point see Franko, *European Multinationals*, and M. Y. Yoshino, *Japan's Multinational Enterprises.*
14. Louis T. Wells, *Third World Multinationals: The Rise of Foreign Investment from Developing Countries* (Cambridge, Mass.: MIT Press, 1983).
15. John Fayerweather, *International Business: Strategy and Administration* (Cambridge, Mass.: Ballinger Publishing Co., 1978), especially Chap. 1.
16. For details on foreign investment theories see Robert Gross, *The Theory of Foreign Direct Investment* (Columbia: University of South Carolina, Center for International Business Studies, 1981). The author provides analysis of five theories: (1) international trade theory, (2) location theory, (3) investment theory, (4) theory of the firm, and (5) industrial organization theory.
17. Louis T. Wells, "Do not Overautomate Your Foreign Plant," *Harvard Business Review* 52, 1 (January-February 1974): 111.
18. Samuel A. Morley and Gordon W. Smith, "The Choice of Technology: Multinational Firms in Brazil," *Journal of Economic Development and Cultural Change* 25, 2 (January 1977): 239–264.
19. Ibid., pp. 245–247.

20. Quoted from Donald A. Ball, and Wendell H. McCulloch, Jr., *International Business* (Dallas: Business Publications, Inc., 1983), p. 426.
21. For detailed discussion on this point, see William H. Davidson, *Global Strategic Management* (New York: John Wiley and Sons, 1982), pp. 184–191.
22. See Negandhi, *Foreign Private Investment Climate in India* especially chapter 1, pp. 1–7.
23. Wayne A. Yeoman, "Selection of Production Processes for the Manufacturing Subsidiaries of US–Brazil Multinational Corporations" (Ph.D. diss., Harvard University, 1968). Quoted from R. Hal Mason, Robert R. Miller, and Dale R. Weigel, *International Business* (New York: John Wiley and Sons, 1981), pp. 256–257.
24. Morley and Smith, "The Choice," pp. 260–261.
25. R. Hal Mason, "Some Observations On The Choice of Technology By Multinational Firms in Developing Countries," *Review of Economics and Statistics* 55, 3, (1973): 349–355.
26. Mason, Miller, and Weigel, *International*, p. 257.
27. A. R. Negandhi and M. Welge, *Beyond Theory Z* (New York: JAI Press, 1984), Chap. 3, pp. 41–45.
28. Jack Baranson, "Automated manufacturing in developing economies," *Finance and Development* 8, 4 (1971):10–17. Also see his *Manufacturing Problems in India: the Cummins Diesel Experience* (Syracuse, NY: Syracuse University Press, 1967):18–45.
29. Wells, "Do not Overautomate," pp. 111–118.
30. Baranson, "Automated Manufacturing," p. 17.
31. Wells, "Do not Overautomate," p. 115.
32. Ibid.
33. Richard Robinson, *International Business Management* (Hinsdale, Ill.: Dryden Press, 1978), p. 156.
34. F. L. Hartley, "World Trade in the '80s: Will We Be Competitive?" (Paper presented at the 1980 World Trade Conference, Chicago, April 17, 1980).
35. A. R. Negandhi and S. B. Prasad, *Comparative Management* (New York: Appleton-Century-Crofts, 1971); A. R. Negandhi and B. R. Baliga, *Quest For Survival and Growth* (New York: Praeger Publishers, 1979); Negandhi and Welge, *Beyond Theory Z*.
36. June Nash, and M. P. Fernandez-Kelly, *Women, Men and The International Division of Labor* (Albany, NY: State University of New York Press, 1983), p. VII.
37. Ibid.
38. Davidson, *Global*, p. 178; D. W. Baerresen, *The Border Industrialization Program of Mexico* (Lexington, Mass.: D. C. Heath, 1971).
39. Nash and Fernandez-Kelly, *Women*, p. VIII.
40. Davidson, *Global*, p. 199.
41. Richard M. Moxon, *Offshore Production in Less Developed Countries* (New York: Graduate School of Business Administration, New York University, 1974).
42. See E. S. Groo, "Choosing Foreign Locations: One Company's Experience," *Columbia Journal of World Business* VI, 5 (September-October 1971): 71–78.
43. Hans Schollhammer, *Locational Strategies of Multinational Firms* (Los Angeles: Center for International Business, 1974), p. 32.
44. Stephen J. Kobrin, "The Environmental Determinants of Foreign Direct Investment: An Ex Post Empirical Analysis," *Journal of International Business Studies* VII, 2 (Fall 1976): 37.
45. Yair Aharoni, *The Foreign Investment Decision Process* (Boston: Division of Research, Harvard Business School, 1966).

46. Hans W. Hagenbuck, *The Selection of Plant Location Abroad* MS thesis, Massachusetts Institute of Technology, 1973, p. 71, quoted from Robinson, *International*, p. 156.
47. The Boston Consulting Group, *Strategy Alternatives for the British Motorcycle Industry* (London: Her Majesty's Stationery Office, 1975).
48. Hugo E. R. Utterhoeven, et al., "The Case of the Multiplant Manufacture," *Harvard Business Review* 43, 2 (March-April 1965): 22–24; (see ref. 1) Polk, pp. 16–28.
49. Quoted from Davidson, *Global*, p. 196.
50. For detailed analysis of the determinants of centralized versus decentralized sourcing strategies, see ibid., pp. 177–214.
51. For detailed discussion on foreign investment policies of various countries, see Negandhi and Baliga, *Quest*, Chap. 4, and Negandhi and Welge, *Beyond Theory Z*, Chap. 5.
52. Quoted from Davidson, *Global*, p. 180.
53. Quoted from Neil Hood and Stephen Young, *The Economics of Multinational Enterprise* (London: Longman, 1979), p. 173.
54. Ibid.
55. Negandhi and Welge, *Beyond Theory Z*, Chap. 3.
56. Lee A. Iacocca, "Address to the National Foreign Trade Convention," November 16, 1976, citied in Robinson, *International*, p. 143.
57. Davidson, *Global*, pp. 177–214.
58. Ibid.
59. Ibid., p. 209.

Additional Readings

Articles

Buckley, Peter J., and Pearce, Richard D. "Overseas Production and Exporting by the World's Largest Enterprise: A Study in Sourcing Policy." *Journal of International Business Studies* X, 1 (Spring/Summer 1979).

Heskett, James L., and Mathias, Peter F. "The Management of Logistics in MNCs." *Columbia Journal of World Business* XI, 1 (Spring 1976): 52–62.

Starr, Martin K. "Global Production and Operations Strategy." *Columbia Journal of World Business* XIX, 4 (Winter 1984): 17–22.

Books

Franko, Lawrence G. *European Business Strategies in the U.S.* Geneva: Business International, 1971.

Otterbeck, Lars. *Location and Strategic Planning.* Stockholm: The Economic Research Institute, 1973.

Schollhammer, Hans. *Locational Strategies of Multinationals.* Los Angeles: Center for International Business, 1974.

Yoshino, Michael Y. *Japan's Multinational Enterprises.* Cambridge, Mass.: Harvard University Press, 1976.

Chapter 10

Assessing the International Markets and Export Marketing

In this and the next chapter, major strategic and important operational aspects of international marketing will be discussed. In analyzing these elements, the focus will be on macro-level and micro-level issues.

Macro-level issues in international marketing involve an assessment of the potential markets and the socioeconomic, political, and legal environments in the foreign industries. Micro-level aspects deal with the parameters and structures of the marketing mix management concerning product, pricing, promotion, and distribution.

As Walsh[1] has pointed out, basically five key strategic decisions are needed in international marketing:

1. The initial decision to sell the product overseas
2. Determining which markets to enter

3. Methods of entry in overseas markets (e.g., exporting, licensing, and manufacturing overseas)
4. The marketing mix management concerning product, pricing, promotion, and distribution
5. Determining the organizational structures for managing overseas markets

The methods of entry and the organizational and structural aspects were discussed in Chapters 3 and 4, respectively. The remaining three elements will be discussed in this and the next chapter.

Both of these chapters highlight only the strategic and policy-level issues. Students interested in various marketing techniques are urged to refer to the standard domestic and international marketing texts.[2]

The second part of this chapter will discuss the important elements of export marketing. As noted in Chapter 4, exporting from the home base is an initial entry method used by many firms entering international marketing. It is the most traditional and well-established means to enter international markets. It is most suitable for inexperienced, small and medium-sized firms, because it requires no investment in the manufacturing operations abroad. Many large multinational companies, such as General Electric, Boeing, McDonnell Douglas, and scores of European and Japanese companies, are the biggest exporters (see Table 10-2).

Decision to Enter Overseas Markets

One can analyze a firm's decision to enter overseas markets in terms of firm-related and market-related variables, which to some extent are interrelated factors.

The Firm-Related Factors

Firm-related factors that motivate a firm to enter foreign markets may include the following situations:

High relation between volume and unit cost. Firms operating in mass production techniques will find it necessary to increase production volume to reduce unit cost, particularly if such firms are facing either tough competition in the domestic market or the domestic market is not growing because of the saturation of demand. To preserve the competitive edge, or even status quo, such firms may find it necessary to enter foreign markets to increase sales volume that could reduce unit cost and increase the competitive advantage at home and abroad.

A large number of Japanese companies, especially automobile and electronics firms, were able to reduce unit cost drastically, thereby achieving economies of scale through high volume and selling the additional output in world markets.[3]

Extension of product life cycle. A firm may desire to extend the life cycle of a given product beyond its natural span by entering into foreign markets in which such products are not available.[4] Many of the United States multinational companies initially introduce new products to domestic markets. During the early stage of the product life cycle, the firm is able to collect monopolistic rents. Through time, however, other firms will enter into these markets, and the excessive profits will disappear. Under such circumstances, entering into foreign markets may be more attractive.

Additionally, the following factors may also induce the firm to enter foreign markets:

1. Unused capital and human resources.
2. Need for incremental revenue to support excessive overhead costs and research and development expenditures. Many times, the product development cost of large firms is extremely high. For example, as reported in the Corfam case, DuPont spent over $250 million to develop a synthetic rubber product. Huge research and development expenditures necessitate a sizeable sales volume. Penetration in overseas markets may provide the needed volume. Many of the Japanese companies, such as Sony, Matshushita, Toyota, and Nissan have successfully used overseas markets to spread their high research and development expenses.
3. Need to learn and keep abreast of technological developments in foreign countries (it is believed that many Japanese and European companies are investing in the United States for this purpose).[5]
4. To avoid seasonal fluctuation in demand in the domestic market.
5. To spread risks in larger geographic areas.[6]
6. To earn money from obsolete machinery.
7. To avoid heavy domestic taxation and earn required foreign exchange for parts and machinery; firms from developing countries investing overseas seem to have such motivation.[7]
8. Subjective and personal preferences of the chief executives; some companies may enter into foreign markets to satisfy their egos and acquire global prestige.

Market-Related Factors

Some important market-related factors influencing the decisions to enter foreign markets are as follows.

Maintain competitive stability and gain competitive advantage at home. In highly concentrated industries, maintaining the firm's status and market share assumes greater importance. One of the important means to achieve these objectives is to enter foreign markets. By doing so, the firm not only is able to maintain its status quo vis-à-vis its competitors, but also gains competitive advantages in the home market. Davidson[8], for example, has analyzed a number of cases of United States firms exhibiting such behavior and strategies. His analysis of the City Bank of New York (Citicorp) shows that "aggressive commitment to foreign markets was primarily responsible for its superior earnings growth among major U.S. banks during the last 25 years. Foreign earnings amounted to 65 percent of Citicorp's net income in 1980, highest among all U.S. banks."[9] This strategy also enabled Citicorp to improve its competitive position in the United States market.

Similarly, Davidson has argued that Caterpillar's aggressive strategies of exporting and investing abroad enabled the company to improve its competitive position in the United States market. Foreign sales through exports resulted in economies of scale, and cost reduction, in turn, "enhanced Caterpillar's ability to compete in the domestic market."[10]

All three major United States tire companies (Goodyear, Firestone, and Goodrich), as well as Gillette in the razor blade industry, used foreign investment to maintain and enhance their competitive positions in the home market.[11]

Other market-related factors inducing the firms to invest overseas are:

1. *Fragmented markets in foreign countries* (entry is easier under such market conditions).
2. *Exchange of threat to maintain competitive stability in the home market.* Some European firms, such as Bayer and Hoechst from West Germany, have invested in the United States to stop the aggressive expansion of the United States companies in their respective home markets. On establishing a balance of mutual threats among the rivals, Vernon, for example, states: "Faced with the competition of U.S.-owned subsidiaries in their main markets, European and Japanese firms have had to weigh the possibility that the Americans might enlarge their foothold by selling at prices that do not fully reflect global costs. . . . By setting up subsidiaries in the United States, the Europeans and Japanese have placed themselves in a position to play the same game on U.S. territory."[12]
3. *Higher profit margins in foreign countries.* The competitive pressures in many developing countries and some European countries are minimal as compared to the United States, and, consequently, the proft margins in those countries are much higher. Table 10-1 outlines the desirable market conditions under which the firm may find it more profitable to invest.

Table 10-1 Foreign investment matrix

Market competition	Market potential	
	Strong	Weak
Strong	United States, (+) Western European countries, Japan, Australia, Canada	Mid-East countries (−)
Weak	China India Indonesia (++) Brazil Pakistan Mexico	Smaller Latin (−) American countries

Note: The positive signs indicate the more profitable places for investment, while the negative signs show the less attractive places. The matrix assumes "other things being equal," such as the political and economic conditions. In the real business world situation, the other things are not always "equal" and play an important role in investment decisions.

Foreign Investment Strategies

The firm can adopt basically four different types of strategies for its foreign investment decisions:

1. Defensive strategy
2. Aggressive strategy
3. Follow-the-leader strategy
4. Avoidance

Defensive Strategy

The defensive strategy, as the name implies, is the "do-nothing" strategy until the competitors start hurting the firm's market share and profitability. International Harvester, for example, was slow in expanding its operations abroad, vis-à-vis its competitor, Caterpillar, which affected its market share in the construction equipment market. As Davidson has remarked, "failure to follow a competitor's initiative into international markets can result in a dramatic change in competitive position."[13]

Aggressive Strategy

In contrast to International Harvester, its competitor Caterpillar followed a growth strategy by entering international markets. By doing so, it increased its market share from 16% in 1950 to over 50% in 1979.

Caterpillar's aggressive strategy enhanced its competitive position in the United States and in the world markets. Many Japanese companies, particularly the automobile, electronics, and heavy industries, have followed aggressive export strategies. In the television industry, for example, the Japanese market share of color television sets in the United States increased from zero in 1967, to 30% in 1977.[14] Large capital investments, to achieve economies of scale and a drastic reduction in unit cost, coupled with aggressive export marketing, were responsible for such dramatic increases in the market share. Aggressive Japanese strategies in the television industry can also be observed through the decline of the United States television firms, from fifty in 1970 to fourteen in 1980. Curiously, of these fourteen United States companies, eight are owned by Japanese, and two are owned by Europeans.[15]

The Japanese competitive strength in the automobile industry is too well known to require further discussion. Within the decades of 1950 to 1980, the Japanese automobile industry has reached top position in both the number of vehicles produced and in profitability. Its share in the United States domestic market has increased from almost nil in 1950 to 22% in 1980.

Follow-the-Leader Strategy

This type of strategy usually occurs in highly concentrated, industrial sectors. The typical situation in this type of investment strategy will be to keep up with the largest and strongest competitor in the field. If the competitor enters into a particular market, others will follow its step. The overall aim of pursuing such a strategy is to minimize risk and to maintain competitive stability in the home market. The three giants of the United States tire industry provide a good example for such a strategy. Goodyear Tire Company has been the leader; Firestone and Goodrich have been the followers.[16]

Avoidance Strategy

This strategy is the opposite of the confrontation strategy, in which the lesser competitor will avoid a direct head-on clash with the major competitor. Control Data *versus* IBM, Chrysler *versus* General Motors, and John Deere *versus* International Harvester are some of the prime examples of using such strategy. Although Control Data had fought a long, legal battle with IBM on antitrust grounds, it consistently avoided following IBM's investment abroad. Instead, the company invested in unexplored areas, such as Hong Kong, Israel, and other developing countries, as well as in Communist Bloc countries in Eastern Europe. Similarly, Chrysler invested in foreign countries where General Motors and Ford Motor Company had not yet established manufacturing operations.[17] To some extent, such a pattern is also found between the two giant German chemical companies, Hoechst and Bayer.

The choices between avoidance *versus* confrontation strategy, to quote Davidson, "rest on firms' assessment of their ability to maintain or improve their position in direct competition and the cost of doing so. . . . In industries, where the principal competitors are other global firms, this consideration should play an important role in market selection decisions."[18]

Such avoidance strategy and reliance on the firm's basic technological strength was clearly exhibited by the American Telephone and Telegraph Company's entry into the computer market. AT&T avoided the direct clash with another United States giant, IBM, by carefully picking products that stressed both communications between computers and the reliability that has been a hallmark of this phone company.[19]

International Market Assessment

In analyzing the market for a given product, two aspects assume considerable importance: (1) the size of the existing markets, and (2) the size of the future markets.

In assessing an international market, the impact of sociocultural, legal, economic, and political environments also needs to be considered.

The factors to be evaluated for analyzing international markets for consumer goods *versus* industrial products will differ considerably. For consumer products, the usual demand-potential measures, such as per capita income, disposable income, consumer preferences, and taste, are useful indicators.

For industrial products, the task of the international marketing manager is to look more at the macro economic level. More specifically, a firm marketing industrial products needs to evaluate its own capital intensity, as well as of the industry and the nation. In addition to the economic planning framework of a nation, economic growth potential, foreign investment policies, national industrial policies, and the role of local private and state-owned enterprises should also be considered.

The national and regional governments in each country, a number of international organizations, such as the International Monetary Fund (IMF), the United Nations, the International Labor Organization, and the Organization for Economic Cooperation and Development (OECD), generate useful statistics for evaluating macro economic conditions. Similarly, various national and international trade organizations, such as the Chamber of Commerce, the International Chamber of Commerce, the U.S. Department of Commerce Publications, *Overseas Business Reports,* and *Foreign Economic Trends,* various publications of Business International, Inc. (consulting firm), and the Bureau of National Business Affairs' publication *The International Trade Reporter,* provide useful data to aid international marketing efforts. A sample of some basic economic and social indicators, provided by the World Bank, is reproduced in the Appendix, Table 10-4. To assess the international market opportunities, Keegan[20] has provided three categories of demand:

1. Existing markets
2. Latent markets
3. Incipient markets

In *existing markets*, consumer needs are known. The potential opportunities can be assessed by estimating the consumption rate and the number of competitors in the market.

In *latent markets*, the potential consumers are not being served, although the need for products exists (e.g., consumer-durable goods such as air conditioners, refrigerators, and ovens in developing countries).

In *incipient markets*, consumer needs are not known or may not exist, but could be stimulated through new product design, packaging, promotion, and pricing mechanisms. Japanese automobiles and motorcycle industries provide good examples of capturing incipient markets.

By producing small, inexpensive, and energy-efficient cars, Japanese companies not only captured the latent demands for such cars in the United States, but also positioned themselves for an emerging incipient market. The same is true with respect to the Japanese motorcycle industry. It produced more sporting motorcycles, and thus opened up entirely new markets unknown to its competitor, the British motorcycle industry. Through innovative product design, quality, pricing, and aggressive advertising strategies, the Japanese motorcycle industry increased its market share by 430% between 1973 and 1977. During the same period, the British share declined from 49% to 9% in the medium- and large-sized motorcycle categories.[21]

Marketing Research

Many conventional research devices, such as consumer surveys, panels, and store audits, are used in the United States and are becoming popular in foreign, particularly in developed, countries. In developing countries, the socioeconomic data may be inadequate to forecast the market potential. Moyer[22] has suggested various short-cut research methods, such as deduction by analogy (deducing the potential consumption pattern by knowing the industrial growth pattern), import substitution elasticities, and regression analysis to forecast potential demands. A more detailed description on various research techniques can be found in marketing research and international marketing textbooks.[23]

Forecasting the Future

Predicting the distant future is a risky task. As the English philosopher Francis Bacon wrote some centuries ago, "Dreams and Predictions ought to serve but for winter talk by the Fireside."[24]

Yet, some sort of forecasting is absolutely necessary for making international investment and marketing decisions.

Recently, *U.S. News and World Report* prepared a fifty-year forecast, affecting our socioeconomic and cultural lives. Table 10-2 summarizes the relevant aspects of this forecast and its implications for international business.

Major Trends

The following extracts from *U.S. News and World Report* highlight major trends affecting the international marketplace.[25]

Smokestack Industries will fade, but a "high" tech boom could create a vibrant business climate.

American industry will be rebuilt and redesigned. Automated factors will replace the aging, inefficient plants of today. Only one out of 10 workers will toil in auto, steel, textile and other smokestack industries that symbolize this country's first industrial revolution.

Big corporations will grow even bigger, but there still will be room for aggressive entrepreneurs, particularly in services and fast-moving high-technology fields.

American industry will give up its grubby, sometimes menial, assembly-line jobs to the lower-wage regions of Asia, India, Africa and South America.

There almost certainly will be fewer auto makers. They will be producing worldwide and will be engaged in more cooperative ventures with foreign manufacturers here and abroad.

The big will become bigger to compete against their foreign counterparts all over the globe. But new giants will emerge, many of them organized as joint ventures and other cooperative arrangements rather than the traditional manufacturer–wholesaler–retailer relationships.

The big companies in 2003 are not going to be General Motors–type vertically integrated companies . . . but trading companies to compete in world markets and financial supermarkets to serve a more sophisticated public.

Table 10-2 Forecasting the future: Major trends and their implications for international business

Major trends	Implications for international business	Assumptions: Conceptual problems
Overall		
Renaissance for U.S. political prestige.	Support for private enterprise system.	Other nations remain stand-still or declining.
Increasing U.S. technological powers.	More trade in high-tech industries.	Other nations remain stand-still.
Exploration of wealth – minerals from space, moon.	Lower cost of minerals, less dependence on other nations, trade reductions unless higher international cooperation.	Higher international cooperation.
Discovery and use of alternative means for energy: atomic, solar, cheaper electricity.	Less dependence on other nations. Less international trade, more reliance on domestic business for economic growth.	More cooperative social environment and inter-group relations.
Less dependence on imported gasoline.	Less trade, less development in oil-producing countries.	Other sources are economically developed.
Increasing challenge by the Third and Fourth World nations for markets in industrialized countries.	Higher imports. Reduced U.S. competitive position, less exports.	Declining bargaining position of countries.
Establishment of new economic and monetary systems.	More tensions, less trade.	
Increasing interdependence of nations around the world for trade and peace.	More trade.	Higher international cooperation, peace in the world.

Table 10-2 Continued

Major trends	Implications for international business	Assumptions: Conceptual problems
A richer America		
Economically Technologically Politically	Higher standard of living, higher economic growth, higher U.S. international prestige.	Other nations remain stand-still or declining or higher level of international cooperation.
A less rich Europe		
Politically Economically Technologically	Less trade with Europe. Less international trade.	Other "unknowns" are still unknown for European growth.
A richer Japan		
Technologically Economically	More trade with Japan.	Other nations remaining stand-still.
Poorer Third and Fourth World countries		
Economically Technologically Politically	Less trade with the developing countries, less trade with Europe, more concentration on domestic markets.	Status quo conditions internationally.
U.S. Society		
Declining birth rate, increasing population of older people, 21% in 2000, versus 11% in 1980.	Lower productivity, lower U.S. competitive advantages.	
Education		
Computerized learning, life-long training, individualized instruction, business in education industry, increasing use of television for education.	Less emphasis on analytical thinking— lower rate of innovations, lower U.S. competitive advantages.	Without analytical training, economic and social growth could be maintained.

Continued

Table 10-2 Continued

Major trends	Implications for international business	Assumptions: Conceptual problems
Resources and quality of life		
Uneven distribution of world's natural resources.	More tensions among nations—reduced trade.	Economic and social growth could be maintained with the increasing tensions. Status quo situation will prevail in the world.
Distribution of population—	Necessity of increasing trade with the developed countries.	Increased cooperation between developed and developing countries.
85% developing nations 15% developed nations		
Economy		
Rising standard of living, wider gaps between "haves" and "have nots"	More tensions among nations—reduced trade.	Social and economic growth could be maintained with the increasing tensions.
Private enterprise-based economy. Less government in business, more government in life.	More trade.	Private enterprise system able to adjust to rapid changes without governmental help.
Expanding sectors		
Government services Finance and insurance trade	Less manufacturing, higher imports of manufactured goods—higher level of international trade.	Sectoral changes are possible without governmental help.
Declining sectors		
Manufacturing	Developing countries becoming manufacturing centers.	Economic progress in industrialized countries could be maintained without growth in manufacturing sector.

Table 10-2 Continued

Major trends	Implications for international business	Assumptions: Conceptual problems
Politics: U.S.		
Minority assuming greater political powers, interregional and inter-state conflicts and competition for bigger role of U.S.	Higher level of international orientations in the U.S.–higher level of international trade.	Social peace exists, intergroup conflicts are kept under control.
Politics: International		
U.S. #1 superpower, USSR role and Europe's role declining, no new-comers except little bit of China.	Higher level of international trade.	Other nations remaining stand-still or declining.
Growth Rates		
Industrialized countries 2% to 4%		
Developing countries 5% to 9%.	More trade with developing countries.	

Source: Excerpted from *U.S. News & World Report* issue of May 9, 1983. Copyright, 1983 U.S. News and World Report.

The very survival of U.S. firms in tougher international markets will depend . . . on the greater willingness of American companies to take long-term investment risks, even at the expense of short-term profits.

For all nations, competition for a share of the world economy will be brisk because expansion of trade is expected to slow from the heady growth that took place in the 1960s and 1970s.

Trade wars and protectionism will increase as governments try to keep jobs from being lost to foreign competition, and international monetary authorities will be hard pressed from time to time to accommodate developing countries' suffering debt problems.

U.S. trade with other nations will equal to 40 percent of the gross national product by year 2000–up from about 20 percent now (1983). In 1950, foreign trade was just about 2 percent of GNP.

Canada will be one of the three most prosperous nations in the world, along with the U.S. and Australia.

Tough times are in store for regions that dominated world commerce for centuries (West European countries).

The problem European countries will have is in horribly sick steel and auto industries. . . . They won't be able to compete on wage scales with far eastern countries. . . . The overall outlook remains grim. . . . Economically and politically Western Europe is very bleak.

The brightest outlook in the next half century's trade picture is in East Asia. Japan will continue to grow more rapidly than the rest of the industrial countries through 1980s and beyond.

Taiwan, Hong Kong, Singapore and South Korea are . . . four economic upstarts, will improve steadily in such fields as textiles, machine tools, chemical products, metals and electronics.

The Philippines, Thailand, Indonesia and Malaysia (will) move to take their places (and) become producers of steel and textiles. . . . India, with its teeming millions, could play a bigger role in low-skill manufacturing.

China . . . is another growing economic power. . . . Their supplies of oil, gas and coal and their agricultural potential also are coveted by foreign business.

Still bigger opportunities await Australia, with its large reserves of coal, oil, natural gas, iron, bauxite and uranium. The land down under will continue to boast one of the highest living standards in the world.

Oil will be the driving force in the Mid-East. A few industries based on petroleum, such as chemicals and plastics, may develop, but the region is given little chance of building an extensive manufacturing base. Nor do economists see much chance of OPEC becoming a powerful force again.

For most of Africa, economists and international experts find little potential . . . most are still traditionally commodity exporters and will remain the same.

Mexico, Brazil and Argentina are expected to take advantage of natural resources and overcome their huge debt burdens to become leading economic powers over the next 30 years. . . . Mexico could become a major steel producer. . . . Brazil will be a leading auto maker. . . . Colombia, Peru and Chile will increase their shares of exports of textiles, shoes and similar goods. . . . Countries in Latin America—and Asia as well—have great potential to become healthy exporters.*

Export Marketing

As mentioned earlier, exporting is perhaps the easiest step in entering the international marketplace. Particularly for small and medium-sized companies, it may be the only way to enter into international business. Even for large established firms, such as General Electric, Boeing Aircraft, Cater-

*Excerpted from *U.S. News & World Report* issue of May 9, 1983. Copyright, 1983, U.S. News & World Report.

Table 10-3 The leading United States exporters for 1984 (billions of dollars)

Company	Product	Exports	Exports as a Percent of Sales
General Motors	Motor vehicles	$7.3	8.7%
General Electric	Electrical equipment	3.9	14.1
Boeing	Aircraft	3.6	35.0
Ford Motor Company	Motor vehicles	6.0	11.5
Caterpillar Tractor	Construction equipment	1.8	26.9
DuPont	Chemicals	2.7	7.4
United Technologies	Aircraft engines	2.4	14.6
McDonnell Douglas	Aircraft and missiles	2.0	22.0
IBM	Information systems	3.1	6.7
Eastman Kodak	Photographic equipment	1.9	18.3
Chrysler	Motor vehicles	2.7	23.8
Westinghouse	Generating equipment	1.1	11.0
Philip Morris	Tobacco products	1.0	10.4

Source: Adapted from Andrew Kupfer, "The 50 Leading Exporters," *Fortune*, August 5, 1985, pp. 60–61, FORTUNE © 1985 Time Inc. All rights reserved.

pillar, and Eastman Kodak, exports constitute a sizeable percentage of their total sales. Table 10-3 provides the importance of export sales of leading companies in the United States.

A majority of governments around the world encourage exports through promotions, trade fairs, outright subsidies, tax rebates, and favorable treatment on granting import licenses. Particularly the developing countries, the last inducement for exporting, assume greater importance because of strict control over foreign exchange and imports. As Keegan has aptly remarked, "National policies toward exports (are) schizophrenic."[26] That is, while governments encourage exports, the flow of goods in the other direction is restricted.

In this section both the macro-level economic and micro-level (firm) issues on export marketing will be discussed. Specifically, I analyze the following elements:

- Importance of export to GNP, national economy, and employment
- The firms' export behavior
- Path to follow successful exporting business
- How to succeed in export marketing

In the Appendix of this chapter, some statistical data on world economy and world markets are provided.

Importance of Export to the National Economy [27]

Exports play an important role in the economic and industrial progress in both industrialized and developing countries. For the latter, it may be the only means to acquire the advanced technological and managerial knowledge of industrialized countries. For many industrialized countries, such as Japan, West Germany, The Netherlands, Belgium, and Switzerland, exports are the real lifeblood of their economies. Recently, even for a country such as the United States, exports are assuming a critical importance in the national economy and employment. For example, consider the following facts:

1. The total dollar volume of exports has increased to 500% during the decade of 1970 to 1980, whereas the gross national product (GNP) rose to only 170% during the same period.
2. Exports are responsible for one out of every six jobs in manufacturing.
3. Eighty percent of all new jobs in manufacturing are linked to exports.
4. One out of three acres of agricultural land in the United States produces crops for export.
5. Export of services (e.g., banking, transportation, consulting) has increased 550% during the decade of 1970 to 1980. It is now a $100 billion business annually for the United States.
6. Every billion dollars of export business creates 40,000 jobs in the United States.

Internationally, the importance of exports is even more striking. For example:

1. In Canada, one dollar in every five is earned outside the country.
2. In England, one dollar in four is earned outside the country.
3. In West Germany, The Netherlands, and Switzerland, roughly one third of the GNP is earned through international trade, mainly exports.
4. For many developing countries, exports contribute 25% to 50% of their GNP.

Why Export?

Exports are not only important for the national economy, but they also assist firms in many ways. These include:

1. Overcome the domestic slack in demand.
2. Even out the seasonal fluctuation in demand.
3. Help the companies lengthen production runs, extend the product

life cycle, and increase sales volume. These in turn enable firms to reduce unit cost and remain competitive in world, as well as domestic, markets.

4. Help keep companies alert to the challenges from international competition.
5. Help companies recoup and spread product development costs.

Export Behavior of Firms

Based on an extensive review of studies on the export behavior of firms, Bilkey[28] identified six different behavior patterns. These are:

1. The firm is unwilling to export; it will not even fill an unsolicited export order. This is caused by apathy, prejudice ("too busy to fill the order"), or whatever reason the company may come up with.
2. The firm fills unsolicited export orders but does not explore the feasibility of exporting.
3. The firm explores the feasibility of exporting (this stage may bypass stage two).
4. The firm exports experimentally to one or more markets.
5. The firm is an experienced exporter to one or more markets.
6. The firm evaluates global market potential and screens the "best" target markets for inclusion in its marketing strategy and plan. This screening is open equally to domestic and foreign markets.

Moving from stage one to stage six is by no means an easy task. A positive management attitude toward international trade is critical for achieving success in exporting. For example, Cavusgil's[29] study indicates the following characteristics of successful exporters:

1. The firms' management has very favorable expectations regarding the effect of exporting on the firms' profitability and growth.
2. Firms plan for the exporting business.
3. Firms have favorable expectations regarding the effects of exporting on their market developments.

Path to Follow for Successful Export Business

Top Management's Commitment

As mentioned earlier, the first step for successful export business is the top management's commitment to international trade. Export cannot be treated as a stepchild and expected to win overseas contracts. Like domestic consumers, overseas customers are sensible and selective regarding product design, pricing, and servicing. They are rightful customers and expect to be treated as such. Many companies fail in generating successful exports largely because of a lukewarm attitude by its top management toward export and international business.

Assess the Strengths and Weaknesses [30]

Assess the company's strengths and weaknesses by asking and answering the following question: "Is the company successful in its domestic business?" Making such an assessment means analyzing the company's performance in such areas as gross and net profit margins, unit costs, overhead costs, return on investments and sales, and financial condition. One has to be successful domestically before one can expect to succeed in the international marketplace. Generally speaking, foreign markets are more competitive, especially in industrialized countries. Thus, foreign markets are not a place to sort out domestic problems.

Decide the Target Markets and Means to Reach Them

The company should decide which level and type of export would be most suitable to start out with. The higher the targeted level, the more resources are required. The easiest level to target is selling to what is called the *United States for export market* – United States firms and foreign trading companies in the United States that buy United States products for delivery abroad. Some examples would be engineering and construction firms that have major products abroad, commission agents, state-controlled buying agents, and trading companies. This method does not require any special knowledge of export sales and is really an extension of domestic selling.

The second level of export marketing is called *easy-to-sell* exporting. This involves selling abroad from a location with delivery to United States destinations. Shipment overseas is handled by the customer. Overseas travel is not necessary at this level of exporting.

The right selection of proper overseas markets is also an important condition for success in exporting. The U.S. Department of Commerce's Foreign Commercial Service's 121 (FCS) offices in 66 countries provide considerable help to United States businesspeople traveling abroad. A computerized *Trade Opportunities Program* (TOP) report is also available from the Commerce Department at a modest cost. This is a worthwhile service even for companies exporting at the easy-to-sell level.

Alternatively, the company could either conduct a market research, make a personal market investigation trip, or present the company's products in one of the many trade fairs.

The next step for exporting should be to select both sales representatives or agents and distributors to handle selling abroad. Selling can be made directly to the end users through advertising.

Still another approach is through an *export management company* (EMC). An EMC acts as the export department for several manufacturers of non-competitive products. It solicits business in the name of the manufacturers it represents for a commission or a retainer plus commission.

Export Trading Company

Selling through an export trading company (ETC) is a further option. ETCs are independent companies that purchase United States goods for resale in foreign markets. Many of these ETCs are based abroad, and have well-established sales, distribution, and service networks in their market areas.

As one good example, trading companies in Japan have taken advantage of economies of scale and large-scale transactions. In contrast, United States trading companies are not the same as the Japanese in terms of product and structure of the ETC. A study indicates that electronics and electrical machinery industries benefit more than other industries, such as aircraft, automobiles, and food processing. Some examples of United States ETCs are General Electric, General Motors, Sears, and Westinghouse.

In general, four types of trading companies are in the United States now. They are project-oriented, industry-oriented, product-oriented, and barter-oriented ETCs. A project-oriented trading company engages in joint ventures and turnkey projects with foreign investors. An industry-oriented trading company handles goods of a specific industry group, such as metals, chemicals, high-technology communications equipment, or pharmaceuticals.

The product-oriented trading company specializes in facilitating the export of a single product that is in steady demand. Examples are major grain trades, such as Continental Grain Co. and Cargill, Inc. A barter-oriented trading company was set up primarily to handle countertrade. Today, countertrade accounts for 25% to 35% of the total international trade. The Sears World Trade Company engages in exporting, importing, third country trade, and countertrade. It buys on its own account and also handles light industrial goods and services for others.

As far as large United States MNCs are concerned, they could also take advantage of tax benefits through the Foreign Sales Corporation (FSC) system. The tax law of 1984 requires United States firms to set up a new subsidiary outside the United States to get tax exemptions on the goods they export. The FSC subsidiary provides roughly the same tax benefit as a Domestic International Sales Corporation (DISC) did. DISCs were paper subsidiaries, set up in 1971, to shelter exports from taxes. Because of continued objectives on DISCs by other General Agreement on Tariffs and Trade (GATT) members, DISC was eliminated and replaced with FSC, by the new tax law, in June 1984.

How to Succeed in Export Marketing[31]

A company must consider carefully two sets of criteria to ensure success in export marketing. They are: general corporate criteria that are related to management philosophy, planning, and practices; and market-specific criteria.

General Corporate Criteria

Commitment to world markets. As discussed earlier, the company must possess a world market perspective for its products and technology rather than treat international business as an appendage to its domestic marketing. A world market perspective is possible only if the top management is committed to overseas markets. Also, the management needs to recognize the cultural difference in the way people do business in other countries, avoiding the self-reference criterion.

Systematic market and competitive research. The management needs to develop a priority list and a long-term plan with which to enter foreign markets through systematic market and competitive research. Some examples of the old stereotypes about the world's markets should be avoided (e.g., India is too poor, Singapore is too small).

Market-Specific Criteria

The five rules for succeeding in exporting can be summarized as market-specific criteria. They are:

1. *Export personnel.* An excellent knowledge of products and production processes is essential for successful export marketing. A high degree of adaptability to adjust to foreign customs, ways of doing business, and even foreign language is necessary.
2. *Product and service.* New products require additional attention and additional service during introduction into foreign markets.
3. *Delivery.* Close adherence to delivery dates, as specified in the contracts, is required. The European and Japanese exporters send

shipments air freight at their own expense to major United States customers to meet the target dates.

4. *Payment.* Acceptable conditions, such as periods of payment and discount commissions, need to be planned in advance and well negotiated with foreign buyers to avoid any contractual problems in the future.

5. *Consistent efforts.* The exporting company is advised to concentrate on a well-defined market, limited to one or two countries in a short-term period.

As noted earlier, useful statistical data on world economy and markets are given in the Appendix.

Summary

This chapter discussed two aspects of world marketing: (1) assessment of international markets, and (2) export marketing.

It began with identifying firm and market-related factors affecting the management decision to enter foreign markets. Firm-related factors included how to use unused capital and capital resources, the need for incremental revenue to cover excessive developmental costs, to keep abreast of technological developments in foreign countries, to avoid the seasonal fluctuations of domestic demands, to spread risks in larger geographical areas, to earn money from obsolete machinery, to avoid domestic taxation, and a subjective preference of decision makers to operate in foreign countries.

The market-related factors included: the desire to maintain a competitive position, taking advantage of fragmented and noncompetitive markets abroad, and realizing foreign profitability and growth potential.

This chapter also discussed four types of foreign investment strategies used by international corporations. These included: (1) defensive ("do nothing" until it "hurts"), (2) aggressive (proreactive and opportunity seekers), (3) follow-the-leader, and (4) avoidance.

For assessing the international markets, a major trend in the world economy was reviewed, based on a fifty-year forecast by *U.S. News and World Report.* The trends seem to indicate a major expansion in international trade and greater dependence of countries on each other. The United States is more likely to retain her superpower status, whereas the USSR and Western Europe may decline. Developing countries will assume greater importance.

The second part of this chapter discussed important elements of export marketing. Topics covered in this part included:

1. Importance of exports to national economy
2. The firms' export behavior

   3. Essential steps to follow in a successful exporting business
   4. How to succeed in export marketing

The case provided for this chapter highlights the problems encountered in assessing the international marketplace.

Case

Appropriate selection of both overseas market and product would be one of the most important success criteria in international marketing. The Stitcher Company case shows an example of a normative guideline for assessing market opportunities.

Case 10-1

The Stitcher Company

Historically, the Stitcher Company had gone into foreign projects as opportunities presented themselves. Decisions had been made on each project as it came up, management being guided by intuition rather than by formalized policies or objectives. The burden on top management became unwieldly, and it was decided to make a formal analysis of (1) what the company was then doing abroad and (2) the strengths and weaknesses of the company in respect to overseas activities. The purpose of the study would be to define company policy in respect to what it should be doing.

To undertake this study, a committee was set up called the Overseas Policy and Planning Committee (OPPC). This group sent "task forces" into each country where the company was then operating and where it might consider operations in the near future. In each case, the initial question was: should the company be in this country? The studies of the task force groups were based on two premises: (1) that the company might consider going into any country and any industry and (2) that the company had complete freedom of action in changing the nature of its investment in respect to either country or industry, or both. Furthermore, no time limit was stipulated during which investment was to be shifted. In other words, in making their studies and forming their recommendations, the task forces were given almost complete flexibility. The OPPC directed that detailed reports be made on 12 African, Asian, and Latin American countries in which Stitcher had interests or projects, plus "less penetrating analysis" of five others in which it had potential interests. The upshot was that on the basis of the task force country reports the OPPC reached certain conclusions as to the outlook for growth in each of these 17 countries relative to opportunities and risks. And in each, the growth industries were singled out for special study. Consideration was given to the company's position in each of the countries, and then related to those industries considered to be especially attractive from the point of view of growth potential. The study finally came down to a recommendation of investment by industry and by country. These recommendations became the criteria against which projects were to be measured. A section of the OPPC report detailed the criteria used in measuring the various "lines of endeavor" of possible interest to the company. It is reproduced in part below:

Summary of OPPC report. From the basic and secondary characteristics of the economics of the seventeen countries, we arrive at definite conclusions as to the criteria by which to determine the right lines of endeavor. If our criteria are correct (and they were one of the first orders of business of the committee when it was formed and have been distilled from all the knowledge that the committee has developed), we have thus a clearly systematic approach to planning for overseas development in Asia, Africa, and Latin America.

Where then do they lead us? What are the guideposts for selecting lines of endeavor?

Primary Specifications

1. As we have already mentioned, as a basic fundamental, ventures should be considered only if they *cut broadly through the ur-banization and industrialization* trends in the economy. These are the deep and sweeping internal movements that will carry all else before them.
2. Investment policy must contribute to overcoming one of the great dangers in all the economies in which we would have serious interest, namely, the stringency of foreign exchange, meaning that lines of endeavor selected should either be *foreign exchange* earners or help meet the exchange problem by substituting local production for imports.
3. There should be low *vulnerability to currency depreciation* with profitability anticipation commensurately higher as the vulnerability increases as in the case with investments involving higher proportions of working capital.

Secondary Specifications

4. The lines of endeavor selected must have the characteristic of filling highly strategic "gap" *opportunities*. It must be in an industry in which consumption is very low compared with what it should be considering the state of the country. It must at the same time have a long range growth potential higher than the rate of growth of economy generally and of personal incomes.
5. There must be long term *growth potential* at a rate greater than the "growth curve" of the economy.
6. "Unique opportunities" that fit into the strategic gaps are

especially desirable—those that give an advantage in a market, especially smaller ones. Investments not having this characteristic in small markets would almost certainly be questionable.

7. There must be an *adequate* existing or clearly foreseeable local *market,* a gap opportunity or extraordinary growth, or there should be already an expanding world market.

8. Availability of *local raw materials* is a primary requisite in view of the foreign exchange problems. If imported materials are used they must be a small fraction of the final value of the ultimately finished product. Can-sealing compounds are a good example.

9. *Foreign entrepreneurship* should be a necessity; i.e., the line of endeavor must still be beyond the possibilities of local nationals now (e.g., due to technology or capital requirements or both), but capable of attracting first-rate foreign personnel.

10. In the absence of a local capital market it must be *capable of financing its own growth* through retained earnings, particularly when further investment from abroad is not attractive or costly.

11. Finally, there is the desirability of *low political exposure.* For instance, the investment should not occupy a strategic position in respect to resources that have high emotional appeal in underdeveloped countries.

We have not mentioned minimum profitability or rate of return here. This is a factor in determining investment policy that can only be considered in relation to the company as a whole and its parts. It cannot be set in accordance with country economic characteristics except that it should be obvious that if the lines of endeavor are selected in accordance with the criteria set forth here, the investment policy requirements for long range profitability will be easier to meet. Whatever minimum base is set on company-wide consideration should, however, be adjusted upward in varying amounts, country-by-country, depending on local risk factors and the specific rationale and expectations for the individual business.

Ranking Lines of Endeavor

The criteria were applied to a wide list of possible industries, particularly those that our surveys in each country brought out as industries that are considered "attractive"; that is, industries that should grow rapidly during the next ten years because of population growth, increases in total and per capita incomes and, most of all, which should tend to move up faster than these indicators. Actually, the industries considered included almost every possible line of endeavor. We put them all through the successive screens of our criteria (basic and secondary) to come up finally with the following main "lines of endeavor" that we concluded were the "opportunity industries":

First we isolated three lines of endeavor that can be considered as having this "opportunity" character without reservation. These are first:

1. Economic intermediates of manufacturing
2. Economic intermediates of distribution
3. Economic intermediates of construction

We should explain what we mean by the term "economic intermediates," as it is a term we had to coin. We mean thereby products that in themselves might be considered "finished products" but whose primary use is in making possible manufacturing, distribution, or construction and that are destroyed, absorbed, or used up in the process. An example of the typical "economic intermediate of manufacturing" would be the hermetically sealed motors produced in Mexico. An example of "economic intermediates of distribution" are packaging materials. Without such materials distribution would be impossible. Yet they are absorbed and used up in the process. Typical examples of "economic intermediates of construction" would be wallboard, paint, structural steel forms, sheet glass, and piping.

The characteristic about economic intermediates that makes them particularly attractive is that their own value is a relatively small part of the total finished product into which they are integrated. A secondary characteristic is that there is a relatively low labor content in their making. They have high capital intensity and they can be produced ordinarily in a fairly continuous flow process. (This, incidentally, is the outstanding characteristic of most of the chemical industry and, therefore—although the products among economic intermediates may be highly diversified—their production will not be entirely unfamiliar to us.) The management requirements are similar in manufacturing where scheduling of raw materials, factory flow, and the overhead to total cost relationships are magnitudinally close.

It is a further characteristic that without the intermediate the final product, whether a building, mine, or a piece of communications equipment, is not capable of being produced. In other words, the "economic intermediates" occupy strategic positions in respect to their essential nature for a whole process, while at the same time negligible in the total cost-structure of the process itself.

We next isolated four "lines of endeavor," which are much more doubtful or which can be considered "opportunity lines" for our company only with reservations and restrictions. These are:

1. Export industries producing primary commodities. We call these "mining" for short even though the production of pulp would belong in this category.

  This category, however, applies only to "minor" extractive industries. "Major" extractive industries such as those mining major materials (rather than rare earths which would be "minor") or producing petroleum do not satisfy the "opportunity criteria" in important aspects.

2. A major "opportunity line" is the building up of a *"distribution system"* (provided it can be organized). By this we mean the actual apparatus needed to distribute goods from the manufacturer to the consumer and any part thereof, warehousing, transporting, financing, and, finally, selling, whether wholesale or retail.

   There is no doubt that the development of streamlined and economical distribution systems is one of the greatest needs of many of these countries. It is doubtful, however, whether such a system can be built without undesirable financial characteristics, though the belief that this is primarily a working-capital investment is perhaps no longer quite valid. There is need for further study here.

3. *Economic intermediates of agriculture.* As we have seen, there is need, and encouragement can be expected to be given to increased agricultural productivity in almost all the countries. This means farm mechanization, fertilizers, insecticides, etc. More rapid introduction of agricultural improvements of this nature is being assisted by developed country assistance and by the economic policies of the respective governments. We should not, therefore, leave out of our thinking an agricultural sector, in at least one aspect of which, fertilizers, the company has expertness. Food imports, as we have seen in the previous chapter, constitute a sizeable drain on the foreign exchange positions of a number of countries. Efforts to substitute local production can be expected to be given emphasis and official encouragement. In relation to the results that can be attained, expenditures for agricultural intermediates represent a fairly small portion of the final product.

4. As a further area that might, with reservations, satisfy the "opportunity characteristics" we list *certain consumer goods, namely those that provide "necessities of status"* rather than "necessities of life" or even "cheap luxuries."

   Consumer goods industries, providing necessities, for example, textiles, clearly do not have the growth potential needed in view of the risk many of these countries pose.

   The situation of "cheap luxuries" consumer goods (packaged foods or biscuits for instance) is much better in that their growth potential is certainly very high, perhaps the highest.

   Such "necessities of status" as durable consumer goods, home appliances, and so on enjoy a growth potential probably as large as that of the "cheap luxuries," though they have greater risks in bad times. At the same time they may be vulnerable in that they depend very much more heavily on the availability of foreign exchange for imports.

The following chart illustrates a checklist method for analyzing lines of endeavor. It is presented only as an approach and to focus the analysis.

Rating of lines of endeavor against criteria

(Illustrative only—not to be used reaching conclusions on lines of endeavor for specific countries)
CODE   + Line of Endeavor
       Rates Favorably
       − Line of Endeavor
       Rates Unfavorably
     0 Line of Endeavor
       Rating Neutral

| | Lines of endeavor | | | | | | | | |
Criteria	A	B	C	D	E	F	G	H	I
Basic Criteria									
Urbanization and Industrialization (Broad cut through)	+	+	+	0	+	0	+	+	0
Foreign Exchange (Earner or Saver)	+	−	−	−	0	+	+	+	+
Maintenance of Values in Face of Inflation & Currency Depreciation	+	+	+	+	−	−	−	−	+
Secondary Criteria									
Dynamic Growth of Potential	+	+	+	+	+	0	+	0	0
Strategic Gap Opportunities	+	+	+	0	+	0	0	0	0
Unique Opportunity Possibilities	+	+	+	0	+	+	0	0	0
Adequate Local or Export Markets	+	+	+	+	+	+	0	+	+
Available Raw Materials	+	+	0	0	0	+	0	+	+
Foreign Management and Capital Desirable	+	+	+	+	+	+	+	−	0
Capable of Self-financing	+	+	+	0	+	0	+	0	+
Political Exposure	+	+	0	−	+	−	−	−	−

A = Economic Intermediates of Manufacturing
B = Economic Intermediates of Distribution
C = Construction
D = "Mining"—Including Pulp
E = Distribution Systems
F = Economic Intermediates of Agriculture
G = Consumer Necessities of Status
H = Some Existing Businesses: Textiles
I = Sugar

Appendix: Statistical Data on World Economy and Markets of the World (Selected Countries)

Table 10-4 Basic indicators: Selected major countries

	Population (millions) mid-1980	GNP per capita U.S. dollars 1980	Average annual growth (percent) 1980	Adult literacy (percent) 1977	Life expectancy at birth (years) 1980
Low-income economies	2,160.9	260	1.2	50	57
China and India	1,649.9	270	–	54	59
Other low-income	511.0	230	1.0	34	48
Bangladesh	88.5	130	–	26	46
India	673.2	240	1.4	36	52
Sri Lanka	14.7	270	2.4	85	66
Tanzania	18.7	280	1.9	66	52
China	976.7	290	–	66	64
Pakistan	82.2	300	2.8	24	50
Sudan	18.7	410	−0.2	20	46
Middle-income economies	1,138.8	1.400	3.8	65	60
Oil exporters	496.8	1.160	3.3	57	56
Oil importers	642.0	1.580	4.1	73	63
Ghana	11.7	420	−1.0	–	49
Kenya	11.7	420	2.7	50	55
Indonesia	146.6	430	4.0	62	53
Egypt	39.8	580	3.4	44	57
Thailand	47.0	670	4.7	84	63
Philippines	49.0	690	2.8	75	64
Albania	2.7	–	–	–	70
Peru	17.4	930	1.1	80	58
Algeria	18.9	1,870	3.2	35	56
Korea, Rep. of	38.2	1,520	7.0	93	65
Turkey	44.9	1,470	3.6	60	62
Malaysia	13.9	1,620	4.3	–	64
Brazil	118.7	2,050	5.1	76	63
Mexico	69.8	2,090	2.6	81	65
Chile	11.1	2,150	1.6	–	67
South Africa	29.3	2,300	2.3	–	61

Continued

Table 10-4 Continued

	Population (millions) mid-1980	GNP per capita U.S. dollars 1980	Average annual growth (percent) 1980	Adult literacy (percent) 1977	Life expectancy at birth (years) 1980
Romania	22.2	2,340	8.6	98	71
Portugal	9.8	2,370	5.0	–	71
Argentina	27.7	2,390	2.2	93	70
Venezuela	14.9	3,630	2.6	82	67
Uruguay	2.9	2,810	1.4	94	71
Iran	38.8	–	–	50	59
Iraq	13.1	3,020	5.3	–	56
Trinidad and Tobago	1.2	4,370	3.0	95	72
Singapore	2.4	4,430	7.5	–	72
Israel	3.9	4,500	3.8	–	72
Industrial market economies	714.4	10,310	3.6	99	74
Spain	37.4	5,400	4.5	–	73
Italy	56.9	6,480	3.6	98	73
New Zealand	3.3	7,090	1.8	99	73
United Kingdom	55.9	7,920	2.2	99	73
Finland	4.9	9,720	4.0	100	73
Australia	14.5	9,820	2.7	100	74
Japan	116.8	9,890	7.1	99	76
Canada	23.9	10,130	3.3	99	74
United States	227.7	11,360	2.3	99	75
Netherlands	14.1	11,470	3.2	99	75
France	53.5	11,730	3.9	99	74
Belgium	9.8	12,180	3.8	99	73
Norway	4.1	12,650	3.5	99	75
Sweden	8.3	13,520	2.3	99	75
Germany, Fed. Rep. of	60.9	13,490	3.3	99	73
Switzerland	6.5	16,440	4.9	99	75
Nonmarket Industrial economies	353.3	4,640	4.2	100	71
Poland	35.8	3,900	5.3	98	72
Hungary	10.8	4,180	4.5	99	71
Czechoslovakia	15.3	5,820	4.0	–	71
Germany, Dem. Rep. of	16.9	7,180	4.7	–	72

Table 10-4 Continued

| Growth of production | Average annual growth rate (percent) | | | |
| | Industry | | Manufacturing | |
	1960–70	*1970–80*	*1960–70*	*1970–80*
Low-income economies	7.0	3.6	6.3	3.7
China and India	8.3	6.6	–	–
Other low-income	7.0	3.2	6.5	3.6
Bangladesh	8.0	9.5	6.6	11.8
India	5.4	4.5	4.7	5.0
Sri Lanka	6.6	4.0	6.3	1.9
Tanzania	–	1.9	–	3.6
China	11.2	8.7	–	–
Guinea	–	–	–	–
Pakistan	10.0	5.2	9.4	4.0
Sudan	–	3.1	–	1.3
Middle-income economies	7.4	6.6	6.8	6.4
Oil exporters	6.2	7.4	6.8	8.0
Oil importers	7.8	6.6	7.5	6.2
Ghana	–	−1.2	–	−2.9
Kenya	–	10.2	–	11.4
Indonesia	5.2	11.1	3.3	12.8
Egypt	5.4	6.8	4.8	8.0
Thailand	11.9	10.0	11.4	10.6
Philippines	6.0	8.7	6.7	7.2
Albania	–	–	–	–
Peru	5.0	3.7	5.7	3.2
Turkey	9.6	6.6	10.9	6.1
Korea, Rep. of	17.2	15.4	17.6	16.6
Malaysia	–	9.7	–	11.8
Algeria	11.6	7.9	7.8	11.4
Brazil	–	9.3	–	10.3
Mexico	9.1	6.6	9.0	5.9
Chile	4.8	0.2	5.5	−0.5
South Africa	–	–	–	–
Romania	12.8	9.7	–	–
Portugal	8.8	4.5	8.9	4.5
Argentina	5.9	1.8	5.7	1.0
Uruguay	1.1	5.2	1.5	4.1
Iran	13.4	–	12.0	–
Iraq	4.7	–	5.9	–

Continued

Table 10-4 Continued

Growth of production	Average annual growth rate (percent)			
	Industry		Manufacturing	
	1960–70	*1970–80*	*1960–70*	*1970–80*
Venezuela	4.6	3.0	6.4	5.7
Trinidad and Tobago	–	–	–	–
Singapore	12.5	8.8	13.0	9.6
Israel	–	–	–	–
Industrial market economies	5.9	3.1	5.9	3.2
Spain	–	3.9	–	6.0
Italy	6.2	1.5	7.1	3.8
New Zealand	–	–	–	–
United Kingdom	3.2	0.7	3.3	0.1
Finland	6.3	3.3	6.2	3.3
Australia	4.6	–	5.6	–
Japan	10.9	5.5	11.0	6.4
Canada	6.3	3.4	6.7	3.6
United States	4.9	1.2	5.3	2.9
Netherlands	6.8	1.2	6.6	2.7
France	6.4	3.1	6.6	3.6
Belgium	5.5	3.0	6.2	2.8
Norway	5.5	5.4	5.3	1.2
Denmark	5.5	–	5.4	–
Sweden	6.2	0.9	5.9	0.8
Germany, Fed. Rep. of	5.2	–	5.4	2.1
Switzerland	–	–	–	–
Nonmarket industrial economies	–	–	–	–
Poland	–	–	–	–
USSR	–	–	–	–
Czechoslovakia	–	–	–	–
Germany, Dem. Rep. of	–	–	–	–

Source: Modified from *World Development Report 1982*, New York: Oxford University Press, 1982, pp. 110–116.

Table 10-5 U.S. trade in 1984 ($ billions)

Top 25 U.S. export markets		*Top 25 U.S. suppliers*	
World total	$217.9	World total	$341.2
1. Canada	46.5	1. Canada	66.9
2. Japan	23.6	2. Japan	60.4
3. United Kingdom	12.2	3. Mexico	18.3
4. Mexico	12.0	4. West Germany	17.8
5. West Germany	9.1	5. Taiwan	16.1
6. Netherlands	7.6	6. United Kingdom	15.0
7. France	6.0	7. Korea	10.0
8. Korea	6.0	8. Hong Kong	8.9
9. Saudi Arabia	5.6	9. France	8.5
10. Belgium & Luxemburg	5.3	10. Italy	8.5
11. Taiwan	5.0	11. Brazil	8.3
12. Australia	4.8	12. Venezuela	6.8
13. Italy	4.4	13. Indonesia	5.9
14. Singapore	3.7	14. Netherlands	4.3
15. Venezuela	3.4	15. Singapore	4.1
16. USSR	3.3	16. Saudi Arabia	4.0
17. Hong Kong	3.1	17. Algeria	3.8
18. China	3.0	18. Sweden	3.4
19. Egypt	2.7	19. China	3.4
20. Brazil	2.6	20. Belgium & Luxemburg	3.3
21. Switzerland	2.6	21. Switzerland	3.2
22. Spain	2.6	22. Australia	2.8
23. South Africa	2.3	23. Malaysia	2.8
24. Israel	2.2	24. India	2.7
25. Malaysia	1.9	25. Spain	2.6

Table 10-6 U.S. merchandise trade balance ($ billions)

U.S. surplus		U.S. deficit	
World total	$20.7	World total	−132.9
1. Netherlands	3.2	1. Japan	−36.8
2. USSR	2.7	2. Canada	−20.4
3. Egypt	2.5	3. Taiwan	−11.1
4. Belgium & Luxemburg	2.0	4. W. Germany	−8.7
5. Australia	1.9	5. Mexico	−6.3
6. Saudi Arabia	1.6	6. Hong Kong	−5.8
7. Pakistan	0.8	7. Brazil	−5.6
8. Turkey	0.8	8. Indonesia	−4.7
9. Iraq	0.5	9. Italy	−4.1
10. Morocco	0.5	10. Korea	−4.0
11. Ireland	0.5	11. Venezuela	−3.4
12. Portugal	0.4	12. Algeria	−3.2
13. Tunisia	0.4	13. United Kingdom	−2.8
14. Panama	0.4	14. France	−2.5
15. Israel	0.4	15. Nigeria	−2.0
16. Kuwait	0.4	16. Sweden	−1.9
17. Jordan	0.3	17. Netherlands Antilles	−1.5
18. Lebanon	0.3	18. India	−1.1
19. Bermuda	0.2	19. Ecuador	−1.1
20. Colombia	0.2	20. Norway	−1.1
21. Libya	0.2	21. Congo	−1.0
22. Leeward & Islands	0.2	22. Malaysia	−1.0
23. Bangladesh	0.1	23. Angola	−1.0
24. Sudan	0.1	24. Denmark	−0.9
25. Bahrain	0.1	25. Philippines	−0.9

Table 10-7 Export markets of selected countries (Export markets for foreign countries means imports of a given country. Therefore, import figures of various countries are provided.)

(1) United States

Main import items	$	(1982, US$ mil) %
Nonelectric machinery	44,175	20.8
Transport equipment	27,824	13.1
Chemicals	19,891	9.4
Electric machinery	15,149	7.1
Grain and cereals	14,747	6.9
Scientific instruments	6,003	2.8
Others	84,486	39.9
Total	212,275	100.0

(2) Canada

Main import items	$	(1982, US$ mil) %
Motor vehicles and parts	6,465	11.7
Petroleum	4,041	7.3
Automobiles	3,278	6.0
Chemicals	2,907	5.3
Industrial machinery	2,766	5.0
Fruit & vegetables	1,518	2.8
Others	34,084	61.9
Total	55,059	100.0

(3) Japan

Main import items	$	(1983, US$ mil) %
Petroleum	58,925	46.6
Other crude materials	17,943	14.2
Food & live animals	14,051	11.1
Manufactured goods	10,147	8.0
Machinery	9,385	7.4
Chemicals	7,207	5.8
Others	8,735	6.9
Total	126,393	100.0

Continued

Table 10-7 Continued

(4) West Germany

Main import items	$	(1983, US$ mil) %
Machinery	33,331	21.8
Petroleum	32,434	21.2
Manufactures as material	24,854	16.3
Manufactures as articles	17,127	11.2
Food & live animals	15,116	9.9
Chemicals	12,492	8.2
Others	17,547	11.4
Total	152,901	100.0

(5) United Kingdom

Main import items	$	(1982, US$ mil) %
Petroleum	10,980	11.0
Vehicles and parts	7,870	7.9
Electric machinery	3,815	3.8
Office machinery	3,715	3.7
Textile yarns and fiber	3,378	3.4
Paper products	2,938	2.9
Others	66,949	67.3
Total	99,645	100.0

(6) France

Main import items	$	(1982, US$ mil) %
Petroleum	30,978	26.8
Machinery	20,294	17.6
Food, drink and tobacco	11,226	9.7
Chemicals	9,898	8.6
Furniture and clothing	9,897	8.6
Manufactures	9,086	7.9
Others	24,075	20.8
Total	115,454	100.0

Table 10-7 Continued

(7) Sweden

Main import items	$	(1982, US$ mil) %
Petroleum	5,137	23.1
Chemicals	1,965	8.8
Road vehicles	1,451	6.5
Food and live animals	1,293	5.8
Iron and steel	857	3.9
Crude materials	843	3.8
Others	10,672	48.1
Total	22,218	100.0

(8) Germany, Democratic Republic of

Main import items	$	(1979, US$ mil) %
Machinery	7,048	33.1
Fuels and metals	6,984	32.8
Raw materials	4,131	19.4
Chemical products	2,001	9.4
Durable consumer goods	1,128	5.3
Total	21,292	100.0

(9) Poland

Main import items	$	(1982, US$ mil) %
Chemical products	1,445	14.6
Petroleum	1,221	12.4
Food products	829	8.4
Agricultural products	814	8.2
Transport equipment	510	5.2
Petroleum products	477	4.8
Others	4,578	46.4
Total	9,874	100.0

Continued

Table 10-7 Continued

(10) Czechoslovakia

Main import items	$	(1982, US$ mil) %
Petroleum	1,410	18.9
Industrial machinery	622	8.3
Gas	507	6.8
Metalliferous ores	275	3.7
Nonferrous metals	247	3.3
Road vehicles	220	3.0
Others	4,170	56.0
Total	7,451	100.0

(11) Hungary

Main import items	$	(1982, US$ mil) %
Petroleum	1,019	14.0
Industrial machinery	553	7.6
Road vehicles	471	6.5
Iron and steel	275	3.8
Textile yarns and fiber	223	3.1
Nonferrous metals	210	2.9
Others	4,529	62.1
Total	7,280	100.0

(12) Bulgaria

Main import items	$	(1980, US$ mil) %
Transport rolling stock	1,543	13.6
Ferrous metals	896	7.9
Sold fuels	468	4.1
Electrical machines	296	2.6
Agricultural machinery	272	2.4
Mining equipment	263	2.3
Others	7,636	67.1
Total	11,374	100.0

Table 10-7 Continued

(13) Yugoslavia

Main import items	$	(1982, US$ mil) %
Petroleum	948	24.0
Nonelectric machinery	653	16.5
Chemicals	508	12.9
Iron and steel	262	6.6
Transport equipment	236	6.0
Electric machinery	203	5.1
Others	1,136	28.9
Total	3,946	100.0

(14) USSR

Main import items	$	(1982, US$ mil) %
Machinery and equipment	26,641	34.4
Rolled stock	1,804	2.3
Knitted wear	820	1.1
Furniture	794	1.0
Cotton fabrics	370	0.5
Others	47,059	60.7
Total	77,488	100.0

(15) China

Main import items	$	(1982, US$ mil) %
Iron and steel	3,330	15.6
Metal and alloys	1,430	6.7
Fertilizers	1,390	6.5
Sets of equipment	1,090	5.1
Sugar	640	3.0
Timber	490	2.3
Others	12,930	60.8
Total	21,300	100.0

Continued

Table 10-7 Continued

(16) India

Main import items	$	(1983, US$ mil) %
Petroleum	5,286	39.6
Nonelectric machinery	1,266	9.5
Iron and steel	1,065	8.0
Precious stones	643	4.8
Transport equipment	566	4.2
Nonferrous metals	263	2.0
Others	4,245	31.9
Total	13,334	100.0

(17) Egypt

Main import items	$	(1982, US$ mil) %
Machinery and equipment	1,651	18.1
Cereals	1,279	14.1
Transport equipment	1,003	11.0
Chemical products	697	7.7
Wood and rubber	469	5.2
Animal and vegetable oil	273	3.0
Others	3,707	40.9
Total	9,079	100.0

(18) Saudi Arabia

Main import items	$	(1982, US$ mil) %
Machinery (incl. electronic)	10,168	25.5
Transport equipment	6,877	17.2
Base metals	5,927	14.9
Foodstuffs	5,194	13.0
Textiles and clothing	2,361	5.9
Chemicals	1,397	3.5
Others	7,943	20.0
Total	39,867	100.0

Table 10-7 Continued

(19) Iraq

Main import items	$	(1978, US$ mil) %
Nonelectric machinery	1,184	29.6
Basic manufactures	917	22.9
Electric machinery	518	12.9
Transport equipment	447	11.2
Food and live animals	434	10.8
Chemicals	190	4.7
Others	311	7.9
Total	4,001	100.0

(20) Kuwait

Main import items	$	(1982, US$ mil) %
Transport equipment	86,638	17.5
Electric machinery	70,377	14.2
Nonelectric machinery	46,346	9.4
Iron ·and steel	29,085	5.9
Textile yarn	24,116	4.9
Clothing	21,992	4.4
Others	217,086	43.7
Total	495,640	100.0

(21) Libya

Main import items	$	(1981, US$ mil) %
Machinery and transport equip.	3,198	38.2
Basic manufactures	1,999	23.8
Food and live animals	1,367	16.3
Manufactured articles	1,074	12.8
Chemicals	376	4.5
Animal and vegetable oil	111	1.3
Others	257	3.1
Total	8,382	100.0

Continued

Table 10-7 Continued

(22) Mexico

Main import items	$	(1982, US$ mil) %
Metalworking machinery	606	4.0
Parts for assembling cars	583	3.9
Iron and steel tubes	337	2.2
Iron and steel sheets	298	2.0
Spare parts for cars	296	2.0
Parts for electric equipment	284	1.9
Others	12,637	84.0
Total	15,041	100.0

(23) Brazil

Main import items	$	(1982, US$ mil) %
Machinery products	10,623	54.8
Machinery equipment	2,826	14.6
Chemical products	1,446	7.5
Vegetables	1,442	7.4
Basic metals	923	4.8
Optical instruments	447	2.3
Others	1,688	8.0
Total	19,395	100.0

(24) Argentina

Main import items	$	(1980, US$ mil) %
Machinery	2,994	28.4
Mineral products	1,257	11.9
Chemical products	1,125	10.7
Transport equipment	1,114	10.6
Basic metals	971	9.2
Scientific equipment	517	4.9
Others	2,563	24.3
Total	10,541	100.0

Table 10-7 Continued

(25) Singapore

Main import items	$	(1982, US$ mil) %
Petroleum	9,656	34.0
Nonelectrical machinery	3,369	11.9
Electric machinery	3,241	11.4
Food and live animals	1,699	6.0
Chemicals	1,317	4.6
Iron and steel	1,225	4.3
Others	7,910	27.8
Total	28,417	100.0

(26) Hong Kong

Main import items	$	(1982, US$ mil) %
Textile yarn	2,233	12.7
Petroleum	1,303	7.4
Electric machinery	1,280	7.3
Chemicals	1,165	6.6
Optical goods	1,028	5.9
Nonmetallic minerals	875	5.0
Others	9,670	55.1
Total	17,554	100.0

(27) Korea

Main import items	$	(1982, US$ mil) %
Petroleum	6,668	27.5
Organic chemicals	1,119	4.6
Ships	980	4.0
Wood	638	2.6
Thermionic valves	641	2.6
Raw cotton	529	2.2
Others	13,676	56.5
Total	24,251	100.0

Continued

Table 10-7 Continued

(28) Taiwan

Main import items	$	(1982, US$ mil) %
Petroleum	3,855	20.5
Logs	406	2.2
Maize (unmilled)	372	2.0
Soybeans	338	1.8
Ships for breakups	309	1.6
Iron and steel sheets	238	1.3
Others	13,296	70.6
Total	18,814	100.0

Source: Modified from *The Europa Year Book*, Europa Publications Limited, London, England 1984.

Discussion Questions

1. Discuss the four major foreign investment strategies by using some examples.
2. Discuss the significant geographical changes likely to occur in international markets in the 1980s and 1990s compared with the 1970s.
3. Why is export so important to the United States' national economy today?
4. What are the key export strategies of Japanese firms?
5. Currently, import restriction policies appear to become a controversial issue in the United States. What are the advantages and disadvantages in establishing protective measures to curb the rapidly growing United States imports? Also discuss in which situations restrictive measures are necessary and most effective.

Endnotes

1. L. O. Walsh, *International Marketing* (Plymouth, Eng.: Macdonald & Evans Ltd., 1981), p. 7.
2. Philip R. Cateora, and John M. Hess, *International Marketing* (Homewood, Ill.: Richard D. Irwin, Inc., 1979).
3. William H. Davidson, *Global Strategic Management* (New York: John Wiley and Sons, 1982), pp. 85–96.
4. See Raymond Vernon, *Storm over the Multinationals* (Cambridge, Mass.: Harvard University Press, 1977), especially Chap. 2.
5. Ibid., pp. 19–37.
6. Ibid.
7. Louis J. Wells, Jr., *Third-World Multinationals: The Rise of Foreign Investment from Developing Countries* (Cambridge, Mass.: MIT Press, 1983), Chap. 1.

8. Davidson, *Global*, pp. 85–92.
9. Ibid., p. 86.
10. Ibid., p. 88.
11. Ibid., pp. 88–89.
12. Vernon, *Storm*, p. 69.
13. Davidson, *Global*, p. 89.
14. Ibid., p. 9.
15. Ibid.
16. Ibid., p. 87.
17. Ibid., pp. 93–94.
18. Ibid., p. 94.
19. *International Herald Tribune*, March 31–April 1, 1984, pp. 15–17.
20. Warren J. Keegan, *Multinational Marketing Management* (Englewood, NJ: Prentice-Hall, 1984), pp. 227–230.
21. Ibid., pp. 229–230.
22. Reed Moyer, "International Market Analysis," *Journal of Marketing Research* V, 4 (November 1968): 353–360.
23. See for example, Harper W. Boyd, Ralph Westfall, and Stanley F. Stasch, *Marketing Research: Text and Cases* (Homewood: Ill.: Richard D. Irwin, Inc., 1981); Keegan, *Multinational*, Chap. 9, pp. 227–251.
24. Quoted from "What the Next 50 Years Will Bring," *U.S. News and World Report*, May 9, 1983, p. A2.
25. Summarized from ibid., pp. A1–A42. Permission of the publisher is gratefully acknowledged.
26. Keegan, *Multinational*, p. 495.
27. Statistical data presented in this section are heavily drawn from the Chamber of Commerce of the United States, Three scripts for the color-slides presentation on exports. These are: (1) *Real World of Exporting: Opportunities and Realities*, (2) *Export for Profit*, (3) *The Case for Two-Way Trade* (Washington, D.C.: Chamber of Commerce of the United States, 1984).
28. Warren J. Bilkey, "Attempted Integration of the literature of the Export Behavior of Firms," *Journal of International Business Studies* 9 (Spring–Summer 1977): 33–46.
29. S. T. Cavusgil, "Organizational Determinants of Firms' Export Behavior: An Empirical Analysis" (Ph.D. diss., The University of Wisconsin (Madison), 1976).
30. These suggestions are drawn from the Chamber of Commerce of the United States' publications.
31. Material discussed in this section is heavily drawn from Jagdish Sheth, and Hans-Martin Schoenfeld, *Export Marketing Lessons to Learn from Europe* (Champaign, Ill.: Bureau of Economic and Business Research, University of Illinois), pp. 185–204; Chamber of Commerce of the United States' publications, 1980.

Additional Readings

Articles

Billey, Warren J. "Attempted Integration of the Literature of the Export Behavior of Firms." *Journal of International Business Studies* VIII, 1 (Summer 1977): 33–46.

Cooper, Robert G., and Kleinschmidt, Elko J. "The Impact of Export Strategy on Export Sales Performance." *Journal of International Business Studies* XVI, 1 (Spring 1985).

Moyer, Reed. "International Market Analysis." *Journal of Marketing Research* XXV, 4 (November 1985).

"What the Next 50 Years Will Bring." *U.S. News and World Report.* May 9, 1983, pp. A1–A42.

Books

Czinkota, Michael R. *Export Management: An International Context.* New York: Praeger Publishers, 1982.

Sheth, Jagdish, and Schoenfeld, Hanns-Martin. *Export Marketing Lessons to Learn from Europe.* Champaign, Ill.: Bureau of Economics and Business Research, University of Illinois, 1980.

Chapter 11

Managing the Marketing Mix in an International Context

Managing the marketing mix involves four familiar aspects: Product, pricing, promotion, and distribution.

In managing these four elements of marketing, the overall aims are to maximize sales, maximize profits and revenues, build up the company's image, and provide a coherent and integrative strategy to guide operational decisions.

In the international marketplace, the fundamental question facing the global firm is how to maintain a balance between standardizing and localizing its marketing practices. In other words, as Fayerweather has stated, "on the one hand, marketing is one phase of business in which companies in advanced countries, especially the United States, have developed a high degree of competence. On the other hand, marketing activities by their nature are associated very broadly and deeply with cultural characteristics, . . . people's tastes and motivation. . . . Fine judgment is therefore required to determine to what extent and how MNC marketing capabilities may be transmitted."[1]

There was a great deal of intellectual debate during the 1960s, suggesting that the marketing practices cannot be standardized. Mr. George Weissman, President of Philip Morris, for example, had argued that "until we achieve one world there is no such thing as international market, only local marketing around the world."[2]

Similarly, Mr. Millard H. Pryor, Jr., Director of Corporate Planning for Singer Sewing Company, had expressed identical views: "Marketing is conspicuous by its absence from the functions which can be planned at the corporate headquarters' level. . . . The operating experience of many international firms appears to confirm the desirability of assigning long-range planning of marketing activities to local managers."[3]

In an often quoted study, Buzzell[4] has shown that, although the problem of deciding the locus of the decision-making authority is a complex phenomenon, local management usually is responsible for developing viable overall local marketing strategies. He identified the following environmental and sociocultural factors as impediments to the standardization of marketing practices:

1. Physical environment
2. Stage of economic and industrial development
3. Custom and tradition
4. Competition
5. The existing marketing and media institutions
6. Legal restrictions

In contrast, Vernon,[5] in analyzing the problems of multinational companies with the nation-states, has argued that there has been a rapid movement toward the homogenization of consumer taste. The following extract highlights the necessity for the standardization of marketing practices:

> The universal instinct of curiosity and the wide-spread propensity for emulation have spread some products rapidly through the world, including not only the markets in which multinational enterprises are present but also the markets in which they are not. Portable radios, Donald Duck dolls, and existentialist novels, for instance, have become ubiquitous items in global markets.[6]

The author goes on to say:

> The manufactured products that appear in the stalls and markets of Accra or Dar es Salaam are no longer very different from those in Djakarta or Car-

tagena or Recife. The plastic pail has replaced the gourd, the earthen pot, and the banana leaf; tin roofs are replacing the local varieties of thatch; electric batteries and electric bulbs are taking over the function of kerosene, wood, vegetable oil, and tallow; the portable radio and the aspirin tablet are joining the list of life's universal necessities.[7]

For consumers at higher levels of income, consumption patterns in different parts of the world show the same overwhelming tendency to convergence.[8] . . . With national distinctions declining in consumer goods and in industrial products, the chances have increased that a product turned out by a firm in one country will be compatible with the requirements of buyers elsewhere.[9] The convergence in the consumers' tastes preferences and income levels are likely to increase the opportunity for standardizing marketing practices (e.g., fast-food chains around the world).

Strategic Options in International Marketing

Basically, three different strategic options are available to the international firm to sell its products in the world markets:

1. Standardized, or undifferentiated, marketing
2. Unstandardized, or differentiated, marketing
3. Concentrated marketing[10]

In a *standardized marketing strategy*, the firm will offer a standard product without much modification to different geographical or national markets. The main advantage of this strategy is the achievement of economies of scale and a reduction of the unit cost of production. The firm's marketing cost will also be reduced to a minimal amount. The strategy assumes a convergence in the consumers' taste and preference, and a minimal impact of socioeconomic, political, and legal environments on the consumers' choices. In other words, as Vernon[11] has argued, a great deal of homogenization of the consumers' preferences must be taking place in the world marketplace for such a strategy to be effective.

A number of soft-drink companies (e.g., Coca-Cola and Pepsi) and pharmaceutical firms seem to follow this undifferentiated marketing strategy. Many firms of manufacturing industrial products also pursue this marketing strategy.

In a *differentiated marketing strategy,* the firm gives in to the environmental demands and differentiated consumers' tastes and preferences. Products are modified and redesigned to accommodate national and geographical differences. In other words, with this strategy, a company segments its market to achieve maximum consumer appeal within each segment of the market. This strategy will increase both the production and the marketing cost. The differentiated marketing strategy could be pursued through both product modification and packaging devices. Automobile companies are the prime example of those firms pursuing such a marketing strategy. Ford Motor Company, for example, has been manufacturing different models of cars for the United States and European markets. The same is true with respect to General Motors. Only in recent years, particularly since the oil crisis of 1973, have those auto companies introduced their small-sized European models in the United States market. Previously, the United States and European markets were highly segmented. Firms in consumer durable goods industries (e.g., refrigerators, stoves, washing machines) are also using the differentiated marketing strategy to accommodate the differences in the consumers' tastes and preferences.

The *concentrated marketing strategy* involves selecting targeted markets and products. Once such a selection is made, the firm will devote considerable marketing efforts to achieve maximum segments of targeted markets. It is an incremental approach in that the firm will proceed cautiously and make advances in unknown markets only after it has succeeded in a relatively known market. Economically, it is a more rational approach in international marketing. Many of the international firms, particularly those with limited capital and human resources, as well as those with little experience, choose this strategy.[12]

The concentrated marketing strategy as such is thus the firm's approach in entering into international markets. Under this approach, it can either use standardized or fragmented marketing practices, depending on the nature of the markets, the products, and the resources available to the firm.

The Hybrid Strategy

This description of the various marketing strategies may create the impression of an either/or type of decision making concerning the strategic choices. In reality, a large number of international companies are using the mix- or hybrid-type of marketing strategy. Under such a strategy, the firm may use some elements from all three of the strategies for its marketing mix management. For example, a pharmaceutical firm may manufacture the same brand name product (e.g., Anacin) in different geographical or national locations but package it differently to accommodate the consumers' preferences and local legal requirements. In other words, one aspect of marketing mix management may be highly standardized whereas other aspects may be partially standardized, and still other elements may be highly fragmented.

Besides the sociocultural, economic, and legal environments, the firm's related factors, products, and industry characteristics play important roles in selecting effective strategies for managing the marketing mix. I shall discuss the influence of important factors on product policy decisions, pricing, promotion, and distribution in the following.

Nationality and Marketing Strategies

Although many of the international companies pursue market penetration and sales growth strategies, there seem to be some differences among the United States, European, and Japanese companies' models for achieving their specific objectives. Hulbert and Brandt, for example, found that approximately two thirds of the United States, European, and Japanese subsidiaries in Brazil specified their objectives in terms of market penetration.[13]

Similarly, a study of German and Japanese subsidiaries in the United States also showed that approximately one half of those companies favored the market penetration strategy.[14] However, the manner of achieving these objectives differed. The European and United States firms emphasized sales-force decisions, whereas the Japanese used the pricing alternative and developed new products and new markets.[15] The Japanese companies also ventured more into unrelated diversifications than did German companies.[16]

Product Policies

Among the four elements of the marketing mix management, the decisions concerning product design are most centralized at the headquarters' levels. The logic of doing so rests on the economies of scale arguments, as well as on the desire to maintain the company's and the product's image, reputation, and brand name.

Besides the advantages of capital, technological, and managerial resources, multinational companies are able to maintain their competitive edge vis-à-vis their local counterparts on the basis of the reputation of their products. Some other advantages of product standardization are:

1. Lower entry costs in foreign markets
2. To extend the life cycle of a given product
3. To fully use the technological and managerial resources of the firm
4. To amortize the research and developmental expenses on large-volume sales
5. Easier to divest from foreign countries if the given product fails, because the cost of redesigning is minimal

These arguments are "generally so persuasive that most companies do have essentially the same product lines throughout the world."[17]

Arguments for Product Modification

The arguments for product modification and redesigning of the firm's product lines for overseas markets are based on the differences in socioeconomic and cultural conditions and on differing consumer tastes and preferences in countries around the world. As Welch has stated, "Internationally, buyers' needs and the benefits they perceive as a result of their purchases, will often vary significantly according to the level of economic development and the social and cultural environment. . . . [Consequently] the most important aspect of international product policy is undoubtedly that of adaptation of existing products to widely differing world markets."[18]

In the following section, I will examine the actual practices of multinational companies and identify the firm's and the environmental-related factors affecting product policies.

Empirical Results

Aylmer's[19] study of some eighty-six European subsidiaries of United States MNCs showed that 55% of those subsidiaries depended on their headquarters for product design decisions. Only 30% of the subsidiaries enjoyed autonomy with respect to product design decisions. In contrast, advertising, pricing, and distribution decisions were considerably decentralized.

Similar results were obtained by Hulbert and Brandt[20] in their study of United States, European, and Japanese subsidiaries in Brazil. Directives from the home office were highest in product design decisions and lowest in salesforce management and pricing decisions.

Sorenson and Wiechmann,[21] in their study of twenty-seven companies for consumer packaged goods in Europe and in the United States, found a high degree of standardization in product designs and brand names. Their specific results, with respect to the various marketing decisions, are described in Table 11-1.

As discussed in Chapter 5, both Franko[22] and Wiechmann,[23] among others, have underscored a high degree of centralization in decision making with respect to product designs.

A study of 120 subsidiaries of United States, German, and Japanese multinational companies indicated that the decisions concerning the introduction of new products were highly centralized in all three types of multinational companies.[24]

Such high levels of centralization in decision making can also be observed through examining research and developmental expenditures of the multinational companies in foreign countries. For example, according to the U.S. Census Bureau, only 15% of the major industrial companies maintain research laboratories in foreign countries.[25] Similarly, a U.S. Senate Com-

Table 11-1 Comparison of product design and brand name standardization

Marketing function	Percentage of companies with high degree of standardization
Brand names	93%
Product characteristics	81
Pricing decisions	56
Advertising message	71
Creative expression in advertisement	62
Sales promotion	56
Media allocation	43
Role of middleman in distribution	80
Role of salesforce management of salesforce	72
Type of retail outlet	59

Source: Adapted from Ralph Z. Sorenson, and Ulrich E. Wiechmann "How multinationals view marketing standardization," *Harvard Business Review* (May–June 1975): 38–55.

mittee Report showed that only 6% of the research and development expenditures of United States MNCs was spent overseas.[26]

Although Behrman and Fischer's recent study seems to indicate increases in research and development expenditures in overseas locations, they also conclude that the research and development activities concerning the introduction of new products are centralized in the home offices of the United States and European multinational companies.[27] The authors state:

> The evidence . . . suggests that transnational corporations with 'host market' orientations are generally most likely to pursue R and D abroad.[28] . . . They are, however, less likely than their 'world market' counterparts to delegate new product research responsibilities to their foreign laboratories.[29]

The extent of product and marketing standardization is also influenced by firm-related factors, listed as follows:

1. *Time orientation in international business.* The shorter the horizon, the higher the degree of product and marketing standardization.

2. *Techological sophistication.* Firms with both high and low levels
   of technological sophistication are likely to have a high degree of
   product and marketing standardization. The high-technology firms
   are motivated to maintain the product's quality, whereas the low-
   technology firms are motivated to preserve brand names (e.g., IBM
   in the computer industry, Colgate and Singer in low-technology
   industries).
3. *Importance of patents and copyrights.* The greater the importance
   attached, the higher the degree of standardization.
4. *Advertising intensity.* The higher the intensity, the greater the
   degree of standardization.
5. *Level of diversification.* Firms with few products tend to standardize more than those with many products. The latter may find it
   difficult to claim a high degree of specialization in varied product
   lines; consequently, standardization in both product design and
   marketing practices is hard to maintain.

Table 11-2 outlines the overall relationships among these factors and the
extent of standardization in product design and marketing practices. It also

Table 11-2 Relationship between the firm's contextual variables and product and
marketing policies

Contextual variable	United States	European	Japanese
Time horizon	Short–5 years	Medium to long	Long–over 10 years
Relative importance of foreign sales	Low	High	High
Technological sophistication	Low to high	High	High
Importance of patents and copyrights	High	Medium	Low
Advertising intensity	High	Low	Low
Level of diversification overseas	Low	Medium to high	High
Extent of standardization in product design and marketing practices	High	Medium	Low

shows the relative postion of United States, European, and Japanese companies.

To sum up, this review of the various empirical studies on multinational corporations points toward a high degree of centralization in decision making with respect to product policies and the introduction of new products into various markets.

The Vital Question

Have multinational and international firms gone too far in standardizing the product lines and centralizing decision making at the headquarters' level? Although the need for economies of scale in the competitive international marketplace is well recognized, many authors in international marketing have expressed grave doubts concerning the high degree of marketing and product standardization.

Sorenson and Wiechmann, for example, in their study of firms of consumer nondurable goods in Western Europe and the United States, observed that: ". . . Actual decisions to standardize might have been carried too far among the firms we studied. . . . Standardization under [differing] conditions could seriously endanger a multinational corporation's marketing success and marketing position."[30]

The authors go on to say that: ". . . MNCs in consumer packaged goods generally could not gain significant competitive advantages by transferring marketing programs across borders. The key to the strength . . . lay rather in . . . better systems of planning and implementing their local marketing efforts."[31]

Similarly, Aydin and Terpstra,[32] as well as Leontiades,[33] have shown that sophisticated marketing programs are not necessary in developing countries. The MNCs' reputation and positive product image are sufficient to compete with their local competitors, if there are any. However, Aydin and Terpstra have shown "that extensive marketing know-how transfers are possible for a developing country."[34]

They have further argued that: ". . . high-powered marketing is not needed to maintain competitive advantages in developing countries. However, competitive advantages stemming from product technology will not last forever. Production technology and marketing sophistication are growing in these countries and market leadership will probably depend increasingly on leadership in marketing."[35]

Hulbert and Brandt, in their study of United States, European, and Japanese subsidiaries in Brazil, came to similar conclusions. They warned that, although the decision to standardize the marketing program is justifiable on the basis of economies of scale, such a decision "should be based on careful analysis of the foreign market being considered."[36]

Pricing Strategy and Decisions

Pricing is a thorny issue in the international marketplace. On the one hand, the international company may be in a position to realize the "real rent" (excessive profits beyond marginal cost) because of its product image and reputation and the prevalence of seller's markets in some foreign countries. On the other hand, the international company can also afford to charge its overseas customers less than the full cost of producing a given product. In the former case, the company will be criticized by the host government and local customers for exercising its monopolistic market power. In the latter, both the home and the host governments will accuse the company of dumping and avoiding taxation.[37]

In other words, unlike distribution and product policy decisions, pricing decisions are politically sensitive issues in the international marketplace.

Types of Pricing

Robinson[38] has identified three basic pricing alternatives:

1. A standard worldwide pricing policy
2. Dual pricing (domestic/export)
3. Market differentiated pricing

A *standardized worldwide pricing policy* may be effective only under monopolistic market conditions with minimal governmental interference in pricing decisions. It also ignores the basic differences in factor costs (labor, capital, materials, and administrative costs) in different countries. Consequently, given the considerable differences in the cost of living, per capita income, and other costs around the world, such a pricing policy is unrealistic and unattainable for the vast majority of foreign investors. Only direct exporters may be able to use a standard worldwide pricing policy.

In *dual pricing,* the international firm will quote two different prices for the identical product: one for the domestic market and a second for exports. The former may be higher than the latter. The economic rationale for charging a lower price for exports is to cover only the variable cost of production to increase its volume, which in turn may eventually reduce the overall unit cost. As Robinson has pointed out, " . . . a firm may use a foreign market in which to dump products. Insofar as somethng over and above the variable cost of production is captured by the firm, a special export price might be justified in the short run so long as such sales do not effect full-cost price sales, either domestically or in other markets. Such a strategy is sometimes called marginal cost pricing."[39]

Japanese companies have widely used this type of pricing method for their exports. Consequently, they have been frequently assailed by various countries for their dumping practices.

Market differentiated pricing offers considerable latitude to the subsidiary managers to fix prices for local markets. The headquarters only provide guidelines and set a floor minimum price. Such a pricing method allows the firm to take into consideration differential factor costs, competitive environments, and governmental interference in different markets around the world. It is a more realistic pricing policy for the international marketplace.

Pricing Strategies

In both domestic and international markets, the firms use three basic pricing strategies:

1. Skimming or discriminating pricing
2. Penetration pricing
3. Follow-the-leader pricing[40]

In the discriminating pricing strategy, the firm will quote the higher prices abroad. Their aim is to obtain a premium price from overseas buyers. Such a pricing strategy usually has a short-term orientation and is attainable under the following circumstances:

1. Absence of viable competition in the markeplace (i.e., pressure of seller's market conditions).
2. Stiff import restrictions that will discourage foreign competition.
3. Product is at the early stage of its life cycle (i.e., a less mature product).
4. Strong brand name and consumer preferences for a given product.
5. Strong barriers to the entry of competitors, both local and foreign, either because of huge resource requirements or governmental restrictions on foreign and local investments. In many developing countries, such conditions are quite prevalent.

Usually, a high-technology firm is able to pursue the skimming pricing strategy in the international marketplace. In a consumer durable goods industry, only the firm with a strong brand name and high advertising and promotional intensities can afford to use such a pricing strategy.[41] As we will see later, United States multinational companies use this pricing policy quite frequently abroad.

Discriminatory pricing also means that the firm will charge different prices in different markets and countries. Both the skimming and the discriminatory pricing strategy invite governmental inquiries. For example, the use by Hoffman-LaRoche, the Swiss pharmaceutical firm, of a discriminating pricing policy for its tranquilizer products, Valium and Librium, invited numerous governmental inquiries in the United Kingdom, Canada, and other countries.[42]

This pricing strategy also invites local and foreign competitors, and encourages smuggling goods from low to high priced markets.

Penetration Pricing

This strategy is aimed at establishing a relatively low price for the purpose of gaining the market share. Once the desired market share is achieved, the firm may opt to raise the price to cover the full cost of production plus some profits. Japanese companies are known to use this pricing strategy. Both in automobile and color television exports to the United States and other industrialized countries, Japanese companies have used this pricing strategy widely. They were able to increase their market share to over 40% in the color television market in the United States by charging $50 to $100 less per comparable unit than United States producers.[43]

The penetration pricing strategy is possible under the following conditions:

1. High relationship between volume and unit cost. The higher the volume, the lower the unit cost (i.e., possibility of achieving economies of scale).
2. High level of product standardization.
3. High price elasticity. The lower the price, the higher the demand.
4. Stable technology and a product at the mature stage of its life cycle.[44]
5. Availability of financial resources to sustain initial losses.

Penetration pricing also invites governmental inquiries, particularly on charges of dumping. Many Japanese companies are accused in the United States and Europe of using this pricing strategy to eliminate local competitors. All of these complaints are not necessarily valid, and only in a few cases have antitrust proceedings been initiated against Japanese companies in the United States by the U.S. Justice Department.

Follow-the-Leader Pricing Strategy

This strategy is basically passive. The firm will set the price on par with the leading competitor in the industry. Tactically, this strategy calls for a close coordination among different firms in the industry to determine the price of a product. Such coordination in pricing is prohibited in many industrialized and some developing countries under antitrust and antimonopoly legislation. Despite the existence of such legislation, coordinated pricing behavior is widespread, particularly in oligopolistic industries.

Transfer Pricing

Many authors in international marketing discuss transfer pricing as one of the available pricing alternatives in the international markeplace. As discussed in Chapter 2, the transfer pricing mechanism has aroused considerable controversy both in the home and the host countries of multinational companies. Although practiced widely by multinational corporations, particularly by those with sizable intracompany sales and purchases, this pricing strategy is rarely articulated by managers as a viable strategy. Besides involving cost and profit transfers, it also affects the company's tax contributions in the home and host countries.

Briefly, transfer pricing is useful for the firm to evaluate the profit performance of each unit involved in intrafirm transactions. Transfer prices may be established on either cost, cost-plus, or a market price basis.

Transfer pricing among units operating in different countries can be adjusted to achieve the following objectives:

1. To transfer funds from a high-risk to a low-risk country
2. To reduce customs duties in high-duty countries by charging low prices to the units in those countries
3. To avoid taxation in a high-tax country[45]

International transfer pricing can also be used as an overall marketing strategy. As Walsh has pointed out, "profits can be concentrated by vertically integrated corporations, at the stage of production where there is least competition. Competitors operating at other stages of production can thus be discouraged by the relatively low profits to be earned."[46] Many United States oil companies, as well as Japanese trading and manufacturing companies, used this pricing strategy to achieve the various objectives just mentioned. However, in using this pricing strategy, the firm must take into account governmental attitudes and concerns about transfer pricing and their impact on the corporate public image.[47]

United States, European, and Japanese Pricing Practices

As mentioned earlier, Japanese multinational companies usually use the penetration pricing strategy both to gain a market share and to reduce unit cost through achieving economies of scale. United States multinational companies either use skimming or discriminating pricing or set prices in relation to the leading firm in the industry. European firms tend to follow the United States pattern.

In a recent study of United States, European, and Japanese companies in the ASEAN region (Thailand, Malaysia, Singapore, Indonesia, and the Philippines), Lecraw[48] seems to have reconfirmed these generalizations. His study, for example, has shown that 44% of the firms studied (N = 42) priced new products below full cost, and an additional 11% priced them below direct cost (penetration pricing). However, a detailed analysis of the results indicates that there is a wide variation in the use of this pricing strategy.[49]

The main factors affecting the pricing strategy were as follows:

1. Type of industry
2. Host country's regulations, industry, and market structures
3. Home country of multinationals
4. Age of product[50]

Lecraw's overall conclusions are summarized in Table 11-3 and as follows:

A higher percentage of Japanese firms initially priced below full cost (63%) or direct cost (22%) than other TNCs (Transnational corporations) from developed countries.[51] . . . Japanese TNCs, however, tended to introduce older, less sophisticated, more price-sensitive products than other TNCs, and of the leading firm in the industry. European firms tend to follow the American pattern.[52]

Table 11-3 Pricing strategies of United States, European, and Japanese multinationals

	MNC's origin			
	U.S. %	*Europe* %	*Japan* %	*LDC* %
When you initially introduce a product, do you price:				
At, or near, full cost including a profit	77	83	33	75
Below full cost	23	17	63	25
Near direct cost	15	11	41	19
Below direct cost	8	6	22	6
Total	100	100	100	100

Source: Donald J. Lecraw "Pricing Strategies of Transnational Corporations," *Asia Pacific Journal of Management*, 1, 2 (January 1984): p. 112.

Promotion Policies

Promotion policies are an integral part of marketing mix management. They play an important role in differentiating the firm's products from its competitors.

Promotion policies are more than advertising. They may include, besides advertising, sales promotions, demonstrating products in various exhibitions and stores, film presentations, trading stamps, premium offers, contests, free coupons, and free samples. Public relations activities can also be included in the firm's promotion policies.

However, advertising may claim a lion's share of the firm's expenditures for promotion activities. Consequently, I will discuss the major aspects of advertising in the international context in this section. Further aspects of promotion activities are fully covered in any standard marketing text.[53]

Advertising is more important for consumer durable and nondurable goods than for industrial products. Table 11-4 shows that firms in the former industries spent considerably more than those in the latter.

Table 11-4 Advertising expenditures as a percentage of sales in consumer nondurable, durable, and industrial products industries (U.S. data in 1978)

Industry	*Advertising expenditures %*
Consumer nondurable products	
Dairy products	1.7
Canned fruits and vegetables	2.3
Beverages	5.1
Cigarettes	6.2
Books	4.2
Soap and cosmetics	10.4
Motion pictures	7.6
Consumer durable products	
Office furniture	0.9
Paints	1.8
Motor vehicles	1.6
Industrial products	
Cement	0.1
Farm equipment	1.1
Construction equipment	0.8

Source: Adapted from Schoenfeld and Associates, Inc., cited in *Advertising Age*, July 23, 1979, p. 40.

Although the international data on advertising expenditures, as presented in Table 11-4, are difficult to obtain, it is generally believed that similar patterns exist in many industrialized countries.[54] In developing countries, the international firm may spend proportionally less because of the existence of seller's markets and the host governments' restrictions on advertising. Nevertheless, many global firms, such as Coca-Cola, Pepsi, Johnny Walker, and Colgate, rely heavily on their brand names. Consequently, advertising and other promotional activities are effectively used to sustain their brand names.

Given the vast differences in sociocultural values, economic standards, and legal conditions in countries around the world, advertising and promotional activities are the most nonstandardizable elements in marketing mix management. In other words, promotion requires the most customization of any element in the marketing mix. In the succeeding section, I will examine the degree of standardization in the advertising practices of multinational companies.

Media Selection

As shown in Table 11-5, media use does not form any discernable pattern. For example, print media are being used widely in such diverse countries as Australia, Egypt, France, Indonesia, Kenya, Spain, and the United States. On the other hand, the modern technology of television is used in many of the developing countries of Latin America.

Data presented in this table reflect the following two situations:

1. Convergence among different nations is taking place with respect to the consumer's taste, preference, and buying behavior, or
2. International companies are attempting to reach educated and affluent customers in different countries who are more comparable in their attitudes, preferences, and buying behavior.

There is an element of truth in both of these contentions. However, judging from the criticism by some in the developing countries that the multinational companies are only patronizing the elite class, the second contention seems more plausible.

Regardless of the validity of these conclusions, a number of studies have underscored a similarity in media use in different countries. For example, Davidson[55] has shown that media use in different industries in Australia, the United States, and Japan was very similar. Urban,[56] Theorelli,[57] and Engledow, Thorelli, and Becher,[58] among others, have reported a considerable convergence in media use in different countries. This may be attributable to government restrictions and, to some extent, to literacy levels and economic standards. France, for example, does not permit television advertising of cigarettes, tobacco, certain alcoholic drinks, books, records,

Table 11-5 Relative media use in advertising in various countries

Heavy reliance on print media (50% and more of the total use)	Heavy reliance on television (30% and more of the total use)	Heavy reliance on radio (20% and more of the total use)
Australia	Argentina	Brazil
Belgium	Brazil	Nigeria
Canada	Colombia	Philippines
Denmark	Greece	Surinam
Egypt	Japan	Trinidad and Tobago
Finland	Mexico	
France	Pakistan	
India	South Korea	
Indonesia	Taiwan	
Israel	Thailand	
Italy	Trinidad and Tobago	
Kenya	Turkey	
Malaysia	United States	
Netherlands	Venezuela	
New Zealand		
Norway		
Singapore		
South Africa		
Spain		
Sweden		
Switzerland		
United Kingdom		
United States		
West Germany		

Source: Adapted from *World Advertising Expenditures* (Mamaroneck, New York: Starch Inra Hooper, 1979): 35–36.

theaters, and cinemas.[59] Similarly, India and West Germany and other European countries not only restrict the availability of television time for advertising, but also restrict the types of products that may be advertised on television.[60]

Standardization of Advertising

To what extent can advertising be standardized? There is no clear-cut answer to this question. Available studies on this issue seem to have arrived at conflicting conclusions. Aylmer, for example, has reported that "the local manage-ment was primarily responsible for 86 percent of the advertising deci-sions."[61] In contrast, Donnelly and Ryans, in their study of sixty-nine multinational companies, found that only 9% of the firms allowed local management to make all of the major advertising decisions.[62] Aydin and Terpstra, in their study of United States and European subsidiaries in Turkey, found much less transfer of advertising knowledge than they had expected. The transfer of knowledge was greatest in television advertising, largely because of the lack of experience of local agencies in preparing television ads.[63]

In assessing the headquarters' involvement in advertising decisions of foreign subsidiaries, Wills and Ryans[64] identified four key areas of advertis-ing decisions. These were:

1. *Establishing objectives* that outline a specific communication task to be achieved; e.g., increase brand awareness or increase recogni-tion of a product's attribute.
2. *Establishing the budget.* This involves determining expenditures for advertising with respect to each market and product line.
3. *Creative strategy decisions.* This involves determining the basic message or appeals, the copy material, and illustrations.
4. *Media decisions.* Determining what media to use and when.

The authors' results are summarized as follows and in Table 11-6.

Overall, the headquarters' management tends to have a significantly higher level of participation in establishing objectives and establishing the budget for international advertising. Open-ended portions of the interviews revealed behaviors of intense involvement when establishing international advertising objectives and budget decisions. The headquarters often had direct inputs into the following areas: (1) target the market to which advertising is directed, (2) specific selling points to be communicated and products to be emphasized, (3) kind of image to be created, (4) advertising expenditure as a percentage of sales, and (5) advertising expenditures according to product lines and items.

Also, the headquarters' management tends to be less involved in creative strategy and media decisions. The headquarters' management behavior in these decision areas tends to be more passive. They may monitor, review, and sometimes give final approval to creative and media decisions. But, for the most part, they rely on local management and agency people to make these decisions.[65]

To sum up, there is no universal solution to promotion and advertising standardization. Although a high degree of standardization brings the "benefits of efficiency in production of advertisement and global control of

Table 11-6 Model of the headquarters' involvement in international advertising decisions

International advertising decision	Type of decision	Level of the headquarters' participation
1. Establishing objectives	Planning and control	Higher
2. Establishing budget	Planning and control	Higher
3. Creative strategy	Strategic; requires specialized expertise	Lower
4. Media	Strategic; requires specialized expertise	Lower

Source: J. R. Wills, Jr., and J. K. Ryans, Jr., "An Analysis of Headquarters Executive Involvement in International Advertising," *European Journal of Marketing* 22, 8 (1983): 579.

the advertising message, it also carries the risks of being insensitive to varying cultural environments and hence being ineffective."[66]

International corporations, therefore, must consider the relevant sociocultural, environmental, and legal constraints before embarking on standardized promotional and advertising policies and practices. A high degree of standardization will be more appropriate and effective under the following conditions:

1. General similarities in socioeconomic, cultural, and legal conditions of home and host countries
2. For industrial products, because purchases are made on more objective criteria

Ricks, in his provocatively titled book, *Big Business Blunders,*[67] has cited numerous real cases of the multinationals' failures in adapting to the sociocultural and environmental conditions of the host countries. A few examples are given to illustrate the lack of adaptation by the multinational companies.

General Motors' Chevrolet "Nova" was poorly received by Puerto Rican auto dealers. "Nova" means "Star" when literally translated, but when spoken, *"no va"* in Spanish means "it does not go." To remedy the situation, General Motors changed the automobile's name to "Caribe."

A New York exporter sent some goods to an Arab country, wrapped in local newspapers for shipment. His customer was arrested and his goods confiscated because the Arab customs inspectors found Jewish newspapers.

A United States golf ball manufacturer's attempt to sell golf balls packaged in groups of four to the Japanese was unsuccessful because the pronunciation of the word "four" in Japanese sounded like the word for death.

The Sunbeam Corporation attempted to enter the German market, advertising its new mist-producing hair curling iron, the "Mist-Stick." In German, the translated meaning of "mist" is actually "excrement" and, of course, Germans had no interest in a "manure" wand.

A private Egyptian airline, Misair, proved to be rather unpopular with the French nationals, probably because the name, when pronounced, meant "misery" in French.

The Vicks Company discovered that in German "Vicks" sounds like the most crude slang term for sexual intercourse, and was able to change its name to an acceptable "Wicks."

Ford's cars were not popular with certain groups in Spain because some of the locals were interpreting the name "Ford" to mean *"Fabrica Ordinaria a Reparaciones Diaviamente"* (translation: "Ordinarily, make repairs daily").

Distribution Policies and Practices

Distribution involves a number of activities, such as transportation, storage, inventory control, packaging, and before and after sales customer services. Arranging these various components logically is useful for the effective distribution of products and services. Many mathematical and statistical models have been developed to carry out these functions in the distribution system effectively. These are amply covered in many standard marketing and international marketing textbooks.[68] It is beyond the objectives of this book to review the various methods and techniques concerning the various elements in the distribution system.

My objectives here are to highlight the importance of distribution in the international marketplace and to examine the impact of socioeconomic, cultural, and legal factors on the distribution activities.

Distribution and channel decisions are greatly affected by the socioeconomic and cultural environments of a given country. As Walsh has pointed out: "Within each nation distribution systems have evolved over many years and they inevitably reflect not merely differences in economic development but social and cultural diversity."[69]

The increasing standard of living in Western Europe, Japan, and some developing countries has resulted in the homogenization of consumers' tastes, preferences, and corresponding similarities in distribution systems. However, vast environmental differences still exist among the countries.

Differences in Channel Structure

Davidson[70] provides the following data that underscore vast differences in channel structures among countries:

1. In the United States, drugstores account for 27% of cosmetic sales. In Japan, they account for only 10% of the total sales, whereas specialty cosmetic outlets score 60% of the total sales. In Spain, department stores sell 55% of the total cosmetic sales, whereas, in West Germany, only 7% of the cosmetics are sold by department stores. In Brazil, door-to-door sales account for over 50% of the total cosmetic sales.
2. Watches are primarily sold in Europe through jewelry stores, whereas in the United States discount stores dominate the sales.
3. Supermarkets account for over 95% of all food retailing in the United States, but in West Germany, they account for only 65% of the total grocery sales. In Italy, "Mom and Pop" stores account for 50% of all food sales.
4. Retail outlets are declining in some industrialized countries, while they are increasing in Japan. For example, the number of small retail outlets in France declined by 75,000 between 1961 and 1971; in the United Kingdom, by 200,000 between 1950 and 1980; and they doubled to 1,400,000 in Japan between 1964 and 1976.[71]

Such differences in channel structures can also be observed by examining the patterns of wholesalers and retailers in various countries.

As Table 11-7 shows, great differences exist in the structures and "powers" of wholesalers in countries around the world. In communist and centrally planned economies, wholesale houses or state trading companies had considerable power. For example, in the USSR, one wholesaler serves 174,922 persons; it supplies 481 retailers. In contrast, one wholesaler in the United States serves 573 persons and supplies only four retailers.[72] Overall, there is a higher concentration of wholesaling business in developing and communist countries than in industrialized countries. Data presented in Table 11-7 thus clearly negate the popular belief that in the United States, "Big business controls the lives of people." Only in developing countries and centrally planned economies is centralized power more pervasive.

In the USSR, Yugoslavia, and India, a few state-owned trading companies control over 50% of the import-export trade. In Malaysia, fewer than a dozen

Table 11-7 Wholesale patterns in selected countries

Selected countries	Number of wholesalers	Employees per wholesaler	Retailers per wholesaler	Population per wholesale establishment
United States	369,791	11	4	573
Japan	292,000	11	6	383
Brazil	41,123	7	14	2,534
Belgium	33,640	5	4	290
Turkey	22,650	1.5	8	1,811
Rep. of Korea	17,471	4	18	1,985
Philippines	15,038	5	27	2,757
Sweden	12,406	15	3	658
New Zealand	5,334	13	6	579
Puerto Rico	2,160	13	14	1,403
USSR	1,441	120	481	174,922
Kenya	1,364	8	3.5	9,466
Yugoslavia	1,231	95	61	17,345
Panama	558	18	2	79

Source: Adapted from *Statistical Yearbook, 1976* (New York: United Nations, 1977).

European trading companies handle over one half of the import trade, whereas hundreds of other local trading companies handle the balance. In Israel, one giant wholesaler, Hamashbir Hamerkazi, takes care of approximately one fifth of all of the wholesaling volume of Israel.[73]

Commenting on the changes taking place in the distribution system, Cateora and Hess have observed:

> There appears to be a worldwide trend toward more vertical integration from the wholesale or retail level back to manufacturing. Such a development, of course, is of great concern to marketers who have been dependent on wholesalers to handle their products, because in many cases they find that the channel is blocked not by a competing manufacturer but by wholesalers handling their own custom-manufactured products. In India, outside companies may have a hard time gaining distribution because the large wholesalers have such an entrenched position that by providing the financial and marketing services, they obtain monopolistic power.[74]

Retailing business shows even greater diversity. In many developing countries, retail shops are family-owned stalls, run by no more than one or two persons, whereas in industrialized countries, the huge chains of departmental stores (e.g., J.C. Penney and Sears in the United States, Mitsukoshi in Japan), discount stores, mail order houses, and supermarkets are claiming increasing shares of total retail sales.

Strategic Choices

This discussion of the differences in distribution and channel structures in various countries clearly indicates that among the four elements of marketing mix management—product, pricing, promotion, and distribution—the last one is the least standardized. In other words, as Cateora and Hess have observed: As marketing structures develop in the years to come, manufacturers will be able to have greater latitude in their policy decisions, but at present, answers to policy questions rest largely in terms of the (possibly unsatisfactory) alternatives that are available.

Questions of control, size of margins, length of channels, terms of sale, and even channel ownership will be decided more on an environmental than a preferential basis.[75]

Under such circumstances, the company can only hope to provide general guidelines to overseas subsidiaries' managers. These managers then should be encouraged to make decisions concerning distribution and channel structures in the context of the availability of outlets, costs, capital investments, the need for control, and the coverage desired.

Within these constraints, the international firm may have to choose from the following alternatives:

1. To use locally established distributors on an exclusive or nonexclusive basis
2. To buy out locally established distributors
3. To build up its own parallel outlets
4. To develop a new type of channel[76]

A thorough analysis of environmental, competitive, institutional, and legal factors will be necessary to arrive at some rational decision concerning these alternatives.[77]

Summary

In Chapters 10 and 11, I discussed the marketing function applicable to world market situations. In the preceding chapter, I outlined the macro-level issues in international marketing. For assessing the potential markets in foreign countries, three aspects were analyzed:

(1) The initial decision to enter foreign markets
(2) Determining which specific markets to enter
(3) Forecasting potential for the future market

The chapter also discussed the major investment strategies of the international firms to enter foreign markets.

In this chapter, attempts were directed toward the strategic and operational policies concerning marketing mix management. Four familiar aspects were discussed: product, pricing, promotion, and distribution.

My analysis has shown that two aspects of the marketing mix, product design and pricing, were highly standardized by international firms; and major strategic decisions concerning these two aspects were made at the headquarters. Promotion and advertising decisions were partly centralized and partly decentralized. The major objectives and budget decisions were centralized, whereas creative (advertising copy) and media decisions were decentralized at the local levels. Distribution and channel decisions were found to be the least standardizable elements in marketing mix management.

Case

The success of a new product in international markets is influenced by many factors. Successful market penetration requires a careful coordination of the marketing mix, depending on sound marketing research and the effective use of the resources of the firm. DuPont's success story with nylon shows a good contrast to its experience with Corfam. The case shows that even the most experienced firm could make a simple but expensive marketing mistake.

Case 11-1

Multinational Expertise Is Not Enough: The Sobering Story of Corfam

*Andrew Robertson**

There is more than a touch of irony in the fact that in 1974 a communist country, Poland, opened a new factory to manufacture a material invented and developed, but unsuccessfully marketed, by one of the largest chemical companies in the capitalist West, E I Du Pont de Nemours of Wilmington, Delaware.

It took Du Pont 18 years and cost an estimated $250 mn to realise that the world did not really need its ingenious synthetic leather, Corfam. Probably the company was a victim of "technology push", the hazardous situation in which science and technology based firms find themselves when they make a discovery in their laboratories which is attractive enough to be worth pursuing through all the phases of the innovation sequence from the initiation of a research and development project to the eventual launch on to the market. Various recent pieces of "research on research" have shown, however, that the majority of *successful* innovations do not begin with the technology but with the perception of a need. About 70 to 75 per cent of successful innovations in a number of samples began with "need pull".

Research, Develop – and Watch Market

This is not to say that firms should discontinue basic research nor that they should not try to develop and market scientific discoveries. It does suggest

*Reader at the School of Management Studies, Polytechnic of Central London.

that they should, however, pay much more attention to the market implications of the scientific and technical advances which they make.

In the case of Corfam, the R & D appears to have come first, with the development of a number of methods of making microporous polymer films in Du Pont's Central Research Department back in the 1930s. This work appears to have been directed at the packaging market, the textile industry and various forms of coating, but not at that stage the footwear manufacturing industry. Also, according to an article published in *Research Management* in 1965 (Vol. VIII, No. 1), written by three executives responsible for the innovation, the early work was done in the Newburgh Research Laboratory where there was a factory making vinyl coated fabrics on the same site. In view of the fact that it was shoes made with uppers of vinyl coated fabric which stopped Corfam from becoming economic in the cheaper, mass end of the footwear market, this is a fact worth remembering.

Corfam Was Expected to Follow Nylon's "Invasion Innovation" Success Route

The work done in the 1930s was not proceeded with as part of the Corfam plan until 1953. By that time Du Pont had experienced the overwhelming success of nylon, the big breakthrough in man made fibres, which also reflected part of the R & D in the 1930s. Nylon was a spectacular example of an "invasion innovation", a new material with superior characteristics to a number of natural and semi artificial fibres in current use. It was far stronger than any of its rivals, including rayon, and was much cheaper than silk, and eventually cotton fabrics too. Its adoption by the textile industry across the world (Du Pont extended a licence to ICI) brought immense benefits to Du Pont and its licensees. There seems little doubt that top management in the company believed that the same would happen with Corfam as happened with nylon: an invasion of the footwear industry that would replace leather.

In the *Research Management* article, which was evidently an authorised version of the story of Corfam up to that date, the then sales manager of the Poromeric Products Division ("poromeric" was a Du Pont coining from "porous" and "polymer"), Charles A Lynch, cites the company philosophy, "that a product must first be new, then serve a purpose, be of value to the user, and fill a need". In other words, the new product was expected to fill a need, rather than there being a need that had been perceived and a new product subsequently developed to meet it.

Leather Was Identified as the Rival, but It Was Not the Main One

In the case of Corfam, Du Pont's economists worked out that there would be a need for a leather substitute for shoe uppers, arising from a predicted shortage of natural leather relative to the growth in world population and the increase in the proportion of people wearing shoes. In these global terms, this projection was neither illogical nor necessarily wrong. At the time of the preparation of the chosen Corfam process for commercial scale application about 1960/61, the US market for all kinds of footwear was of the order of 600 mn pairs a year. This grew to about 800 mn pairs over the next ten years. But every one of the additional 200 mn pairs a year was imported, mainly from Japan and Italy, and the majority of them were with synthetic upper materials, designed for the cheap end of the women's fashion shoe market. This unexpected eventuality did not form part of Du Pont's economic forecast. Indeed, they appeared to be quite unaware, until they were fully committed to the Corfam programme, that non-porous synthetic sheet was the main rival.

Technology Push

The sequence of events, in brief, was that in 1953 Du Pont had three industrial departments working on the development of a poromeric based on the research done before the war. These were the Fabrics and Finishes and the Film Departments, backed up by the Textile Fibers Department which was working on the fibre for the substrate. The material structure of Corfam was designed as an analogue to natural leather, with a smooth surface on a porous or permeable base, the substrate. Early versions of the material were three layers: the felted web or batt, made of compacted and needle punched polyester fibres of as fine a count as could be drawn (one to two denier), an interlayer to prevent foot perspiration attacking the surface, and a coating of polyurethane which was coloured and embossed with rollers to give it the appearance of natural leather.

At Du Pont research projects are overseen and evaluated by an executive committee and, in 1955, the appropriate committee ruled that the development work on what was to become Corfam should be concentrated in the Fabrics and Finishes Department. At this point the product was being made on two pilot plants, one in Fabrics and Finishes and the other in Film. The former had a product lacking in acceptable leather like characteristics, while the latter was able to make a similar material but more easily. The official account does not reveal why the Fabrics and Finishes Department won the competition. But there is a telling comment in that account which helps the understanding of Du Pont's predicament. Quoting from the *Research Management* article we find that "In 1956 and 1957 these materials were field tested, and more thorough consideration was given to where these products might find utility in the American economy". Clearly this innovation was technology push.

Hush Puppies Denied One Market –

By mid 1959 the company's commitment was almost complete. For one thing the price of leather had reached a new peak. For another, suede had become extremely popular. This was important technically, and appeared to be a brilliant piece of good luck, because a suede or napped finish meant that Corfam could be made more quickly and cheaply by cutting out the coating and embossing stages of the process. Unfortunately, it was at that time that the Wolverine Shoe and Tanning Corporation, makers of horsehide work shoes but facing a shrinking market, decided to plunge on their pigskinning machine. They did a deal with the Chicago meat packers (their home was not far away, Rockford, Michigan) who paid in pig skins for the rent of the machine, capable of skinning a pig carcase without leaving the tallow on the hide. The brand name of these shoes was Hush Puppy. No one at Du Pont will admit that this was the reason for switching the production programme away from napped finishes to coated, but they do concede that "suede is a cyclical market" and they wanted a steady offtake. Anyway, no suede type Corfam was put on the market.

−While the Tanning Industry Responded to Synthetic Leather's Threat−

In terms of production complexity this change meant the addition of two processes, coating and embossing, and contributed to the unit cost of a square foot of the new material, which had been estimated at about $1 to be competitive with leather. There can be no doubt now that the whole research and marketing effort was aimed at replacing natural leather, a threat to which the American tanning industry responded energetically. The latter phenomenon was recognised in principle by S Gilfillan as early as 1935. In his *Sociology of Invention* he refers to what he calls the "sailing ship effect", the fact that the best and fastest sailing ships came into service after the arrival of the steamship. In this case the leather tanners began to make their leathers have Corfam characteristics−scuff resistance, toughness and durability.

−And a Simpler, Cheaper Product Was in the Mass Market

Yet here was another marketing enigma for Du Pont. Their plan for Corfam was logical. The footwear market would be invaded with this synthetic substitute for upper leather, which has the advantage of being uniform, unlike cowhide which is of an irregular shape and bears the scars of active life. At first it would compete only at the top end of the market but as the market grew and production increased and unit costs fell, it would descend into the lower ranges and eventually replace leather right across the board (except that cheap leather had already been ousted by vinyl coated fabrics at the really low priced end of the market). So as far as the cheap end of the domestic market was concerned, the Corfam plan was nipped both by cheap imports and by synthetic sheet of the kind produced by Du Pont themselves.

An Encouraging Start, Then Little Growth

Corfam was launched in the United States in 1963, just ten years after the restart of the research programme into microporous sheet. It appeared to have had instant success in the market, selling the equivalent of 1 mn pairs of shoes in 1964, 5 mn in 1965, 12 mn in 1966, 20 mn in 1967 and 40 mn in 1968. After that sales seemed to have reached a plateau, and the domestic market share never reached even 10 per cent.

The International Rivals

Nevertheless, competitors for Corfam were already on the market. In 1967 *Chemical Week* (Sept 23) noted that Goodrich had become a danger to Corfam with its follow up product Aztran. Indeed, there were by that time four American rival materials, four Japanese, one German and one British. The British contender was Ortix from the Fibres Division of Imperial Chemical Industries, hopefully building upon the development work done at Du Pont. The intention seems to have been to try to pip Corfam at the post in Europe.

Du Pont had signalled its punches by making an attempt to launch Corfam in Europe as early as 1967, two years before they realised that the invasion of the domestic market was not succeeding. Conforming with the general plan, the material had been offered to the top fashion shoe makers, such as Edward Rayne in London, but although some of the British manufacturers were willing to experiment, resistance was much tougher in France and Italy.

It is worth noting that while the Germans, the Dutch and the British, as well as the Japanese, made attempts to get into the temporarily attractive market for poromeric materials, neither the French nor the Italians bothered. It does look, with hindsight, as if the shoemakers of those fashion conscious countries were alert to the twin facts that their premium market wanted leather, while the ephemeral fashion conscious low priced segment had no preference for materials but rather for price and style. Asked about this shortly before Du Pont pulled out of the whole business in 1971, one of the chemists in Poromeric Products Division said, a shade wistfully, "we should have asked our daughters".

The Mass Market Did Not Need Corfam's Qualities, Nor Could It Afford Them

The hard truth of the market resistance to Corfam at the cheap end seems to have been that the majority of buyers in this price bracket are young women, with little money but a lot of fashion sense. As the shoes which they buy tend to be designed in various "open" styles (better ventilated than men's shoes, said a Du Pont marketing man bitterly) permeability or porosity does not matter, indeed is lacking in any marketing significance. Not only that, but the toughness and durability of Corfam are equally irrelevant. Who wants fashionable footwear to last? Most of the pluses built into Corfam became minuses in this unfamiliar market. Perhaps it was the fixation with nylon that blinded Du Pont senior executives to the shortcomings of their amazing Corfam. As we have seen, they were not alone in being misguided. As many as 20 other companies in half a dozen countries followed their lead.

One of the economic difficulties with all the poromerics was their high cost of production. Unlike the vinyl sheet plastic materials, they could not just be extruded, they had to be laid up. The felt or web substrate had to be provided with a protective layer and that layer covered with a coating. Advanced versions of the poromerics were two layer rather than three, but still the unit cost remained higher per square foot than the cost of cheap "side" leathers. It is possible that really high volume production would have changed this cost basis and made the poromerics competitive, but the vinyl coated fabrics prevented that happening.

Shoemakers, Retailers and Customers Found Fault with the Product

In addition there were mundane marketing problems. Du Pont went to great lengths to convince footwear manufacturers that their new material was going to succeed. They encouraged 200 shoemakers to produce 16,000 test pairs of shoes. These were given to a wide cross section of users in the United States, from hard wearers like postmen and policemen to children and housewives. The researchers and marketing men were satisfied with the results from these user tests. The makers had technical problems, because their machinery was designed to make shoes from soft leather rather than tough, unyielding Corfam. And even when these production problems were overcome, there remained three more obstacles.

One was the retailer, interested mainly in the volume of his sales rather than the material from which shoes are made. The same applies to his sales assistants whose commission depends not on what kind of shoes they sell but how many and at what price. Finally the customer, not particularly keen on substitutes for the familiar leather, especially at high prices, but anxious to have the sort of shoes with which she or he is familiar, to like their looks and to have them fit and feel comfortable.

The Cost of Not Having Natural "Stress Decay"

A characteristic of Corfam which did not come to light until after full commitment (not indeed until 1964) is that it could not be regarded in any real sense as a synthetic substitute for leather, because of its relative coarseness. In 1964, for the first time, the scanning electron microscope, developed in Britain, became available to Du Pont. This device enables the user to scrutinise the structure of a material in complete detail. As soon as microphotographs of Corfam were examined and compared with those of natural leather it was obvious what was wrong. The fibre in natural leather is at least ten times as fine and therefore ten times as soft and pliable as that in Corfam as it then was. To spin manmade fibres down to the fineness of animal hair was not technically possible. The result was that the poromerics lacked an important quality as far as shoe uppers were concerned—they would not "break in". In the words of the Du Pont scientists they had no "stress decay", or in other words would not deform to fit the foot.

Making a Virtue out of Necessity

In 1964, with sales rising fast, this technical setback was taken in the company's stride. The marketing angle was subtly changed. Instead of Corfam being heralded as a manmade substitute for natural leather in shoe uppers, the line became that Corfam was in many ways superior to leather, not a mere replacement but something even better. This was making a virtue out of necessity. It was a good tactical move but it made little difference to the long term outcome.

There were other, comparatively minor, difficulties. Whereas in the United States it has become unusual to repair shoes, in Europe, at the time when Du Pont made the first attempt to introduce Corfam, 1967 and again in 1969, it was still customary. Apparently no one in Wilmington had paid any attention to this small international difference, but when Corfam shoes went to the cobblers trouble began. When heels or soles have been replaced it is usual to polish the shoe using a high speed rotary brush. The friction of the brush raises the surface temperature to several hundred degrees centigrade, enough to melt the polyurethane coating on Corfam. Shoes came back from the repairer with grooves in the uppers where the brush had destroyed the surface. Feedback on this defect was very slow.

There were other unforeseen problems. Manufacturers, used to leather uppers, forgot that Corfam relied on permeability for one of its unique selling points and lined their shoes with impermeable vinyl. They would line leather with leather or canvas, but this was a plastic, wasn't it? At the same time shoemaking technology was changing, from nailing and stitching uppers to the soles, to bonding them, and from using leather soles to using manmade materials. Again, the result was that quite a number of Corfam shoes went on to the middle range of the market, with bonded and manmade soles, allowing little or no permeability. There had been no serious problems with nylon in the textile industry (except a few, such as photodisintegration of net curtains, static and discoloration of white nylon with age). Here the invasion innovation was not quite up to it.

The Cost of the Venture

The competition from native and foreign firms was comparatively negligible. The only leather like material to be marketed internationally against

Corfam was Clarino, the brand name adopted by Kurashiki Rayon, Japan. Du Pont, having tried out numerous chemical routes to its poromeric, had also protected many of the more promising ones by patent in the industrialised countries of the world. Their Japanese imitators were caught by one of these and eventually had to pay royalties on the sales of Clarino to Du Pont. But this was a hollow victory. No one but the top management of Du Pont knows what the venture cost the company. When in 1971 they announced to a surprised world that they were withdrawing Corfam, shutting down the plant in Old Hickory, Tennessee, and selling the machines to the Poles, they said that the 18 years had left them at least $100 mn out of pocket. It was known that the launch in 1963 and 1964 had cost $25 mn on top of the R & D investments. Later estimates (unofficial) pushed the probable loss to $250 mn at least and a possible billion dollars. When it is remembered that they invested in a marketing department in Geneva, in a finishing plant at Malines in Belgium and in launches in the major countries of Europe, not to mention their legal costs and the continuous programme of education and service in the United States and Canadian footwear manufacturing industries, a ten figure shortfall sounds at least possible.

The bigger they come, the harder they fall.

Schedule of Significant Events in the Corfam Story*

1802	E. I. Du Pont de Nemours of Delaware is founded.
1923	Du Pont decides to allow company scientists freedom to pursue pure research, a policy that results in the discovery of the means of combining small molecules to make larger ones. As a result of this discovery, future discoveries of Nylon, synthetic rubber, polyester, and acrylic fibers are possible.
1930	Research and development on microporous polymer film in Du Pont's Central Research Department is directed towards the packaging market, textile industry, and various forms of coating materials.
1931	Synthetic rubber is perfected.
1935	Work begins on Corfam.
1938	Nylon is patented by Du Pont and a pilot plant is completed for producing the synthetic fiber.
1939	Nylon is introduced to the public at the New York World's Fair.
1941	America's source of silk, Japan, is closed.
1953	Nylon is successful and adopted by the textile industry worldwide.

*This history was compiled by Marie H. Eighmey, Roger E. Martin, and Paul L. Medlin, students of the Executive MBA class of 1982–1984.

1955	The development of Corfam is assigned to Du Pont's Fabric and Finishes Department, the same unit that produced nylon.
1958	Du Pont establishes its International Division.
1959	The price of leather has reached a new peak. Suede is popular. The Wolverine Shoe & Tanning Corporation implements its pigskinning machine to produce material for Hush Puppy shoes, closing that portion of the market for Corfam.
1960–61	The United States shoe market totals 600 million pairs. Corfam is chosen by Du Pont for commercial development as a shoe upper.
1960–1970	The United States shoe market grows by 200 million pairs per year; however, the growth in the market is neutralized by foreign imports.
1963	Du Pont fully commits itself to Corfam, which initially is to be launched as a substitute for leather.
1964	Corfam is launched in thirty-six major United States market areas. One million pairs are sold; the product is advertised as being superior to leather even though Du Pont learns that the fibers are too thick to deform to fit the foot as leather does.
	Du Pont employs nearly 16,000 people in thirty-five foreign plants in thirteen countries. It has invested $320.0 million in its foreign operations, which now represent 15% of its total business.
1965	5 million pairs of Corfam shoes sold.
1966	12 million pairs of Corfam shoes sold.
1967	20 million pairs sold. Ten of the ultimate twenty competitors to the Corfam product now exist. Du Pont goes international, offering Corfam to top shoemakers in Britain, France, and Italy with little success.
1969	Du Pont recognizes its inability to invade the domestic market. Sales have reached a plateau of less than 10% of the domestic market share.
1971	Du Pont withdraws Corfam from the marketplace, suffering a total estimated $100 million to $1 billion loss on its Corfam investment.

Discussion Questions

1. Discuss the differences in pricing practices among United States, Japanese, and European MNCs in the international market.

2. How do marketing channels in developing countries differ from those in industrialized countries?

3. What would the advantages or disadvantages be in standardizing marketing mix management globally? Give some examples of standardization and differentiation of the marketing management.

4. What factors would affect the choice of concentration *versus* differentiation in marketing strategy?

5. Develop a comprehensive marketing plan for exporting oranges and other fruits to Japan.

Endnotes

1. John Fayerweather, *International Business: Strategy and Administration* (Cambridge, Mass.: Ballinger Publishing Co., 1978), p. 316.
2. George Weissman, "International Expansion" in *Planning Marketing Strategy: A New Dimension*, ed. Lee Adler (New York: Simon and Schuster, 1967), p. 229.
3. Millard H. Pryor, Jr., "Planning in a Worldwide Business," *Harvard Business Review* 43, 1 (January–February 1965): 137.
4. Robert D. Buzzell, "Can you Standardize Multinational Marketing?," *Harvard Business Review* 46, 6 (November–December 1968): 102–113.
5. Raymond Vernon, *Storm over the Multinationals* (Cambridge, Mass.: Harvard University Press, 1977), pp. 1–17.
6. Ibid., p. 3.
7. Ibid., p. 4.
8. Ibid.
9. Ibid., pp. 4–5.
10. L. S. Walsh, *International Marketing* (Plymouth, Eng.: Macdonald & Evans Ltd., 1981), pp. 11–14.
11. Vernon, *Storm*, pp. 4–6.
12. William H. Davidson, *Global Strategic Management* (New York: John Wiley and Sons, 1982), pp. 113–118.
13. James M. Hulbert, and William K. Brandt, *Managing the Multinational Subsidiary* (New York: Holt, Rinehart and Winston, 1980), pp. 65–87.
14. Anant R. Negandhi, and B. R. Baliga, *Tables are Turning: German and Japanese Multinational Companies in the United States* (Cambridge, Mass.: Oelgeschlager, Gunn & Hain, Publishers, Inc., 1981), Chap. 3, pp. 45–59.
15. Hulbert and Brandt, *Managing*, pp. 71–75.
16. Negandhi and Baliga, *Tables*, pp. 48–49.
17. Fayerweather, *International*, p. 222.
18. Walsh, *International*, p. 33.
19. J. Aylmer, "Who Makes Marketing Decisions in the Multinational Firm?," *Journal of Marketing* 34 (October 1970): 25–30.
20. Hulbert and Brandt, *Managing*, pp. 74–76.
21. Ralph Z. Sorenson, and Ulrich E. Wiechmann, "How Multinationals View Marketing Standardization," *Harvard Business Review* 53, 3 (May–June 1975): 38–55.
22. Lawrence G. Franko, *European Business Strategies in the United States* (Geneva: Business International, 1976).

23. Ulrich E. Wiechmann, *Marketing Management in Multinational Firms* (New York: Praeger Publishers, 1976).
24. Anant R. Negandhi, and Martin K. Welge, *Beyond Theory Z* (Greenwich, Conn.: JAI Press, 1984), Chap. 5.
25. Quoted from Jack N. Behrman, and William A. Fischer, "Transnational Corporations: Market Orientations and R & D Abroad," *Columbia Journal of World Business* XV, 3 (Fall 1980): 55.
26. U.S. Congress, Senate Committee on Finance, *Implications of Multinational Firms for World Trade and Investment and U.S. Trade and Labour* (Washington, D.C.: Government Printing Office, 1973), pp. 581–593.
27. Behrman and Fischer, "Transnational," op. cit., p. 60.
28. Ibid., p. 19.
29. Ibid.
30. Sorenson and Wiechmann, "How Multinationals," quoted from Fayerweather, *International*, p. 229.
31. Fayerweather, *International*, p. 229.
32. Nizam Aydin, and Vern Terpstra, "Marketing Know-How Transfers by Multinationals: A Case Study in Turkey," *Journal of International Business Studies* XII, 3 (Winter 1981): 35–48.
33. James Leontiades, from ibid., footnote 20, p. 48.
34. Ibid., p. 47.
35. Ibid.
36. Hulbert and Brandt, *Managing*, p. 84.
37. The current debates concerning Japanese imports to industrialized countries relate to the dumping charges.
38. Richard Robinson, *Internationalization of Business* (Chicago: Dryden Press, 1984), pp. 49–52.
39. Ibid., p. 51.
40. For extensive discussion on the pricing policies of multinational companies, see Davidson, *Global*, pp. 135–146.
41. Ibid., pp. 136–138.
42. Ibid., p. 137.
43. *Business Week*, April 1973, p. 26.
44. See Davidson, *Global*, pp. 138–146.
45. Walsh, *International*, pp. 117–119; see also Sanjaya Lall, "Transfer Pricing by Multinational Manufacturing Firms," *Oxford Bulletin of Economics and Statistics* 35, 3 (August 1973): 173–195.
46. Walsh, *International*, p. 118.
47. For fuller discussion on this point, see Lall, "Transfer," pp. 188–191.
48. Donald J. Lecraw, "Pricing Strategies of Transnational Corporations," *Asia Pacific Journal of Management* 1, 2 (January 1984): 112–119.
49. Lecraw uses penetration and predatory pricing terms interchangeably. However, Davidson has argued there are some basic differences between these two pricing strategies. Predatory pricing, according to Davidson, involves "short-term cuts intended to financially weaken the competition rather than expand the market." In contrast, penetration pricing may be a long-term or medium-term strategy. See Davidson, *Global*, p. 140.
50. Ibid., pp. 140–146.
51. Ibid., pp. 115–116.
52. Ibid., pp. 116–117.
53. P. Kotler, *Marketing Management* (Englewood Cliffs, NJ: Prentice-Hall, 1980).

54. J. J. Boddewyn, and Katherin Marton, *Comparison Advertising: A Worldwide Study* (New York: International Advertising Association, 1978).
55. Davidson, *Global*, p. 153.
56. C. D. Urban "A Cross-National Comparison of Consumer Media Use Patterns," *Columbia Journal of World Business* XV, 4 (Winter 1977): 53–63.
57. Hans B. Theorelli, "Concentration of Information Power Among Consumers," *Journal of Marketing Research* VIII, 4 (November 1971): 427–463.
58. J. Engledow, H. B. Theorelli, and H. Becher, "The Information Seekers – A Cross-Cultural Consumer Elite" in *Advances in Consumer Research*, ed. M. J. Schlinger (Atlanta: Association for Consumer Research, 1975).
59. Walsh, *International*, p. 126.
60. Ibid., p. 123.
61. Aylmer, "Who Makes," p. 26.
62. J. M. Donnelly, Jr., and J. K. Ryans Jr., "The Role of Culture in Organizing Overseas Operations: The Advertising Experience," *University of Washington Business Review* 29 (Autumn 1969): 59–62.
63. Aydin and Terpstra, "Marketing," p. 40.
64. J. R. Wills, Jr., and J. K. Ryans, Jr., "An Analysis of Headquarters Executive Involvement in International Advertising," *European Journal of Marketing* 22, 8 (1983): 11–8.
65. Ibid., p. 583.
66. Boddewyn and Marton, *Comparison*, pp. 102–115.
67. David A. Ricks, *Big Business Blunders: Mistakes in Multinational Marketing* (Homewood, Ill.: Dow Jones-Irwin, 1983).
68. See Kotler, *Marketing*, and Philip R. Cateora and John M. Hess, *International Marketing* (Homewood, Ill.: Richard D. Irwin, Inc., 1979).
69. Walsh, *International*, p. 90.
70. Davidson, *Global*, pp. 160–161.
71. Ibid., p. 161; see also M. Kanabayashi in Cateora and Hess, *International*, pp. 606–610.
72. Cateora and Hess, *International*, pp. 588–590.
73. Ibid., p. 588.
74. Ibid., p. 589.
75. Ibid., p. 578.
76. Walsh, *International*, p. 92.
77. Simon Majaro, *International Marketing: A Strategic Approach to World Markets* (London: George Allen & Unwin Ltd., 1977).

Additional Readings

Articles

Davidson, William, and Harrigan, Richard. "Key Decisions in International Marketing: Introducing New Products Abroad." *Columbia Journal of World Business* XII, 4 (Winter 1977): 15–23.

Keegan, Warren I. "International Competition: The Japanese Challenge." *Journal of International Business Studies* XV, 3 (Winter 1984): 173–189.

Keegan, Warren I. "Strategic Marketing: International Diversification versus National Concentration." *Journal of International Business Studies*, XI, 3 (Winter 1980): 120–130.

Books

Kaynak, Erdener. *Marketing in the Third World.* New York: Praeger Publishers, 1982.

Majaro, Simon. *International Marketing: A Strategic Approach to World Markets.* London: George Allen & Unwin Ltd., 1977.

Ricks, David A. *Big Business Blunders: Mistakes in Multinational Marketing.* Homewood, Ill.: Dow Jones-Irwin, 1983.

Chapter 12

Financial Management in International Corporations

This chapter discusses the various aspects of financial management in international corporations. For manufacturing firms, the financial system is only a secondary aspect. Its primary objective is to deliver goods and services to the marketplace. Although money is the lifeblood of any business enterprise, and to that matter any sovereign government, manufacturing firms are not in the business of making money through money. Only banking and financial institutions are primarily involved in generating money through the use of money.[1] In spite of its secondary importance, the financial system occupies the central position in managerial decision making.

This chapter will discuss, in more detail, the following aspects of the financial system:

- Strategic choices in establishing the financial flow system
- Decision making in financial management (centralization-decentralization issue)
- Sources of obtaining needed finance
- Management of the working capital and cash flow
- Remittance policies
- Management of the foreign exchange risk

In analyzing these elements, I will provide comparative profiles of United States, European, and Japanese companies' financial practices.

Strategic Choices

Financial management in international corporations is basically concerned with two fundamental elements: (1) providing funds for financing overseas business, and (2) remittance of profits, interest, and royalty fees back to the home office. Table 12-1 outlines the financial flow system of international corporations.

As shown in Table 12-1, strategic choices have to be made with respect to the nature of the financing, whether it will be done through equity or debt, and the sources to be used for equity and debt.

Earnings flow will be dependent on the type of financing chosen. For equity financing, it will be mainly dividends; for loans, it is interest on capital transferred from headquarters or other affiliates. Intracompany transfers,

Table 12-1 Important elements in financial management of international corporations

Financing overseas operations	*Income flow from overseas operations*
Equity: Parent company	Dividends
Local sources	
Loans: Parent company	Interest
Local sources	
International agencies	
Intracompany translations	Royalty fees, transfer pricing

Source: Adapted from John Fayerweather, *International Business Strategy and Administration,* Cambridge, Mass.: Ballinger Publishing Co., 1978, p. 371.

royalties, and management fees are additional earnings alternatives available to international corporations.

Factors affecting strategic choices concerning the method of financing overseas operations and the nature of the earnings flow are:

1. Home and host government controls on outflow and inflow of capital
2. Interest rate differentials in various countries
3. Tax rate differentials
4. Foreign exchange rates, fluctuations, and controls
5. Inflation and political and economic instability and risks
6. The firm's technological, capital, and human resources
7. The firm's long-range strategic policies, goals, and objectives[2]

Although rational policies should be based on cost considerations, focusing on interest rates, political and economic risks, and taxes, the actual financial practices of international corporations fall short of the ideal situation. For example, Robbins and Stoubaugh's study of United States MNCs indicates that they could increase their profits by 25% if they were able to exploit the full potential of all financial alternatives. To quote Robbins and Stoubaugh:

> The financial manager of a multination enterprise has many opportunities to earn profits through the appropriate use of the many external sources of funds and the large number of intercompany financial links at his disposal. However, the number of alternatives is so great that the manager copes by adapting simplifying decision rules . . . and emphasizes short-term local borrowing.[3]

The important constraining forces responsible for the suboptimization of available financial alternatives are government restrictions on capital inflow and outflow, royalty and management fees and remittances, and repatriation policies, as well as the firm's desire to maintain and enhance its public image and long-range strategy. As Fayerweather has noted:

> The emphasis . . . must . . . be placed on the primary status of the product delivery system and on issues determining its effectiveness. Government actions affecting market access, operational control, logistic flexibility, and other elements of the product delivery system are fundamental. Major financial system features affecting basic profitability are . . . essential. But it is questionable whether incremental gains by sophisticated use of financial flow options are desirable . . . if they affect overall government relations to the ultimate disadvantage of more fundamental strategy needs.[4]

Decision Making in Financial Management

One of the important issues concerning financial management in international corporations is the locus of the decision making. Although many authors have argued that the main objective of an overseas subsidiary is to maximize the net returns of the global unit rather than the subsidiary itself, in practice it is hard to achieve this objective because of environmental forces and governmental restrictions and demands.

The critical problem, therefore, is how to establish an optimum combination of centralization and decentralization in decision making with respect to the various elements of financial management. I will first examine the advantages and disadvantages of the centralized and decentralized systems and then briefly review the actual practices of international corporations.

The main advantages of a centralized approach are:

1. Use of specialized skills by financial managers.
2. Economies of scale. Borrowing a large amount may provide leverage to secure a low interest rate, and investing a large amount of cash may secure higher interest.
3. Possibilities of using intracompany resources to finance international operations.
4. Better hedging against foreign exchange fluctuations; that is, the centralized financial management may provide an opportunity to restructure the firm's cash assets of foreign currencies more effectively.

The main disadvantages of centralized management are:

1. Autonomy and motivation of the subsidiary's managers will be reduced, which may decrease their effectiveness in coping with the host countries' demands.
2. May create problems with the host and home governments, especially to those with serious problems of balance of payments and a loss of tax revenues.[5]

The main advantages and disadvantages of a decentralized system are the opposite of the centralized system just listed.

Actual Practices of International Enterprises

Robbins and Stoubaugh's study of 187 United States MNCs indicated a relationship between the size of the firm and the nature of decision making. Their main conclusions are as follows.

Small MNCs usually gave wide latitude to their subsidiaries because of a lack of skilled centralized staff at the headquarters and a lack of large financial resources of the parent company. Consequently, each subsidiary was considered as an independent operation, taking care of its own financial needs and using its resources for growth.

The study showed that only 20% of the small MNCs invested additional funds in a foreign subsidiary as compared to 70% of the medium-sized and large companies, which invested additional funds in overseas operations.

Medium-sized MNCs used a skilled central staff and adapted the "system optimization" perspective. This approach allowed them to exercise more control over their overseas subsidiaries through a continuous flow of information, instructions, procedures, and policy guidelines. The centralized orientation enabled their firms to optimize the financial benefits. For example, all firms in this category were able to take advantage of the lower interest rates in home countries as compared to 60% of the small and large MNCs who did the same. Also, during the monetary squeeze in the host country, medium-sized firms were able to provide their overseas subsidiaries with funds from outside of the country. For these firms it was relatively easier to implement centralized controls over financial matters.

Large MNCs leaned toward a "system optimization" perspective, but the implementation of this strategy was difficult. This is largely because of the complexity of their business activities and their need to maintain the public image of "good corporate citizens" in the host countries. Consequently, the headquarters' staff issued overall guidelines and provided available information to the financial managers of the subsidiary.[6]

Other variables affecting decision making were the nature of equity participation and the technological sophistication of the parent firm. Companies with more joint ventures exercised less central financial control than those with fully-owned subsidiaries. Similarly, a firm with high research and development expenditures was more concerned with new product development and less concerned with financial costs. In contrast, low-technology firms were more concerned with minimizing costs.

Other Studies

As discussed in Chapter 5, a number of other studies have shown relatively higher centralized decision making with respect to finances. For example, Wiechmann's study of European MNCs revealed that the finance function is the most centralized.[7] Of the companies surveyed (N = 27), 85% had a high degree of headquarters direction over finances. Barlow, in his study of United States firms, also found that the majority of the companies established higher financial control over their subsidiaries.[8] Similarly, Franko's study of European MNCs revealed that the financial decisions were the most controlled by the headquarters.[9]

Lastly, our recent study of 120 subsidiaries of United States, German, and Japanese MNCs also shows considerable centralization of decision making in financial matters[10] (Figures 5-2 and 5-3).

Turning from a broad financial perspective to specific elements, the following trends have been found:

1. Overall foreign investment decisions are mostly centralized.[11]
2. Remittance policies are mostly centralized.[12]
3. Licensing policies and policies concerning royalties and management fees are centralized.[13]
4. Transfer pricing decisions are centralized, especially in United States MNCs.[14]

Policy Guidelines

This review of some of the studies seems to suggest that, by and large, the financial function should be centralized at the headquarters level. Much can be said to support this viewpoint. First, it allows the headquarters to employ and use highly trained financial managers. Second, it assures tight control over the subsidiaries' activities. Third, through centralized control, the headquarters may be able to estimate the costs and benefits of foreign investments more accurately.

Notwithstanding these advantages of centralized finances, one can argue against centralized control on the basis of the primary goals and objectives of a firm, increasing competition in the world marketplace, increasing sources of capital, and increasing complexity of environmental (host and home countries') demands.

As discussed earlier, Fayerweather has strongly argued in favor of a rather decentralized system on the basis of the main objectives of the firm.[15] For manufacturing firms the delivery of product and services is most fundamental for a firm's survival and growth. Consequently, concentration on its primary objectives is more important than establishing the optimum financial system.

Increasing competition in the world marketplace will also necessitate more autonomy by the subsidiary in financial matters. The subsidiary manager is likely to have a better understanding of the local capital market than the headquarters' financial wizard, sitting some eight to ten thousand miles away.

Since World War II, and especially since the 1960s, financial institutions have undergone many fundamental changes. Major banks have been internationalized. New stock and security markets, such as Eurocurrency,

Eurodollars and Eurobonds, the Tokyo stock market, and the Singapore Exchange Market have emerged.

To illustrate these fast-changing, international money markets, I will briefly review developments in international banking, the Eurocurrency market, and Japan's growing international money market.

International Banking

Although international banking was originally developed in the early nineteenth century in England, the real growth has occurred only since 1960. Earlier, international banking was no more than a network of corresponding banks in various countries through which domestic banks conducted international business for their clients.

Until 1960, even major United States banks such as the Bank of America, the First National City Bank of New York, and Chase Manhattan were largely domestically oriented. Since then, United States, European, and Japanese banks have expanded their overseas branches and international business tremendously. During the fifteen-year period from 1960 to 1975, the foreign assets share in the total assets of United States banks grew from 3.5% in 1966 to 18.5% in 1975.[16]

As shown in Table 12-2, the major United States banks obtain 35% to 65% of their total earnings from overseas.[17]

In recent years, foreign banks also have expanded considerably in the United States. They have doubled their share of commercial and industrial loans from 10% in 1980 to 20% in 1985. They have expanded assets from $37 billion to $121 billion, and opened some 252 new offices during this period. Among the foreign banks in the United States, the Japanese banks are the most aggressive. They represent 50% of foreign banks' commercial and indus-

Table 12-2 Earnings of major United States banks

United States Banks	*Percent of Foreign Earnings in 1980*
Chase Manhattan	47
Citicorp	65
Morgan	52
Manufacturer's Hanover	49
Chemical Bank of New York	35
Banker's Trust	52

Source: Corporate Reports. Adapted from William H. Davidson, *Global Strategic Management* New York: John Wiley and Sons, 1984, p. 86.

trial loans. With 208 branches, 25 agencies, and 14 subsidiaries, the Japanese main banks, such as Dai-ichi Kangyo, Fugi, Mitsubishi, Mitsui, Sumitomo, Sanwa, and the Bank of Tokyo, have firmly established a nitch in the United States money market.[18]

Decentralization of finance functions may be necessary to use effectively these various options.

The Eurocurrency Market

Although the Eurocurrency market existed before World War I, its phenomenal growth only came since the 1950s. Its original creators and users were the socialist countries that chose to hold their foreign currencies outside of the United States for fear of a possible freeze of their assets during the Cold War years.

Eurocurrencies are defined as "currencies that are held and used outside the country where they have legal tender status." The main characteristics of Eurocurrencies are:

1. Euromarkets are a deposit and loan market, not a foreign market
2. Holders of Eurodollars are not residents of the United States
3. Eurodollars are the same as United States dollars
4. There are no lenders of last resort to Euromarket operators[19]

As can be seen from Table 12-3, during the last decade the Eurocurrency market has grown tenfold, from U.S. $110 billion in 1970 to U.S. $1,120 billion in 1979. Europe and OPEC countries are the main depositors in the Eurocurrency market (Table 12-4).

The main reasons for expansion of the Eurocurrency market are:

1. Interest rate ceilings on deposits in the United States (Regulation Q), imposed by the Federal Reserve, allowed banks overseas to at-

Table 12-3 Size of Eurocurrency market (in billion U.S. dollars)

	1970	1971	1972	1973	1974	1975	1976	1977	1978	1979
Gross	110	145	200	305	375	460	565	695	895	1120
Net	65	85	110	160	215	250	310	380	485	610
Dollars as % of gross	81	76	78	73	77	78	79	76	74	73*

*Estimated figure.
Source: Adapted from *World Financial Markets*, Morgan Guaranty Trust, New York, December 1978, February 1979, and March 1980.

Table 12-4 Sources of Euromarket deposits (in billion U.S. dollars)

Source	Dec. 1978	Percent	Dec. 1979	Percent	Dec. 1980	Percent
Europe	144.5	38.3	181.0	39.4	235.0	42.3
OPEC	54.7	14.5	68.6	14.9	98.6	17.7
Nonoil LDCs	39.8	10.5	46.0	10.1	38.0	6.8
Offshore bank centres	45.4	11.8	56.9	12.3	64.0	11.5
East Europe	8.8	2.3	8.2	1.8	7.2	1.3
Other developed countries	26.2	6.9	31.1	6.7	34.5	6.2
Canada & Japan	13.0	3.5	14.2	3.2	14.5	2.6
USA	37.0	10.1	46.5	10.1	56.5	10.3
Unallocated	7.6	2.1	7.0	1.5	7.3	1.3
Total	377.0	100.0	459.5	100.0	555.6	100.0

Source: Adapted from *AMEX Bank Review* 7, 1 (December 1980). Figures are estimates. The data recorded in this table only refer to banks located in the European Reporting Area. Totals are therefore smaller than for the offshore market as a whole.

tract dollar deposits whenever the equilibrium rates rose above the Regulation Q limit.
2. Eurobanks are not required to maintain reserves against the dollar deposits they take in, whereas Federal Reserve Regulation M in the United States mandates fractional reserves.
3. The Interest Equalization TAX (IET), introduced in 1963, taxed interest on foreign debt sold in the United States, thereby raising to prohibitive levels the cost of borrowing in United States capital markets by foreign corporations and governments. This meant that borrowers had to look outside of the United States for funds, often turning to the Eurodollar market.
4. The 1968 U.S. Office of Foreign Direct Investment (OFDI) regulation restricted United States corporations in their use of domestic dollars overseas. This meant future expansion had to be financed overseas, greatly increasing the demand for external dollars or Eurodollars.[20]

Although the IET and OFDI regulations have been abolished and Regulation Q is no longer binding on certificates of deposits exceeding U.S. $100,000, the Eurodollar market is still expanding.[21] It will continue to exist as long as there are lucrative opportunities in offshore financing. Besides the United States MNCs, the European and Japanese MNCs are increasingly using this market to finance their foreign operations.

Japan's International Money Market

Japanese economic growth has made Tokyo the international financial center. The amount of inflow and outflow of yen from Japan has increased tenfold during 1971 to 1981. Foreign capital into Japan has increased from U.S. $1.1 billion in 1971 to U.S. $13.1 billion in 1981. Similarly, Japanese capital investments abroad have increased from U.S. $2.2 billion in 1971 to U.S. $22.8 billion in 1981. This can be seen from Figure 12-1. Japan is now on par with other major international money markets with respect to loan availability to nonresidents and residents. For example, banks operating in Japan loaned U.S. $149 billion by 1981, as compared to U.S. $66 billion by West German

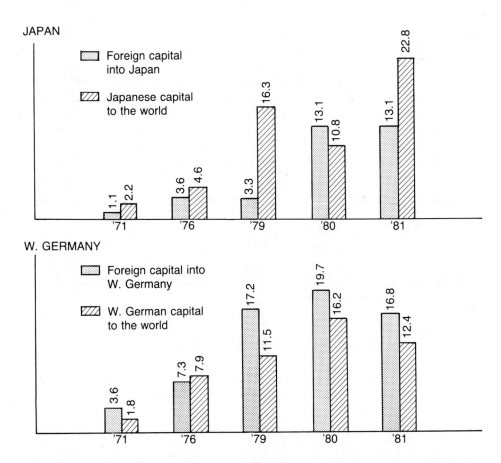

Figure 12-1 Balance of long-term capital ($ billion) (*Source: Focus Japan,* July 1982 JS-A.)

Table 12-5 Bond markets of major countries ($ billion)

	Japan	U. S.	W. Germany	U. K.
Outstanding issue as of end of 1980	732	1,516	346	124*
Turnover in 1981	725	3,700**	228	322

*1979　**1980
Source: Focus Japan, July 1982 JS-A.

banks, and U.S. $165 billion and U.S. $214 billion by French and United States banks, respectively[22] (Table 12-5).

The main reason for the increasing foreign capital inflow into Japan is the growing attractiveness of the Japanese bond and securities market. As Figure 12-2 shows, the Japanese bond market is the second largest after the United States. Similarly, Tokyo stock market transactions also ranked the second heaviest (Figure 12-3). Japan also has a well-developed short-term market; it reached U.S. $62 billion in 1981, and the strength of the Japanese yen and its importance among world currencies is increasing.

Governmental Demands

Coupled with the increased complexities and options in money markets as just discussed, increasing governmental demands and controls on inflow and outflow of capital, remittance, repatriation of capital, dividends, royalty fees, transfer pricing, and foreign exchange may render a centralized finance function less operational and effective.

Financing of Foreign Subsidiaries

The international firm has a larger number of alternatives to finance its overseas business operations than the domestic firm. These include:

1. *Parent company*
   Equity
   Loans from its own resources or through banks
   Loans by other affiliates
   Intracompany transfers

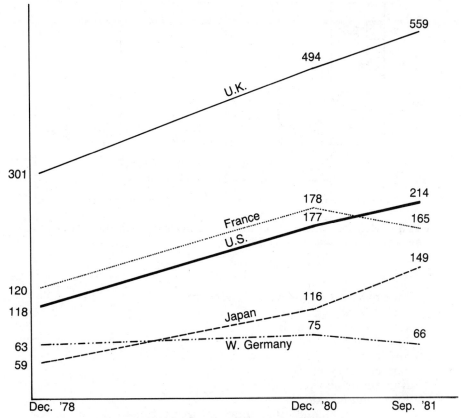

*Loans to nonresidents and foreign currency loans to residents

Figure 12-2 International loans* outstanding extended by banks ($ billion) (*Source: Focus Japan,* July 1982 JS-A. Data were provided by the Ministry of Finance (Japan).)

       Transfer pricing mechanism
       Home governmental agencies, e.g., Export-import bank, over-
         seas private investment corporations
  2. *Host country*
       Stock and bond markets
       Local partner
       Local banks
       Local financial institutions
       Host government's development agencies
       Home government's Foreign Aid Program (PL 480 Funds)
  3. *International Agencies*
       International Bank for Reconstruction and Development (IBRD)

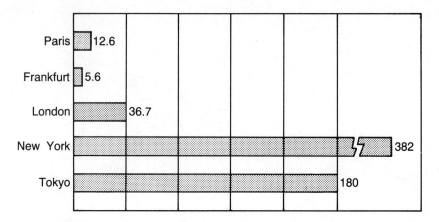

Figure 12-3 1980 major stock market turnovers in major countries ($ billion) (*Source:* Adapted from *Focus Japan*, July 1982 JS-A.)

       International Development Association
       World Bank
       Asian Development Bank
       Export-import Banks
  4. *Third Country Sources*
       Eurocurrency market
       Eurodollar market
       Eurobond market
       Foreign banks and other financial institutions

These larger numbers of alternatives also mean greater complexity in managing the financial affairs of a company. Numerous factors need to be taken into consideration for determining the source of financing overseas operations. These include: foreign exchange controls, taxation, exchange rate fluctuations, rate of inflation in given country, interest rates, and the balance of payment situations in the host country.

    Preceding the analysis of the actual financial practices of United States, European, and Japanese companies, a brief discussion of the advantages and disadvantages of the various sources and methods of financing follows.

Advantages and Disadvantages

Conceptually, the various methods of financing can be grouped into two basic categories: (1) equity financing and (2) debt financing. For both equity and debt financing the sources of obtaining funds, as we saw earlier, are numerous.

Tradeoffs between debt and equity are discussed extensively in the international business literature.[23] The main issue is the cost of debt *versus* equity. However, a number of studies in international finance[24] have indicated that firms are generally not making decisions on the basis of the cost of the capital. Other factors, such as political risks, currency stability, foreign exchange fluctuations and exposure risks, control on remittance and repatriation of capital, tax structure, and expropriation risks play important roles in financial decision making.

The main advantages of equity financing are the greater flexibility in exercising controls over overseas operations; use of economies of scale in borrowing a large pool of money from low-cost countries; and the increased debt capacity of the firm.

The chief disadvantages of equity financing are the greater risk of exposure to foreign exchange fluctuations. In developing countries, where severe restrictions are placed on remitting dividends and repatriating capital, the firm with a heavy equity base will find it difficult to transfer earnings and invested capital.

The main advantages for debt financing are the tax deduction on interest paid by the subsidiaries, access to low-cost funds, and low risks in repatriating borrowed capital. The prime disadvantage of debt financing is the higher foreign exchange exposure risk if the subsidiaries have borrowed from foreign sources.

The advantages of borrowing from the host country are the low political risks and no foreign exchange exposure risks. At the same time, it offers a possibility of tax deduction because most countries will allow interest paid on borrowed capital as tax deductible. It also provides an opportunity to establish good relationships with local businesses and other financial institutions. This assumes, however, that the funds are available in the host countries. This may not be the case in many developing countries.

Given the multitude of factors and risks, it is not simple to decide the optimum source and method of financing international operations. However, some guidelines could still be derived from this discussion.

1. If political and exchange risks are high, debt financing through host country sources is most advisable
2. If there are severe restrictions on remittance of earnings and repatriation of invested capital, financing through loans from the parent company is more preferable
3. For the rapidly growing subsidiary, internal equity financing may be more appropriate[25]

Table 12-6 outlines the main advantages and disadvantages of different sources and methods of financing.

Table 12-6 Advantages and disadvantages of different sources and methods of financing overseas operations

Sources/methods	Advantages	Disadvantages
Debt financing through host country sources	Low political risk Tax deduction on interest paid	Availability of capital
	Elimination of foreign exchange exposure risks	Less control over subsidiary operations
	Possibility of establishing good relationship with local businesses and other financial institutions	
Debt financing through home base sources parent company, affiliates and home country)	Tax deductions on interest paid Ease in remittance and repatriation Access to low-cost funds	Higher foreign exchange exposure risks for subsidiaries
Equity financing through parent company sources	Possibility of enhancing debt capacity of overseas subsidiaries	Higher foreign exchange exposure risks
	Higher parental controls on subsidiary operations Access to low-cost funds	Higher risks for remittance of earnings and repatriation of invested capital
		Higher risks for expropriation and nationalization
Equity financing through host country source	Less foreign exchange exposure risks Stronger identity with host country and local interest groups	Less parental control on overseas operations

Source: Adapted from William H. Davidson, *Global Strategic Management*, New York: John Wiley and Sons, 1982, p. 233.

Financing Through Intrafirm Transactions

Intrafirm transactions, such as international payables and receivables, are another important source of financing international operations. They have been used both for initial capital investments and as working capital. The several types of intrafirm transactions include:

1. Management service fees
2. Royalty payments
3. Dividends and interest payments
4. Payables and receivables for intrafirm trade
5. Transfer pricing

The last two could be used for financing overseas operations.

The main advantage of these sources of financing are the ease in obtaining the required funds in a short time, the reduced cost of borrowing, and the hedge against foreign exchange fluctuations.

Transfer pricing among units operating in different countries can be adjusted to achieve the following objectives:

1. Transfer funds from a high-risk to low-risk country (political and foreign exchange risks)
2. Reduce import duties in high-duty countries by charging low prices to the units in those countries
3. Avoid taxation in a high-tax country

Besides transfer pricing, both the nature and the timing of the payments among the trading units can be adjusted to consolidate funds in low-risk countries or in countries earning high interest rates. Leads and lags in payments and netting approaches have been used by many international corporations in which the home office or the financial holding company in some tax haven country becomes a clearing house for all intracompany transactions.

The actual transfer pricing policies of international corporations range from an arm's length market-oriented pricing, to strict cost-plus formula, to export pricing at less than the marginal cost. For example, Arpan's study of United States and foreign firms indicates that in the United States firms, setting prices remained in the hands of the home office, whereas in the foreign firms, market-oriented pricing is being used. More specifically, he found the following patterns among the different multinationals:

1. French companies attempted to minimize income tax worldwide; they set the prices accordingly to achieve this objective.
2. Italian companies attempted to maximize the parent company's income.

3. Japanese companies used cost-oriented pricing for competitive advantages.
4. British companies maximized return on investment (ROI) because of the pressures from the banking system.
5. Canadian companies used market-oriented pricing because of the close ties with United States Canadian legal regulations.
6. German companies were not much concerned about transfer pricing and aimed at long-term profitability of subsidiary operations.
7. Scandinavians used market-oriented pricing to cope with the host countries' demands.[26]

Many countries have imposed severe restrictions on transfer pricing, especially on those practices that reduce the tax base of the country.

Besides the legal violations, transfer pricing also creates a serious problem in evaluating the subsidiary's performance. It makes it difficult to identify the profitability of each subsidiary.

Sources of Financing in United States, European, and Japanese Multinational Companies

As Robbins and Stoubaugh's study has shown, the managers of multinational companies expect the foreign subsidiary to grow on its own with minimum financial help from the parent company.[27] Penrose[28] and Barlow and Wender[29] have also shown that the foreign subsidiaries borrow very little capital from the headquarters.

Robbins and Stoubaugh's study of 187 United States multinational companies revealed the following patterns:

> Most foreign subsidiaries are started with a modest sum. After incubation, internal fund flows are the dominant source of funds, and when coupled with local borrowing, leave relatively little need for fresh funds from headquarters.[30]

United States, as well as European and Japanese, subsidiaries depend on local borrowing for both short-term and long-term financing. This is done regardless of interest rate differentials. In other words, international corporations' financial practices are less than optimum. As discussed earlier, the main advantages of local borrowing are to:

1. Secure protection against losses caused by currency devaluation
2. Reduce the liabilities of the parent company by not consolidating the subsidiary's debt, occurred through local borrowing, in the annual report
3. Meet governmental restrictions on capital inflow and outflow

4. Foster good relations with local banks and other financing institutions.

Overall, approximately 40% of United States foreign subsidiaries' funds are secured through loans and 60% from within the MNCs' system, of which internally generated funds constitute 46%.[31] A similar situation exists in European companies. For example, the study of Brooks and Remmers of European MNCs shows that:

1. The largest single source of finances for foreign subsidiaries is the cash flow from their operations.
2. The second largest source of finances is local borrowing.
3. The smallest proportion of subsidiary finances comes from foreign sources.[32]

Sarathy and Chatterjee's study of the financial structure of United States and Japanese companies indicates the following patterns:

1. Japanese firms rely heavily on banks for short-term debt.
2. Japanese firms have low levels of working capital.
3. Japanese firms operate with about one half as much equity as United States firms.
4. Japanese firms hold about twice as much in long-term investments as United States firms.[33]

Debt-Equity Ratios

The financial structure norms in terms of debt-equity ratios differ significantly among different nations. Environmental, institutional, and governmental regulations seem to play important roles in establishing these norms. For example, the debt-equity ratios in the United States is the lowest in the world, whereas Japan, West Germany, and Sweden have relatively high debt-equity ratios. In the United States, the main source of industrial capital is the stock market. To acquire needed capital United States firms have to conform to the established financial norms, that is, a low debt-equity ratio.[34] In Japan and some European countries, banks and governmental agencies constitute the major source of capital.

Tables 12-7, 12-8, 12-9, and Figure 12-4 show the debt-equity ratios in United States, European, and Japanese multinational companies. It can easily be seen that there is a trend toward greater use of debt financing by United States, European, and Japanese multinationals.

Although the different industries may differ in financial norms, a number of studies seem to indicate that country norms are more important than in-

Table 12-7 Debt ratios in selected industries and countries, 1964–1965

	Alcoholic beverages	Automobiles	Chemicals	Electrical	Foods	Iron and steel	Nonferrous metals	Paper	Textiles	Total
Benelux	45.7	–	44.6	37.5	56.2	50.0	59.2	35.9	54.2	47.9
France	35.8	36.0	34.3	59.1	24.7	33.7	55.0	35.5	20.9	37.2
West Germany	59.2	55.1	54.8	67.5	42.5	63.8	68.1	71.8	44.9	58.6
Italy	64.9	77.3	68.2	73.6	66.4	77.9	67.5	–	66.6	70.3
Japan	60.9	70.3	73.2	71.1	78.3	74.5	74.5	77.7	72.2	72.5
Sweden	–	76.4	45.6	60.1	46.8	70.0	68.7	60.7	–	61.2
Switzerland	–	–	59.7	50.8	29.3	–	26.3	–	–	41.5
United Kingdom	43.8	56.5	38.7	46.9	47.6	44.9	41.7	46.6	42.4	45.5
United States	31.1	39.2	43.3	50.3	34.2	35.8	36.7	33.9	44.2	38.7
Total	48.8	58.7	51.4	57.4	47.3	56.3	55.3	51.7	49.4	

Source: Copyright © (1969) by the Regents of the University of California. Reprinted from CALIFORNIA MANAGEMENT REVIEW, Vol. XII, No. 1, p. 92, by permission of the Regents.

Table 12-8 Debt ratios in selected industries and countries, 1979–1980

	Alcoholic beverages	Automobiles	Chemicals	Electrical	Foods	Iron and steel	Nonferrous metals	Paper	Textiles	Total
Benelux	41.4	61.8	60.0	50.8	64.3	66.2	41.4	63.2	54.2	55.9
France	56.3	67.3	72.1	72.5	77.7	74.1	66.3	74.4	73.9	70.5
West Germany	–	57.1	56.2	66.4	48.8	51.6	67.8	69.8	65.0	60.3
Italy	–	21.7	67.7	79.2	83.4	90.2	86.1	77.4	77.7	72.9
Japan	–	71.3	81.2	65.7	76.3	87.5	88.2	76.6	77.6	78.1
Sweden	79.1	75.2	67.5	76.9	62.8	69.3	56.1	55.5	59.7	66.9
Switzerland	–	–	–	63.2	53.7	63.8	–	–	–	60.2
United Kingdom	41.9	72.8	49.8	59.9	55.3	50.7	56.7	55.9	50.7	54.5
United States	51.1	58.0	54.7	53.6	55.4	54.3	57.6	58.2	47.5	54.5
Total	54.0	60.7	63.7	65.4	64.5	67.5	65.0	66.4	63.3	

Source: J.M. Collins, and W. S. Sekely, "The Relationship of Headquarters, Country and Industry Classification to Financial Structure," *Financial Management* 12, 3 (Autumn 1983): 48.

Table 12-9 Equity ratios by country*

Country	1977	1978
Japan (103 firms average)	21.77%	22.86%
United States (177 firms average)	49.92	49.40
Canada (15 firms average)	46.59	45.13
United Kingdom (38 firms average)	42.05	41.87
West Germany (25 firms average)	28.59	28.92
France (21 firms average)	24.99	26.80
Italy (7 firms average)	22.90	26.31
The Netherlands (3 firms average)	40.17	40.18
Belgium (3 firms average)	30.55	30.81
Switzerland (6 firms average)	49.68	50.88
Sweden (11 firms average)	25.69	25.66

*Weighted averages.
Source: Ministry of International Trade and Industry, *Sekai no Kiayo no Keei Bunseki*, Tokyo, Japan: International Comparison of Management, 1980, pp. 84–87. Taken from S. Suzuki, and R. W. Wright, "Financial Structure and Bankruptcy Risk in Japanese Companies," *Journal of International Business Studies* XVI, 1 (Spring 1985): 98.

dustry norms.[35] The increasing trend toward debt financing reflects firms' desires to hedge against political and foreign exchange risks and to reduce taxes because the interest on loans is deductible in most countries.

It has been argued that Japanese firms have more financial leverage than do United States companies. A recent study by Michel and Shaked cast doubts on this prevailing notion.[36] Their study showed that when capitalization ratios are based on the book value of equity, Japanese companies appear to have a higher leverage than do United States companies. However, when capitalization ratios are based on the market value of equity, there are no large differences between Japanese and United States firms.

Working Capital and Cash-Flow Management

International cash-flow management usually relates to the management and control of short-term liquid assets and liabilities, namely, cash, marketable securities, and payables. In multinational companies, the transfer of funds is either done through the mail or by cable. Transferring money across countries by cable is quicker, more efficient, and less expensive.

International cash flow is of two types: (1) intercompany transfers, and (2) intracompany transfers. For intercompany transfers, the timing of the settlement is critical, because overdue receivables lose interest on capital. Inter-

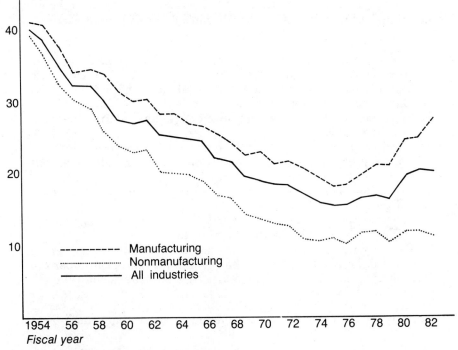

Note: Equity ratio = Equity ÷ total assets

Figure 12-4 Average equity ratios of major Japanese companies (*Source:* Ministry of International Trade and Industry, *Wagakuni Kigyono Keiei Bunksei* (Analysis of Japanese Corporation), 1981. Taken from S. Suzuki, and R. W. Wright, "Financial Structure and Bankruptcy Risk in Japanese companies," *Journal of International Business Studies* (Spring 1985): 98.)

national corporations generally are more concerned with intracompany transfers. Here two alternatives are possible.

1. Pooling money at one central location, either at the home office or in the foreign country that offers distinct tax and other advantages
2. Keeping the liquid cash in the subsidiary in which the money has been made

The main advantage of centralizing liquid cash is better control over available current assets for effective allocation and investment. A large pool of money also provides better leverage with the bankers to earn higher interest or to secure needed capital at a reduced risk. Shapiro lists the following additional advantages of a centralized cash management system:

1. The corporation is able to operate with a smaller amount of cash; pools of excess liquidity are absorbed and eliminated. Each operation will maintain only transaction balances and not hold speculative or precautionary ones.
2. By reducing total assets, profitability is enhanced and financing costs are reduced.
3. The headquarters' staff, with its purview of all corporate activity, can recognize problems and opportunities that an individual unit might not perceive.
4. All decisions can be made using overall corporate benefit as the criterion.
5. Greater expertise in cash and portfolio management exists if one group is responsible for these activities.
6. The corporation's total assets at risk in a foreign country can be reduced. Less will be lost in the event of an expropriation or the promulgation of regulations restricting the transfer of funds.[37]

Arguing for the centralized cash management system, Shapiro states:

Today, the combination of volatile currency and interest rate fluctuations, questions of capital availability, increasingly complex organizations and operating arrangements, and a growing emphasis on profitability virtually mandates a highly centralized international cash management system. The impetus is not simply to obtain some advantages; there is an additional motivation which is to ensure the corporations can be flexible and decisive. A strong movement is readily evident to place much greater responsibility in corporate headquarters. This trend applies to European as well as U.S. firms.[38]

Besides centralizing money at one central point, the international company uses netting techniques to settle intrafirm transactions. The netting technique is basically an in-house clearing system that identifies the net inflows and outflows of each subsidiary. This method is useful when there are frequent transactions among the various affiliates of the firm. It saves service fees and transaction expenses. It is also effective in avoiding exchange and capital control by governments.

Although the financial manager spends considerable time in managing the working capital and cash reserves, the research on this topic is minimal. Gentry, et al. cite the following reasons for the lack of research studies in this area:

1. Decisions concerning working capital and liquid assets are made frequently, and they are routine. Consequently, the impact of individual decisions is insignificant.
2. Decisions are reversible over time, and corrective solutions are easy to implement.
3. Because of the frequency of decision making, an immediate feedback system is needed, thus requiring a dynamic analysis that management usually considers to be too expensive and not worthwhile.
4. Difficulties in forecasting cash flows.
5. For manufacturing firms, as noted earlier, the financial system is secondary. Production and sales are the primary functions. Thus financial decisions "are virtually eclipsed by marketing (credit granting) or production (inventory) decisions which have direct impact on the firm's cash flow position."[39]

Objectives of the Management of Working Capital: Cross-National Comparisons

The financial manager considers the following four objectives as the most important:

1. *Supporting sales*
   To provide the cash, accounts receivable, inventories, and short-term credit necessary to support the anticipated sales in a defined planning period.
2. *Financial buffer*
   To minimize the effect of surprises in sales or materials, production, labor, credit, and transportation.
3. *Minimization*
   To minimize the balances in cash, receivables, inventories, and short-term debt.
4. *Investment decision*
   To evaluate changes in each current asset as an investment decision and to minimize the cost of short-term credit.[40]

As Table 12-10 shows, the majority of managers in four countries, Belgium, France, the United States, and India, mentioned that the most important short-run objective was to support sales with cash, receivables, and short-term credit. They also agreed on the ranking of the short-run objectives.

Gentry, et al. also showed that the short-run objectives do not correspond with long-range goals. The practicing managers "show a more finely tuned and distinctive attitude toward managing working capital than toward long-term goal hierarchy and presumably thereby forward financial strategies."[41]

Table 12-10 Most important working capital management objectives of companies in Belgium, France, India, and the United States

Objectives	(Percent of total respondents)				
	Belgium	*France*	*India*	*U.S.*	*Total*
(Number of respondents)	(37)	(54)	(38)	(450)	(579)
• Supporting sales	45.9	53.7	50.0	55.6	54.4
• Financial buffer	35.1	7.4	18.4	6.4	9.2
• Minimization	13.5	25.9	18.4	21.3	21.2
• Investment decision	5.4	11.1	13.2	15.1	14.0

Source: James Gentry, et al., "An International Study of Management Perceptions of the Working Capital Process," *Journal of International Business Studies* X, 1 (Spring–Summer 1979): 31.

In contrast to specific objectives concerning the management of working capital and liquid cash, Stonehill, et al. indicate no clear-cut preference for long-run financial planning objectives.[42] Consequently, Gentry, et al. have argued that a "development of a generalized model for working capital management is likely to be more fruitful than the modeling efforts in the direction of strategy formulation."[43]

Remittance Policies

Remittance policies refer to a firm's guidelines concerning payments from the overseas subsidiary operations with respect to management fees, contributions toward the headquarters' overhead and research and development expenses, interest on loans, royalties for technical knowledge, and dividends on equity capital.

The firm's policies are dependent on the economic and political risks, the tax rates in the home and host countries, the nature of investments, and the long-term strategies of the foreign investment. More specifically Summa, a tax consultant, has underscored the importance of the following factors in formulating remittance policies:

1. The firm's business goals and objectives
2. Reinvestment requirements and opportunities for growth in the host countries

3. Availability of capital in the host countries
4. Stability of currency
5. Economic and political considerations in the home and host countries
6. Cost of converting foreign funds into domestic currency
7. The government's restrictions on remittances
8. Tax structures in the home and host countries
9. Impact of remittances on the firm's image in the host countries[44]

Based on these factors, the following guidelines can be outlined:

1. In economically and politically high-risk countries, an immediate payback cycle will be more desirable
2. For a fast-growing subsidiary, a slower payback cycle will be more desirable
3. A mature subsidiary should send a larger remittance (this will be treated as cash cow)
4. A slower payback cycle from high-tax countries to reduce taxation on earned profits, if the reinvested profits are not taxed
5. Remittance of profits through countries with low withholding taxes (e.g., a financial holding company in Bermuda)

With respect to the type of income flows, Fayerweather has suggested the following guidelines.

Technologically sophisticated firms are in a better position to earn profits through royalties and management fees, as well as through intracorporate pricing of spare parts, than through dividends. Medium-range technological firms can earn profits through dividends via equity investments. Low-technology firms are more likely to earn only moderate profits only through dividends.[45]

The host government's restrictions and the firm's public image are of overriding importance in designing remittance policies. As noted in Chapter 2, many developing countries restrict royalty payments ranging from 3% to 8% of the total sales and dividends and ranging from 10% to 15% of profits. Even industrialized countries are critical of the large outflow of remittances from foreign investors, especially during adverse balance of payment situations. For example, in 1977, when Ford Motor Company and the Utah Development Company transferred a large remittance to the United States, a public uproar arose in Australia. The leading Australian newspaper, *The Sydney Morning Herald*, echoed public sentiments over the behavior of the MNCs in these words:

> Companies like Utah may claim to be backing Australia, but ultimately any company must put its corporate interests first . . . [unless] we realize this and

Table 12-11 Funds received from foreign operations by United States firms (in millions of dollars)

Nature of payments	Percentage
Dividends	51
Royalties	17
Management fees	17
Income from sales to affiliates	9
Interest	6

Source: Adapted from Sidney Robbins, and Robert Stabough, *Money in the Multinational Enterprise*, New York: Basic Books, 1973, p. 76.

begin some shrewd bargaining . . . companies like Utah will continue backing Australia . . . all the way to the bank.[46]

Remittance Practices of International Corporations

Dividends seem to be the most common means of withdrawing funds from overseas subsidiaries. As shown in Table 12-11, Robbins and Stobaugh's study of 187 United States MNCs indicated that 51% of the companies transfer money through dividend payments; royalties and management fees constituted 34% of the total money received from overseas operations.[47]

Dividend policies vary greatly among different firms and different industries. As noted earlier, mature technological firms are more inclined to remit larger funds than firms with higher growth potential.

Dividend policy decisions are more centralized in United States companies than in European and Japanese companies. Generally, the latter are more permissive in allowing subsidiaries to retain profits for building up their capital for further investment.[48]

Foreign Exchange Risks[49]

The three different types of risk exposure international companies face in doing business overseas are:

1. *Transaction risk.* It arises when a company has agreed to make a payment or to receive a payment, at a future date, and the payment is in a foreign currency.
2. *Translation risk.* It occurs with changes in the valuation of overseas assets and liabilities, because of exchange rate fluctuations.
3. *Operational risk.* It is an overall economic exposure that arises

Table 12-12 Currency value changes

Currency	Jan. 25, 1985	Feb. 1, 1985	Feb. 8, 1985
German mark	3.1710	3.1945	3.257
Swiss franc	2.664	2.6725	2.7750
Japanese yen	254.100	254.4	260.25
Singapore dollar	2.2030	2.2085	2.2585

from the indirect effects of exchange rate changes on a company's revenues and expenses from overseas operations.

In recent months the volatility of currency values, especially the changing value of the United States dollar against the Swiss franc, the German mark, the Japanese yen, and the Singapore dollar, has significantly increased the foreign exchange risk exposure of MNCs. A sample of data, taken from *The International Herald Tribune* for a few selected days, is appropriate for appreciating the level of risk involved.

Using the data from Table 12-12, we can clearly see the U.S. $10,000, when converted would yield 31,710, 31,945, and 32,570 German marks on January 25, February 1, and February 8, respectively. These data suggest it is not unusual for an exchange rate to change 2.7% in two weeks; changes in excess of 5% are also common. Such degrees of fluctuation impose severe hardships on the multinational companies that are fully risk-prone because of the transaction, translation, or operational exposure.

Serfass[50] points out that the pursuit of speculative profits on currency exchange markets is a pastime about as rewarding as Russian roulette for corporate money managers. However, calculated guesses of the likely range of short-term exchange rates do serve a purpose, to provide a rough idea of the range of possible gains or losses that may result, given a particular net exposure. By computing the upper and lower limits of the probable gains or losses, the corporate treasurer of a multinational corporation can possibly forestall threats arising out of these fluctuations. In such an uncertain environment, a corporate treasurer has a number of important tasks to perform. First, he or she must try to forecast the lower and upper limits of a currency in relation to his or her home currency, and then select an optimum hedging policy. Finally, he or she must choose the least costly method of covering the relevant risk.

How to Minimize Currency Risks

A financial manager can use several hedging policies to minimize currency risks.

Buying and Writing Call and Put Options. These options are written in currencies to which the firm is exposed. The firm develops forecasts for the currencies in which it has exposure. Specifically, a confidence interval may be developed for each currency, providing an upper and a lower limit within which the currency is expected to fluctuate. If the exchange loss is expected to be greater than the cost of the hedge, hedging a percentage of the currency exposure would be recommended.

Hedging in the Futures Market. This refers to the sale or purchase of future contracts. The firm often takes a position in the market either to substitute temporarily the cash transaction to be carried out in the future or to offset an equal and opposite transaction or position in the market. The hedge tries to compensate the loss anticipated in the cash market with the gain expected in the futures market, with the result that uncertainty, arising from the volatility, will be substantially reduced.

Currency Swap. The firm that has branches in many countries may use the currency swap as a form of hedging. Typically, a currency swap is a current exchange of two currencies and an agreement to reexchange these currencies after a set period of time. The initial exchange of currencies is made at the current spot rate and the same currency rate is used for the subsequent exchange, regardless of the intervening exchange rate fluctuation. The benefit of this strategy is that it eliminates the exchange risks completely. A marginal cost may be involved in such arrangements in the form of differential fees to reflect the interest rate differential.

Parallel and Back-to-Back Loans. Parallel and back-to-back loans are other possible hedging alternatives. They require two multinationals with headquarters in different countries, each having subsidiaries in the other's country. Further, these companies must have similar liquidity positions and financing requirements.

Using Foreign Exchange Reserves. If the firm has adequate foreign exchange reserves, these could then be used to offset the impact of unpredictable forces in the foreign exchange market. It could effectively self-hedge and avoid paying a significant price for protection. Using the reserve may not amount, in strict terms, to hedging. Hedging is done in the marketplace and involves someone else bearing the risks. However, reserves serve the same purpose; that is, to smooth out adverse foreign exchange fluctuations.

Leads and Lags. Another widely used hedging strategy is leading and lagging. This strategy facilitates the transfer of liquidity among the affiliates in an accelerated (leading) or decelerated (lagging) way in settling interaffiliate accounts. In other words, leading and lagging changes the credit terms extended by one unit to the other.

The firm's decision to choose an optimum short-term cover may be influenced by the choices available for local and foreign currency financing, comparative interest rates, degree of currency risk, expected exchange gain or loss, foreign reserves, currency swap, and back-to-back loan arrangements. In the long run, if a firm were well diversified across currencies, its losses without protection would approximate the costs of obtaining protection on efficient foreign exchanges and money markets. Thus the purchase of protection is a cost, required when the conditions for the diversification of foreign exchange exposures are not available to the firm.

Short-Term Financing and Borrowing Strategy. In instituting a borrowing strategy, the major concern of the firm is to discover those circumstances under which a policy of selective borrowing is warranted. In the absence of a forward market in the local currency, it will pay to choose among currencies in arranging financing if (1) local currency borrowing is the cheapest method of hedging a firm's exchange risk in that currency, or if (2) the expected borrowing costs differ among the currencies. In either case, the approximate currency mix of a firm's financing would depend on the firm's degree of exposure, its risk tolerance, and the relative financing costs involved. If a forward market in the local currency does exist, then loans should be compared on a covered basis, with financing performed in the cheaper currency. Any resulting exposure can be offset in the forward market.

Macro-Level Problems

The techniques just discussed dealt with micro-level decisions. The international company also has to consider macro-level factors, such as the exchange reserve position of the host and home countries, trade restrictions, changes in balance of payment positions, and the growing foreign debt of developing countries.

Lieater[51] has developed a technique for specifying an optional strategy for a firm that has exposure to devaluation-prone currencies. Basically, this involves comparing exposed assets—accounts receivable, local currency bank, bank deposits, inventories, and other current assets—with exposed liabilities—local bank loans, accounts and notes payable, and local taxes payable. The larger the exposed liabilities, the greater the devaluation gain. Thus, the treasurer of the firm should have adequate information, derived from the data base and market intelligence, to evaluate and analyze the foreign exchange position of the firm's overseas operations. The treasurer has to consider the exposures in different currencies and evaluate the possible value changes in the exposed assets and liabilities. Although it is impossible to ensure against all foreign exchange risks, some protection will be necessary to cover the transaction and translation exposure. Firms that indulge in speculative trading in currencies often lose out heavily in the currency market. It is the ultimate responsibility of the treasurer to ensure corporate earnings at a minimum cost and risk.

Summary

This chapter analyzed the following important elements of financial management in international corporations:

- The strategic choices to be made in managing financial aspects
- Decision making in financial management (centralization-decentralization issue)
- Sources of obtaining funds for overseas operations
- Management of working capital and cash flow
- Remittance policies of international corporations
- Management of foreign risk exposures

In analyzing these elements, I provided a comparative profile of United States, European, and Japanese companies' practices.

With respect to the strategic choices, it was shown that the financial system is only a secondary system in the manufacturing firm. The primary aspects for these firms are production and marketing. However, in spite of its secondary role, the financial system occupies central position in international corporations. Consequently, decision making is by and large centralized at the headquarters' level.

Multinational corporations finance their overseas operations through debt rather than through equity. Local borrowing is preferred to foreign borrowing, largely because of foreign exchange and political risks.

The main objectives of working capital and cash-flow management are to support the production and marketing functions. Nationality differences are minor in formulating the objectives of working capital.

Remittance policies of international corporations vary a great deal. Dividends are the main source of remittance from foreign operations. United States companies seem to remit larger proportions of their overseas income than do European and Japanese counterparts.

There are three kinds of foreign exchange risks: (1) transaction, (2) translation, (3) operational. This chapter outlined the various hedging practices available to international corporations to cover their risk exposures.

Discussion Questions

1. Discuss the major strategic choices involved in formulating and implementing financial practices in international corporations.
2. Analyze the major sources of funds for financing overseas operations.
3. Discuss the advantages and disadvantages of financing the foreign operations through equity *versus* debt.
4. Discuss the differences in financial management practices among United States, Japanese, and European MNCs.
5. What are the major profit transferring mechanisms from the subsidiary to its headquarters?
6. Discuss several financial management techniques available for reducing foreign exchange risks.
7. Analyze decision making in United States, European, and Japanese companies concerning financial management.

Endnotes

1. John Fayerweather, *International Business Strategy and Administrations* (Cambridge, Mass.: Ballinger Publishing Co., 1978), p. 369.
2. Ibid., pp. 375–379.
3. Sidney M. Robbins, and Robert B. Stobaugh, "Financing Foreign Affiliates," *Financial Management* 2, 4 (Winter 1973): 65.
4. Fayerweather, *International*, p. 405.
5. William H. Davidson, *Global Strategic Management* (New York: John Wiley and Sons, 1982), pp. 217–218, 240–242.
6. Sidney M. Robbins, and Robert B. Stobaugh, "Financing of Foreign Subsidiaries," *Journal of International Business* 1, 1 (Summer 1970): 43–64.
7. Ulrich E. Weichmann, *Marketing Management in Multinational Firms* (New York: Praeger Publishers, 1976).
8. E. R. Barlow, *Management of Foreign Subsidiaries* (Boston: Harvard Graduate School of Business Administration, 1953), pp. 84–113.
9. Lawrence G. Franko, *European Business Strategies in the United States* (Geneva: Business International, 1971).
10. Anant R. Negandhi, and Martin K. Welge, *Beyond Theory Z* (Greenwich, Conn.: JAI Press, 1984), especially Chap. 2.
11. Yair Aharoni, *The Foreign Investment Decision Process* (Boston: Harvard Graduate School of Business Administration, 1966).
12. David Zenoff, "Remittance Policies of U.S. Subsidiaries in Europe," *The Banker* 117, 495 (May 1967): 418–427.
13. Enid Baird Lovell, *Appraising Foreign Licensing Performance* (New York: National Industrial Conference Board, 1969).
14. Jaffrey S. Arpan, "International Intercorporate Pricing: Non-American Systems and Views," *Journal of International Business Studies* (Spring 1972): 1–8.
15. Fayerweather, *International*, pp. 405–410.
16. Olivier Pastre, *Multinationals: Banks and Corporations' Relationships* (Greenwich, Conn.: JAI Press, 1981), pp. 168–169. (Literature search for international

banks and financial institutions was conducted by Mr. A. Alan Rividi. I am grateful for his help and insights.)

17. Davidson, *Global*, p. 86.
18. Rabecca Tsurumi, "Japanese Banks in U.S. Expanding Domestic Operations," *Pacific Basin Quarterly* (1980): pp. 10–11.
19. E. L. Versluysen, *The Political Economy of World Finance* (New York: St. Martins Press, 1981).
20. Alan C. Shapiro, *Multinational Financial Management* (Boston: Allyn and Bacon, Inc., 1982), p. 502.
21. Ibid.
22. *Japanscene: Focus Japan*, July 1982, pp. JS-A, JS-B.
23. Davidson, *Global*, pp. 230–234.
24. Arthur Stonehill, et al., "Financial Goals and Debt Ratios Determinants: A Survey of Practice in Five Countries," *Financial Management* 4, 3 (Autumn 1975): 27–41.
25. Davidson, *Global*, p. 233.
26. Arpan, "International," pp. 1–18.
27. Robbins and Stobaugh, "Financing Foreign Subsidiaries," pp. 58–59.
28. E. T. Penrose, "Foreign Investment and the Growth of the Firm," *Economic Journal* LXVI, 262 (June 1956): 220.
29. E. R. Barlow and I. T. Wender, *Foreign Investment and Taxation* (Englewood Cliffs, NJ: Prentice-Hall, Inc., 1955), pp. 11–14.
30. Robbins and Stobaugh, p. 56.
31. Ibid., p. 57.
32. Michael Z. Brooke, and M. Lee Remmers, *International Management and Business Policy* (Boston: Houghton Mifflin Company, 1978), pp. 13–15.
33. Ravi Sarathy, and Sangit Chatterjee, "The Divergence of Japanese and U.S. Corporate Financial Structure," *Journal of International Business Studies* XV, 3 (Winter 1984): 75–89.
34. David A. Ricks, *International Dimensions of Corporate Finance* (Englewood Cliffs, NJ: Prentice-Hall, Inc., 1978), pp. 73–74.
35. Stonehill, et al., "Financial,"; J. M. Collins, and W. S. Sekely, "The Relationship of Headquarters Country and Industry Classification to Financial Structure," *Financial Management* 12, 3 (Autumn 1983): 45–51.
36. Allen Michel, and Israel Shaked, "Japanese Leverage: Myth or Reality?" *Financial Analysts Journal*, 41, 4 (July-August 1985): 61–67.
37. Shapiro, *Multinational*, pp. 236–237.
38. Ibid.
39. James A. Gentry, et al., "An International Study of Management Perceptions of the Working Capital Process," *Journal of International Business* X, 1 (Spring-Summer 1979): 28–29.
40. Ibid., p. 31.
41. Ibid., p. 36
42. Stonehill, et al., "Financial," pp. 32–33.
43. Gentry, et al., "International," p. 36.
44. Donald J. Summa, "Remittance by U.S. Owned Foreign Corporations: Tax Considerations," *Columbia Journal of Word Business* X, 2 (Summer 1975): 40.
45. Fayerweather, *International*, pp. 408–410.
46. "Foreign Backing," *The Sydney Morning Herald*, November 3, 1977, p. 9.
47. Sidney M. Robbins, and Robert G. Stobaugh, *Money in the Multinational Enterprise* (New York: Basic Books, 1973).
48. Zenoff, "Remittance," pp. 421–427.

49. This section is drawn from Bobby Srinivasan and Anant R. Negandhi, "Hedging in Currency Futures: A Singapore Dollar Case Study," *Asia Pacific Journal of Management* 2, 3 (May 1985): 170–179.

50. W. D. Serfan, "You Cannot Outguess the Foreign Exchange Market," *Harvard University Business Review* 54, 2 (March-April 1976): 64–67.

51. B. A. Lieater, *Financial Management of Foreign Exchange: An Operational Technique to Reduce Risk* (Cambridge, Mass.: MIT Press, 1971).

Additional Readings

Articles

Collins, J. M., and Sekely, W. S. "The Relationship of Headquarters, Country, and Industry Classification to Financial Structure." *Financial Management* 12, 3 (Autumn 1983): 45–51.

Gentry, James A., et al. "An International Study of Management Perceptions of the Working Capital Process." *Journal of International Business Studies* X, 2 (Fall 1979): 28–38.

Sarathy, Ravi, and Chatterjee, Sangit, "The Divergence of Japanese and U.S. Corporate Financial Structure." *Journal of International Business Studies* XV, 3 (Winter 1984): 75–89.

Srinivasan, Bobby, and Negandhi, Anant R. "Hedging in Currency Futures: A Singapore Dollar Case Study." *Asia Pacific Journal of Management* 2, 3 (May 1985): 173–179.

Stonehill, Arthur, et al. "Financial Goals and Debt Ratios Determinants: A Survey of Practices in Five Countries." *Financial Management* 4, 3 (Autumn 1975): 27–41.

Books

Eiteman, David K., and Stonehill, Arthur. *Multinational Business Finance*, ed. 4. Reading, Mass.: Addison-Wesley, 1986.

Shapiro, Alan C. *Multinational Finance Management*. Boston: Allyn and Bacon, Inc., 1982.

Indexes

Names

Inoue, Y., 376
International Business Machines (IBM), 5,
    24, 32, 164, 165, 169, 172, 173, 184,
    185–186, 195, 203–219, 321, 363,
    392–393, 440
  World Trade Corporation, 32
International Chamber of Commerce, 49,
    393–394
International Harvester, 391–392
International Labor Organization, 48
International Machine Union, 56
International Monetary Fund (IMF), 393
International Petroleum, 38
International Telephone and Telegraph
    (ITT), 5, 37, 38, 49, 250
Ishibashi, Kanchiro, 372, 374
Ishibashi, Shojiro, 373
Ishikure, K., 372–373, 376
Ivancevich, John N., 311, 343

Jacoby, Neil, 94
Jaeger, Alfred M., 117, 179
Janata Government, 163, 164, 165
Janata Party, 206
Japan External Trade Organization
    (JETRO), 5, 10, 13, 14, 28, 121, 122–123
J. C. Penney Company, 454–455
John Brown Company, 56
John Deere Company, 392
Johnes, Peter T., 95
Johnnie Walker Company, 448
Johnson, Richard T., 188–189, 222, 308

Kanabayashi, M., 468
Kanungo, Rabindra, 345
Kapoor, Ashok, 255
Kaufman, S., 227, 253
Kaynak, Erdener, 469
Kayser, G., 144, 178
Keegan, Warren J., 28, 221, 238, 254, 394,
    401, 431, 468, 469
Kendall, Donald M., 32, 93
Kennedy, Jr., Charles R., 255
Kerr, Clark, 261, 306
Khera, Inder P., 28
Kiernan, Paul H., 343
Kilmann, R. M., 178
Kindleberger, Charles P., 29
King, W. R., 238, 254
Kleinschmidt, Elko J., 432
Kobrin, Stephen J., 34–35, 56, 93, 239, 254,
    255, 336–337, 345, 363, 385
Koike, R., 344
Kono, Toyohiro, 137, 141, 177
Koontz, Harold, 137, 141, 177
Kotler, P., 467, 468
Kraar, Louis, 250

Kraut, A. I., 307
Kumar, Krishna, 28
Kumazawa, Sadao, 260, 306
Kupfer, Andrew, 401

Lall, Sanjaya, 467
Lammers, C. J., 323, 327, 344
Land, Edwin, 252
Lander, Don, 77
Lauter, Peter G., 345
Lauterbach, Albert, 331, 344
Lawrence, Paul R., 184, 220
League, Burton W., 343
Lecraw, Donald J., 124, 138, 446, 467
Leksell, Laurent, 222
Leontiades, James, 441, 467
Lever, Harold, 71, 75
Lieater, B. A., 499, 503
Lindsay, William K., 228, 253
Litton Industries, 152
Lockheed Aircraft Corporation, 37, 49, 55
Lorange, P., 228, 253
Lord, Alan, 78
Lorsch, Jay W., 184, 220
Lovell, Enid Baird, 109, 137, 501
Luter, Edward R., 56–57, 95

Mahathir, Datuk Seri, 252–253
Maisonrouge, Jacques, 32, 93
Majak, Roger M., 43, 94
Majaro, Simon, 468, 469
Mandelbaum, D. G., 307
Mangone, G. J., 314, 343
March, James, 137
Martin, Roger E., 464
Marton, Katherin, 468
Martyn-Johns, T. A., 322, 344
Marubeni Trading Company (Japan), 55
Maruyama, R., 376
Mascarenhas, Briance, 240, 243, 255
Mason, Hal R., 354–355, 385
Mathias, Peter F., 386
Matsuki, R., 376
Matsushita, Konasuke, 373
Matsushita Industrial Electric Company
    (Panasonic), 361, 373, 389
McArdle, James, 126
McCann, Eugene, 344
McClelland, David C., 261
McClenanthen, J. S., 307
McCulloch, Jr., Wendell H., 385
McDonnell Douglas Corporation, 388
McIsaac, George S., 308
McLeod, Maxwell G., 28
McMillan, Jr., Claude, 262, 306
Meade, R. D., 344
Meadow, Jr., A., 262, 306

Subjects